LONDON MUSIC IN 1888–89 AS HEARD BY CORNO DI BASSETTO (LATER KNOWN AS BERNARD SHAW) WITH SOME FURTHER AUTOBIOGRAPHICAL PARTICULARS

LONDON MUSIC IN 1888-89 AS HEARD BY CORNO DI BASSETTO (LATER KNOWN AS BERNARD SHAW) WITH SOME FURTHER AUTOBIO-GRAPHICAL PARTICULARS

DODD, MEAD & COMPANY
NEW YORK   1961

PRINTED IN THE U. S. A. BY
Quinn & Boden Company, Inc.
BOOK MANUFACTURERS
RAHWAY, NEW JERSEY

LONDON MUSIC IN 1888–89

PREFACE

WHEN my maiden novel, called Immaturity, was printed fifty years after it was written, I prefaced it with some account of the unhappy-go-lucky way in which I was brought up, ending with the nine years of shabby genteel destitution during which my attempts to gain a footing in literature were a complete and apparently hopeless failure.

I was rescued from this condition by William Archer, who transferred some of his book reviewing work to me, and pushed me into a post as picture critic which had been pushed on him, and for which he considered himself unqualified, as in fact he was. So, as reviewer for the old Pall Mall Gazette and picture critic for Edmund Yates's then fashionable weekly, The World, I carried on until I found an opening which I can explain only by describing the musical side of my childhood, to which I made only a passing allusion in my Immaturity preface, but which was of cardinal importance in my education.

In 1888, I being then 32 and already a noted critic and political agitator, the Star newspaper was founded under the editorship of the late T. P. O'Connor (nicknamed Tay Pay by Yates), who had for his very much more competent assistant the late H. W. Massingham. Tay Pay survived until 1936; but his mind never advanced beyond the year 1865, though his Fenian sympathies and his hearty detestation of the English nation disguised that defect from him. Massingham induced him to invite me to join the political staff of his paper; but as I had already, fourteen years before Lenin, read Karl Marx, and was preaching Socialism at every street corner or other available forum in London and the provinces, the effect of my articles on Tay Pay may be imagined. He refused to print them, and told me that, man alive, it would be five hundred years before such stuff would become practical political journalism. He was too good-natured to sack me; and I did not want to throw away my job; so I got him out of his difficulty by asking him to let me

3

have two columns a week for a feuilleton on music. He was glad to get rid of my politics on these terms; but he stipulated that—musical criticism being known to him only as unreadable and unintelligible jargon—I should, for God's sake, not write about Bach in B Minor. I was quite alive to that danger: in fact I had made my proposal because I believed I could make musical criticism readable even by the deaf. Besides, my terms were moderate: two guineas a week.

I was strong on the need for signed criticism written in the first person instead of the journalistic "we"; but as I then had no name worth signing, and G. B. S. meant nothing to the public, I had to invent a fantastic personality with something like a foreign title. I thought of Count di Luna (a character in Verdi's Trovatore), but finally changed it for Corno di Bassetto, as it sounded like a foreign title, and nobody knew what a corno di bassetto was.

As a matter of fact the corno di bassetto is not a foreigner with a title but a musical instrument called in English the basset horn. It is a wretched instrument, now completely snuffed out for general use by the bass clarionet. It would be forgotten and unplayed if it were not that Mozart has scored for it in his Requiem, evidently because its peculiar watery melancholy, and the total absence of any richness or passion in its tone, is just the thing for a funeral. Mendelssohn wrote some chamber music for it, presumably to oblige somebody who played it; and it is kept alive by these works and by our Mr Whall. If I had ever heard a note of it in 1888 I should not have selected it for a character which I intended to be sparkling. The devil himself could not make a basset horn sparkle.

For two years I sparkled every week in The Star under this ridiculous name, and in a manner so absolutely unlike the conventional musical criticism of the time that all the journalists believed that the affair was a huge joke, the point of which was that I knew nothing whatever about music. How it had come about that I was one of the few critics of that time who really knew their business I can

PREFACE

explain only by picking up the thread of autobiography which I dropped in my scrappy prefix to Immaturity. For the sake of those who have not read the Immaturity preface, or have forgotten it, I shall have to repeat here some of my father's history, but only so far as is necessary to explain the situation of my mother.

Technically speaking I should say she was the worst mother conceivable, always, however, within the limits of the fact that she was incapable of unkindness to any child, animal, or flower, or indeed to any person or thing whatsoever. But if such a thing as a maternity welfare centre had been established or even imagined in Ireland in her time, and she had been induced to visit it, every precept of it would have been laughably strange to her. Though she had been severely educated up to the highest standard for Irish "carriage ladies" of her time, she was much more like a Trobriand islander as described by Mr Malinowski than like a modern Cambridge lady graduate in respect of accepting all the habits, good or bad, of the Irish society in which she was brought up as part of an uncontrollable order of nature. She went her own way with so complete a disregard and even unconsciousness of convention and scandal and prejudice that it was impossible to doubt her good faith and innocence; but it never occurred to her that other people, especially children, needed guidance or training, or that it mattered in the least what they ate and drank or what they did as long as they were not actively mischievous. She accepted me as a natural and customary phenomenon, and took it for granted that I should go on occurring in that way. In short, living to her was not an art: it was something that happened. But there were unkind parts of it that could be avoided; and among these were the constraints and tyrannies, the scoldings and browbeatings and punishments she had suffered in her childhood as the method of her education. In her righteous reaction against it she reached a negative attitude in which, having no substitute to propose, she carried domestic anarchy as far as in the nature of

5

things it can be carried.

She had been tyrannously taught French enough to recite one or two of Lafontaine's fables; to play the piano the wrong way; to harmonize by rule from Logier's Thoroughbass; to sit up straight and speak and dress and behave like a lady, and an Irish lady at that. She knew nothing of the value of money nor of housekeeping nor of hygiene nor of anything that could be left to servants or governesses or parents or solicitors or apothecaries or any other member of the retinue, indoor and outdoor, of a country house. She had great expectations from a humpbacked little aunt, a fairy-like creature with a will of iron, who had brought up her motherless niece with a firm determination to make her a paragon of good breeding, to achieve a distinguished marriage for her, and to leave her all her money as a dowry.

Manufacturing destinies for other people is a dangerous game. Its results are usually as unexpected as those of a first-rate European war. When my mother came to marriageable age her long widowed father married again. The brother of his late wife, to whom he was considerably in debt, disapproved so strongly that on learning the date of the approaching ceremony from my mother he had the bridegroom arrested on his way to church. My grandfather naturally resented this manoeuvre, and in his wrath could not be persuaded that his daughter was not my granduncle's accomplice in it. Visits to relatives in Dublin provided a temporary refuge for her; and the affair would have blown over but for the intervention of my father.

My father was a very ineligible suitor for a paragon with great expectations. His family pretensions were enormous; but they were founded on many generations of younger sons, and were purely psychological. He had managed to acquire a gentlemanly post in the law courts. This post had been abolished and its holder pensioned. By selling the pension he was enabled to start in business as a wholesaler in the corn trade (retail trade was beneath his family dignity) of which he knew nothing. He accentuated this deficiency by becoming the partner of a Mr Clibborn, who had served an apprenticeship to the cloth trade. Their combined ignorances kept the business going, mainly by its own inertia, until they and it died. Many years after this event I paid a visit of curiosity to Jervis St. Dublin; and there, on one of the pillars of a small portico, I found the ancient inscription "Clibborn & Shaw" still decipherable, as it were on the tombs of the Pharaohs. I cannot believe that this business yielded my father at any time more than three or four hundred a year; and it got less as time went on, as that particular kind of business was dying a slow death throughout the latter half of the nineteenth century.

My father was in principle an ardent teetotaller. Nobody ever felt the disgrace and misery and endless mischief of drunkenness as he did: he impressed it so deeply on me in my earliest years that I have been a teetotaller ever since. Unfortunately his conviction in this matter was founded on personal experience. He was the victim of a drink neurosis which cropped up in his family from time to time: a miserable affliction, quite unconvivial, and accompanied by torments of remorse and shame.

My father was past forty, and no doubt had sanguine illusions as to the future of his newly acquired business when he fell in love with my mother and was emboldened by her expectations and his business hopes to propose to her just at the moment when marriage seemed her only way of escape from an angry father and a stepmother. Immediately all her relatives, who had tolerated this middle-aged gentleman as a perfectly safe acquaintance with an agreeable vein of humor, denounced him as a notorious drunkard. My mother, suspicious of this sudden change of front, put the question directly to my father. His eloquence and sincerity convinced her that he was, as he claimed to be, and as he was in principle, a bigoted teetotaller. She married him; and her disappointed and infuriated aunt disinherited her, not foreseeing that the consequences of the marriage would include so remarkable a phenomenon as myself.

7

PREFACE

When my mother was disillusioned, and found out what living on a few hundreds a year with three children meant, even in a country where a general servant could be obtained for eight pounds a year, her condition must have been about as unhappy and her prospects as apparently hopeless as her aunt could have desired even in her most vindictive moments.

But there was one trump in her hand. She was fond of music, and had a mezzo-soprano voice of remarkable purity of tone. In the next street to ours, Harrington Street, where the houses were bigger and more fashionable than in our little by-street, there was a teacher of singing, lamed by an accident in childhood which had left one of his legs shorter than the other, but a man of mesmeric vitality and force. He was a bachelor living with his brother, whom he supported and adored, and a terrible old woman who was his servant of all work. His name was George John Vandaleur Lee, known in Dublin as Mr G. J. Lee. Singing lessons were cheap in Dublin; and my mother went to Lee to learn how to sing properly. He trained her voice to such purpose that she became indispensable to him as an amateur prima donna. For he was a most magnetic conductor and an indefatigable organizer of concerts, and later on of operas, with such amateur talent, vocal and orchestral, as he could discover and train in Dublin, which, as far as public professional music was concerned, was, outside the churches, practically a vacuum.

Lee soon found his way into our house, first by giving my mother lessons there, and then by using our drawing-room for rehearsals. I can only guess that the inadequacies of old Ellen in the Harrington Street house, and perhaps the incompatibilities of the brother, outweighed the comparative smallness of our house in Synge Street. My mother soon became not only prima donna and chorus leader but general musical factotum in the whirlpool of Lee's activity. Her grounding in Logier's Thoroughbass enabled her to take boundless liberties with composers. When authentic

8

band parts were missing she thought nothing of making up an orchestral accompaniment of her own from the pianoforte score. Lee, as far as I know, had never seen a full orchestral score in his life: he conducted from a first violin part or from the vocal score, and had not, I think, any decided notion of orchestration as an idiosyncratic and characteristic part of a composer's work. He had no scholarship according to modern ideas; but he could do what Wagner said is the whole duty of a conductor: he could give the right time to the band; and he could pull it out of its amateur difficulties in emergencies by sheer mesmerism. Though he could not, or at any rate within my hearing never did sing a note, his taste in singing was classically perfect. In his search for the secret of *bel canto* he had gone to all the teachers within his reach. They told him that there was a voice in the head, a voice in the throat, and a voice in the chest. He dissected birds, and, with the connivance of medical friends, human subjects, in his search for these three organs. He then told the teachers authoritatively that the three voices were fabulous, and that the voice was produced by a single instrument called the larynx. They replied that musical art had nothing to do with anatomy, and that for a musician to practise dissection was unheard-of and disgusting. But as, tested by results, their efforts to teach their pupils to screech like locomotive whistles not only outraged his ear but wrecked the voices and often the health of their victims, their practice was as unacceptable to him as their theory.

Thus Lee became the enemy of every teacher of singing in Dublin; and they reciprocated heartily. In this negative attitude he was left until, at the opera, he heard an Italian baritone named Badeali, who at the age of 80, when he first discovered these islands, had a perfectly preserved voice, and, to Lee's taste, a perfectly produced one. Lee, thanks to his dissections, listened with a clear knowledge of what a larynx is really like. The other vocal organs and their action were obvious and conscious. Guided by this knowledge, and by his fine ear, his fastidious taste, and his instinct, he found out what Badeali was doing when he was singing. The other teachers were interested in Badeali only because one of his accomplishments was to drink a glass of wine and sing a sustained note at the same time. Finally Lee equipped himself with a teaching method which became a religion for him: the only religion, I may add, he ever professed. And my mother, as his pupil, learnt and embraced this musical faith, and rejected all other creeds as uninteresting superstitions. And it did not fail her; for she lived to be Badeali's age and kept her voice without a scrape on it until the end.

I have to dwell on The Method, as we called it in the family, because my mother's association with Lee, and the *ménage à trois* in which it resulted, would be unpleasantly misunderstood without this clue to it. For after the death of Lee's brother, which affected him to the verge of suicide, we left our respective houses and went to live in the same house, number one Hatch Street, which was half in Lower Leeson Street. The arrangement was economical; for we could not afford to live in a fashionable house, and Lee could not afford to give lessons in an unfashionable one, though, being a bachelor, he needed only a music room and a bedroom. We also shared a cottage in Dalkey, high up on Torca Hill, with all Dublin Bay from Dalkey Island to Howth visible from the garden, and all Killiney Bay with the Wicklow mountains in the background from the hall door. Lee bought this cottage and presented it to my mother, though she never had any legal claim to it and did not benefit by its sale later on. It was not conveniently situated for rehearsals or lessons; but there were musical neighbors who allowed me to some extent to run in and out of their houses when there was music going on.

The *ménage à trois*, alternating between Hatch St. and Dalkey, worked in its ramshackle way quite smoothly until I was fifteen or thereabouts, when Lee went to London and our family broke up into fragments that never got pieced together again.

In telling the story so far, I have had to reconstruct the part of it which occurred before I came into it and began, as my nurse put it, to take notice. I can remember the ante-Lee period in Synge St. when my father, as sole chief of the household, read family prayers and formally admitted that we had done those things which we ought not to have done and left undone those things which we ought to have done, which was certainly true as far as I was personally concerned. He added that there was no health in us; and this also was true enough about myself; for Dr Newland, our apothecary, was in almost continual attendance to administer cathartics; and when I had a sore throat I used to hold out for sixpence before submitting to a mustard plaster round my neck. We children (I had two sisters older than myself and no brothers) were abandoned entirely to the servants, who, with the exception of Nurse Williams, who was a good and honest woman, were utterly unfit to be trusted with the charge of three cats, much less three children. I had my meals in the kitchen, mostly of stewed beef, which I loathed, badly cooked potatoes, sound or diseased as the case might be, and much too much tea out of brown delft teapots left to "draw" on the hob until it was pure tannin. Sugar I stole. I was never hungry, because my father, often insufficiently fed in his childhood, had such a horror of child hunger that he insisted on unlimited bread and butter being always within our reach. When I was troublesome a servant thumped me on the head until one day, greatly daring, I rebelled, and, on finding her collapse abjectly, became thenceforth uncontrollable. I hated the servants and liked my mother because, on the one or two rare and delightful occasions when she buttered my bread for me, she buttered it thickly instead of merely wiping a knife on it. Her almost complete neglect of me had the advantage that I could idolize her to the utmost pitch of my imagination and had no sordid or disillusioning contacts with her. It was a privilege to be taken for a walk or a visit with her, or on an excursion.

My ordinary exercise whilst I was still too young to be allowed out by myself was to be taken out by a servant, who was supposed to air me on the banks of the canal or round the fashionable squares where the atmosphere was esteemed salubrious and the surroundings gentlemanly. Actually she took me into the slums to visit her private friends, who dwelt in squalid tenements. When she met a generous male acquaintance who insisted on treating her she took me into the public house bars, where I was regaled with lemonade and gingerbeer; but I did not enjoy these treats, because my father's eloquence on the evil of drink had given me an impression that a public house was a wicked place into which I should not have been taken. Thus were laid the foundations of my lifelong hatred of poverty, and the devotion of all my public life to the task of exterminating the poor and rendering their resurrection for ever impossible.

Note, by the way, that I should have been much more decently brought up if my parents had been too poor to afford servants.

As to early education I can remember our daily governess, Miss Hill, a needy lady who seemed to me much older than she can really have been. She puzzled me with her attempts to teach me to read; for I can remember no time at which a page of print was not intelligible to me, and can only suppose that I was born literate. She tried to give me and my two sisters a taste for poetry by reciting "Stop; for thy tread is on an empire's dust" at us, and only succeeded, poor lady, in awakening our sense of derisive humor. She punished me by little strokes with her fingers that would not have discomposed a fly, and even persuaded me that I ought to cry and feel disgraced on such occasions. She gave us judgment books and taught us to feel jubilant when after her departure we could rush to the kitchen crying "No marks today" and to hang back ashamed when this claim could not be substantiated. She taught me to add, subtract, and multiply, but could not teach me division,

PREFACE

because she kept saying two into four, three into six, and so forth without ever explaining what the word "into" meant in this connection. This was explained to me on my first day at school; and I solemnly declare that it was the only thing I ever learnt at school. However, I must not complain; for my immurement in that damnable boy prison effected its real purpose of preventing my being a nuisance to my mother at home for at least half the day.

The only other teaching I had was from my clerical Uncle William George (surnamed Carroll) who, being married to one of my many maternal aunts (my father had no end of brothers and sisters), had two boys of his own to educate, and took me on with them for awhile in the early mornings to such purpose that when his lessons were ended by my being sent to school, I knew more Latin grammar than any other boy in the First Latin Junior, to which I was relegated. After a few years in that establishment I had forgotten most of it, and, as aforesaid, learnt nothing; for there was only the thinnest pretence of teaching anything but Latin and Greek, if asking a boy once a day in an over-crowded class the Latin for a man or a horse or what not, can be called teaching him Latin. I was far too busy educating myself out of school by reading every book I could lay hands on, and clambering all over Killiney hill looking at the endless pictures nature painted for me, meanwhile keeping my mind busy by telling myself all sorts of stories, to puzzle about my vocabulary lesson, as the punishments were as futile as the teaching. At the end of my schooling I knew nothing of what the school professed to teach; but I was a highly educated boy all the same. I could sing and whistle from end to end leading works by Handel, Haydn, Mozart, Beethoven, Rossini, Bellini, Donizetti and Verdi. I was saturated with English literature, from Shakespear and Bunyan to Byron and Dickens. And I was so suscept-ible to natural beauty that, having had some glimpse of the Dalkey scenery on an excursion, I still remember the moment when my mother told me that we were going to

13

live there as the happiest of my life.

And all this I owed to the meteoric impact of Lee, with his music, his method, his impetuous enterprise and his magnetism, upon the little Shaw household where a thoroughly disgusted and disillusioned woman was suffering from a hopelessly disappointing husband and three uninteresting children grown too old to be petted like the animals and birds she was so fond of, to say nothing of the humiliating inadequacy of my father's income. We never felt any affection for Lee; for he was to excessively unlike us, too completely a phenomenon, to rouse any primitive human feeling in us. When my mother introduced him to me, he played with me for the first and last time; but as his notion of play was to decorate my face with moustaches and whiskers in burnt cork in spite of the most furious resistance I could put up, our encounter was not a success; and the defensive attitude in which it left me lasted, though without the least bitterness, until the decay of his energies and the growth of mine put us on more than equal terms. He never read anything except Tyndall on Sound, which he kept in his bedroom for years. He complained that an edition of Shakespear which I lent him was incomplete because it did not contain The School for Scandal, which for some reason he wanted to read; and when I talked of Carlyle he understood me to mean the Viceroy of that name who had graciously attended his concerts in the Antient Concert Rooms. Although he supplanted my father as the dominant factor in the household, and appropriated all the activity and interest of my mother, he was so completely absorbed in his musical affairs that there was no friction and hardly any intimate personal contacts between the two men: certainly no unpleasantness. At first his ideas astonished us. He said that people should sleep with their windows open. The daring of this appealed to me; and I have done so ever since. He ate brown bread instead of white: a startling eccentricity. He had no faith in doctors, and when my mother had a serious illness took her case in hand unhesitatingly and at the end of a week or so gave my trembling father leave to call in a leading Dublin doctor, who simply said, "My work is done" and took his hat. As to the apothecary and his squills, he could not exist in Lee's atmosphere; and I was never attended by a doctor again until I caught the smallpox in the epidemic of 1881. He took no interest in pictures or in any art but his own; and even in music his interest was limited to vocal music: I did not know that such things as string quartets or symphonies existed until I began, at sixteen, to investigate music for myself. Beethoven's sonatas and the classical operatic overtures were all I knew of what Wagner called absolute music. I should be tempted to say that none of us knew of the existence of Bach were it not that my mother sang My Heart Ever Faithful, the banjo like obbligato of which amused me very irreverently.

Lee was like all artists whose knowledge is solely a working knowledge: there were holes in his culture which I had to fill up for myself. Fortunately his richer pupils sometimes presented him with expensive illustrated books. He never opened them; but I did. He was so destitute of any literary bent that when he published a book entitled The Voice, it was written for him by a scamp of a derelict doctor whom he entertained for that purpose, just as in later years his prospectuses and press articles were written by me. He never visited the Dublin National Gallery, one of the finest collections of its size in Europe, with the usual full set of casts from what was called the antique, meaning ancient Greek sculpture. It was by prowling in this gallery that I learnt to recognize the work of the old masters at sight. I learnt French history from the novels of Dumas *père*, and English history from Shakespear and Walter Scott. Good boys were meanwhile learning lessons out of schoolbooks and receiving marks at examinations: a process which left them pious barbarians whilst I was acquiring an equipment which enabled me not only to pose as Corno di Bassetto when the chance arrived, but to add the criticism of pic-

tures to the various strings I had to my bow as a feuille-
tonist.

Meanwhile nobody ever dreamt of teaching me anything. At fifteen, when the family broke up, I could neither
play nor read a note of music. Whether you choose to put
it that I was condemned to be a critic or saved from being
an executant, the fact remains that when the house became
musicless, I was forced to teach myself how to play written
music on the piano from a book with a diagram of the
keyboard in it or else be starved of music.

Not that I wanted to be a professional musician. My
ambition was to be a great painter like Michael Angelo (one
of my heroes); but my attempts to obtain instruction in his
art at the School of Design presided over by the South
Kensington Department of Science and Art only prevented
me from learning anything except how to earn five shilling
grants for the masters (payment by results) by filling up
ridiculous examination papers in practical geometry and
what they called freehand drawing.

With competent instruction I daresay I could have
become a painter and draughtsman of sorts; but the School
of Design convinced me that I was a hopeless failure in that
direction on no better ground than that I found I could not
draw like Michael Angelo or paint like Titian at the first
attempt without knowing how. But teaching, of art and
everything else, was and still is so little understood by our
professional instructors (mostly themselves failures) that
only the readymade geniuses make good; and even they
are as often as not the worse for their academic contacts.

As an alternative to being a Michael Angelo I had
dreams of being a Badeali. (Note, by the way, that of
literature I had no dreams at all, any more than a duck has
of swimming.) What that led to was not fully explained
until Matthias Alexander, in search, like Lee, of a sound
vocal method, invented his technique of self-control.

I had sung like a bird all through my childhood; but
when my voice broke I at once fell into the error unmasked

by Alexander of trying to gain my end before I had studied
the means. In my attempts to reproduce the frenzies of the
Count di Luna, the sardonic accents of Gounod's Mephistopheles, the noble charm of Don Giovanni, and the supernatural menace of the Commendatore, not to mention all
the women's parts and the tenor parts as well (for all parts,
high and low, male or female, had to be sung or shrieked or
whistled or growled somehow) I thought of nothing but the
dramatic characters; and in attacking them I set my jaws
and my glottis as if I had to crack walnuts with them. I
might have ruined my voice if I had not imitated good
singers instead of bad ones; but even so the results were
wretched. When I rejoined my mother in London and she
found that I had taught myself to play accompaniments
and to amuse myself with operas and oratorios as other
youths read novels and smoke cigarets, she warned me that
my voice would be spoiled if I went on like that. Thereupon
I insisted on being shewn the proper way to sing. The instructive result was that when, following my mother's
directions, I left my jaw completely loose, and my tongue
flat instead of convulsively rolling it up; when I operated
my diaphragm so as to breathe instead of "blowing"; when
I tried to round up my pharynx and soft palate and found
it like trying to wag my ears, I found that for the first time
in my life I could not produce an audible note. It seemed
that I had no voice. But I believed in Lee's plan and knew
that my own was wrong. I insisted on being taught how to
use my voice as if I had one; and in the end the unused and
involuntary pharyngeal muscles became active and volun-
tary, and I developed an uninteresting baritone voice of
no exceptional range which I have ever since used for my
private satisfaction and exercise without damaging either
it or myself in the process.

Here I must digress for a moment to point a moral.
Years after I learnt how to sing without spoiling my voice
and wrecking my general health, a musician-reciter
(Matthias Alexander aforesaid) found himself disabled by

the complaint known as clergyman's sore throat. Having the true scientific spirit and industry, he set himself to discover what it was that he was really doing to disable himself in this fashion by his efforts to produce the opposite result. In the end he found this out, and a great deal more as well. He established not only the beginnings of a far reaching science of the apparently involuntary movements we call reflexes, but a technique of correction and self-control which forms a substantial addition to our very slender resources in personal education.

Meanwhile a Russian doctor named Pavlov devoted himself to the investigation of the same subject by practising the horrible voodoo into which professional medical research had lapsed in the nineteenth century. For quarter of a century he tormented and mutilated dogs most abominably, and finally wrote a ponderous treatise on reflexes in which he claimed to have established on a scientific basis the fact that a dog's mouth will water at the sound of a dinner bell when it is trained to associate that sound with a meal, and that dogs, if tormented, thwarted, baffled, and incommoded continuously, will suffer nervous breakdown and be miserably ruined for the rest of their lives. He was also able to describe what happens to a dog when half its brains are cut out.

What his book and its shamefully respectful reception by professional biologists does demonstrate is that the opening of the scientific professions to persons qualified for them neither by general capacity nor philosophic moral training plunges professional Science, as it has so often plunged professional Religion and Jurisprudence, into an abyss of stupidity and cruelty from which nothing but the outraged humanity of the laity can rescue it.

In the department of biology especially, the professors, mostly brought up as Fundamentalists, are informed that the book of Genesis is not a scientific document, and that the tribal idol whom Noah conciliated by the smell of roast meat is not God and never had any objective existence.

18

PREFACE

They absurdly infer that the pursuit of scientific knowledge: that is, of all knowledge, is exempt from moral obligations, and consequently that they are privileged as scientists to commit the most revolting cruelties when they are engaged in research.

Their next step in this crazy logic is that no research is scientific unless it involves such cruelties. With all the infinite possibilities of legitimate and kindly research open to anyone with enough industry and ingenuity to discover innocent methods of exploration, they set up a boycott of brains and a ritual of sacrifice of dogs and guinea pigs which impresses the superstitious public as all such rituals do. Thereby they learn many things that no decent person ought to know; for it must not be forgotten that human advancement consists not only of adding to the store of human knowledge and experience but eliminating much that is burdensome and brutish. Our forefathers had the knowledge and experience gained by seeing heretics burnt at the stake and harlots whipped through the streets at the cart's tail. Mankind is better without such knowledge and experience.

If Pavlov had been a poacher he would have been imprisoned for his cruelty and despised for his moral imbecility. But as Director of the Physiological Department of the Institute of Experimental Medicine at St Petersburg, and Professor of the Medical Academy, he was virtually forced to mutilate and torment dogs instead of discovering the methods by which humane unofficial investigators were meanwhile finding out all that he was looking for.

The reaction against this voodoo is gathering momentum; but still our rich philanthropic industrialists lavish millions on the endowment of research without taking the most obvious precautions against malversation of their gifts for the benefit of dog stealers, guinea pig breeders, laboratory builders and plumbers, and a routine of cruel folly and scoundrelism that perverts and wastes all the scientific enthusiasm that might otherwise have by this

19

time reduced our death and disease rates to their natural minimum. I am sorry to have to describe so many highly respected gentlemen quite deliberately as fools and scoundrels; but the only definition of scoundrelism known to me is anarchism in morals; and I cannot admit that the hackneyed pleas of the dynamiter and the assassin in politics become valid in the laboratory and the hospital, or that the man who thinks they do is made any less a fool by calling him a professor of physiology.

And all this because in 1860 the men who thought they wanted to substitute scientific knowledge for superstition really wanted only to abolish God and marry their deceased wives' sisters!

I should add that there is no reason to suppose that Pavlov was by nature a bad man. He bore a strong external resemblance to myself, and was well-meaning, intelligent, and devoted to science. It was his academic environment that corrupted, stultified, and sterilized him. If only he had been taught to sing by my mother no dog need ever have collapsed in terror at his approach; and he might have shared the laurels of Alexander.

And now I must return to my story. Lee's end was more tragic than Pavlov's. I do not know at what moment he began to deteriorate. He was a sober and moderate liver in all respects; and he was never ill until he treated himself to a tour in Italy and caught malaria there. He fought through it without a doctor on cold water, and returned apparently well; but whenever he worked too hard it came back and prostrated him for a day or two. Finally his ambition undid him. Dublin in those days seemed a hopeless place for an artist; for no success counted except a London success. The summit of a provincial conductor's destiny was to preside at a local musical festival modelled on the Three Choirs or Handel Festivals. Lee declared that he would organize and conduct a Dublin Festival with his own chorus and with all the famous leading singers from the Italian opera in London. This he did in connection with an Exhibition in

PREFACE

Dublin. My mother, of course, led the chorus. At a rehearsal the contralto, Madame de Meric Lablache, took exception to something and refused to sing. Lee shrugged his shoulders and asked my mother to carry on, which she did to such purpose that Madame Lablache took care not to give her another such chance.

At the Festivals Lee reached the Dublin limit of eminence. Nothing remained but London. He was assured that London meant a very modest beginning all over again, and perhaps something of an established position after fifteen years or so. Lee said that he would take a house in Park Lane, then the most exclusive and expensive thoroughfare in the West-end, sacred to peers and millionaires, and—stupendous on the scale of Irish finance—make his pupils pay him a guinea a lesson. And this he actually did with a success that held out quite brilliantly for several seasons and then destroyed him. For whereas he had succeeded in Dublin by the sheer superiority of his method and talent and character, training his pupils honestly for a couple of years to sing beautifully and classically, he found that the London ladies who took him up so gushingly would have none of his beauty and classicism, and would listen to nothing less than a promise to make them sing "like Patti" in twelve lessons. It was that or starve.

He submitted perforce; but he was no longer the same man, the man to whom all circumstances seemed to give way, and who made his own musical world and reigned in it. He had even to change his name and his aspect. G. J. Lee, with the black whiskers and the clean shaven resolute lip and chin, became Vandaleur Lee, whiskerless, but with a waxed and pointed moustache and an obsequious attitude. It suddenly became evident that he was an elderly man, and, to those who had known him in Dublin, a humbug. Performances of Marchetti's Ruy Blas with my sister as the Queen of Spain, and later on of Sullivan's Patience and scraps of Faust and Il Trovatore were achieved; but musical society in London at last got tired of the damaged Svengali who could manufacture Pattis for twelve guineas; and the guineas ceased to come in. Still, as there were no night clubs in those days, it was possible to let a house in Park Lane for the night to groups of merrymakers; and Lee was holding out there without pupils when he asked me to draft a circular for him announcing that he could cure clergyman's sore throat. He was still at Park Lane when he dropped dead in the act of undressing himself, dying as he had lived, without a doctor. The postmortem and inquest revealed the fact that his brain was diseased and had been so for a long time. I was glad to learn that his decay was pathological as well as ecological, and that the old efficient and honest Lee had been real after all. But I took to heart the lesson in the value of London fashionable successes. To this day I look to the provincial and the amateur for honesty and genuine fecundity in art.

Meanwhile, what had happened to the *ménage à trois*; and how did I turn up in Park Lane playing accompaniments and getting glimpses of that art-struck side of fashionable society which takes refuge in music from the routine of politics and sport which occupies the main Philistine body?

Well, when Lee got his foot in at a country house in Shropshire where he had been invited to conduct some private performances, he sold the Dalkey cottage and concluded his tenancy of Hatch Street. This left us in a house which we could afford less than ever; for my father's moribund business was by now considerably deader than it had been at the date of my birth. My younger sister was dying of consumption caught from reckless contacts at a time when neither consumption nor pneumonia were regarded as catching. All that could be done was to recommend a change of climate. My elder sister had a beautiful voice. In the last of Lee's Dublin adventures in amateur opera she had appeared as Amina in Bellini's La Somnambula, on which occasion the tenor lost his place and his head, and Lucy obligingly sang most of his part as well as her own. Unfortunately her musical endowment was so complete that it cost her no effort to sing or play anything she had once heard, or to read any music at sight. She simply could not associate the idea of real work with music; and as in any case she had never received any sort of training, her very facility prevented her from becoming a serious artist, though, as she could sing difficult music without breaking her voice, she got through a considerable share of public singing in her time.

Now neither my mother nor any of us knew how much more is needed for an opera singer than a voice and natural musicianship. It seemed to us that as, after a rehearsal or two, she could walk on to the stage, wave her arms about in the absurd manner then in vogue in opera, and sing not only her own part but everybody else's as well, she was quite qualified to take the place of Christine Nilsson or Adelina Patti if only she could get a proper introduction. And clearly Lee, now in the first flush of his success in Park Lane, would easily be able to secure this for her.

There was another resource. My now elderly mother believed that she could renounce her amateur status and make a living in London by teaching singing. Had she not the infallible Method to impart? So she realized a little of the scrap of settled property of which her long deceased aunt had not been able to deprive her; sold the Hatch Street furniture; settled my father and myself in comfortable lodgings at 61 Harcourt St.; and took my sisters to the Isle of Wight, where the younger one died. She then took a semi-detached little villa in a *cul-de-sac* in the Fulham Road, and waited there for Lucy's plans and her own to materialize.

The result was almost a worse disillusion than her marriage. That had been cured by Lee's music: besides, my father had at last realized his dream of being a practising teetotaller, and was now as inoffensive an old gentleman as any elderly wife could desire. It was characteristic of the Shavian drink neurosis to vanish suddenly in this way. But

23

that Lee should be unfaithful! unfaithful to The Method!
that he, the one genuine teacher among so many quacks,
should now stoop to outquack them all and become a
moustachioed charlatan with all the virtue gone out of him:
this was the end of all things; and she never forgave it. She
was not unkind: she tolerated Lee the charlatan as she had
tolerated Shaw the dipsomaniac because, as I guess, her
early motherless privation of affection and her many disap-
pointments in other people had thrown her back on her
own considerable internal resources and developed her
self-sufficiency and power of solitude to an extent which
kept her up under circumstances that would have crushed
or embittered any woman who was the least bit of a clinger.
She dropped Lee very gently: at first he came and went at
Victoria Grove, Fulham Road; and she went and came at
13 Park Lane, helping with the music there at his At Homes,
and even singing the part of Donna Anna for him (elderly
prima donnas were then tolerated as matters of course) at
an amateur performance of Don Giovanni. But my sister,
who had quarrelled with him as a child when he tried to give
her piano lessons, and had never liked him, could not bear
him at all in his new phase, and, when she found that he
could not really advance her prospects of becoming a prima
donna, broke with him completely and made it difficult for
him to continue his visits. When he died we had not seen
him for some years; and my mother did not display the
slightest emotion at the news. He had been dead for her
ever since he had ceased to be an honest teacher of singing
and a mesmeric conductor.

Her plans for herself came almost to nothing for several
years. She found that Englishwomen do not wish to be made
to sing beautifully and classically: they want to sing eroti-
cally; and this my mother thought not only horrible but
unladylike. Her love songs were those of Virginia Gabriel
and Arthur Sullivan, all about bereaved lovers and ending
with a hope for reunion in the next world. She could sing
with perfect purity of tone and touching expression

PREFACE

Oh, Ruby, my darling, the small white hand
Which gathered the harebell was never my own.

But if you had been able to anticipate the grand march of
human progress and poetic feeling by fifty years, and asked
her to sing

You made me love you.
I didnt want to do it.
I didnt want to do it.

she would have asked a policeman to remove you to a
third-class carriage.

Besides, though my mother was not consciously a snob,
the divinity which hedged an Irish lady of her period was
not acceptable to the British suburban parents, all snobs,
who were within her reach. They liked to be treated with
deference; and it never occurred to my mother that such
people could entertain a pretension so monstrous in her
case. Her practice with private pupils was negligible until
she was asked to become musical instructress at the North
London College. Her success was immediate; for not only
did her classes leave the other schools nowhere musically,
but the divinity aforesaid exactly suited her new rôle as
schoolmistress. Other schools soon sought her services; and
she remained in request until she insisted on retiring on the
ground that her age made her public appearances ridiculous.
By that time all the old money troubles were over and forgotten, as my financial position enabled me to make her
perfectly comfortable in that respect.

And now, what about myself, the incipient Corno di
Bassetto?

Well, when my mother sold the Hatch Street furniture,
it never occurred to her to sell our piano, though I could
not play it, nor could my father. We did not realize, nor did
she, that she was never coming back, and that, except for
a few days when my father, taking a little holiday for the
first time in his life within my experience, came to see us
in London, she would never meet him again. Family revo-

lutions would seldom be faced if they did not present themselves at first as temporary makeshifts. Accordingly, having lived since my childhood in a house full of music, I suddenly found myself in a house where there was no music, and could be none unless I made it myself. I have recorded elsewhere how, having purchased one of Weale's Handbooks which contained a diagram of the keyboard and an explanation of musical notation, I began my self-tuition, not with Czerny's five finger exercises, but with the overture to Don Giovanni, thinking rightly that I had better start with something I knew well enough to hear whether my fingers were on the right notes or not. There were plenty of vocal scores of operas and oratorios in our lodging; and although I never acquired any technical skill as a pianist, and cannot to this day play a scale with any certainty of not foozling it, I acquired what I wanted: the power to take a vocal score and learn its contents as if I had heard it rehearsed by my mother and her colleagues. I could manage arrangements of orchestral music much better than piano music proper. At last I could play the old rum-tum accompaniments of those days well enough (knowing how they *should* be played) to be more agreeable to singers than many really competent pianists. I bought more scores, among them one of Lohengrin, through which I made the revolutionary discovery of Wagner. I bought arrangements of Beethoven's symphonies, and discovered the musical regions that lie outside opera and oratorio. Later on, I was forced to learn to play the classical symphonies and overtures in strict time by hammering the bass in piano duets with my sister in London. I played Bach's Inventions and his Art of Fugue. I studied academic textbooks, and actually worked out exercises in harmony and counterpoint under supervision by an organist friend named Crament, avoiding consecutive fifths and octaves, and having not the faintest notion of what the result would sound like. I read pseudo-scientific treatises about the roots of chords which candidates for the degree of Mus. Doc. at the universities had to

26

swallow, and learnt that Stainer's commonsense views would get you plucked at Oxford, and Ouseley's pedantries at Cambridge. I read Mozart's Succinct Thoroughbass (a scrap of paper with some helpful tips on it which he scrawled for his pupil Sussmaier); and this, many years later, Edward Elgar told me was the only document in existence of the smallest use to a student composer. It was, I grieve to say, of no use to me; but then I was not a young composer. It ended in my knowing much more about music than any of the great composers, an easy achievement for any critic, however barren. For awhile I must have become a little pedantic; for I remember being shocked, on looking up Lee's old vocal score of Don Giovanni, to find that he had cut out all the repetitions which Mozart had perpetrated as a matter of sonata form. I now see that Lee was a century before his time in this reform, and hope some day to hear a performance of Mozart's Idomeneo in which nothing is sung twice over.

When I look back on all the banging, whistling, roaring, and growling inflicted on nervous neighbors during this process of education, I am consumed with useless remorse. But what else could I have done? Today there is the wireless, which enables me to hear from all over Europe more good music in a week than I could then hear in ten years, if at all. When, after my five years' office slavery, I joined my mother in London and lived with her for twenty years until my marriage, I used to drive her nearly crazy by my favorite selections from Wagner's Ring, which to her was "all recitative", and horribly discordant at that. She never complained at the time, but confessed it after we separated, and said that she had sometimes gone away to cry. If I had committed a murder I do not think it would trouble my conscience very much; but this I cannot bear to think of. If I had to live my life over again I should devote it to the establishment of some arrangement of headphones and microphones or the like whereby the noises made by musical maniacs should be audible to themselves only. In Germany

27

it is against the law to play the piano with the window open. But of what use is that to the people in the house? It should be made felony to play a musical instrument in any other than a completely soundproof room. The same should apply to loud speakers on pain of confiscation.

Readers with a taste for autobiography must now take my Immaturity preface and dovetail it into this sketch to complete the picture. My business here is to account for my proposal to Tay Pay and my creation of Bassetto. From my earliest recorded sign of an interest in music when as a small child I encored my mother's singing of the page's song from the first act of Les Huguenots (note that I shared Herbert Spencer's liking for Meyerbeer) music has been an indispensable part of my life. Harley Granville-Barker was not far out when, at a rehearsal of one of my plays, he cried out, "Ladies and gentlemen: will you please remember that this is Italian opera."

I reprint Bassetto's stuff shamefacedly after long hesitation with a reluctance which has been overcome only by my wife, who has found some amusement in reading it through, a drudgery which I could not bring myself to undertake. I know it was great fun when it was fresh, and that many people have a curious antiquarian taste (I have it myself) for old chronicles of dead musicians and actors. I must warn them, however, not to expect to find here the work of the finished critic who wrote my volumes entitled Music in London, 1890-94, and Our Theatres in the Nineties. I knew all that was necessary about music; but in criticism I was only a beginner. It is easy enough from the first to distinguish between what is pleasant or unpleasant, accurate or inaccurate in a performance; but when great artists have to be dealt with, only keenly analytical observation and comparison of them with artists who, however agreeable, are not great, can enable a critic to distinguish between what everybody can do and what only a very few can do, and to get his valuations right accordingly. All artsmen know what it is to be enthusiastically praised for

28

PREFACE

something so easy that they are half ashamed of it, and to receive not a word of encouragement for their finest strokes.

I cannot deny that Bassetto was occasionally vulgar; but that does not matter if he makes you laugh. Vulgarity is a necessary part of a complete author's equipment; and the clown is sometimes the best part of the circus. The Star, then a hapenny newspaper, was not catering for a fastidious audience: it was addressed to the bicycle clubs and the polytechnics, not to the Royal Society of Literature or the Musical Association. I purposely vulgarized musical criticism, which was then refined and academic to the point of being unreadable and often nonsensical. Editors, being mostly ignorant of music, would submit to anything from their musical critics, not pretending to understand it. If I occasionally carried to the verge of ribaldry my reaction against the pretentious twaddle and sometimes spiteful cliquishness they tolerated in their ignorance, think of me as heading one of the pioneer columns of what was then called The New Journalism; and you will wonder at my politeness.

You may be puzzled, too, to find that the very music I was brought up on: the pre-Wagner school of formal melody in separate numbers which seemed laid out to catch the encores that were then fashionable, was treated by me with contemptuous levity as something to be swept into the dustbin as soon as possible. The explanation is that these works were standing in the way of Wagner, who was then the furiously abused coming man in London. Only his early works were known or tolerated. Half a dozen bars of Tristan or The Mastersingers made professional musicians put their fingers in their ears. The Ride of the Valkyries was played at the Promenade Concerts, and always encored, but only as an insanely rampagious curiosity. The Daily Telegraph steadily preached Wagner down as a discordant notoriety-hunting charlatan in six silk dressing-gowns, who could not write a bar of melody, and made an abominable noise with the orchestra. In pantomime harlequinades the clown produced a trombone, played a bit of the pilgrims' march from Tannhäuser fortissimo as well as he could, and said, "The music of the future!" The wars of religion were not more bloodthirsty than the discussions of the Wagnerites and the Anti-Wagnerites. I was, of course, a violent Wagnerite; and I had the advantage of knowing the music to which Wagner grew up, whereas many of the most fanatical Wagnerites (Ashton Ellis, who translated the Master's prose works, was a conspicuous example) knew no other music than Wagner's, and believed that the music of Donizetti and Meyerbeer had no dramatic quality whatever. "A few arpeggios" was the description Ellis gave me of his notion of Les Huguenots.

Nowadays the reaction is all the other way. Our young lions have no use for Wagner the Liberator. His harmonies, which once seemed monstrous cacophonies, are the commonplaces of the variety theatres. Audacious young critics disparage his grandeurs as tawdry. When the wireless strikes up the Tannhäuser overture I hasten to switch it off, though I can always listen with pleasure to Rossini's overture to William Tell, hackneyed to death in Bassetto's time. The funeral march from Die Götterdämmerung hardly keeps my attention, though Handel's march from Saul is greater than ever. Though I used to scarify the fools who said that Wagner's music was formless, I should not now think the worse of Wagner if, like Bach and Mozart, he had combined the most poignant dramatic expression with the most elaborate decorative design. It was necessary for him to smash the superstition that this was obligatory; to free dramatic melody from the tyranny of arabesques; and to give the orchestra symphonic work instead of rosalias and rum-tum; but now that this and all the other musical superstitions are in the dustbin, and the post-Wagnerian harmonic and contrapuntal anarchy is so complete that it is easier technically to compose another Parsifal than another Bach's Mass in B Minor or Don Giovanni I am no longer a combatant anarchist in music, not to mention that I have

30

learnt that a successful revolution's first task is to shoot all revolutionists. This means that I am no longer Corno di Bassetto. He was pre- and pro-Wagner; unfamiliar with Brahms; and unaware that a young musician named Elgar was chuckling over his irreverent boutades. As to Cyril Scott, Bax, Ireland, Goossens, Bliss, Walton, Schönberg, Hindemith, or even Richard Strauss and Sibelius, their idioms would have been quite outside Bassetto's conception of music, though today they seem natural enough. Therefore I very greatly doubt whether poor old Bassetto is worth reading now. Still, you are not compelled to read him. Having read the preface you can shut the book and give it to your worst enemy as a birthday present.

MID-ATLANTIC,
Sunday, 2nd June 1935.

LONDON MUSIC IN 1888-89

THE number of empty seats at the performance of Bach's Mass in B Minor at St James's Hall on Saturday afternoon did little credit to the artistic culture of which the West-end is supposed to be the universal centre. This Mass towers among the masterpieces of musical art like Everest among the mountains; but we still prefer Elijah. The performance suffered from the want of energy and impetus which is one of the hampering traditions of Herr Goldschmidt's conducting, and which Mr Villiers Stanford, as a younger hand, and an Irishman, ought to have proved the very man to correct. But under him, as under Herr Goldschmidt, the wonderful Kyrie dragged tediously along without fire or emphasis, and without a touch of expression in the recurring cadence, which is so moving a point in the score. The later choruses were more effective, though there was a want of power in certain passages which demand a crushing sonority from the mass of voices and instruments. This was notably the case in the Cum Sancto Spiritu. In the Et Ressurexit Mr Stanford made the astonishing mistake of retarding the great passage for the basses, Et iterum venturus. But, in spite of these shortcomings, the stupendous march of Bach's polyphony, and the intense and touching expression of his harmonies produced their inevitable effect. The restored trumpet part, first played for us at the Albert Hall by Herr Kosleck at the bi-centenary performance in 1885, was played on Mr Mahillon's two-valved trumpet by Mr Morrow, who vanquished nearly all the impossibilities until just at the end, when his lip tired, and the notes above the high A became uncertain. At the famous Sanctus Mr Stanford made an attempt, successful unfortunately, to manufacture a tradition similar to that by which English audiences stand during the Hallelujah Chorus in the Messiah. When such an act of homage is the spontaneous

33

impulse of the people it is worthy of jealous conservation. But when a conductor deliberately attempts to produce an imitation of the Hallelujah custom by making his solo singers stand up and then turning to the audience and beckoning to them to rise, which they of course do under the impression that it is an established practice, he is really guilty of a sort of forgery. Probably, however, people will not be so easily persuaded to stand up when they come to know how long the Sanctus is.

It should be mentioned that there were plenty of shilling seats: a great improvement on the high prices of the early days of the Bach Choir.

14 *May* 1888

THE late conflict between the Bishop of London and the Rev. Stewart Headlam as to the godliness of dancing ended practically in the excommunication of the dancers and the inhibition of the popular clergyman, whose version of the Thirty-nine Articles includes Land Nationalisation, Free Speech, Communion for Stage Players, and a Democratic Constitution for the Church. Mr Headlam's teaching nevertheless seems to have travelled further than the Bishop's, for we hear from Georgia of a troop of factory hands removing the benches from their church on a Friday evening, and having a hearty dance. At a church in North Carolina, a brass band was allowed to perform some stirring rhythmical hymn-tunes for the edification of a negro congregation. These pious colored persons, we are told, 'began to grow a little nervous and restless about the feet, and in a short time the whole crowd was indulging in a regular old break down.' This is shocking, no doubt, to our insular conception of a church as a place where we must on no account enjoy ourselves, and where ladies are trained in the English art of sitting in rows for hours, dumb, expressionless, and with the elbows uncomfortably turned in. But since people must enjoy themselves sometimes, why not in their own churches

34

as well as in places where drinking bars, gambling tables, and other temptations to enjoy themselves unhealthily and indecently are deliberately put in their way? 'Dancing is an art,' says Mr Headlam. 'All art is praise,' says Mr Ruskin. Praise is surely not out of place in a church. We sing there: why should we not dance?

The Puritans, from whom we inherit our prejudice against such a proposal, objected to dancing and singing in all places and at all seasons. Merry England never shared that objection: we admit it in church only because we can afford to dance elsewhere. But how about the people who have no such opportunities: no drawing-rooms, no money, no self-control in the presence of temptation and licence? We do not want to see Westminster Abbey turned into a ballroom; but if some enterprising clergyman with a cure of souls in the slums were to hoist a board over his church door with the inscription, 'Here men and women after working hours may dance without getting drunk on Fridays; hear good music on Saturdays; pray on Sundays; discuss public affairs without molestation from the police on Mondays; have the building for any honest purpose they please— theatricals, if desired—on Tuesdays; bring the children for games, amusing drill, and romps on Wednesdays; and volunteer for a thorough scrubbing down of the place on Thursdays'—well, it would be all very shocking, no doubt; but after all, it would not interfere with the Bishop of London's salary.

3 *July* 1888

HERR RICHTER has added to his Nibelung's Ring selections for concert use the great scene of the forging of the sword in the forest stithy, from the first act of Siegfried. It is one of the most effective he has made, and proves again that Wagner can work on the imagination with voice and orchestra in ways beyond the arts of the actor and stage manager. Mr Edward Lloyd, pretending to forge a sword on the stage, with one eye on the conductor, would be ridiculous; but last night in St James's Hall the leviathan breath of the bellows with its great train of sparks, the roar of the flame, the fierce hiss of the red-hot steel plunged into the water, the ringing of the hammers, the crooning of the old dwarf in the corner, and the exultant shouting of Siegfried at his work, culminating in a yell of excitement from the orchestra as the finished sword smites the anvil in two, made a tremendous effect, and gained an ovation for Mr Lloyd and the conductor.

There was no other novelty except a Bach concerto, one of those incomparable works which tax every quality of a first-rate player, and which, to tell the truth, speedily found out some of the weak places in the wind band. The concert ended in Beethoven's Symphony in A, the final movement of which went off with astonishing dash and vigor. The next concert will be the last, and will be devoted to Beethoven's Mass in D.

4 *July* 1888

To old opera-goers a performance of Verdi's Ballo in Maschera brings reminiscences of bygone days and forgotten singers: of Titiens in the trio in the cave scene and Giuglini in the quintet. Fortunately for you, dear reader, it produces no such effect on me; for I never heard the opera on the stage before, and never heard Giuglini, though I knew most of the music in my cradle or thereabouts. As to the young opera-goers, one can really only wonder what they think about it. Its interminable string of cavatinas, its absurdly Offenbachian finale to the first act, its inexhaustible vein of melodramatic anguish, its entire impossibility from any rational point of view from beginning to end, must all help to puzzle those who were never broken in to that strange survival of Richardson's show, the so-called acting of genuinely Italian opera. These are untimely reflections, perhaps; but they rise unbidden at a performance of Un Ballo.

36

The work, nevertheless, contains one capital scene: that in which Samuel and Tom (who are called Armando and Angri in the bills in these squeamish days) meet Renato innocently escorting his own wife, veiled, from an assignation with his dearest friend, and force her to unveil. Verdi has done nothing better than the combination of the raillery of the two rascals, the humiliation of the woman, and the distress of the husband. But at Covent Garden they do not seem to think that there is much in this. Samuel and Tom were solemn as sextons; and M. Lassalle merely stretched forth his sword to the stalls, as if he were about to perform the familiar feat of cutting an apple in two on Signor Mancinelli's head. He sang the part very well from a French point of view, which the audience, it was most encouraging to observe, flatly declined to accept. Mdlle. Rolla does not understand the English people. She may sing consistently sharp here with impunity. Though the assembled Britons will not like it, they will pretend to, thinking that she knows best. But to begin a note in tune, and then force it up quarter of a tone is neither popular nor humane. It is better, on the whole, to sing in tune all through, as Mdlle. Rolla decided to do towards the end of the performance. Her acting consisted of the singular plunge, gasp, and stagger peculiar to the Verdi heroine, whose reason is permanently unsettled by grief. Miss Arnoldson added Oscar to the list of her successes. Jean de Reszke was Riccardo. Some of the tediousness of the opera was due to the senseless conventionality of the representation and to the slow *tempi* adopted by Signor Mancinelli; but Mr Harris will do well to face the fact that, until fortune sends him an extraordinarily sensational dramatic soprano, he will do well to leave such old-fashioned affairs as Un Ballo on the shelf.

16 July 1888

Aïda filled the house at Covent Garden on Saturday quite as effectually as Il Trovatore emptied it earlier in the week.

Not that Aïda, comparatively fresh and varied in interest as it is, is at bottom at all a more rational entertainment than Il Trovatore, but simply because Aïda is now put on to give the best artists in the company a chance, whereas Il Trovatore is put on only to give them a rest. The performance of the first two acts was unsatisfactory. Madame Nordica, brown enough as to face and arms, was colorless as to voice. Signor Mancinelli conducted the court and temple scenes barbarically, evidently believing that the ancient Egyptians were a tribe of savages, instead of, as far as one can ascertain, considerably more advanced than the society now nightly contemplating in "indispensable evening dress" the back of Signor Mancinelli's head. Not until the scene of the triumphal return of Radames from the war did the gallery begin to pluck up and applaud. Fortunately, an incident which occurred at the beginning of the fourth act confirmed the good humor thus set in. Ramphis, Amneris, and their escort were seen approaching the temple in a state barge. On its tall prow, which rose some five feet out of the water, stood an Egyptian oarsman, urging the craft along the moonlit bosom of the Nile. Now this was all very well whilst the royal party were on board to balance him: but when they stepped ashore on to the stage, the barge went head over heels; the native went heels over head; and Signor Navarrini's impressive exhortation to *Vieni d'Iside al tempio* was received with shrieks of laughter. Whether the operatic gods were appeased by the sacrifice of the luckless boatman (who never reappeared from beneath the wave), or whether his fate made his surviving colleagues more serious, is a matter for speculation; but the fact is beyond question that the representation greatly improved from that moment. Madame Nordica's voice, no longer colorless, began to ring with awakened feeling. Her admirable method, to which she is, unfortunately, not invariably faithful, was exemplified in the ease, skill, and perfect intonation with which the higher notes were produced. It is an inexpressible relief to the jaded opera-goer to hear notes above the treble stave taken otherwise than with the neck-or-nothing scream of the ordinary *prima donna ma ultima cantatrice.* M. Jean de Reszke also rose to the occasion, and so astonished the house by a magnificent delivery of *Io son disonorato! Per te tradii la patria!* . . . *Sacerdote, io resto a te,* that the curtain descended to an explosion of applause. It is true that M. de Reszke utterly missed the simple dignity of his part of the duet with Amneris in the first scene of the last act; but that did not obscure his great success: the audience, delighted with him, accepting his version with enthusiasm. Signor d'Andrade, in coffee color and tiger skins, ranted as Amonasro in a manner against which common sense ought to have guarded him. Why the Ethiopian captive king should be conceived on the Italian stage, not even as an antique Cetewayo, but as a frenzied Hottentot, is hard to understand. Verdi certainly had no such intention, as the character of the music proves. Madame Scalchi played Amneris with passion and a certain tragic grace that might make her an actress, if it were possible for anyone to become an actress in such an atmosphere of incongruity and nonsense as that which an operatic artist is condemned to breathe.

20 September 1888

JAMES HENRY MAPLESON, alias Enrico Mariani, commonly and unaccountably spoken of as Colonel Mapleson, one time professional viola player, later operatic vocalist, and finally for twenty-seven years London *impresario* at Drury Lane and Her Majesty's Theatre, has written The Mapleson Memoirs. They are very amusing, especially to readers who, like the Colonel himself, have no suspicion that his record covers a period of hopeless decay. The financial record is depressing enough; but that is nothing new in the history of Italian Opera in England, since all the *impresarios,* from Handel to Laporte and Lumley, lost money, and lived, as far as one can make out, chiefly on the splendor of the scale on which they got into debt. Nevertheless they kept the insti-

39

tution afoot in the good old style, with absurd high-falutin'
prospectuses, expensive ballets, rapacious star singers and
star dancers, and unscrupulous performances in which the
last thing thought of was the fulfilment of the composer's
intentions. What was wanted, after Lumley's retirement,
was a manager with sufficient artistic sensibility to perceive
that these abuses, which Wagner and Berlioz had quite sufficiently exposed, must be done away with if the opera house
was to hold its own against the ordinary theatre. Unfortunately, Colonel Mapleson's most indulgent friends can
hardly claim for him any such musical and dramatic conscience. The period between the disappearance of Mario and
the advent of Jean de Reszke is hardly to be recalled without
a shudder, in spite of Christine Nilsson, and such fine artists
as De Murska, Trebelli, Santley, and Agnesi. Costa maintained rigid discipline in the orchestra; and Titiens's geniality,
her grand air, the remains of her great voice, and even her
immense corpulence covered for a time her essential obso-
lescence as an artist; but the prevailing want of life, purpose,
sincerity, and concerted artistic effort would have destroyed
a circus, much less the Opera; and the enterprise went from
bad to worse, until it finally collapsed from utter rottenness.

Colonel Mapleson's negative contributions to this result
may have been considerable. His positive contribution was
the selection of such a line of tenors, all straight from La
Scala, and all guaranteed beforehand to replace and eclipse
Mario and Giuglini, as we may fervently hope never to hear
again. Colonel Mapleson hopes to take the field again next
season; and no one can help wishing that his perseverance
may be rewarded with success. But if he proceeds on his old
plan, or want of plan, he will only add another failure to his
list. If he has learnt at last that the lyric stage cannot lag a
century behind the ordinary theatre; that the days of
scratch performances are over; that Donizetti is dead; that
Wagner is the most popular composer of the day; that the
Costa conception of orchestral conducting has been succeeded by the Richter conception; and that people will not

pay to see heroes and gentlemen impersonated by tenors who are not distinguishable in manners, appearance, voice, or talent from the average vendor of penny ices, then, and not otherwise, he may succeed. It is only fair to add, by the way, that Colonel Mapleson is by no means the only *impresario* who has hitherto failed to take this lesson to heart.

26 November 1888

A NEW quintet by Dvorak brought a large audience to St James's Hall on Saturday afternoon. The success of a popular concert is always a question of luck; for if the leader of the quartet be out of sorts, or the pianist indisposed, the affair is a grief and a disappointment to all except those devotees whose enthusiasm for great compositions and great artists is a manufactured literary product, capable of standing any quantity of wear and tear. Nobody will ever know how much Messrs Chappell owe to their having made St James's Hall a fool's paradise, and how much to genuine musical taste and culture. On Saturday, happily, all went well. By the time the trio of the opening quartet (Mozart's in B flat: the first of the Haydn set) was reached, it was apparent that Madame Neruda was in the vein, and was about to display all her superb qualities: her fire and precision, her perfect artistic relation to her fellow artists, her unerring intonation and unflagging and unforced expression. Her playing was especially admirable in the Mozartian slow movement, which is, as great artists know, one of the most delicate and searching tests a player can undergo. After it the quintet was a trifle; and it goes without saying that she carried Dvorak through brilliantly, making his work seem as delightful as her playing of the first violin part, which it by no means is. With worse executants it would have been found too full of odds and ends from the common stock of musical phrases, with the usual Dvorakian dressing of Bohemian rhythms and intervals, which give the analytical programmist an opportunity of writing about "national traits," and save the composer the trouble of developing his individual traits. The quintet is chiefly remarkable for the advance it marks in the composer's constructive ability, both as regards polyphony and the sonata form. The first movement is well balanced and shapely; and in the *andante* Dvorak has successfully contrived a form of his own. If the quintet were as fresh as it is well put together it would be a valuable addition to our store of chamber music. As it is, it will not be so popular without Madame Neruda's help as it proved on Saturday.

Of Miss Bertha Moore's singing it is only necessary to say that she selected Sullivan's Orpheus, as all ladies do who can take a high B flat pianissimo, and Grieg's setting of Solveig's song from Ibsen's great poetic drama Peer Gynt.

Sir Charles Hallé played Beethoven's sonata in D Major, No. 3 of Op. 10. Sir Charles is not a sensational player; but nobody who has heard him play the *largo* of this sonata has ever accepted the notion that his playing is "icy and mechanical." Is there any audience in the world that would come to hear Rubenstein play a Beethoven sonata for the twentieth time? Yet Hallé (to drop the prefix which he shares with the ex-Chief Commissioner of Police) is always sure of his audience, no matter how often he has repeated the sonata he chooses. The secret is that he gives you as little as possible of Hallé and as much as possible of Beethoven, of whom people do not easily tire. When Beethoven is made a mere *cheval de bataille* for a Rubenstein, the interest is more volatile. The "classical" players have the best of it in the long run.

3 December 1888

MR MANNS might have arranged his programme at the Crystal Palace on Saturday afternoon more considerately. Schumann's concerto in A minor is a beautiful work; and the Rhenish symphony is not to be despised. But to play them one after the other, with only one incongruous interruption

42

in the shape of Rossini's *Bel raggio* between, is, to say the least, not a tactful proceeding. Why an inoffensive Saturday audience, all devoted to Mr Manns, should be compelled to wallow for an hour and a half in the noisy monotony and opacity of Schumann's instrumentation, is not to be guessed on any benevolent theory of concert administration. However, what is done is done. In the present instance it is not even necessary to describe how it was done, further than to say that the pianist was Madame Essipoff. That lady's terrible precision and unfailing nerve; her cold contempt for difficulties; her miraculous speed, free from any appearance of haste; her grace and finesse, without a touch of anything as weak as tenderness: all these are subjects for awe rather than for criticism. When she played Chopin's waltz in A flat, it did not sound like Chopin: the ear could not follow the lightning play of her right hand. Yet she was not, like Rubenstein at that speed, excited and furious over it: she was cold as ice: one felt like Tartini on the celebrated occasion when he got the suggestion for his Trillo del Diavolo. Additional impressiveness was given to the performance by the fact that Madame Essipoff has no platform mannerisms or affectations. When the applause reached the point at which an encore was inevitable, she walked to the pianoforte without wasting a second; shot at the audience, without a note of prelude, an exercise about 40 seconds long, and of satanic difficulty; and vanished as calmly as she had appeared. Truly an astonishing—almost a fearful player. Mademoiselle Badia's songs would have done excellently at a concert in Paris in the year 1850; but after Schumann they were anachronisms.

12 *December* 1888

LONDON has now had two opportunities of tasting Mr Hubert Parry's Judith, the oratorio which he composed for this year's Birmingham festival. It was performed on the 6th of this month at St James's Hall, and again on Saturday last at the Crystal Palace, with Dr Mackenzie in the seat of Mr Manns (gone to Scotland), and the Palace choir replaced by that of Novello's oratorio concerts. The truth about the oratorio is one of those matters which a critic is sorely tempted to mince. Mr Parry is a gentleman of culture and independent means, pursuing his beloved art with a devotion and disinterestedness which is not possible to musicians who have to live by their profession. He is guiltless of potboilers and catchpennies, and both in his compositions and in his excellent literary essays on music he has proved the constant elevation of his musical ideal. Never was there a musician easier and pleasanter to praise, painfuller and more ungracious to disparage. But—! yes, there is a serious but in the case on the present occasion; and its significance is that when a man takes it upon himself to write an oratorio—perhaps the most gratuitous exploit open to a nineteenth century Englishman—he must take the consequences.

Judith, then, consists of a sort of musical fabric that any gentleman of Mr Parry's general culture, with a turn for music and the requisite technical training, can turn out to any extent needful for the purposes of a Festival Committee. There is not a rhythm in it, not a progression, not a modulation that brings a breath of freshness with it. The pretentious choruses are made up of phrases mechanically repeated on ascending degrees of the scale, or of hackneyed scraps of fugato and pedal point. The unpretentious choruses, smooth and sometimes pretty hymnings about nothing in particular, would pass muster in a mild cantata: in an oratorio they are flavorless. It is impossible to work up any interest in emasculated Handel and watered Mendelssohn, even with all the modern adulterations. The instrumentation is conventional to the sleepiest degree: tromboned solemnities, sentimentalities for solo horn with tremolo accompaniment, nervous excitement fiddled *in excelsis*, drum points as invented by Beethoven, and the rest of the worn-out novelties of modern scoring.

Of the music assigned to the principal singers, that of

LONDON MUSIC IN 1888–89

Judith is the hardest to judge, as Miss Anna Williams labored through its difficulties without eloquence or appropriate expression, and hardly ever got quite safely and reassuringly into tune. Mdme. Patey as Meshullemeth discoursed in lugubrious dramatic recitative about desolate courts and profaned altars. She was repaid for her thankless exertions by one popular number in the form of a ballad which consisted of the first line of The Minstrel Boy, followed by the second line of Tom Bowling, connected by an "augmentation" of a passage from the finale of the second act of Lucrezia Borgia, with an ingenious blend of The Girl I Left Behind Me and We be Three Poor Mariners. It will be understood, of course, that the intervals—except in the Lucrezia Borgia case—are altered, and that the source of Mr Parry's unconscious inspiration is betrayed by the accent and measure only. Manasseh, a paltry creature who sings Sunday music for the drawing room whilst his two sons are cremated alive before his eyes, was impersonated by Mr Barton McGuckin, who roused a bored audience by his delivery of a Handelian song, which has the fault of not being by Handel, but is otherwise an agreeable composition, and a great relief to the music which precedes it. Indeed matters generally grow livelier towards the end.

The Israelites become comparatively bright and vigorous when Judith cuts Holofernes' head off. The ballad is gratefully remembered; the enchanting singing of Manasseh's son is dwelt upon; the Handelian song is quoted as a fine thing; and so Judith passes muster for the time.

One of the painful features of oratorio performances in this country is the indifference of most English singers to the artistic treatment of their own language. Hardly any of them shew the results of such training as that by which Italian singers used to be kept at *do, re, mi, fa* until they acquired a certain virtuosity in the sounding of the vowel and the articulation of the consonant. On Saturday afternoon it was not pleasant to hear Mr Barton McGuckin singing line after line as if he were vocalizing for the sake of practice on the very disagreeable vowel "*aw*." By a singer who knows this department of his business, such a word, for example, as "command" is a prized opportunity. Mr Barton McGuckin pronounced it "co-monnd" and spoiled it. It is somewhat unlucky that artists who are aware of the full importance of pronunciation, and whose cultivated sense of hearing keeps them acutely conscious of distinctions to which the ordinary singer seems deaf, are also for the most part persons with a strong mannerism, which makes it unsafe to recommend them as models for imitation. Advise a student to pronounce as Mr Irving does, as Mr Sims Reeves does, as Mrs Weldon does, or as Madame Antoinette Sterling does, and the chances are that that student will simply graft on to his own cockney diphthongs and muddled consonants, an absurd burlesque of Mr Irving's resonant nose, of Mr Sims Reeves' lackadaisical way of letting the unaccented syllables die away, of Mrs Weldon's inflexible delivery and shut teeth, or of Madame Sterling's peculiar cadence and Scottish-American accent.

The importance of this question of English as she is sung is emphasized just now by the advertisement which announces Mr Leslie's very laudable and far-sighted plan of making the new Lyric Theatre an English opera house. English opera suggests at once the Carl Rosa style of entertainment. Now, with all due honor to Mr Carl Rosa's enterprise and perseverance, the performances of his company have never, even at their best, achieved a satisfactory degree of distinction and refinement. But what is peculiar to its representation is the slovenliness in uttering the national language. In an institution which ought to be a school of pure English this is disgraceful, the more so as the defect is, of course, not really the result of social and educational disadvantages, but only of indifference caused by colloquial habit, and by want of artistic sensibility and vigilance.

The Gilbert-Sullivan form of opera caused a remarkable improvement in this respect by making the success of the whole enterprise depend on the pointed and intelligible delivery of the words. It is an encouraging sign, too, that in the success of Dorothy a very important share has been borne by Mr Hayden Coffin, an American, who is a much more accomplished master of his language than many older and more famous baritones of English birth. If Mr Leslie is well advised he will test the artists whom he engages for his new theatre no less carefully as speakers than as singers.

The other day a small but select audience assembled in one of Messrs Broadwood's rooms to hear Miss Florence May play a pianoforte concerto by Brahms. An orchestra being out of the question, Mr Otto Goldschmidt and Mr Kemp played an arrangement of the band parts on two pianofortes. Brahms's music is at bottom only a prodigiously elaborated compound of incoherent reminiscences, and it is quite possible for a young lady with one of those wonderful "techniques," which are freely manufactured at Leipzig and other places, to struggle with his music for an hour at a stretch without giving such an insight to her higher powers as half a dozen bars of a sonata by Mozart. All that can be said confidently of Miss May is that her technique is undeniable. The ensemble of the three Broadwood grands was not so dreadful as might have been expected, and the pretty finale pleased everybody.

(The above hasty (not to say silly) description of Brahms's music will, I hope, be a warning to critics who know too much. In every composer's work there are passages that are part of the common stock of music of the time; and when a new genius arises, and his idiom is still unfamiliar and therefore even disagreeable, it is easy for a critic who knows that stock to recognize its contributions to the new work and fail to take in the original complexion put upon it. Beethoven denounced Weber's Euryanthe overture as a string of diminished sevenths. I had not yet got hold of the idiosyncratic Brahms. I apologize. (1936).)

LONDON MUSIC IN 1888–89

Mr August Manns evidently made up his mind last week that nobody should reproach him again with want of variety in the Saturday programme. Mozart, Schubert, Berlioz, Mr Hamish MacCunn, and Sir Arthur Sullivan were represented by some of their most characteristic work. The concert began with the overture to the Yeomen of the Guard, by way of signalizing the replacement in Gilbert-Sullivan opera of potpourri prelude by orthodox overture. Then the orchestra got to serious business in the G minor symphony. The performance of the first and last movements only showed that Mozart can utterly baffle a band for which Beethoven, Berlioz, and Wagner have no terrors. It is useless to try to make the G minor symphony "go" by driving a too heavy body of strings through it with all the splendor and impetuosity of an Edinburgh express. That has been tried over and over again in London, with the result that Mozart's reputation positively declined steadily until Hans Richter conducted the E flat symphony here. Wagner has told us how, when he first began to frequent concerts, he was astonished to find that conductors always contrived to make Mozart's music sound vapid. Vapid is hardly the word for any performance conducted by Mr Manns; but on Saturday, except in the slow movement and minuet, his energy was unavailing. It was magnificent; but it was not Mozart. When M. Marsick began Wieniawski's concerto in D, it at first seemed that a disappointment was in store. Wieniawski's work, which is much more truly violin music than the Beethoven and Mendelssohn concertos, requires above all a violinist who can play with perfect spontaneity, and even with abandonment. M. Marsick was constrained and mechanical, and his instrument, not at all in the vein, whined comfortlessly. Not until the movement was half over did his spirits improve. In the andante he completely recovered himself, and the final allegro was a triumph for him. A handsome recall at the end put him on the best of terms with the

48

audience, who subsequently applauded him enthusiastically for a very pretty Dans Slavacque, which he played exquisitely. The vocal pieces were sung by Miss Antoinette Trebelli, who imitates, with the facility of a child, what she has heard other people doing around her all her life; but who certainly displays as yet no individuality, style, purpose, or even earnest respect for her work. For the sake of the distinguished artist whose name she bears, Miss Trebelli has been allowed a very favorable start. But she will lose that start if she allows herself to be spoilt by the foolish people who recalled her for an immature trifling with *Non mi dir*, an aria which only very intelligent, refined, and sympathetic singers should attempt. Miss Trebelli not only attempted it without these qualifications, but actually tampered with the concluding bars by way of improvement upon Mozart. Mr Hamish MacCunn's happy thought of setting Lord Ullin's Daughter in the freest and easiest way for chorus and orchestra was as successful as ever. Pearsall would have laughed at the cheapness of the success; but Pearsall would have been wrong; the *naïveté* with which Mr MacCunn has gone to work in the simplest fashion is his great merit. The concert ended with Berlioz's first overture, Les Francs Juges, one of the most striking examples of his curious gift of brains and brimstone. A few old-fashioned bars of Rossinian tum-tum in it sounded oddly beside the poignantly expressive section in C minor, the effect of which will not readily be forgotten by those who heard it for the first time.

12 December 1888

THE Wagner Society has just completed the opening volume of its journal The Meister by the issue of the fourth quarterly part at the modest price of a shilling. At first sight The Meister suggests a quarto edition of The Hobby Horse; but closer inspection reveals a cover from the slapdash drawing of which the Century Guild would recoil, and a printed page which certainly cannot be compared to the "solid set" letterpress which enabled The Hobby Horse, at the Arts and Crafts Exhibition, to hold its own beside the most beautiful of old Italian books. It is the content rather than the form that makes The Meister respectable. Mr Charles Dowdeswell's Schopenhauer articles are admirably done; and the translation of Art and Revolution is one that no Socialist should be without. The editorial tone, however, is not Wagnerian: there is an evident indisposition to provoke hostility. This, with respect be it spoken, was not an indisposition to which The Meister himself was at all subject. There is one editorial footnote in the volume which he would have regarded as recreant. To be quite satisfactory, The Meister wants three things: a title-page by Mr Selwyn Image or Mr Walter Crane; a printer who appreciates The Hobby Horse, and is not above taking a hint from it; and a fighting editor.

Messrs Rud, Ibach, and Co. are exhibiting, at 113 Oxford Street, Beckmann's picture of Wagner in the music room at his Bayreuth home, Wahnfried. Cosima is seen in profile, seated on the composer's right; and Liszt sits with his back to the window and the score of Parsifal on his knees. The picture is already known by the photogravure reproduction which has found its way into one or two shop windows. Mr Ibach was a personal friend of Wagner's; and the picture is to be seen free of charge at his pianoforte rooms until its voyage to America, which is close at hand.

3 January 1889

On New Year's night at the Albert Hall, Messiah is the affair of the shilling gallery, and not of the seven-and-sixpenny stalls. Up there you find every chair occupied, and people standing two or three deep behind the chairs. These sitters and standers are the gallery vanguard, consisting of *prima donna* worshippers who are bent on obtaining a bird's-eye view of Madame Albani for their money. At the back are those who are content to hear Handel's music. They sit on the floor against the wall, with their legs converging straight towards the centre of the dome, and terminating in an inner circumference of boot soles in various stages of wear and tear. Between the circle of boots and the circle of sightseers moves a ceaseless procession of promenaders to whom the performance is as the sounding brass and tinkling cymbals of a military band on a pier. The police take this view, and deal with the gallery as with a thoroughfare included in the Trafalgar Square proclamation, calling out, "Pass along, pass along," and even going the length of a decisive shove when the promenade is at all narrowed by too many unreasonable persons stopping to listen to the music. The crowd is a motley one, including many mechanics, who have bought Novello's vocal score of the oratorio and are following it diligently; professional men who cannot afford that luxury and are fain to peep enviously over the mechanics' shoulders; musicians in the Bohemian phase of artistic life; masses of "shilling people" of the ordinary type; the inevitable man with the opera-glass and campstool; and one enthusiast with a blanket on his shoulder, who has apparently been ordered by the police to take up his bed and walk.

To those who heard the Albert Hall Choral Society for the first time on Monday evening, the performance cannot have been a very lively one. The "cuts" (*i.e.* numbers omitted) were many and audacious. They actually included For He shall purify, one of the finest and most popular of Handel's choruses. And with His stripes, Their Sound has gone out, The Trumpet shall sound, and others were also ruthlessly excised. The choruses retained for the occasion were sung in the old prosaic jog-trot. Unto Us a Child is Born was sung correctly, and with admirable purity of tone; but in spirit and feeling it might have been the congratulations offered to a respectable suburban family on the latest addition to the nursery: one whose name could not by any stretch of imagination be called Wonderful! Counsellor! The Everlasting Father, the Prince of Peace. Through that fierce and sardonic tumult of mockery, He trusted in God that He would deliver Him, the choir picked its way with a gingerly decorum that suggested a hampering sense of the danger of prosecution for blasphemy. And, later on, in the most famous of all famous choruses, there was not one real, rapturous, transporting Hallelujah. The truth is that Mr Barnby has done with those thousand choristers everything that a conductor can do—except kindle their imagination. That exception places Messiah beyond their reach. Until he can make them rejoice and exult like all the hosts of heaven, and scorn and deride like all the fanatics in Jewry, young London will grow up ignorant of the wonderful qualities which underlie the mere brute amplitude of one of the greatest treasures in their musical heritage. How fast those qualities are being forgotten—how little they are missed, is shewn by the conventional praise which each performance like that of Monday elicits from their appointed assayers in the press.

But if the foregoing must be said in justice to Handel and music, a word must also be said in justice to Mr Barnby. Only those whose memories of the choir go back at least a dozen years can appreciate the wonders he has done with it. In its raw state, its aptitudes for everything except the production of pure vocal tone were manifold and extraordinary. It could hiss, it could growl, it could choke, buzz, gasp, seethe, and whistle until the Albert Hall was like the King's Cross Metropolitan station, with four trains in, all letting off steam, and an artillery waggon coming full gallop up the Gray's Inn Road, whilst somewhere at the heart of the hurly-burly All We like Sheep were being imperfectly kept from going too much astray by Dr Stainer thundering at the organ. Then the orchestra, the indolent, callous, slovenly orchestra, that thought the accompaniments to the old Messiah the cheapest of easy jobs, that was killing Covent Garden by its slovenliness, killing the Philharmonic by its perfunctoriness, under the anxious and estimable Mr Cusins, respecting nobody but Mr August Manns, and fearing nobody but Sir Michael Costa! Mr Weist Hill, too, got some notable work out of them, but he did not shake their conviction that they could not be done without, and in that conviction they hardened

themselves until Richter came and beat them easily with
what they considered a scratch band of rank outsiders.
Those were terrible days for Mr Barnby; but his present
achievement gathers lustre from their darkness and confusion. The choir now sings, and abstains from unlovely
noises. The tone might be more voluminous considering the
multitude of singers; but it could hardly be purer and clearer.
And the orchestra, thoroughly reformed, respects itself and
its conductor. Mr Smith's conquest of the House of Commons is a joke in comparison. Mr Barnby has made a noble
position as an immense, indefatigable worker and a consummate musician. Now is the time for him to consider
whether he has not also a poet somewhere in him. If *he*
were forthcoming, what a conductor Mr Barnby would
be!

There is not much to be said about the four principal
singers of Monday. Their work required a very beautiful and
eloquent delivery of some of the most touching and impressive passages in our language. It also required complete
forgetfulness of the vanities of vocal display. On both points
Madame Patey got the better of Madame Albani; but
neither lady succeeded in perfectly realizing her true artistic
relation to the oratorio. Madame Albani altered the ending
of her songs for the worse in the bad old fashion which is
now, happily for London, vanishing to the provinces. This
time no old gentleman got up to exclaim, "Woman, for this
be all thy sins forgiven thee" at the end of He shall feed his
Flock; for the singer of that exquisite strain was too bent on
finishing "effectively" to finish well. However, the two voices
were grand voices, and so could not wholly miss the mark at
any time. Mr C. Banks was the tenor. The English tradition
as to the tenor music of The Messiah is distinctly a maudlin
tradition, and it is much to Mr Banks's credit that he was
not unmanly in his pathos. For the rest, his performance
lacked distinction. By the bye, he—or Mr Barnby—took
Every Valley so fast that it was spoiled. The audience was
much pleased by Mr Watkin Mills's delivery of Why do the

Nations, and was a little astonished at his omitting The
Trumpet shall Sound.

23 *January* 1889

MADAME PATTI kissed hands last night, in her artless way,
to a prodigious audience come to bid her farewell before her
trip to South America. The unnecessary unpleasantness of
the most useful of Mr Louis Stevenson's novels makes it impossible to say that there is in Madame Patti an Adelina
Jekyll and an Adelina Hyde; but there are certainly two
very different sides to her public character. There is Patti
the great singer: Patti of the beautiful eloquent voice, so
perfectly produced and controlled that its most delicate
pianissimo reaches the remotest listener in the Albert Hall:
Patti of the unerring ear, with her magical *roulade* soaring to
heavenly altitudes: Patti of the pure, strong tone that made
God save the Queen sound fresh and noble at Covent
Garden: Patti of the hushed, tender notes that reconcile
rows of club-loving cynics to Home, Sweet Home. This was
the famous artist who last night sang *Bel raggio* and Comin'
thro' the Rye incomparably. With Verdure Clad would also
have been perfect but that the intonation of the orchestra
got wrong and spoiled it. But there is another Patti: a Patti
who cleverly sang and sang again some pretty nonsense from
Delibes' Lakmé. Great was the applause, even after it had
been repeated; and then the comedy began. Mr Ganz, whilst
the house was shouting and clapping uproariously, deliberately took up his *bâton* and started Moszkowski's Serenata
in D. The audience took its cue at once, and would not have
Moszkowski. After a prolonged struggle, Mr Ganz gave up
in despair; and out tripped the *diva*, bowing her acknowledg-
ments in the character of a petted and delighted child. When
she vanished there was more cheering than ever. Mr Ganz
threatened the serenata again; but in vain. He appealed to
the sentinels of the greenroom; and these shook their heads,
amidst roars of protest from the audience, and at last, with

elaborate gesture, conveyed in dumb show that they dare not, could not, would not, must not, venture to approach Patti again. Mr Ganz, with well-acted desolation, went on with the serenata, not one note of which was heard. Again he appealed to the sentinels; and this time they waved their hands expansively in the direction of South America, to indicate that the prima donna was already on her way thither. On this the audience showed such sudden and unexpected signs of giving in that the diva tripped out again, bowing, wafting kisses, and successfully courting fresh thunders of applause. Will not some sincere friend of Madame Patti's tell her frankly that she is growing too big a girl for this sort of thing, which imposes on nobody—not even on the infatuated gentlemen who write columns about her fans and jewels. No: the queens of song should leave the coquetry of the footlights to the soubrettes. How much more dignified was Madame Neruda's reception of the magnificent ovation which followed her playing of Bazzini's Ronde des Lutins!

It is unnecessary to say more of the rest of the programme than that *È che! fra voi la tema* brought back pleasantly the days when Mr Santley trod the stage, and that Wallace's ridiculous Let me like a Soldier Fall was treated as it deserves, even though it was Mr Edward Lloyd's breast that "expanded to the ball." Miss Gomez made a very favorable impression by her singing of Sir Arthur Sullivan's Sleep, my love, sleep. Madame Patti, it may be added, looks very well and strong, and her voice is as good as ever.

23 January 1889

The unexpected death of Dr Hueffer is a loss to the best interests of music in London. Fortunately, his warfare was accomplished before he fell. The critics who formerly opposed him on the ground that Wagner's music had no form and no melody, that it was noisy and wrong, and never ought to have been written, and could never be popular, came at last to be only too grateful to Hueffer for his willingness to forget their folly. He was a thorough and industrious worker in many departments, and much better equipped for his work both by his capacity and acquirements than many of his colleagues who were by no means so modest.

Personally he was an amiable man, shy and even timid; but he did not look so, and he often produced the most erroneous impressions on those who were only slightly acquainted with him. His long golden-red beard, shining forehead, and accentuated nostrils made him a remarkable figure at musical performances. Formerly he was careless of his dress and appearance; but of late years he became rather the reverse. His work as a critic was not confined to music: the present writer last met him at the press view of the Arts and Crafts Exhibition at the New Gallery, and at his own request introduced him to Mr Walter Crane, certainly without the slightest presentiment that the meeting was final.

25 January 1889

EVERY reader of this column is, I presume, a lover of music, aware, as such, that noise is not music, and shrinking from the multiplication of drums and cymbals as from an outrage on all true and delicate art. This cultivated state of mind comes of reading high-toned criticism. I cannot say that I have attained it myself—unless noise is defined as mere empty toneless clatter. But if it means magnitude of sound, then I may as well confess at once that I hardly ever get noise enough to satisfy me. I despise an orchestra if its fortissimo does not leave me as if an avalanche had come thundering and roaring upon me, sweeping me away like a feather with its mere wind. Until every man has gone to the bottomless depths of sonority potential in his instrument— until the basses are lifting the ground like an earthquake— until the trebles are whistling like a storm through the giant teeth of the Alps—until the middle parts can drown with their impetuous charge the rush of an express train through a tunnel—until even Philharmonic fogeydom believes and trembles, my craving for immense sound is unsatisfied.

I enjoy the Richter orchestra because its fortissimo is unapproached by that of any other band in London. After its gorgeous tone paintings the performances of the Philharmonic seem but pretty water-color sketches. On Monday nights this season I have been so much occupied with the opera—which requires a good deal of parental looking after —that I have missed the whole Richter series so far with the exception of the Wagner Society concert this week. Now, I am not going to waste time in describing how stupendously they played the Rienzi overture and the Kaisermarsch, or how the orchestra made itself a Cyclopean bellows in the forest smithy of Mime, and wafted the air of the mediaeval burgher town about the meditations of Hans Sachs. No; my business is perpetually to find fault until the limit of attainable perfection is reached. A moment ago I disparaged the Philharmonic orchestra. Now let me say that, though it could not have played the Rienzi overture so as to give me concussion of the brain (which is the right way), yet it would certainly have accompanied Mr Edward Lloyd in the first part of Lohengrin's farewell speech with much more refinement than the Richterians. The wood wind lacked delicacy of touch; and the Grail music was—of all things—mundane.

Mr Edward Lloyd delivers his words better than many English singers; but he was not half so intelligible as Mr Max Heinrich, an admirable baritone singer, whom I had not heard before (probably he has not been singing here for more than a couple of years). Mr Lloyd does Siegfried very well, just as Mrs Kendal would do Schiller's Joan of Arc very well if she were put at it. Still, his laugh, though a very well-bred laugh, is hardly the exultant shout of a young giant over his anvil. Mr William Nicholl should try to get Mime's music safely on his ear. He sings it as if he were reading it at sight, and felt hopelessly bothered by the harmony. In short, he sings it out of tune. The performance of the wonderful Parsifal music was a little labored and uneasy: its divine atmosphere was much clouded and troubled by its

technical unfamiliarity; but on the whole it was meritori-
ously done. The set of sonorous cylinders seem to me to give
satisfactory bell effects; but surely the fifth in the peal is
atrociously flat. Can it not be replaced next time by a fresh
cylinder?

On Tuesday I was again in St James's Hall at the concert
of the Chevalier Emil Bach. I applaud the Chevalier for
engaging the Philharmonic orchestra and Mr Cusins; I
deplore his ambition to compose a pianoforte concerto; I
protest against his sending me the most uncomfortable seat
in St James's Hall: a seat which drove me away, groaning
with artificially induced sciatica and lumbago, at the end of
the first part. It was the fault of that seat that I did not hear
the Chevalier's songs, nor his playing of the Weber polonaise; and I hereby solemnly warn Mr Vert and the musical
profession in general that if they ever again send me a ticket
numbered AA15 I shall destroy it as I would a mad dog.

Mr Cusins seized the opportunity to let us have that
charming Fingal's Cave overture of Mendelssohn's, which it
is almost as hard to hear nowadays as it is to avoid hearing
Cherubini's Anacreon. Madame Sembrich sang *Giunse al fin*;
and never have I writhed as I did when Madame Sembrich
altered the exquisite and perfect ending of Mozart's exquisite and perfect song. After that her arts were lost on me. I
listened sternly to the *scena* from Lucia, with its two touching melodies, and its ridiculous and old-fashioned florid
frippery in which the flute enters into a contest of pure fool-
ishness with the human voice. I could not laugh at it as I
usually do. Nor was my eye dimmed with emotion when a
huge bouquet was brought up by no less a person than
Christine Nilsson, who ought to have known better, and the
air was filled with bowing and handshaking and wafting of
kisses and all the old undignified humbug that even the
Opera has outgrown. Sarasate was looking on. I wonder
what he thought of it all!

As to the Chevalier's concerto, I shall be brief and frank.
The proper place for the first movement is the fireplace. The

other two, with a little trimming, may be allowed to survive as pretty little sketches. The program of the concert, by the bye, must have been printed at The Star office. Such a champion misprint as *Spargi d'amaro puanto* could have been achieved nowhere else. As to Miss Isaacson's concert of chamber music at Princes' Hall the same afternoon, with Mr Carrodus and Mr E. Howell, I can only offer my sincere apologies for being unable to get there. Ordinary critics find it almost impossible to be in two places at the same time. I find considerable difficulty in being in one.

I regret to have to announce that The British Bandsman, an excellent paper devoted to the interests of the brass banditti, has had the mad presumption to "strongly suspect that I am deficient in knowledge of wind instruments." This is true; but I am not going to be told so by any British bandsman alive. How am I to make myself respected as a critic if the public for a moment suspects that there is anything I dont know? Besides, the B.B. is really too hard on me. The euphonium is not to me "an instrument unknown." I learnt to be gentle and modest, not at my mother's knee, but by listening to the diffident mooings of British bandsmen trying to play Oh, happy days! on the euphonium, in selections from L'Étoile du Nord. As to the ophicleide being obsolete, I did not say it was not. The "chromatic bullock" was born obsolete; but it is no more obsolete today than it ever was. It seems only the other day that Mr Hughes was playing. Oh, ruddier than the cherry! on it at Covent Garden.

However, I am not punctilious on the subject of the ophicleide. When its part is played on a tuba in the Midsummer Night's Dream overture, I never dream of objecting to the substitution. But when The British Bandsman goes on to speak of the trumpet in the same strain, then I put down my foot. I am aware that there is a delusion rife among bandsmen that the great composers have written trumpet parts out of mere amateurish ignorance of the cornet. I am also rather disposed to laugh occasionally when

Mr Morrow or Mr M'Grath, in a sudden fit of classic reverence, solemnly produce the slide trumpet of commerce—a surpassingly obdurate and disagreeable instrument—and blare away with it through Mendelssohn's violin concerto. These trumpets, if it were worth anyone's while to learn to play them, would doubtless give the peculiar close, ringing, penetrating sound that the cornet so completely misses; but then they would probably fail in the soft cornet effects in which Wagner's and Gounod's scores abound. What we really want is a revival of the old Handel and Bach trumpet, which Kosleck, of Berlin, handled so brilliantly at the Albert Hall a few years ago, and which Mr Morrow (I think it was Mr Morrow) tried last year for the Bach Choir. I do not suggest that it should oust the cornet from the orchestra, but only from those trumpet parts in which the cornet is out of place.

(It was after this that the cornet vanished from our symphony orchestras. I do not know what conductor kicked it out; so I may as well claim the credit for the above protest. The slide trumpet, being now played by trumpeters, and not by cornettists forced to take a very occasional turn at an unfamiliar instrument, is no longer obdurate or disagreeable; though I still deny that it is a true trumpet. We need a great artist reformer, a musical William Morris, to recover for us the character and variety of our wind instruments.

23 *January* 1889

THE Saturday Popular concerts are almost too popular to be comfortable. Standing room is exhausted before three o'clock. This on the last occasion was not due to Haydn's quartet in C, with the variations on the Austrian hymn. It was not wholly due even to Mr Santley with The Erl King, and To Anthea. It was very largely caused by the announcement of Beethoven's septet. The way in which people flock to St James's Hall when a few wind instruments are added to the fiddles, is only one out of many symptoms of the thirst for orchestral music which remains unsatisfied in London. Private enterprise is a curious thing. When an eminent French engineer suggests an impossible canal through Central America millions are forthcoming instantly. Yet London clamors in vain for a West-end concert-room capable of accommodating on every Saturday afternoon enough people at a shilling a head to support an orchestra 200 strong. It not only clamors, but gives repeated proofs of the sincerity of its demand, and the readiness of its shillings. But no; Panama will be dug through, the Channel Tunnel finished, and the North-west Passage carpeted before we escape from St James's Hall, where either the orchestra is too small, as with Mr Henschel, or the prices too high, as with Herr Richter. Will not some American millionaire take the matter in hand; build the hall; and give the baton to Mr Theodore Thomas to revenge on the English conductors the wrongs of the American actors?

Howbeit, this particular concert squeezed itself into St James's Hall until, as has been intimated, St James himself could not have been accommodated with a place. It is unnecessary to say how the quartet was played. Listening to the septet, it was impossible to avoid indulging in some stray speculations as to the age of Mr Lazarus. Fifty or sixty years ago, when the great clarionettist was beginning to rank as a veteran, the subject might have been a delicate one. Today it is difficult to know how to treat him critically; for it would be absurd to encourage him as if he were a promising young player; and yet there is no use in declaring that he "played with his usual ability," because his ability is still, unfortunately for us, as far as ever from being usual. The usual clarinet player is stolid, mechanical, undistinguished, correct at best, vulgar at worst. A phrase played by Mr Lazarus always came, even from the unnoticed ranks of the wood wind at the opera, with a distinction and fine artistic feeling that roused a longing for an orchestra of such players. And his phrases come just that way still. When, in the slow movement of the septet, Mr Lazarus would not have it so fast as

Madame Neruda wanted, the question arose whether the difference was one of taste or of age. But when Madame Neruda led off the final presto at full speed without sparing a flash of her Hungarian fire, Mr Lazarus answered the question by following her spirited challenge, without slackening one demisemiquaver. For the rest, Mr Paersch managed the horn part with perfect discretion, and Mr Hollander handled his viola admirably; but Signor Piatti was out of sorts, and got quite amazingly out of tune in the trio.

But the highest plane of musical enjoyment during the concert was attained in Beethoven's pianoforte sonata in A flat (Op. 110). Unfortunately, this plane is a select one: it is not everyone who feels at home on it. Among the people who dont may generally be classed those who hunt after popular vocalists and never brave the inclemency of classical music except when Mr Sims Reeves or some other famous singer is in the bill. On Saturday, all the chinks and crannies in the audience were stuffed with ballad-concert enthusiasts who had come solely to hear Mr Santley. When Madame Haas began to play Beethoven's Op. 110 they held out for a while in silent misery. Then they began to cough. Now Madame Haas was beginning an exquisite work, most beautifully— most poetically—and was indeed so rapt in it that it is quite possible that the spell may have been too delicately woven to reach her more distant hearers. It may be, too, that even the regular frequenters of the concerts are accustomed to have Beethoven's later works soundly thumped into them; and Madame Haas is certainly no thumpist. But when every possible excuse is made for the people who coughed, it remains a matter for regret that the attendants did not remove them to Piccadilly, and treat their ailment there by gently passing a warm steam-roller over their chests. It is to be hoped that they did not succeed in shaking Madame Haas's faith in her artistic instinct; for it guided her unerringly through the first movement of the sonata. As to the other movements, my impotent exasperation at the idiots on whom such playing seemed lost, deprived me of all power of forming a trustworthy judgment. Beethoven in his third manner, and Madame Haas in her smoke-colored silk domino, were got rid of in due course, to be replaced by the idolized baritone.

Mr Santley was a little nervous, and both in The Erl King and To Anthea he forced the pace at the end, and tried to "rush" the effect. It is a pity that he should lack the calm confidence which so many of his rivals derive from their complete innocence of the art of singing. His voice is as fresh and his method as unfailing as ever. He had to repeat To Anthea to console his more obstreperous admirers for their sufferings at the hands of Madame Haas.

Madame Ilma de Murska is dead; and an ungrateful world is describing her obituarily as a person remarkable for a compass that extended to F in alt. Reader, believe it not. What lack has there ever been of F's in alt? Is not that note attainable by Etelka Gerster, Miss van Zandt, our sister's schoolfellow Miss Smith, and many others? Yet they are not de Murskas. It is true that the F's in those famous fioriture of the Queen of Night used, when de Murska sang the part, to chime with a delicate ring and inimitable precision of touch which made *Gli angui d'inferno* her especial property, and gave her a monopoly of the part of Astriffiamante. But she was no less unapproachable as Elvira, in Don Giovanni, a creation to which only a great artist can do justice, and which is usually thrown over to a second-rate "dramatic soprano." The highest note in it is a fifth below the vaunted F, so that "exceptional range" has certainly nothing to do with success in it. Yet who but de Murska was ever rapturously encored for *Mi tradi quell' alma ingrata*, which the general public so often finds "classical," by which it means rather dull and too long? Even Christine Nilsson was nothing to her in this crucial part.

In Italian opera proper she was also unique. Out of a confused memory of dozens of Lucias one remembers only de Murska's. This, remember, was the de Murska of twenty years ago, even then a fabulously old woman and a mons-

63

trously made-up woman, the middle of whose voice was not unjustly compared to an old tin kettle. Her make-up had the curious effect of making her seem very young and pretty at close quarters and very artificial and vague in facial outline at a distance. Probably she was by no means the Ninon de L'Enclos that gossip made her out to be. Her eccentric ways of travelling, her menagerie of pets, and such whims as her objection to be watched upon the stage by people in the wings, started a vein of small talk about her, which all somehow tended to the exaggeration of her age.

Grove's dictionary gives the date of her birth in Croatia as 1843. A usually well-informed critic suggests 1835 as nearer the truth. The first date is certainly wrong: it is impossible to believe that the consummate artist of 1870 was only twenty-seven. It is to be hoped that the story of her daughter's suicide is as untrue as most of the odd stories that attached themselves to her during her lifetime. In her great days here, she was a small, slight, fragile woman, with a refinement of manner and delicacy of taste that made itself felt in everything she did on the stage, and that led to all the de Murska legends beginning with the statement that she was "a lady of position." However that may have been, she was unquestionably a woman of exceptional intelligence and peculiar artistic gifts; and her skill at vocal pyrotechnics was only a small part of the powers which give her a claim to a place among the greatest operatic artists of her day.

21 February 1889

On Monday the editor of The Star summoned me to a private conference. "The fact is, my dear Corno," he said, throwing himself back in his chair and arranging his moustache with the diamond which sparkles at the end of his pen-handle, "I dont believe that music in London is confined to St James's Hall, Covent Garden, and the Albert Hall. People must sing and play elsewhere. Whenever I go down to speak at the big Town Halls at Shoreditch, Hackney, Stratford, Holborn, Kensington, Battersea, and deuce knows where, I always see bills at the door announcing oratorios, organ recitals, concerts by local Philharmonic and Orpheus societies, and all sorts of musical games. Why not criticise these instead of saying the same thing over and over again about Henschel and Richter and Norman Neruda and the rest?" I replied, as best I could, that my experience as a musical critic had left me entirely unacquainted with these outlandish localities and their barbarous minstrelsy; that I regarded London as bounded on the extreme north-east by Stonecutter Street, on the extreme south-west by Kensington Gore, on the south by the Thames, and on the north by the Strand and Regent-street. He assured me that the places he had mentioned actually existed; but that, as I was evidently hurt by the suggestion that I should condescend to visit them, he would hand the ticket he had just received for a Purcell-Handel performance at Bow, to Musigena. "What!" I exclaimed, "Purcell! the greatest of English composers, left to Musigena! to a man whose abnormal gifts in every other direction have blinded him to his utter ignorance of music!" "Well, the fact is," said the editor, "Musigena told me only half an hour ago that he was at a loss to imagine how a writer so profound and accomplished as di Bassetto could be in music a mere superficial amateur." I waited to hear no more. Snatching the tickets from the editor's desk, I hastily ran home to get my revolver as a precaution during my hazardous voyage to the East-end. Then I dashed away to Broad-street, and asked the booking-clerk whether he knew of a place called Bow. He was evidently a man of extraordinary nerve, for he handed me a ticket without any sign of surprise, as if a voyage to Bow were the most commonplace event possible. A little later the train was rushing through the strangest places: Shoreditch, of which I had read in historical novels; Old Ford, which I had supposed to be a character in one of Shakespear's plays; Homerton, which is somehow associated in my mind with pigeons; and

Haggerston, a name perfectly new to me. When I got into the concert-room I was perfectly dazzled by the appearance of the orchestra. Nearly all the desks for the second violins were occupied by ladies: beautiful young ladies. Personal beauty is not the strong point of West-end orchestras, and I thought the change an immense improvement until the performance began, when the fair fiddlers rambled from bar to bar with a certain sweet indecision that had a charm of its own, but was not exactly what Purcell and Handel meant. When I say that the performance began, I do not imply that it began punctually. The musicians began to drop in at about ten minutes past eight, and the audience were inclined to remonstrate; but an occasional apology from the conductor, Mr F. A. W. Docker, kept them in good humor.

Dido and Eneas is 200 years old, and not a bit the worse for wear. I daresay many of the Bowegians thought that the unintentional quaintnesses of the amateurs in the orchestra were Purcellian antiquities. If so, they never were more mistaken in their lives. Henry Purcell was a great composer: a very great composer indeed; and even this little boarding-school opera is full of his spirit, his freshness, his dramatic expression, and his unapproached art of setting English speech to music. The Handel Society did not do him full justice: the work, in fact, is by no means easy; but the choir made up bravely for the distracting dances of the string quartet. Eneas should not have called Dido Deedo, any more than Juliet should call Romeo Ro-*may*-oh, or Othello call his wife Days-*day*-mona. If Purcell chose to pronounce Dido English fashion, it is not for a Bow-Bromley tenor to presume to correct him. Belinda, too, was careless in the matter of time. She not only arrived after her part had been half finished by volunteers from the choir, but in Oft She Visits she lost her place somewhat conspicuously. An unnamed singer took Come away, fellow sailors, come away: that salt sea air that makes you wonder how anyone has ever had the face to compose another sailor's song after it. I quote the concluding lines, and wish I could quote the incomparably jolly and humorous setting:—

> Take a bowsy short leave of your nymphs on the shore;
>> And silence their mourning
>> With vows of returning,
> Though never intending to visit them more.

SAILORS (*greatly tickled*). Though never—!

OTHER SAILORS (*ready to burst with laughter*). Though never—!

ALL (*uproariously*). Inte-en-ding to vi-isit them more.

I am sorry to have to add that the Handel choir, feeling that they were nothing if not solemn, contrived to subdue this rousing strain to the decorum of a Sunday school hymn; and it missed fire accordingly. Of Alexander's Feast I need only say that I enjoyed it thoroughly, even though I was sitting on a cane-bottomed chair (Thackeray overrated this description of furniture) without adequate room for my knees. The band, reinforced by wind and organ, got through with a healthy roughness that refreshed me; and the choruses were capital. Mr Bantock Pierpoint, the bass, covered himself with merited glory, and Mr John Probert would have been satisfactory had he been more consistently careful of his intonation. Miss Fresselle acquitted herself fairly; but her singing is like that of the society generally: it lacks point and color. Mr Docker must cure his singers of the notion that choral singing is merely a habit caught in church, and that it is profane and indecorous to sing Handel's music as if it meant anything. That, however, is the worst I have to say of them. I am, on the whole, surprised and delighted with the East-end, and shall soon venture there without my revolver. At the end of the concert, a gentleman, to my entire stupefaction, came forward and moved a vote of thanks to the performers. It was passed by acclamation, but without musical honors.

P.S. The Handel Society appeals urgently for tenors, a second bassoon, and horns. Surely every reader of The Star

can at least play the second bassoon. Apply to Mr P. L. G.
Webb, 3 Chandos Street, Cavendish Square, W.

ONE of the reflections suggested by the musical events of the
last seven days is a comparison of Mr Hamish MacCunn's
luck with Wagner's. It is exactly six years since Wagner died
at Venice, aged 70. Mr Hamish MacCunn was born yesterday—or thereabouts. Yet whereas Mr MacCunn's Last
Minstrel was performed at the Crystal Palace last Saturday,
even the overture to Wagner's Die Feen was not heard in
London until Tuesday last, when Mr Henschel kindly gave
it a turn at the London Symphony Concert. This Die Feen
(The Fairies) was written in 1833 for the Würzburg Theatre,
where Wagner was chorus master at ten florins a month,
which was probably considered a handsome thing for a young
man of twenty. It must by no means be supposed that at
that age he was a crude amateur. He was certainly a crude
Wagner; but if his object had been to turn out a business-like
opera overture, he could evidently have managed as well as
Sir Arthur Sullivan or Mr Ebenezer Prout; for the shortcomings of Die Feen are not those of mere illiteracy in music.
And there is something of the enchantment of twenty about
it. At that age fairyland is not forgotten. The impulse to
hear "the horns of elfland" is genuine and spontaneous. At
twenty-six fairyland is gone: one is stronger, more dexterous,
much more bumptious, but not yet much deeper: sometimes not so deep. Accordingly, it was not surprising to find
a charm in this "Vorspiel" that is wanting in the empty and
violently splendid overture to Rienzi. It is more Wagnerian,
for one thing. For another, it has youthful grace and fancy
as well as earnestness. At the end, after a little juvenile tearing and raging, it weakens off into an echo of Weber's jubilant
mood, and the coda is spoilt by the boyish repetition of a
piece of energetic commonplace. But the earlier part is well
worth the trouble Mr Henschel took with it. The only later

work foreshadowed in it is the Faust overture of 1840.

I was astonished, and indeed somewhat hurt, at Mr Henschel's apparent oversight of my proposal that there should be two concerts instead of one. However, he doubtless had my comments in his mind when conducting the Magic Flute overture; for though he did not allow the band to try how fast they could rattle the notes off, as the fashion used to be with Mozart's orchestral works, neither was he able to sound the depths of this great composition, nor is he likely to until he can afford to make a thorough study of it, and devote several rehearsals to its preparation. The Haydn symphony (B flat, No. 12), a masterpiece in every sense, went delightfully; and Liszt's Hungarian rhapsody in D, after the usual preliminary bunkum from the horns and bassoons, sparkled, tinkled, warbled, soared, swooped and raced along so that it was almost impossible to resist the itching to get up and dance. Mr Johann Kruse's performance of Beethoven's violin concerto was not particularly bad except in the opening strokes of the first cadenza, and not particularly good except in a few of the simpler passages. This was the last of the subscription performances. An extra concert, at which we shall have the Leeds choir and the Ninth Symphony, will finish the season next Wednesday afternoon.

Whatever faults the St James's Hall audience may have, susceptibility to panic is not one of them. Although the cooking arrangements connected with the restaurant occasionally scorch the concert-room and produce the most terrifying odors of shrivelling paint and reddening iron, nobody budges. On Tuesday night I sat trembling, convinced that the whole building was in flames, until a lady gently slipped out and came back with an assurance from the attendants that there was no danger, a smell of fire being one of the well-known attractions of the hall. Then my past life ceased to run panoramically before my mind's eye; and I settled down to listen to the music. But I respectfully submit that everybody is not gifted with my iron nerve, and that in a very heavy crush the consequences of an inopportune scorch might be disastrous.

The Popular Concert last Saturday afternoon would hardly have provoked me to comment if there had been nothing else to remark than Dr Mackenzie's set of six pieces for the violin, even though three of them were played for the first time by Madame Neruda. They are sentimentally pretty, especially where the programist tells us that in the Benedictus "rapture succeeds to awe"; but there is nothing to prevent Dr Mackenzie carrying out his expressed intention of composing some more. If Madame Neruda would like to contract for such pieces by the dozen, I do not see why the accomplished president of Tenterden Street should make any difficulty. Neither do I mean to say much about Miss Zimmerman's playing of the Waldstein sonata. Everybody acknowledges that the first movement of the Waldstein is a colossal piece of pianoforte music. I confess I have never been able to see it. It certainly was not colossal as Miss Zimmerman scampered through it, and for the life of me I do not know what else she could have done with a long, scrappy movement which is neither bravura nor tone poem, though it asserts itself occasionally in both directions. The allegretto, which is the really popular and interesting part of the sonata, was admirably played, the exposition of the theme being particularly happy. Miss Zimmerman got a double recall.

But what I really bring this concert in for is to ask why Mendelssohn's quartet in E flat major is to be thrust into our ears at the point of the analytical programme, as one of "the happiest productions of the composer's genius." Also why Mendelssohn is described as "a master yielding to none in the highest qualifications that warrant the name." The man who would say these things nowadays would say anything. Long ago, when the Mendelssohn power was at its height they were excusable; but programs dating from that period are out of date by this time. We now see plainly enough that Mendelssohn, though he expressed himself in

music with touching tenderness and refinement, and sometimes with a nobility and pure fire that makes us forget all
his kid glove gentility, his conventional sentimentality, and
his despicable oratorio mongering, was not in the foremost
rank of great composers. He was more intelligent than
Schumann, as Tennyson is more intelligent than Browning:
he is, indeed, the great composer of the century for all those
to whom Tennyson is the great poet of the century. He was
more vigorous, more inventive, more inspired than Spohr,
and a much abler and better educated man than Schubert.
But compare him with Bach, Handel, Haydn, Mozart,
Beethoven, or Wagner; and then settle, if you can, what
ought to be done to the fanatic who proclaims him "a
master yielding to," etc., etc., etc.

These remarks will doubtless have the effect of instantaneously inducing Messrs Chappell to discard their stereotyped program of the E flat quartet. To replace it they
should select some person who is not only void of superstition
as to Mendelssohn, but also as to the sacredness of sonata
form. If the first movement of this quartet was not "a model
of construction," it would perhaps be a genuine piece of
music instead of the mere dummy that it is. Surely the
musical critics ought to leave to their inferiors, the literary
reviewers, the folly of supposing that "forms" are anything
more than the shells of works of art. Though Bach's natural
shell was the fugue, and Beethoven's the sonata, can anybody but an academy professor be infatuated enough to
suppose that musical composition consists in the imitation
of these shells: a sort of exercise that is as trivial as it is
tedious? The fugue form is as dead as the sonata form; and
the sonata form is as dead as Beethoven himself. Their
deadliness kills Mendelssohn's St Paul and the "regular"
movements in his symphonies and chamber music. Fortunately, the people are sound on this question. They are
not indifferent to the merits of the first and second subjects
in a formal sonata; but to the twaddling "passages" connecting them, to the superfluous repeat, the idiotic "working

out," and the tiresome recapitulation they are either deaf or wish they were. I once asked an energetic and liberal-minded young conductor what he thought of Liszt's music. He replied with the inelegant but expressive monosyllable, "Rot." I was much less scandalized than I should have been had he applied that term to Mendelssohn's music; and yet I have no hesitation in saying that we have in Liszt's *Preludes* a far better example of appropriate form than any of the "regularly constructed" works of Mendelssohn.

1 March 1889

THERE are twenty-four concerts this week. Consequently I give myself a holiday; for if anyone asks me what I thought of this or that performance, I reply, "How can I possibly be in twenty-four places at the same time? The particular concert you are curious about is one of those which I was unable to attend." And, indeed, only a few out of the two dozen require any more special notice than an ordinary day's business at a West-end shop. Musigena has told you all about Otto Hegner, and has undertaken to look after the two performances of the Ninth Symphony by Mr Henschel on Wednesday and Mr Mann's on Saturday. The Hackney choir gave St Paul on Monday; but as they did not invite me to be present—instinctively divining, perhaps, that I detest St Paul, and might pitch into them for its contrapuntrocity—I did not go. As to Mr Grieg, at the Popular Concerts, I tried to get in on Saturday, but found the room filled with young ladies, who, loving his sweet stuff, were eager to see and adore the confectioner. So on Monday I forbore St James's Hall altogether, lest my occupying a seat should be the means of turning away even one enthusiastic worshipper. Mr Isidore de Lara is to be at the Steinway Hall this afternoon, and were I a dark-eyed Oriental beauty from Maida Vale or Sutherland Gardens doubtless I should go; but being what I am, I refrain. Not that Mr de Lara cannot sing very well from my point of view when he likes; but I am always

72

mortally afraid of his beginning to sing well from the dark-eyed point of view, which infuriates me. I have already taken and described my Farewell of Madame Patti at the Albert Hall; and although she is kind enough to repeat the ceremony, I shall not repeat the description. For the other concerts, they are not yet; and sufficient unto the day, etc.

Still, one must go somewhither, after all. That was my feeling, last Tuesday, when, turning over my invitations, I found a card addressed to me, not in my ancestral title of Di Bassetto, but in the assumed name under which I conceal my identity in the vulgar business of life. It invited me to repair to a High School for Girls in a healthy south-western suburb, there to celebrate the annual prize-giving with girlish song and recitation. Here was exactly the thing for a critic. "Now is the time," I exclaimed to my astonished colleagues, "to escape from the stale iterations of how Mr Santley sang The Erl King, and Mr Sims Reeves Tom Bowling; of how the same old orchestra played Beethoven in C minor or accompanied Mr Henschel in Pogner's Johannistag song or Wotan's farewell and fire charm. Our business is to look with prophetic eye past these exahusted contemporary subjects into the next generation—to find out how much beauty and artistic feeling is growing up for the time when we shall be obsolete fogies, mumbling anecdotes at the funerals of our favorites. Will it be credited that the sanity of my project and the good taste of my remarks were called in question, and that I was absolutely the only eminent critic who went to the school!

I found the school on the margin of a common, with which I have one ineffaceable association. It is not my custom to confine my critical opinions to the columns of the Press. In my public place I am ever ready to address my fellow-citizens orally until the police interfere. Now it happens that once, on a fine Sunday afternoon, I addressed a crowd on this very common for an hour, at the expiry of which a friend took round a hat, and actually collected 16s. 9d. The opulence and liberality of the inhabitants were thus very forcibly impressed on me; and when, last Tuesday, I made my way through a long corridor into the crowded schoolroom, my first thought as I surveyed the row of parents, was whether any of them had been among the contributors to that memorable hatful of coin. My second was whether the principal of the school would have been pleased to see me had she known about the 16s. 9d.

When the sensation caused by my entrance had subsided somewhat, we settled down to a performance which consisted of music and recitation by the rising generation, and speechification by the risen one. The rising generation had the best of it. Whenever the girls did anything, we were all delighted: whenever an adult began, we were bored to the very verge of possible endurance. The deplorable member of Parliament who gave away the prizes may be eloquent in the House of Commons; but before that eager, keen, bright, frank, unbedevilled, unsophisticated audience he quailed, he maundered, he stumbled, wanted to go on and couldnt, wanted to stop and didnt, and finally collapsed in the assuring us emotionally that he felt proud of himself, which struck me as being the most uncalled-for remark I ever heard, even from an M.P. The chairman was self-possessed, not to say hardened. He quoted statistics about Latin, arithmetic, and other sordid absurdities, specially extolling the aptitude of the female mind since 1868 for botany. I incited a little girl near me to call out "Time" and "Question," but she shook her head shyly and said "Miss —— would be angry"; so he had his say out. Let him deliver that speech next Sunday on the common, and he will not collect 16s. 9d. He will be stoned.

* * *

But the rest of the program was worth a dozen ordinary concerts. It is but a few months since I heard Schubert's setting of The Lord is my Shepherd, sung by the Crystal Palace Choir to Mr Mann's appropriate and beautiful orchestral transcript of the accompaniment; but here a class of girls almost obliterated that memory by singing the opening

74

strain with a purity of tone that was quite angelic. If they could only have kept their attention concentrated long enough, it might have been equally delightful all through. But girlhood is discursive; and those who were not immediately under the awful eye of the lady who conducted, wandered considerably from Schubert's inspiration after a while, although they stuck to his notes most commendably. Yet for all that I can safely say that if there is a little choir like that in every high school the future is guaranteed. We were much entertained by a composition of Jensen's, full of octaves and chords, which was assaulted and vanquished after an energetic bout of fisticuffs by an infant pianist who will not be able to reach the pedals for years to come.

Then there was the inevitable scene from Athalie, rather anglicized as to the vowels and "t's" and "r's," but intelligently and intelligibly done. Josabeth had the *maintien* of the French stage in a degree that would have enraptured A. B. Walkley. Joas was so spirited and artless that one forgave Racine the atrocious priggishness of the character; and Athalie did very well indeed. The recitations reached a climax in The Power of Life, a verse dialogue in which the lead was cleverly taken by a sharp and almost bumptious child, who brought out her mother in a wonderful way. I am almost tempted to mention the name of the young lady who spoke the mother's lines, so admirably was it done. It was more in the manner of Miss Beatrice Lamb than that of any other public performer I can recall. There were many other numbers in the program, but let it suffice to add that when God save the Queen was sung, the substitution of two quavers for the triplet at the beginning of the last line so completely spoiled it that I instantly suspected the headmistress of being a Fenian. She was a slender, elegant lady, who somehow reminded me of Mrs Kendal in Coralie; and there was certainly nothing revolutionary in her aspect. But, unless my suspicion is well founded, she had better restore that triplet.

On the whole, as I hurried back by the common, with a fine driving snow dispelling all chance of an impromptu

75

repetition of the sixteen-and-ninepenny experiment, I was able to rejoice in the thought that we may look forward to the persistence of the enormous improvement which has taken place within the last fifteen years in the average taste, general culture, and artistic capacity of our singers, players, and the audiences of appreciative amateurs, upon which everything really depends in the long run. And of you, wise and discriminating reader, I ask whether my account of the high school does not interest you more than the highly scientific account of Dr Mackenzie's Dream of Jubal, which I have left myself no room for, but which may descend on you at any time when I happen to be short of humanly readable copy?

8 March 1889

BEFORE I hurry away to St James's Hall to hear the Bach Choir and Joachim, I must snatch a moment to reply to the numerous correspondents who have been struck by my recent remarks as to the salutary effects of wind-instrument playing. It is impossible to answer all their questions in detail, but a few general observations will cover most of the cases.

First, then, as to the constantly recurring question whether the practice of musical instruments is likely to annoy the neighbors. There can be no doubt whatever that it is; and when the man next door sends in to complain there is no use in quarrelling over the point. Admit promptly and frankly that the noise is horrible, promise to cease practising after half-past twelve at night, except when you have visitors; and confess that if he in self-defence takes up another instrument you will be bound to suffer in turn for the sake of his health and culture as he is now suffering for yours. This is far more sensible and social than to place the bell of your instrument against the partition wall and blow strident fanfares in defiance of his nerves, as I foolishly did when a complaint of the kind was made to me. But I was little more than a boy at the time, and I have never since thought of it without remorse.

As to my correspondent who inquires whether there is such a thing as "a dumb French horn," analogous to the "dumb piano" used for teaching children to finger the keyboard, I am happy to be able to assure him that no such contrivance is needed, as the ordinary French horn remains dumb in the hands of a beginner for a considerable period. Nor can anyone, when it does begin to speak, precisely foresee what it will say. Even an experienced player can only surmise what will happen when he starts. I have seen an eminent conductor beat his way helplessly through the first page of the Freischutz overture without eliciting anything from the four expert cornists in the orchestra but inebriated gugglings.

The amateur will find, contrary to all his preconceptions, that the larger the instrument the easier it is to play. It is a mistake to suppose that he has to fill the instrument with expired air: he has only to throw into vibration the column of air already contained in it. In the German bands, which were dispersed by the Franco-Prussian war, mothers of households used to observe with indignation from the windows that these apparently lazy and brutal foreigners always placed the burden of the largest instrument on the smallest boy. As a matter of fact, however, the small boy had the easiest job; and I recommend amateurs to confine themselves to the tuba or bombardon, the chest encircling helicon, the ophicleide, or at most the euphonium. The euphonium is an extraordinarily sentimental instrument, and can impart a tender melancholy to the most ferocious themes. The accents of the Count di Luna, raging to inflict *mille atroci spasimi* on Manrico, in the last act of Trovatore, are blood-curdling. Transcribed for the euphonium in a military band selection they remind you of The Maiden's Prayer.

Of course, you will not take my advice. You are bent on learning the flute or the cornet. As to the flute I do not greatly care: you will get tired of it long before you can play

Ah, non giunge, even without variations. But the cornet is a most fearful instrument, and one with which self-satisfaction is attainable on easy terms. The vulgarity of the cornet is incurable. At its best—playing *pianissimo* in heavenly sweet chords scored by Gounod, or making the sword motive heard, in the first act of Die Walküre—it is only pretty. But in trumpet parts it is simply perdurable. Yet there is no getting rid of it.

Two cornet performances have left an abiding memory with me. One was M. Lévy's variation on Yankee Doodle, taken *prestissimo,* with each note repeated three times by "triple tonguing." This was in the open air, at the inauguration of Buffalo Bill; and it was preceded by a spirited attempt on the part of Mdme. Nordica to sing The Star Spangled Banner to an entirely independent accompaniment by the band of Grenadier Guards. The other was The Pilgrim of Love, played by an itinerant artist outside a public-house in Clipstone Street, Portland Place. The man played with great taste and pathos; but, to my surprise, he had no knowledge of musical etiquette, for when, on his holding his hat to me for a donation, I explained that I was a member of the press, he still seemed to expect me to pay for my entertainment: a shocking instance of popular ignorance.

I dwell on the cornet a little, because in my youth I was presented by a relative with absolutely the very worst and oldest cornet then in existence. It was of an obsolete rectangular model, and sounded in B flat with the A crook on. Its tone was unique; my master—an excellent player, of London extraction—once described it as "somethink 'ellish"; and he did it no more than justice. I never come across Scott's line, "Oh, for a blast of that dread horn," without thinking of it. After devastating the welkin with this remarkable instrument for some months, I was told that it would spoil my voice (perhaps in revenge for having had its own spoiled); and though I had not then, nor ever have had, any voice worth taking care of, I there and then presented the cornet as a curiosity to my instructor, and abandoned it for aye. It turned his brain eventually; for he afterwards spread a report that *I* was mad.

I believe that a taste for brass instruments is hereditary. My father destroyed his domestic peace by immoderate indulgence in the trombone; my uncle played the ophicleide—very nicely, I must admit—for years, and then perished by his own hand. Some day I shall buy a trombone myself. At the Inventions Exhibition Messrs Rudall and Carte displayed a double-slide trombone, which I felt insanely tempted to purchase. Of the merits of this instrument I was, and am, wholly ignorant, except that I inferred that its "shifts" were only half as long as on the ordinary trombone; and I ascertained that its price was 13 guineas. If ever I have so vast a sum at my command I shall probably buy that trombone, and ask Herr Richter to engage me for the next concert at which the Walkürenritt or Les Francs Juges is in the program.

By the bye, I do not agree with Musigena that Mr Manns keeps his brass too quiet at the Crystal Palace. I admire two things at Sydenham: the brass and Mr Manns himself. The strings are often snappish and mechanical, the wood wind stolid; but the brass is generally noble. I have never heard the statue music in Don Giovanni more finely played than at Mr Mann's centenary recital of that masterpiece; and this is as much as to say that Mr Manns feels for the trombone like Mozart and myself. But I certainly believe that the time is approaching when it will be admitted that the doubling, trebling, and quadrupling of the strings which has taken place in the modern orchestra requires a proportional multiplication of the wind instruments to balance them. In spite of the splendors of the Boehm flute, it is often lost in passages where the old flute used to tell when violins were less numerous. For ensemble playing there ought to be at least six bassoons instead of two. And though I never want Mr Manns's trombones to play four times as loud—the trombone being a tender plant that must not be forced—I sometimes want twelve trombones instead of three. This would satisfy Musigena, though it would run into money.

But I must not leave my inquiring amateurs without a word for those who most deserve my sympathy. They are people who desire to enjoy music socially: to play together, to explore the riches of concerted chamber music for mere love of it, and without any desire to expand their lungs or display their individual virtuosity. Yet they are too old to learn to fiddle, or, having learnt, cannot do it well enough to produce tolerable concord. Their difficulty is, fortunately, quite easy to solve. The instrument for them is the concertina: not the Teutonic instrument of the midnight Mohock, but the English concertina of Wheatstone. I presume Wheatstone and Co. are still flourishing in Conduit Street, although Mr Richard Blagrove and his quartet party have not been much in evidence lately. You can play any instrument's part on a concertina of suitable compass, the B flat clarinet being most exactly matched by it in point of tone. The intonation does not depend on you any more than that of a pianoforte. A good concertina is everlasting: it can be repaired as often as a violin. It costs from 16 guineas for a treble to 24 for a contrabass.

16 *March* 1889

I AM sorry to say that a postcard has been forwarded to me inscribed as follows:—" 'My uncle played the ophicleide for years, and then perished by his own hand.'—Corno di Bassetto, in Star.

"Bassetto, so expert you are
  With anecdote and wrinkle,
To keep the readers of The Star
  For ever on the twinkle;
Of playing ophicleides, in sooth,
  You make us feel quite funky;
But, tell us—*was* it gospel truth,
  That death of poor old Nunky?

"With this ancestral tale of woe
Youve set us all a-sighing,
Until we deeply crave to know
The manner of his dying.
Did he fall slain by field or lake,
By poison, or stiletto,
Or did his nephew's stories take
His breath away, Bassetto?

S."

Nature must be dead in the man who can thus trifle with a family feeling. I regret now that I mentioned the matter. My statement was true; but I decline, for two reasons, to satisfy the morbid curiosity of S. (Henry Salt). The reasons are: (1) the evidence at a coroner's inquest does not come under the head of musical memoranda; and (2) the details are so grotesquely extraordinary—so absolutely without precedent in the records of self-destruction—that, often as I have told the story, it has never once been believed.

Another correspondent, writing in vivid prose, describes me as "an ignorant ass" for having spoken of "four cornets" in the overture to Der Freischütz. I own the soft impeachment generally, but demur to the particular instance of it. Sir Isaac Newton confessed himself an ignorant man; and though I know everything that he knew, and a good deal more besides, yet relatively—*relatively*, mind—I am almost as ignorant as he. The term "ass" I take to be a compliment. Modesty, hard work, contentment with plain fare, development of ear, underestimation by the public: all these are the lot of the ass and of the last of the Bassettos. But I think the superior information and sagacity of my censor might have enabled him to detect an obvious misprint. "Four expert cornets" (*vide* last week's column) is nonsense, and would be so even if the instruments referred to—horns, of course—were really cornets. What I wrote was "Four expert cornists." My correspondent is an idiot.

Hitherto I have not been a great admirer of Edvard

81

Grieg. He is a "national" composer; and I am not to be imposed on by that sort of thing. I do not cry out "How Norwegian!" whenever I hear an augmented triad; nor "How Bohemian!" when I hear a tune proceeding by intervals of augmented seconds; nor "How Irish!" when Mr Villiers Stanford plays certain tricks on subdominant harmonies; nor "How Scotch!" when somebody goes to the piano and drones away on E flat and B flat with his left hand, meanwhile jigging at random on the other black keys with his right. All good "folk music" is as international as the story of Jack the Giant Killer, or the Ninth Symphony. Grieg is very fond of the augmented triad; but his music does not remind me of Norway, perhaps because I have never been there. And his sweet but very cosmopolitan modulations, and his inability to get beyond a very pretty snatch of melody, do not go very far with me; for I despise pretty music. Give me a good, solid, long-winded, classical lump of composition, with time to go to sleep and wake up two or three times in each movement, say I.

However, let us be just. The pretty snatches are not only pretty, but both delicately and deeply felt by the composer. And they are, at least, long enough to make exquisite little songs, which Madame Grieg sings in such a way as to bring out everything that is in them. There is a certain quaintness about the pair. Grieg is a small, swift, busy, earnest man, with the eyes of a rhapsode, and in his hair and complexion the indescribable ashen tint that marks a certain type of modern Norseman. For Madame's appearance I cannot answer so fully, as I have had no opportunity of observing her quite closely; but she holds herself oddly and sings with unrestrained expression. The voice, unluckily, does not help her much. I know half a dozen commonplace young ladies with better, fresher, more flexible voices; but they will not take Madame Grieg's place yet awhile. Most of them, too, would regard a habit of musical composition on their husband's part as one of those conceited follies to which men are subject. It is really a stupendous feat, this of making your wife believe in you.

Grieg's Peer Gynt suite, which he conducted at the Philharmonic on Thursday, was written for use in the theatre at the performance of the play. Now Peer Gynt (Pare Yoont is about as near as you can get to it in English) is a great play: a masterpiece of Norwegian literature, as Faust is a masterpiece of German literature. Like Faust, it is a fantastic drama in rhymed verse. Like Faust, again, it is full of scenes that haunt a composer and compel him to give them musical expression. Grieg, however, has not attempted to wrestle with a giant like Ibsen. His Aase's death music, for instance, does not deal with that wonderful imaginary ride to the castle east of the sun and west of the moon with which Peer, having harnessed the cat to his mother's deathbed, beguiles the worn-out old woman painlessly from the world. Grieg deals rather with the earlier part of the scene, where Aase lies deserted, awaiting her last hour. The music, a quiet crooning harmonic motive, is deeply pathetic. On Thursday it moved an audience which knew nothing of Peer Gynt. For the rest, the dawn music is charming, and so is Anitra's dance, which begins like the waltz in Berlioz's Fantastic Symphony. The Dovregubben orgy is a riotous piece of weird fun. All four numbers are simply frank repetitions, in various keys and with different instrumentation, of some short phrase, trivial certainly, but graceful and fancifully expressive. But they pleased the Philharmonic audience more and more as they went on; and finally Grieg, after two recalls, had to repeat the Dovregubben piece.

On next Wednesday afternoon Grieg will have a concert all to himself. He will play his Holberg suite (Holberg was the Molière of the North); Madame will sing five of his songs, besides playing duets with him; and Johannes Wolff will play a violin sonata of his. Mr Wolff is a Dutchman, like Mr Henry Seiffert, who played the other day at the Ice Carnival, which I did not attend, as my skates are out of order. The violin is capricious in its choice of nations. Formerly all fiddlers were Italian. Then the French had a turn,

83

and then the Hungarians, Sarasate being a brilliant exception to all rules. But no one ever dreamt of a modern Dutch
musician until the year of the Inventions Exhibition, when
a Mr de Lange and his brother, conductor and organist respectively, gave two concerts of the music of the great old
Netherlandish school of Sweelinck, Okeghem, Orlandus
Lassus, and the rest of them, the execution of which, by
eight singers from Amsterdam, made an extraordinary impression on the few musicians who happened to be present.
After that, when at a concert at Steinway Hall I heard Mr
Seiffert play a couple of pieces by Max Bruch and Wieniawski,
with remarkably powerful tone and startling execution, I
was not surprised to hear that he was a Dutchman. Subsequently, at the same hall, I heard Mr Wolff, who struck me,
before he began to play, as the most goodnatured-looking
violinist I ever saw: a man whom no one would have the
heart to criticize adversely. I do not remember what he was
set down to play: it may have been the Kreutzer Sonata for
all I know; but, in answer to an encore, he gave us the oddest
tune I ever heard in a concert room. He must have picked
it up from some very old itinerant fiddler in the street. It
was only about forty bars, played with immense humor and
perfectly appropriate expression. I have not forgotten it
yet. Advance, Holland!

23 *March* 1889

A. B. WALKLEY has had the unspeakable audacity to advise
"the frolic Bassetto" to go to Richard III at the Globe
Theatre. This is a gibe at my earnestness, which perhaps
makes my column appear heavy to those who are accustomed to the trivialities of dramatic criticism. But I believe
I have the support of those who are weary of levity, of
egotism, of senseless facetiousness, of self-advertisement,
and, I will add, of ignorance and presumption. If, as Walkley
implies, I have no sense of humor—and I do not deny it nor
regret it—at least my readers are protected against mis-

placed jests and fleers at men who feel their responsibility
and do not trifle with their mission.

As a matter of fact, I did go to the Globe, not because
Walkley wished me to hear "Mr Edward German's fine
music, with its *leitmotivs* after Wagner's plan" (ha! ha! ha!),
but because a musician only has the right to criticize works
like Shakespear's earlier histories and tragedies. The two
Richards, King John, and the last act of Romeo and Juliet,
depend wholly on the beauty of their music. There is no deep
significance, no great subtlety and variety in their numbers;
but for splendor of sound, magic of romantic illusion, majesty
of emphasis, ardor, elation, reverberation of haunting echoes,
and every poetic quality that can waken the heart-stir and
the imaginative fire of early manhood, they stand above all
recorded music. These things cannot be spectated (Walkley
signs himself Spectator): they must be heard. It is not
enough to see Richard III: you should be able to *whistle* it.

However, to the music! Mr Mansfield's execution of his
opening *scena* was, I must say, deeply disappointing. When
I heard his rendering of the mighty line—

> In the deep bosom of the ocean buried,

which almost rivals "the multitudinous seas incarnadine" I
perceived that Richard was not going to be a musical success. And when in that deliberate staccato—

> I am determinéd to be a villain,

he actually missed half a bar by saying in modern prose
fashion, "I am determin'd to be a villain," I gave him up as
earless. Only in such lines as—

> Framed in the prodigality of nature,

which simply cannot be put out of joint, was his delivery
admirable. And yet his very worst achievement was—

> Bound with triumphant garlands will I come,
> And lead your daughter to a conqueror's bed.

85

Spectator, with reckless frivolity, has left his readers to infer that the magnificent duet with Miss Mary Rorke in which these lines occur, with the famous section beginning,

> Send to her, by the man that slew her brothers,
> A pair of bleeding hearts,

is by Cibber. "*Ecce iterum!* this scene is Cibber again," says Spectator. And this, mind, not that he does not know as well as I do that the lines are Shakespear's, but simply because, as Cibber was a sort of dramatic critic (he was an actor who wrote an apology, by no means uncalled for, for his own existence, though in justice I must add that it is still the best book on the English theatre in existence, just as Boswell's Journey to the Hebrides is still the best guidebook), Spectator wishes to prove him superior to Shakespear!

To return to Mr Mansfield. It is a positive sin for a man with such a voice to give the words without the setting, like a Covent Garden libretto. Several times he made fine music for a moment, only to shew in the next line that he had made it haphazard. His acting version of the play, though it is an enormous improvement on the traditional Cibberesque, notably in the third and fourth acts, yet contains some wanton substitutions of Cibber's halting, tinpot, clinking stuff for noble and beautiful lines by Shakespear, which would occupy no longer time in delivery. Why, for instance, is this passage avoided?

> RICHARD'S MOTHER: . . . I prithee hear me speak;
> For I shall never speak to thee again.
> RICHARD: So.
> HIS MOTHER: Either thou wilt die, by God's just ordinance,
> Ere from this war thou turn a conqueror;
> Or I with grief and extreme age shall perish,
> And never more behold thy face again.

And so on. Is Mr Mansfield deaf, that he allows the dead hand of Cibber to filch this passage from Miss Leclercq and the audience? Or is a gentleman connected with this paper

who has shewn a suspicious familiarity with the Globe arrangements, the real author of the Mansfield version? If I
were playing Richard I would sacrifice anything else in the
play sooner than that monosyllable "So"; which tells more
of Richard than a dozen stabbings and baby smotherings.

The last act also presents some unaccountable incon-
sistencies. Mr Mansfield valiantly gives every word of the
striking solo following the nightmare scene; and he rejects
"Richard's himself again" with the contempt it deserves.
But instead of finishing the scene in mystery and terror by
stealing off into the gloom to eavesdrop with Ratcliff, he
introduces that vulgar Cibberian coda in the major key:—

Hark! the shrill trumpet sounds. To horse! Away!
My soul's in arms and eager for the fray.

Imagine a man at dead midnight, hours before the battle,
with cold, fearful drops still on his trembling flesh, suddenly
gasconading in this fashion. Shakespear waits until Richard
is in the field, and the troops actually in motion. That is the
magnetic moment when all the dreadful joy of the fighting
man surges up in him, and he exclaims—

A thousand hearts are great within my bosom.

And now, as to Mr Edward German's music, "with its
leitmotivs after Wagner's plan." Here is the principal theme
of the overture:—

 etc.

And whenever Richard enters you hear the bassoons going:
Pum-pum-pum, pum, pum, Paw! It is a *leitmotiv* certainly;
but this very primitive employment of it is not "after
Wagner's plan." Hang it all, gentlemen critics of the drama,
have you never been to the opera? Surely you have heard at
least Der Freischütz or Robert le Diable, or even Satanella,
with their one or two comparatively undeveloped, unaltered,
and uncombined *leitmotivs* labelling stage figures rather than
representing ideas. Yet you can hardly have supposed that
these were "after Wagner's plan."

87

What Mr Edward German has done is this: Having had about twenty-two players at his disposal, he has wisely written for the old Haydn-Mozart symphony orchestra: two flutes, two oboes, two clarinets, two bassoons, two horns, drums, and strings: no trumpets or trombones. He has also necessarily economized in the strings by doing without 'cellos. For these hardly Wagnerian forces he has written an overture and a series of intermezzos, all pretty and well put together, but none presenting a single point of novelty. The style is the style of—say Max Bruch: that is, everybody's style: Gounod's, Bizet's, Mendelssohn's, Verdi's, all styles *except Wagner's.*

The first *entr'acte* begins with a prolonged bassoon note and a slow triplet, which makes you rub your eyes and ask whether the curtain is not about to rise on the tower scene from Il Trovatore. The prelude to the last act is a reminiscence, and a very vivid one too, of the prelude and gipsy dance at the beginning of the tavern scene in Carmen. In short, Mr German knows his business, and has come off with credit; but his music is not specially dramatic in character, and would suit The Lady of Lyons just as well as Richard III. By the bye, why has he not taken the pastoral opportunity offered by the scene in which Richmond and his army scent the morning air on Bosworth Field? He should have divided the honors of this most effective bit of scene painting with Mr Telbin.

I have been asked to say something about Tamberlik; but I imagine he must have flourished a little before my time. At any rate, I only heard him once, about twelve years ago, and then he was not a good singer, nor did he convince me that he was even the remains of one. The opera was Rossini's Otello, which proved worth half-a-dozen Semiramides. At the end of the duet with Iago, Tamberlik rushed at the footlights and delivered an eldritch squeal, which was all that was left of the famous *ut dièse de poitrine.* I had almost as lief have been played upon by a fire-engine. He had a superb figure, and certain traditional phrasings which the old-

fashioned training used to knock into singers, usually knocking the voice out of them at the same time. No doubt when
he was young, with a fresh larynx, and able as well as willing
to shout, he found no difficulty in carrying off some of the
very doubtful honors of middle Victorian Italian opera. But
if ever he was a fine artist, then I do not know what a fine
artist is—which, as you justly observe, kindly reader, is a
perfectly admissible hypothesis.

30 March 1889

I GRIEVE to say that a member of the Globe orchestra has
written a long letter to the editor most unbecomingly allud-
ing to me as "the captious frolic," and seeking to prove that
I am no musician. As well try to prove the earth flat. With
all the gentleman's ingenuity and exceptional opportunities
of knowing Mr German's score, he has succeeded in con-
victing me of only fifteen mistakes in an entire column of
The Star: a result which speaks for itself.

On one or two points I have a remark to offer—I trust
respectfully, and with good temper. If the music printer of
The Star subjects my quavers to a course of Darwinian evo-
lution from which they issue without tails, and so, to quote
my critic, "gets the value of four crotchets in a bar of three-
four time," is that my fault? Further, when I am told that
"the two trumpets and trombone were there right enough,"
the implication is that I regarded their apparent absence as
a culpable omission. So far was this from my thoughts that
I am now disposed to reproach Mr German with wasting
three players on instruments which made no effect. For they
were lost to hearing as completely as to sight, except in a
few warlike passages, which I innocently accounted for by
concluding that the four stage trumpeters had been for the
moment pressed into the orchestra, and of course pressed
carefully out of sight, as their costumes would have been
anachronic off the stage.

If there were really "about thirty" players instead of

twenty-two, where were they? The editor's correspondent, a man of humor as well as of music, suggests that "my eye was off color"; but my eye, during the overture, counted twenty-two. This, assuming that "off color" means temporary incapacity for duty, makes exactly eleven men seen double. But, as a matter of fact, my eye retained its normal ultramarine; and I believe I counted accurately. True, there may have been not only the trumpets and the solitary trombone "right enough" under the stage, but also a bass clarinet in the scene dock, an English horn in the flies, third and fourth horns in the box office, and a harp on the roof. I can answer only for what I saw and heard; and I can assure Mr German that the Bayreuth device of an invisible orchestra is also inaudible on the floor of the Globe, whatever may be the case upstairs. Besides, I confess I do not feel quite easy concerning the estimate of "about thirty," made by one who is in a position to be exact. It suggests more than twenty-nine and less than thirty: possibly twenty-nine and a boy.

My critic, who signs himself The Amused One, becomes almost sarcastic over my suggestion that the scene of the dawn on Bosworth Field is a fit opportunity for a pastoral symphony. "Fancy a Pastorale where Bassetto wants it: *i.e.* in the Bosworth Field scene, which is full of mail-clad warriors!" Well, my friend, why not? Does not the mail-clad Ratcliff tell us that the early village cock hath thrice done salutation to the morn? Am I to be told that the early village cock is not pastoral? And again: "Mr German *has* grasped the pastoral opportunity and written a beautiful Pastorale as a prelude to the Road to Chertsey scene: a fitting place for it, I say." Will it be believed that this more fitting place than Bosworth Field is a road full of corpses and mourners? Surely a field is more pastoral than a road!

However, these matters are but trifles, like my amused correspondent's mistaking the prelude to the first act for the Pastorale before the second, and, consequently, correcting me where I was, as usual, perfectly right. The true force of his letter is in the feeling it expresses that I have been unjust to

Mr Edward German. No doubt I have: who am I that I should be just? But if I had said that Mr Edward German had written an original and adequate overture and *entr'actes* to Shakespear's Richard III, I should have set his music on a level with Beethoven's Egmont, and himself above Verdi, Gounod, Dvořák, Grieg, and Brahms; for I do not believe that one of these composers could tackle Richard III successfully. Some of the dramatic critics have lightheartedly gone this length. If I followed that example, Mr Edward German would probably be the first to protest that I was making him ridiculous. So I shall confine myself to suggesting that the overture and one or two of the preludes might very well be subjected to expert criticism at one of our orchestral concerts this season. Many less meritorious compositions by Moszkowski and others have been admitted there.

(*Sir Edward German's overture, re-scored for full orchestra, has survived as a concert overture, and is familiar to wireless listeners. It is a much more serious composition than my readers could have gathered from my remarks 47 years ago; but its excellence has nothing to do with Richard III: it stands by itself as a composition in overture form. 1936.*)

At the last Philharmonic Concert, by the bye, I paid a shilling for my program. The editor informs me that, with the law of libel in its present unsatisfactory condition, I must not call this a fraud, a cheat, a swindle, an imposition, an exorbitance, or even an overcharge. Therefore, I have resolved to sulk and call it nothing. Formerly the Philharmonic programs were sixpenny yellow-covered quartos, written by Macfarren. The Crystal Palace Saturday programs are still sixpence. But the Richter programs are a shilling; and shilling books are creeping in at special oratorio performances even at the Crystal Palace.

Doubtless, these prices pay. It is more lucrative to sell 200 programs at a shilling than 2000 at a penny, the maximum of profit coinciding with the minimum of utility. In the same way, it paid Messrs Chappell the other day, at Grieg's recital, to turn away the shilling frequenters of the orchestra —their most faithful patrons—by charging three shillings instead of one; and to allow more than half, but not quite two-thirds, of the seats to remain empty. Though that cannot be helped at present, there is a way of smashing the program fr—— I mean of bringing down the prices of programs, as follows.

Let some publisher employ a competent person—myself, for instance—to write analytical programs of all the standard symphonies, overtures, Wagner selections, and the like, keeping the collection up to date by punctual piracies from German programs; and, in the case of works produced in England, paying the composer a reasonable sum for the necessary particulars. Translations of songs, and opera libretti, combining sane if unsingable English versions, with a few remarks descriptive of the chief points of the opera, might also come into the scheme. Then put these on the market at $\frac{1}{2}$d. apiece, or 2d. the half-dozen. Packets containing the pieces of any concert could be made up from the advertisements. There is no reason to fear that concert givers would at once dish the outside competitor by lowering their prices; for the outside competitor, supplying all audiences, could sell with profit at a price that would not cover the cost of production to separate concert givers, each having only his own particular audience to fl—— that is, to deal with.

Besides, analytical programs are wanted elsewhere than at St James's Hall. Amateurs would buy them for information, for guidance in purchasing music, and for distribution at private performances. Critics would buy them for reference. Literary men would buy them for the charm of their style. Composers would buy them to find out what their compositions meant. Fellow citizens: there is a Golconda in this idea. For the sake of its public utility I dedicate it freely to whoever will advance the capital.

LONDON MUSIC IN 1888–89

IF the performance of Benoît's Lucifer had been put off for
four days Madame Lemmens-Sherrington would have made
her re-entry on the 33rd anniversary of her first appearance
in London. On that occasion she was, if I mistake not,
twenty-two. Experienced mathematicians will find no difficulty in calculating Madame Sherrington's age from these
data. It is an age at which singers usually find themselves
incapacitated by what physiologists call "ossification of the
larynx." I do not pretend to be a physiologist; but I may
mention that I have frequently known cases of "ossification"
occur at twenty-four and earlier in the cases of singers who
did not know how to sing, whereas the other sort of singers
—who are, I admit, a rare species—hold out unimpaired
until the public absolutely refuses to believe its ears, and
concludes that a singer over eighty *must* retire. And yet it
will crowd Bingley Hall to hear Mr Gladstone, who might
be Madame Sherrington's father, speak for an hour and
fifty minutes at a stretch.

Madame Sherrington's method was always of the safest;
and she has the advantage, not common among artists, of
being a clever and sensible woman. Within the natural limitations of her talent almost her only fault was a somewhat
too ready recognition of the undeniable advantage, from a
commercial point of view, of a spice of claptrap. And though
she never carried it so far as Madame Patti and others of her
contemporaries, still, when that basket of flowers was handed
up the other evening, it awakened memories; and it is perhaps as well to say at once that preconcerted ovations of
this kind are by this time happily acquiring a *rococo* air
which warns artists with an alert sense of modernity to avoid
them. Untamed young prima donnas from America occasionally insist on them in spite of advice; but the result is
now generally disappointing. At Covent Garden last year
it was more than once rather worse than disappointing,
except to those who, like myself, regard the ovation ma-

chinery as an impertinence, a nuisance, and a sham. Madame Sherrington's basket of florist's goods, and the *claque* which the management had judiciously provided for the reception of Lucifer, were fortunately swept into insignificance by a hearty spontaneous reception which she acknowledged with all her old grace. And, save once, when she pulled down the pitch during an unaccompanied chorus, and so made the entry of the organ an appalling catastrophe, there was no falling-off to complain of.

When I say that there was no falling-off discernible in Madame Lemmens-Sherrington, I wish I could say the same for Musigena, who sat next me. He fell off repeatedly; and when I awakened him he yawned as I have never seen even a musical critic yawn before. I am bound to admit that there was nothing whatever in M. Benoît's music to keep him awake; but I think he went too far when, on my venturing a criticism as we left the building, he cut me short with: "How do *you* know? You were asleep all the time."

If criticism is to have any effect on concerts, it must clearly be published before they come off. On this principle it behoves me at once to say a word about the Richter Concerts, which will take place every Monday, except Whit Monday, from 6 May to 8 July inclusive. First, then, I want to know whether the orchestra is going to be any better than it was last year. Because last year, as Dr Hans Richter knows quite as well as I do, it was not up to the mark. I remember one scramble through the Walkürenritt which would have disgraced a second-rate military band; and the general want of refinement in detail, especially in the wind, was apparent in nearly all the Beethoven symphony performances. Nobody was more delighted than Bassetto by the breadth and force which Richter taught our orchestras after a period of stagnation that cannot be recalled without a shiver. Nobody thrilled with more savage and vengeful glee when the old, heartless, brainless, purposeless, vapid, conceited, jack-in-office, kid-glove, St James's-street, finicking Philharmonic fastidiousness was blown into space by

94

him. But, contemptible and inadequate as this genteel fastidiousness was in the mass, it had its good points in detail;
and Sir Arthur Sullivan's delicate taste, individuality, and
abhorrence of exaggeration and slovenliness raised it to a
point at which, if it still did nothing, it at least did it with
exquisite refinement.

The possibility of such refinement being thus demon-
strated, and being in no way essentially bound up with the
nothingness, why should we tolerate any degeneracy in this
respect from the Richter orchestra? For it is degeneracy.
Some seasons ago they played Schubert's Unfinished
Symphony with unsurpassable delicacy, the wood wind attaining a *piano* which I can only compare to the rustling of
leaves in the gentlest of breezes. At that time, too, they
could play a Liszt rhapsody with precision, a habit of which
they have since broken themselves. There is a book—I forget
the author's name, but it is the Posthumous Papers of some
club or other—in which a man says to his son, "Vidth and
visdom go together, Sammy." I rather doubt the statement;
for I have noticed that as Hans Richter grows wider season
after season he is more inclined to let things take their
chance, and to depend on snatching an occasional magnificent success from the inspiration of the moment.

A word or two about the season's program. I am not
sorry to see the Seventh Symphony, which Richter has done
to death in past seasons, replaced by the joyous Eighth, in
which I hope we shall hear the beautiful trio taken slowly,
on Wagner's lines, and not raced to destruction on Mendelssohn's. Talking of Mendelssohn, one of the happiest ad-
ditions to the list is the poetic Athalie overture. The *maestoso*
which closes that work is a masterpiece of harmonic structure:
one of the grandest pages Mendelssohn ever penned. Liszt's
Mazeppa is sufficiently novel, though it has been played
here more than once. When I first heard it at the Crystal
Palace I tried vainly to recollect what the rushing, swishing
triplets which represent the galloping of the horse were like.
At last a rustic-looking young lady behind me said very

audibly, "Oh, *isnt* it like frying rashers?" And so it was, exactly.

Richter's affection for Weber's vulgar Euryanthe overture is one of the things I do not understand. Nor, considering that perhaps his greatest triumph here as a conductor has been his resuscitation of the great symphony in E flat, can I imagine why he is so chary of the works of Mozart. However, he promises the symphony in D. There are lots of Mozart symphonies in D; but this is Köchel No. 504, a mark of identification which—Köchel not being at hand as I write —conveys no impression whatever to my mind, though doubtless it does to yours. A less hackneyed example of Cherubini than the Anacreon overture might have been found without much trouble; and Glinka's Komarinskaja will be the better for a rest after this season.

(*"Weber's vulgar Euryanthe overture" rather staggers me nowadays. But in Euryanthe Weber's music is thickening into Wagner's, and losing the unique charm and perfume of Der Freischütz, Oberon, and the Concertslück for piano and orchestra. Knowing as we do now what Wagnerism was going to mean to music, the loss to Weberism does not affect us as a vulgarization; but then!—well, there the word is; and I really meant it. 1936.*)

The Wagner selections are to be increased by the duet with Venus in the first act of Tannhäuser. The vein in which this scene, and much of Tristan und Isolde, is written is restless, passionate, harsh, and intolerable to those who agree with the composer who displayed his tact by saying to Berlioz, "I like music that puts me to sleep." A nobler addition to the repertory is the scene from Die Walküre, in which the Valkyrie warns Siegmund that he is fated presently to die and accompany her to Valhalla, which, on carefully examining her as to how he will be situated there, he flatly declines to do. The music is perfectly simple and indescribably impressive.

The extension of the musical arrangements at the Shakespearean theatres is bearing fruit. I hear remarks on the ap-

pearance of the Flying Dutchman overture in the bill at the
Lyceum. By the way, I was at the Lyceum on Tuesday, and
found Mr. Irving playing very finely indeed, and quite irre-
proachable in my department. He and I are the only two
men—not professional phonetic experts—in England who
can distinguish a vowel from a diphthong. What a Lady
Macbeth Miss Terry is! I would trust my life in her hands.
It was a luxury to hear her speak of "the owl, the fatal bell-
man which gives the stern'st goodnight." I had not heard
"goodnight" said in that exact tone since I saw her in the
balcony scene in Romeo and Juliet.

13 *April* 1889

A GENTLEMAN recently condoled with me on the immense
number of concerts a critic has to attend. He then asked me
somewhat abruptly when I had last been at one. His intention being plainly to suggest that I am in the habit of neglecting my duties, I explained to him that the ear of a critic is a
far more delicate organ than the larynx of a singer, and to
keep it fresh and sensitive it must be used sparingly. But the
fact is that I have so much to say about music that I forget
about the concerts. For example, I made a special excursion
last month to a concert in a place called Bermondsey, at the
invitation of the Popular Musical Union, and then clean forgot to write a word about it.

The Popular Musical Union was formed in 1882 for the
musical training and recreation of the "industrial classes."
By subscribing a guinea you become an "honorary member"
(I always thought that the point in honorary membership
was that you paid nothing) and have a concert all to yourself at Grosvenor House once a year. You are patronized by
the Lord Mayor, presided over by the Duke of Westminster,
and vice-presided over and councilled by nearly five dozen
illustrious persons, including Sir Charles Russell, Sir Frederick Leighton, handfuls of earls, a dean, a county councillor, an oculist, an amateur actress, three bishops, half-a-

dozen members of Parliament, *et hoc genus omne.*

The Union opens singing or other musical classes wherever "a sufficient number of ladies and gentlemen" signify to the hon. sec. (Mrs Ernest Hart) their intention of joining. And here I would dubiously ask whether ladies and gentlemen belong to the industrial classes? Surely the quintessence of gentility is doing nothing, and making the industrial classes keep you. I submit that the Popular Musical Union should resolutely refuse to train and recreate ladies and gentlemen who can presumably very well afford to recreate and train themselves.

The Union has given two imposing concerts lately. At the last one Gounod's Redemption was performed in the People's Palace. I did not go, because I cannot stand listening to a band and chorus practising the chromatic scale in slow time for nearly three hours even when it is harmonized by Gounod. Progression by semi-tones is too gradual for my ardent nature. I understand that various members of the industrial classes of Mile End pretended to enjoy it, which shews how the hypocrisy of culture, like other cast-off fashions, finds its last asylum among the poor. Now, in my opinion, the East-enders ought to be ashamed to have anything to do with the affectations of their parasites in the West. If the East listens patiently for a while, and never condescends to pretend to like what bores it, it will save itself from much tedium and consequent prejudice against pseudo-sacred music. Roughly, the novices of the East End may take it that the only Scriptural oratorios worth listening to are those of Bach, Handel, and Haydn. After Mozart struck the modern secular humanitarian note in The Magic Flute, and Beethoven took it up in his setting of Schiller's Ode to Joy, oratorio degenerated into mere sentiment and claptrap. With the exception of a few cantatas by Mendelssohn, all the Biblical music of this century might be burnt without leaving the world any the poorer. If the Musical Union is wise, it will train its audiences to nineteenth century vocal music by means of opera recitals.

Here I am, as usual, wasting all my space on the concert I was *not* at. The one at Bermondsey was in the Town Hall of that region. The vocalists announced in small print were Mdlle de Lido, Miss Helen Trust, Mr Dyved Lewis, "the Welsh tenor," Mr Albert Reakes, and Mr Bertram Latter. The vocalist announced in colossal letters suitable to a star of the first magnitude was Lady Colin Campbell. This piece of snobbery annoyed me to begin with. Then I was not formally received, as I should have been, by the Mayor and Corporation of Bermondsey. Further, in spite of my card of invitation, I was only admitted to a seat worthy of my dignity on payment of sixpence extra. But I never spare money in the service of the public. Bang went that coin without a murmur from me.

The generosity with which "the industrial classes" applaud you if they think you have "done your bit" heartily, even if you have not done it particularly well, was not abused on this occasion, as it too often is at concerts for the people. The Welsh tenor was excellent, and kept his temper in spite of grievous maltreatment from the accompanist in Deeper and deeper still. That gentleman when he came to Waft her, angels, discovered that the accompaniment of alternate dotted semiquavers and demisemiquavers would make a rattling galop, which he forthwith led off with such spirit that he got nearly to the end of the page before Mr Dyved Lewis had finished the first bar. However, Handel and the Welsh tenor triumphed in the end, for the aria was encored. To avoid further Terpsichorean difficulties, the successful singer substituted Gounod's setting of Victor Hugo's serenade, highly bowdlerised in the course of translation so as to spare the blushes of Bermondsey.

Mr Bertram Latter greatly distinguished himself by singing a duet with a baby. His intention was to sing Sullivan's Thou'rt Passing Hence as a solo; but the baby joined in at the end of the first line and continued *sempre crescendo e piu lamentevole* until a little before the end, when it collapsed, leaving Mr Latter, like Orpheus, master of the situation. Great and deserved was the applause elicited by his fortitude and his artistic singing under exceptionally trying circumstances.

Messrs W. Marshall & Co., of 70 Berners Street, have sent me some music for review. Here, for instance, is a volume of airs from Maritana for violin and piano. But of what use is that to me? I cannot play the violin and piano at the same time. Musigena can play violin parts with exquisite virtuosity through a sheet of tissue paper on a comb, his wide-toothed register being remarkable for its fulness and capability of dramatic expression; but he scorns Maritana. And, indeed, I think Messrs Marshall might have sent me the Kreutzer or the Strinasacchi sonata instead of Herr Meissler's waltzes arranged for the flute, The State Ball Album, The Children's Ball, and M. de Faye's arrangements of Braga's Serenata, and the like. My good sirs: do you think that di Bassetto regards this sort of thing as serious music?

20 April 1889

I REGARD with immense approval the formation of a Concert Guild by ex-scholars and ex-students of the Royal College of Music. Three of the rules deserve to be quoted. 1. Members of the Guild are not to employ for professional purposes any title or designation of their membership. 2. The services of members taking part in the performances shall be gratuitous. 3. Any surplus arising from the concerts shall go towards the foundation of a benevolent fund for the members. The spirit of these rules is full of promise. They suggest the question whether political economy is included in the curriculum of the Royal College of Music. Highly interesting examination papers could be set by an experienced professor. For instance:—How do you propose to reconcile the artistic interests of society with the individual pecuniary interest of an exceptionally gifted artist? Explain why Madame Patti, instead of assisting at least twice a week all through the year in complete artistic performances of the best operas before large audiences, is at present doing mere jobbing work in South America. Point out, from the point of view of sound national economy, the advantage of a system which makes it the interest of the greatest artists to perform as seldom as possible, and that, too, only before the fewest and richest people. Expatiate on the native vulgarity and insensibility to the refining influences of art evinced by those who insist on the interest which the public has in getting for their collective moneys as many performances out of an artist as may be compatible with his or her health and reasonable happiness. Enumerate the benefits conferred on the French nation by the secession of Madame Bernhardt and M. Coquelin from the Comédie Française on the ground that strolling pays them better. Show how a progressive income tax would affect art. Is it or is it not a corrupt proceeding for a singer to sing a worthless song for the sake of a royalty on every copy sold? To what extent has the spread of education reduced the percentage of private pupils who are unaware that they can buy their own music for less than half the marked price, or a pianoforte for from 20 to 25 per cent less than the figure named in the catalogue?

I could extend this list of questions considerably if I had nothing else to do just now. Sometimes it is not the artist, but the manager, who needs a lesson in political economy. The late Patti concerts at the Albert Hall were curious examples of managerial innocence. At them the singer obtained £700 for each concert. The managers of the hall should have demanded £200 extra as the rent of the hall, to be deducted from Madame Patti's fee. She would have objected, of course; but the managers need only have invited her to go elsewhere. As there is no other eligible hall in London capable of seating a sufficiently large audience to cover the ordinary return to the investment and leave £500 for the prima donna, Madame Patti could not have gone further without faring worse. The fact is, there were two monopolies concerned: Madame Patti's monopoly of herself, and the Albert Hall's monopoly of its unique size. Both monopolies have their "rents"; and the managers were childlike and bland enough to allow her to add £200 of the rent of their monopoly to that of hers. Had Bassetto been the manager that would not have occurred.

We are to have Italian opera at two houses this season: Verdi's Otello at the Lyceum, after the departure of Shakespear's Macbeth, and the usual series at Covent Garden. I take the opportunity of contrasting the modesty of Mr Augustus Harris with the ambition of actor-managers like Mr Wilson Barrett, Mr Irving, and Mr Mansfield, who produce no plays except those in which they themselves figure prominently. Mr Harris has been so self-denying in this respect that very few people in London know that he is an operatic artist as well as an *impresario*. The first time I had the pleasure of seeing him was in Der Freischütz, in which he played Zamiel, the demon huntsman. The part is not a singing part, so I am unable to speak critically of Mr Harris's voice; but his vivid and agile pantomime made a deep impression on me, and I felt strongly that I had witnessed the performance of an enthusiast: so strongly, indeed, that I prophesied that if ever he became bankrupt it would be by trying to revive Italian opera.

I lost sight of him for some time after this until, happening to be present one evening at a performance of Pink Dominoes, I recognized in one of the characters the strange personality of Zamiel. The moment I heard that he had entered upon a career as manager, I foresaw all the glories of the present *régime* at Covent Garden. May I now venture to suggest that Mr Harris should revive Weber's masterpiece, and permit the present generation of Londoners to see him in a character which he has made his own?

If Mr Harris has a fault as an *impresario* it is his too indiscriminate attachment to the traditions of the operatic stage. Instead of making up his mind to a clean sweep of all its barn-storming absurdities, he has cultivated them on the largest scale. He should go to his singers and say gently, "Do not saw the air thus. You think yourselves fine fellows when you do it; but the public thinks you idiots. The English nation, among whom I am a councillor, no longer supposes that attitudinizing is acting. Neither would I have you suppose that all amative young men wear dove-colored tights, and have pink cheeks with little moustaches. Nor is it the case that all men with grown-up daughters have long white beards reaching to the waist, or that they walk totteringly with staves, raising hands and eyes to heaven whenever they offer an observation. The daughters of Albion do not, when in distress, leave off wearing bonnets in the open air, assume mourning, keep their hands continually on their hearts, and stagger and flop about like decapitated geese." And so on. Harris's advice to the opera singers would become more celebrated than Hamlet's to the players.

27 *April* 1889

Two new operas were produced last Saturday: Doris at the Lyric Theatre in London, and Brinio at the Park Theatre in Amsterdam. There has been of late a Dutch fashion in art setting in here. We all know that the Netherlands formerly produced such painters as Rembrandt, Jan Steen, and de Hooghe, and such musicians as Sweelinck and Orlandus Lassus. These glories were supposed to have departed until the modern school of Dutch landscape and seascape painters arose and brought Holland again to the front as a rheumatic mother of great painters. And, we naturally asked, if great painters, why not great composers, too? Are there no Dutchmen who do in music what James Maris, his brother Matthew, Mesdag, Weissenbruch, Neuhuys, Bosboom, and others are doing in painting? Somebody suggested Peter Benoit; and it is only a few weeks since Mr Barnby went to the trouble of producing Lucifer at the Albert Hall. The work, as it turned out, had not an original bar in it. However, the announcement of a new opera on a national subject at Amsterdam was not to be neglected. I have been described as "a shirk" in an envious headline by the sub-editor

of The Star. But I was at my post in Amsterdam nevertheless; and I think that if the sub-editor had seen me on my
way thither, when I had been rocked in the cradle of the
deep for an hour, he would have blushed for the first time in
his life.

Brinio is a grand opera in four acts by S. van Milligen.
The book is by Flower of the Snow, a memorable name. The
characters include William Tell and Ophelia in the relation
of brother and sister, our old friend Oroveso the Druid from
Norma, Pollio from the same opera, and an unpopular
Roman governor, who is addressed throughout by the
Ethiopian title of Massa, and who may possibly have been
suggested by Pontius Pilate. The action takes place in
Batavia during the ascendency of the Romans. Brinio (W.
Tell) is a patriotic Batavian with two sisters, one of whom
is mad and the other sane, although I am bound to add that
there is but little to choose between them except that Rheime
overdoes the make-up of her eyes and plays hysterically
with straws and poppies. Ada, the uncertified one, is beloved
by Aquilius, a Roman officer, and by Massa, both of whom,
accordingly, cultivate Brinio's acquaintance. Massa, however, is out of the question, for he not only drinks—he
emptied a large goblet seven times in the course of one act
without turning a hair—but he seems to have had something to do with Rheime's mental affliction. Consequently
Brinio invites Aquilius to dinner, and shuts the door in
Massa's face.

In the second act Massa further exhibits his sybarite
nature by reclining on a couch whilst a bevy of maidens sing
a chorus and strew flowers on him. Then comes an amazing
scene in which Vulpes, the confidant of Massa, conducts a
sort of conscription among the Batavians, much as Falstaff
did at Justice Shallow's house on his way to Coventry. The
rest of the act I totally forget, except that Massa ordered
the Roman soldiery to arrest Aquilius, which they refused
to do on any terms.

The third act takes place at night, in the depths of a

104

primeval forest. Ada and Rheime happen to be strolling there in their ordinary indoor costume. Rheime sings to a tambourine accompaniment, which indicates that she is distraught. Ada sings then without the tambourine; and finally the two repeat their parts simultaneously in a manner much affected by Sir Arthur Sullivan in his operas. Massa then enters, unobserved, with two villains in cloaks, to whom he laboriously points out Ada—mind! *Ada*, not Rheime, because the villains of course subsequently get hold of the wrong woman. Massa and his hateful hirelings then retire in order to give a chance to Aquilius, who comes in and has a love duet with Ada, Rheime meanwhile sitting on a stump in a dumb paroxysm of flower and straw mania. Aquilius and Ada then elope, leaving Rheime an easy prey to the two villains, who re-enter and approach her by a series of strategic movements from tree to tree, as if she were a regiment of sharpshooters. At last they bear her off, wrapping her head in a veil, lest they should recognize her and spoil the last act. Brinio comes in with Ada and Aquilius: at least, I think it happened this way. Anyhow, Oroveso the Druid comes in with a host of mistletoe worshippers, and, after declaiming unintelligently at insufferable length in a colorless bass voice, appeals to the heavenly powers, who ring a bell, which causes the limelight man to cast a dazzling ray on Brinio, thus unmistakably pointing him out as the savior of his country.

In the last act, Massa is found with his bevy of maidens, drinking like a Roman Coupeau, and inviting everybody to hail his approaching bride. The bride appears with her head wrapped up; but even before she is unveiled, the friskings of the tambourine convince Massa, to his entire disgust, that in spite of his plain directions the two villains have mistaken the sisters. Vulpes now announces the advance of the foe, who come charging cautiously over the battlements, preoccupied with the real danger of breaking their necks rather than with the illusory perils of a stage battle. Massa, after a tremendous draught of Dutch courage, takes his sword, with which, to the utter astonishment of the audience, and in flat defiance of poetic justice, he kills Brinio, whereupon most of the Mistletonians fall down dead. Suddenly, however, Aquilius appears; and the Roman soldiery in turn fall down dead, apparently of heart disease precipitated by excitement. Massa is disarmed and removed in custody; and Ada and Aquilius are happily united. Rheime's reason is perhaps restored by the sight of her brother's mortal pangs, for the tambourine is heard no more; but on this point I cannot in the present stage of my acquaintance with sung Dutch, speak with certainty.

The opera was received with a considerable show of enthusiasm. At the end of the first act Rheime rushed to the conductor's desk and shook hands impulsively with Heer van Milligen amid cheers. When the forest scene was over the poet and the manager came upon the boards. Vast trophies of laurel and national bunting were handed up and hung upon the arms of the manager, who peered through the greenery like Birnam forest coming to Dunsinane, and made a glowing speech about his heart (just like Mr Wilson Barrett), about the Amsterdam public, about the Netherlands public, about the public of the whole universe, about the triumphant establishment of a great national school of opera, about the inspiration of della Neve, the genius of van Milligen, and heaven knows what not. When he had finished he began again, as public speakers will, and repeated his speech at least twice. Finally, he handed over the trophies to the blushing van Milligen; the applause broke out afresh; the trumpets blared forth victorious fanfares; and the audience dispersed in quest of refreshments.

With all due respect for the manager, I am unable to agree with him in his estimate of Brinio. Had the poem been as rational as even an exceptionally bad Drury Lane melodrama, it might have passed as an opera libretto with that unfortunately large section of the public which does not consider opera-making a serious or responsible profession. But it was not so rational, nothing like it. The music was vigorous, ambitious, elaborately scored, glib in the sentimental parts and strenuous in the martial, but without a phrase, progression, or rhythmical figure that could by any stretch of international courtesy be described as moderately fresh. As to any attempt at that distinctively dramatic power of suiting the music to the character as well as to the action and emotion, Heer van Milligen seems to have exhausted his endowment of it in devising the tambourine part to which I have alluded.

On the whole, though Brinio is not without the sort of plausibility that has secured for Lucifer a troublesome and expensive hearing in London, there is no reason why it too should be brought across the North Sea. But the example of the manager who produced it might be imitated by our impresarios. Mr Goring Thomas can do Heer van Milligen's work, and do it far better. So can Mr Villiers Stanford, who is sprightly enough when he is not gratifying his fancy for the pedantries of sonata form. Why Mr Augustus Harris does not get a grand opera out of Sir Arthur Sullivan, who is never dull, is one of the unaccountable things in modern management. Perhaps Mr Harris does not understand that he is expected to produce new work. If so, he is mistaken. Far too many nights last season were wasted in rattling the drying bones of Un Ballo and Il Trovatore; whilst works like Goetz's Taming of the Shrew and Wagner's Die Walküre, both of them beautiful and popular works, were left on the shelf. If that happens again, the readers of The Star shall learn my opinion of such senseless proceedings.

I *May* 1889

THE importance which was attached yesterday to the news of Mr Carl Rosa's death measures the position he had made for himself in England. His special work was the organization of opera in English, as opposed to the fashionable opera in Italian. In this he was so far successful that he leaves his company firmly established in London and the provinces, not without a certain artistic prestige, though the artistic side was never the strong side of his undertakings. His career as an impresario grew out of his marriage with Madame Parepa, whom he met in the United States in 1867, in the course of a concert tour, for which the late Mr Bateman had engaged him as violinist. He was then twenty-four years of age, and had played in this country at the Crystal Palace. With Madame Parepa's talent to support him, he turned conductor and manager, in which capacities he proved so competent that, after some years' experience in America, he directed his attention to England. The death of Madame Rosa in 1874 upset his calculations; but he persevered until his reputation was established in the provinces. In the winter of 1875 he tried a season in London. Mr Santley's performance of the part of the water-carrier in Cherubini's *Deux Journées* immediately gave the enterprise an artistic position which it certainly could not have gained by its performances of Faust and Il Trovatore in English. Next year, at the Lyceum, the great success of Wagner's Flying Dutchman, with Mr Santley as the Dutchman and Madame Torriani as Senta, still further raised the status of the company, emboldening Mr Carl Rosa to produce a real English opera, entitled Pauline, of which, in consideration for the composer and librettist, no further particulars need here be raked up. The next stride was made in 1879, when there was a season of opera in English at Her Majesty's Theatre. Rienzi was produced with the late Mr Joseph Maas in the title part; and Miss Georgina Burns burst on us as the Messenger of Peace. Nothing comparable with this achievement has been since done here in choral and spectacular opera with the exception, perhaps, of the revival of William Tell by Mr Harris last season at Drury Lane. In 1880 Goetz's Taming of the Shrew, with Miss Minnie Hauk as Katherine, was produced at Her Majesty's. This also was an excellent performance; and it was the last really great work introduced to us by Mr Carl Rosa. The operas by Dr Mackenzie, Mr Goring Thomas, and Massenet, which he afterwards undertook, had their

merits; but they were far inferior in their artistic importance
to the works of Wagner or Goetz.

Mr Carl Rosa was a capable man of business; and as conductor and impresario his judgment was to be depended upon
to a certain point. But it had its limits. His finest artists—
Mr Santley, Miss Minnie Hauk, and Madame Marie Roze,
for instance—were not discovered by him; and though he
brought forward several singers with bright, strong voices
and plenty of hard work in them, yet it is impossible to
believe that he enlisted the best talent available in his time
in young England, in point of grace, refinement, and intelligence. His recruits, though robust enough, were often rather
raw, with Irish, Scotch, Canadian, provincial English or
Welsh dialects, and no stage training. With him they found
no traditions of the Comédie Française order to improve them.
To this day the diction and deportment of the Carl Rosa
artists leave everything to be desired; and it is this deficiency
which compels the criticism that their spiritual director was
not as eminent an artist as he unquestionably was an eminent organiser and man of business. On the purely musical
side he had sufficient vigor, individuality, and even enthusiasm; and he certainly knew how to get himself respectably
served in the matter of stage management and decoration.
As impresarios go, all this was no mean endowment; and we
could have better spared many worse men whilst we wait for
Providence or Bayreuth to train us a manager with the
requisite administrative ability—one fully sensible of the
pictorial, the poetic, the dramatic, and the musical sides of
great operas, and able to co-ordinate them into an ideal
representation towards which it shall be the business of an
English opera-house constantly to work.

The name of Rosa was a phonetic version of the German
"Rose." The deceased impresario's complete title was Carl
August Nicolas Rose, and he was born at Hamburg in 1843.

4 *May* 1889

I have been amusing myself this week by comparing English opera at the West End of the town with English opera at the East. The most important result so far has been the discovery of a magnificent theatre in a place called Shoreditch: a palatial opera house in which you get an orchestra stall for two shillings, or a ruby velvet chair in the front row of the balcony for half-a-crown. More modest arrangements can be made for fourpence; and there are no fees, except a penny for a program. Here have we all been for years paying half-guineas and half-crowns for admission to paltry Strand playhouses, unwitting that there was an East-end Covent Garden accessible for fourpence. I had heard of Shoreditch as the home of an industrious population, of persons who never will be slaves earning their modest shilling a day by 16 hours' work; but its celebrity as a theatrical centre was unknown to me.

When Mr Melville, the proprietor and manager of the National Standard Theatre, informed me of his intention to produce Macfarren's Robin Hood on Monday last, I resolved to be there. I do not mind confessing that though, as a professional critic, I know everything, yet there are a few matters that I have not yet got quite at my fingers' ends. Among them are the works of Macfarren, who, like Cherubini, acquired such a reputation as a pedant that it was almost forgotten that he had once been a composer. And just as people with a dread of Cherubini's pedantry are always agreeably surprised by the overture to Anacreon, so was I years ago pleasantly taken aback by the overture to Chevy Chace. Indeed, it was partly on the strength of Chevy Chace that I went to hear Robin Hood.

Robin Hood was written for Her Majesty's Theatre in 1860. In that year English opera sung by Sims Reeves, Santley, and Madame Lemmens-Sherrington, and conducted by Hallé, was given night about with Italian opera conducted by Arditi and sung by Titiens and Giuglini. Such things have been, and may be again. As far as I know, Robin Hood has been shelved ever since; so that the performance on Monday was practically a first one to most of the audience.

Twenty-nine years after Robin Hood, and one and a half after the death of its composer, we have Mr Alfred Cellier's new English opera Doris produced at the Lyric Theatre, Shaftesbury Avenue, under the disadvantage of the absence from England of Corno di Bassetto. He, however, frequented the first two acts on Tuesday evening last, and proceeded to compare Doris with Robin Hood, with a view to determining how far English opera had advanced in the meantime. He regrets to have to announce quite decisively that it has not advanced at all. Macfarren put forth his musicianship and strained his fancy to trick out a libretto which barely pretended to be serious; and history has repeated itself with some minor variations, as, for instance, that Mr Cellier's songs are gayer, and his finales and concerted pieces flimsier, than Macfarren's. Mr Stephenson, too, lightheartedly drops even the pretence of seriousness. Otherwise there is not a pin to choose between the opera of 1860 and the opera of 1889. In one case the trifling is solemn: in the other, it is inane and flippant, that is all.

Doris is the more aggravating of the two at first, because the music seems to interrupt the action until it becomes apparent that there is no action to interrupt. When Martin, catching Carey in the act of kissing Doris's hand, stops to sing her a song before he takes any further steps, you pay no more attention to the story, and feel defrauded of what you have paid already. In Robin Hood the music generally advances matters: you feel that you are getting along, even though you are obviously in a no-thoroughfare. And although after a certain age—say ten—it is not easy to laugh very heartily at the Sumpnour, he is a veritable Falstaff compared with the buffoon at the Lyric, who, in spite of such pleasantries as changing his breeches and getting too drunk to find the keyhole of his door, would be quite intolerable if it were not for a certain natural drollery in Mr Arthur Williams which enables him to pretend to write a letter as Mr Crummles's comic countryman pretended to catch a fly: that is, funnily enough to make a cockney laugh.

Where the East-End audience suffered in comparison with the West was not in the quality of the opera, but in the manner of its performance. Mr Hawes Craven's Highgate scene at the Lyric is full of the true Bank Holiday feeling for nature, besides being thoroughly carried out in detail so as to make the illusion as easy to the spectator as possible. Further, Mr Ivan Caryll has trained his orchestra to play with such spirit and daintiness that it ranks as quite the best orchestra of its kind in London when the individuality of the conductor is placed to its credit. Then all the artists are good enough for their work: some of them, indeed, much too good. Mr Hayden Coffin's artistic intelligence is so completely wasted on his parts that by the time he has played three or four more of them—he will then be about fifty, judging from the run of Dorothy—his higher faculties will certainly have decayed from disuse. Meanwhile the West End hears its Doris to great advantage.

Not so the East-End Robin Hood. With the singers at the Standard I have no serious fault to find, although I may remark that Mr Turner has probably no idea of how unsatisfactory his intonation is when he is not bringing down the house with stentorian high notes. For the chorus I have nothing but praise: the men deserved the thundering encore they got for the unaccompanied chorus in the second act. The scenery, though of the old-fashioned sort, was sufficiently plausible. But the orchestra should not have been inflicted on Shoreditch, as it certainly durst never have been inflicted on Shaftesbury Avenue. And here, again, I make magnanimous allowances. The economies in the wood wind I pass over: the sufficiency of the brass I acknowledge. But imagine the effect, in a theatre of the largest size, of a string band consisting of five violins, one tenor, and two 'cellos, none of the players being, to say the least, Nerudas or

Hollmans! When the feeble and mistuned scraping got very bad—and once or twice it could hardly have been worse—doubtless the packed pittites said reverently, "This is classical music. This is above our heads, this is." Perhaps they even thought that it was quite the operatic thing for the conductor to wield his *bâton* with one hand and play the harmonium with the other. If so, they were far too kind in their estimate of the management's sense of its artistic duty to them. I hate to see the East End imposed upon; and I felt strongly inclined to rise between the acts and inform the house that more and better strings would have made an enormous difference for the better, and ought to have been provided.

The last time I ventured on a remark about music in the East End, I brought upon myself a letter from a correspondent at Camberwell which exasperated me beyond measure. He accused me of having said that working-men "could not enjoy the high-class oratorios of their superiors"; of running down the Peckham Choir in order to disparage the Tonic Sol-fa; and of wanting to burn "all the cantatas written since Mendelssohn's Ode to Joy." These intolerable aspersions are apparently founded on my opinion that Gounod's Redemption is, as a whole, such a bore that the audience of the People's Palace cannot have been sincere in pretending to enjoy it; on a distinct and unqualified compliment paid by me to the Peckham Tonic Sol-fa Choir; and on my disparagement of all scriptural oratorios written since Mozart's Magic Flute and Beethoven's setting of Schiller's Ode to Joy, *except* certain cantatas by Mendelssohn. It is infuriating to be misunderstood in this way, particularly as it is admitted in literary circles that I write the best English in the world. For the future, I positively decline to answer letters founded on inexcusable misreadings of my column.

Another correspondent—this time a model one—asks whether Miss Grace Pedley really said, as The Star reported, that her compass was four octaves. I cannot answer the question, as it was not I who interviewed Miss Pedley; but a compass of four octaves is not impossible. I believe Mr Corney Grain is gifted to that extent. However, people are apt to make statements of very doubtful value on this subject. For instance, between my lowest growl and my highest squeak there lies a compass of more than three octaves; but if I attempted to range far outside an octave and a fifth in singing, I should be asked to leave off. The service from which my correspondent quotes the bass must have been written either *by* a greenhorn or *for* a Russian choir. I was not aware that the text-books differed as much on the subject as my correspondent says; but surely no text-books encourage a student to expect bass chorus singers to be equally ready with C's below the stave and E naturals above it. The average basso cannot be trusted below G or above E flat.

7 May 1899

Mr Hamish MacCunn, at twenty-one years of age, is better known than most of the rising young men of forty-five or so who infuse some of the light and promise of early youth into the productive branches of the fine arts in London. The fame of the more important of his works will have reached every amateur who takes any interest in modern music; and even the main facts of the composer's personal history are already known wherever any curiosity exists concerning them. It is no news that he was born at Greenock in 1868; that his home was an actively musical one; that he was often brought to London, and spent one season, when he was eight years old, at Sydenham, where he heard Mr Manns's orchestra every day; that he took a scholarship at the Royal College of Music when he was fifteen, and worked under Dr Parry, picking up his orchestral experience as a viola player; that his works, which came out without the slightest flavor of Dr Parry or South Kensington, were first heard in the studio of Mr J. Pettie, R.A., the attraction of whose household for Mr MacCunn will probably be explained in the course of the year; and that the last commission given by the late Mr Carl Rosa was to the composer of The Lay of the Last Minstrel for an opera on the subject of Waverley, to be written by Mr Bennett, the musical critic of the Daily Telegraph. Personally Mr MacCunn is such a very significant-looking young man that he appears taller than he actually is. His hair is dark; he speaks with the accent of a Scottish gentleman; he is by no means unlike the bust of him by Mr D. W. Stevenson at the Royal Academy. There are certain youthful portraits of Mendelssohn, Chopin, and Weber, a composite of which would give some interesting suggestions of Hamish MacCunn. His noble forehead, fine, clear eyes, and particularly pleasant and open expression, partly account for the reminiscence of Mendelssohn. A glance at our portrait will show that his nose is his own and Scotland's, and that in the length of his head and the development at the base of the skull behind (where these men of war have their powder magazines) his photograph recalls Mr Herkomer's portrait of Wagner.

First, then, as to Mr MacCunn's view of the musical situation in England. He has no doubt that we are entering on a period of genuine musical activity. The necessary conditions for it are: the men, the money, and the public. As to the men, what difficulty should there be about that? We have produced the greatest of men in the fine arts, from Shakespear downwards; and there is no magician's circle drawn about music more than about any other art. Money we have in plenty. As for the public, you want one with enthusiasm, idealism, and—purchasing power. The idealism of the British public is proved, not by the fact that a few of them are fond of Beethoven's symphonies, but by the extent to which they suffer themselves to be aristocracy-ridden. Needless to say, Mr MacCunn, at twenty-one, and proud of a newly taken place in the Republic of Art, is no worshipper of aristocracy. But he sees that others worship it, and he finds comfort in the spectacle; for he knows that we do not worship aristocrats wholly because we are a nation of snobs: we idealize them first, and only give our homage to our ideal.

Now, says Mr MacCunn, with a salt touch of humor that goes along with the clearest earnestness in him, whilst the British are able to idealize the British aristocracy, nobody can say that they have not a tremendous fund of idealizing capacity ready for the service of Music as soon as she comes to claim it. Questioned as to his favorite composers, Mr MacCunn simply protested: "You might as well ask me which I like best, my arms or my legs." Yet he has tenderness towards certain composers. Weber—the Weber of the Freischütz and Oberon rather than of Euryanthe—is a special favorite of his; and he is strong in praise of M. Gounod, for the beauty and dramatic force of the prelude to whose Faust he has no words to express his admiration. With reference to the old composers, he said more than once, "They carry us very far back; even Gounod takes you very far back"—which means that Mr MacCunn is going to take us as far forward as he can. Mr MacCunn has made no secret of his conviction that the music of the future will be dramatic and descriptive, not "abstract." He has always put programs to his works on the simple ground that, as he always meant something when he wrote them, he may as well tell people what the meaning is. In this there is a touch of Scotch rationalism which cropped up again when, replying to a question as to whether he ever felt impelled to adopt Wagner's practice of writing his own words, he said: "I have not the vocabulary. I can find music but not words. Besides, if I write the book, you will be expecting me to paint the scenery too, on the same principle." He added that if a librettist brought inadequate words, the composer could always refuse to set them; but on this score he is evidently void of anxiety and fraternal jealousy. Indeed, he rather insists on the social character of opera production than on the composer's individual share in it. His view about symphonies and abstract music generally is that we have as much of it as we want, and that we cannot advantageously replace the old symphonies with new ones. If he were to write a symphony, he says, Beethoven's in C minor would be better worth listening to; that would be all. As to professors' music generally—"organist's music," as Wagner called it—the professor is always ashamed to do the very thing he is there to do—namely, to make an effect—and so he does nothing.

I at last had the hardihood to ask Mr MacCunn for his notions of press criticism.

"I think," said the composer, fixing his eye on me to indicate that he felt confident of my approval, "that criticism, above all things, should not be flippant, because if it is, nobody respects it."

THE PHILHARMONIC

7 *May* 1889

MADAME BACKER-GRÖNDAHL last night played the E flat concerto again for the Philharmonic Society. She is a famous Norwegian pianist, great in strength and feeling, now urging the pianoforte almost violently to do what a piano cannot do, and anon caressing it to exquisite ripples of sound and streams of keen plaintive melody. I shall not forget her playing of the second subject of the first movement. Her diminuendo in the long octave passage near the end of the Allegro came as an enchanting surprise after the curious rough, sluggish forte at which she began it. The point for pianoforte and drum came out as I never heard it come out before; I feel sure that that fine artist, Mr Chaine, must adore Madame Gröndahl for doing him justice in this passage. The circumstances under which the concerto was played were unusually sensational. During the opening movement subdued rumblings, with which Mr Chaine had nothing to do, were heard from time to time. Just as we had all settled down, intent on the hushed melody of the Adagio, the sky suddenly flashed into view through the windows; the electric light staggered as if from a mortal shock; and the rumbling broke into a crash. Everybody thought of the recent earthquake. A gentleman next me seized his hat and jammed it on his head too tightly for any convulsion of nature to dislodge it, which done, he folded his arms, and glared at Mr Cowen's back. I refrained with difficulty from crawling under the seat. As Madame Gröndahl dashed at the finale, a torrent of rain dashed at the windows; the lights, which had partly recovered, again burnt blue; and the pianist had to compete with the elements for our attention, and came out of the competition victorious. Young Mr Frederick Cliffe's symphony in C minor also weathered the storm. It has life and youth in it. A few pardonable displays of scholarship disfigure it here and there; and it is of course not quite free from reminiscences: a drum point from Beethoven, a theme in the trio taken from a beautiful melody in Liszt's Preludes, and so on. But, on the whole, it is fresh, genuine, and interesting. Fräulein Fillunger, who gave us Ocean, thou Mighty Monster, is not like the gentleman in Shakespear who could sing both high and low. She can sing high, but not low. The concert began with Cherubini's barren Anacreon overture, and ended with that to Mozart's Zauberflöte, which Mr Cowen darted through as I should not have cared to do with so much lightning about.

13 *May* 1889

THIS week seems to be devoted to celebrating the French Revolution of 1789 which produced such an effect on music that it has never been the same since. I can bring the connection down to this very week; for the first musical product of the Revolution was the Eroica Symphony, utterly unlike anything that had ever been heard in the world before. That very symphony, though nobody feels particularly excited about it now, was performed at the first Richter concert the other day. This would be an excellent opportunity to introduce a criticism of the concert; but unluckily I was not there —though that, of course, need not prevent me from writing a notice of it. I had gone down to Surrey to inspect the newest fashions in spring green; and when the concert began I was communing perplexedly with Nature as to the probability of catching the last train but one from Dorking.

Between ten and eleven, as I sat at Redhill Junction awaiting the arrival of the ten minutes to ten train, I meditated on the Revolution music—on its grandioseness, splendioseness, neuroseness, and sensationaloseness; on its effort, its hurry, its excitement, its aspiration without purpose, its forced and invariably disappointing climaxes, its exhaustion and decay, until in our own day everything that was most strenuously characteristic of it seems old-fashioned, platitudinous, puerile, forcible-feeble, anything but romantic and original. Just think of the mental condition of the enthusiastic musicians who believed that the operas of Meyerbeer were a higher development of those of Mozart, that Berlioz was the heir and successor of Beethoven, Schubert an immortal tone poet as yet only half come to light, Rossini such another as Handel, and Wagner a cacophonous idiot! It is not twenty years since this was quite an advanced program.

If, however, we are to have a Revolution, do not let us sing the Marseillaise. The incurable vulgarity of that air is a disgrace to the red flag. It corresponds so exactly in rhythmic structure with the Irish tune called The Red Fox, or, as Moore set it, Let Erin Remember the Days of Old that the two airs can be harmonized, though not in what Cherubini would have considered strict two-part counterpoint. But compare the mechanical tramp and ignobly self-assertive accent of Rouget de Lisle's composition with the sensitiveness of the Irish melody and the passion that is in all its moods. My own belief is that the men of Marseilles were horribly frightened when they went to the front, as any sensible person would be; and Rouget de Lisle's tune enabled them to face it out, exactly as "Ta-ran-ta-ra" encouraged the policemen in The Pirates of Penzance.

On Saturday evening, during one of my East End expeditions, I discovered the People's Palace, which consists of a board with an inscription to the effect that if I choose to produce £50,000, the palace will be built for me forthwith. This rather took me aback; for I had thought that the palace was an accomplished fact. But no: there was a huge concert-room, a reading-room, and shanties containing a bath, a gymnasium, and a restaurant; also a little clubhouse, but no palace. In the concert-room some unfortunate artists were bawling ballads in the vain hope of fixing the attention of an immense audience. But the thing was impossible: the place was too big. Hundreds of young people loafed and larked, or stared and wandered in and out, at the end of the room. I thought of the late Edmund Gurney—of his useless big book to prove that Wagner's music was *wrong*, and his invaluable little plea for an orchestra for the East End. One hundred and twenty good players, under an able conductor, could make that concert-room useful. They would cost money, too; but why not stick up a board and ask for it?

But there is another way of getting music afoot there. Why not buy first-rate wind instruments; engage a really competent instructor-bandmaster; and then invite the East End to come in and play for itself. There is plenty of musical talent knocking about misused or misdirected among the wage-workers. I have often heard a knot of East End amateurs with a few brass instruments helplessly making the most hideous discord, because they had never been taught to tune their slides or warned against the impossibility of making up a band with a fortuitous concourse of deadly weapons tuned to different pitches and only agreeing in the single point of having been purchased at a pawnbroker's. With properly assorted instruments and a little simple instruction, these enthusiasts would have made excellent music. The proletarian bands of the industrial north and of the Salvation Army prove it.

From the People's Palace I went to the Bow and Bromley Institute. There I found a sixpenny and threepenny audience, of discouragingly middle-class aspect, listening to M. Gigout, who was performing on the "kist o' whustles," which is the pride of the Institute. Presently came Madame Belle Cole, a robust lady with an extraordinary voice and an effective adaptation of the style of Madame Antoinette

Sterling. She sang Gounod's Entreat me not to Leave Thee
to such purpose that the audience, instead of entreating her
to leave them, insisted on her singing again, whereupon she
gave Home, sweet Home. The next artist that turned up was
Henry Seiffert, the Dutch violinist, whose breadth of tone
and command of his instrument completely confirmed the
very favorable opinion I formed of him when he first played
in London. The audience clamored for an encore; but a gentleman came forward in the midst of the hubbub, and when
his evident wish to speak had produced a breathless and ex-
pectant silence, said he wanted somebody to give a theme
for M. Gigout to improvize upon. This simply struck us
dumb. Then he smiled reassuringly, and his eye began to
travel slowly along the bench where I sat. Ere it reached my
vacant chair I was safe on the roof of an Aldgate tram.

17 May 1889

I DO not know anything more annoying at a concert than a
man who beats time. He is a sort of modern prophet with a
Kentish fire shut up in his bones, so that, like Jeremiah, he
is weary with forbearing and cannot stay. He generally does
stay, notwithstanding, right through to the very end. It
seems unreasonable to hate him so venomously for attempting what the big drum and cymbals may be achieving at the
same time with your entire approval; but, reasonably or not,
the thumping of his boot distracts and annoys you beyond
expression, and you gloat vindictively over his defeat when
a syncopated passage throws him out.

Among these death-watches of the concert room there
are some terribly destructive varieties. I remember a tenor
who used to mark time by shooting his ears up and down. If
you have ever seen a circus clown twitch his ear you know
how it makes your flesh creep. Imagine the sensation of looking at a man with his ears pulsating 116 times per minute in
a quick movement from one of Verdi's operas. That man permanently injured my nervous system by rehearsing in my

presence (unsuccessfully) the arduous part of Ruiz in Il Trovatore. But he was eclipsed by a rival who marked time with his eyes. You know the fancy clock in which an old man with a pistol looks out of a rustic window, glancing from side to side for burglars as the clock ticks. That was how he did it; and never shall I forget the shrinking of my whole nature from his horrible ocular oscillations. Feeling that I should go mad if I ever saw such a thing again, I left the country (he was not an Englishman), and have never revisited it.

Time, the great healer, eventually effaced his detested image from my memory. But on Wednesday afternoon I happened to be at Mr Henry Phillips's concert at St James's Hall, contemplating Mr Frederic King, who was singing *O du mein holder Abendstern*. To confess the truth, I was not minding the song so much as Mr King's fashionable trousers, made according to the new mode in which the tailor measures you round the chest, in order to get the correct width for the knee. I am rather an outsider in these matters, as it is my practice to make a suit of clothes last me six years. The result is that my clothes acquire individuality, and become characteristic of me. The sleeves and legs cease to be mere tailor-made tubes; they take human shape with knees and elbows recognizably mine. When my friends catch sight of one of my suits hanging on a nail, they pull out their pen-knives and rush forward, exclaiming, "Good Heavens! he has done it at last."

However, the musical critic presently prevailed over the clothes philosopher; and I lifted my gaze to Mr King's face as the piano began the six-eight rhythm of the Romance. To my intense horror, he instantly beat time horizontally with his eyes for a whole bar. Unbearable memories crowded upon me. I held on to the back of my seat in a silent struggle with homicidal mania. It was a terrible moment; for my place was within a few yards of Mr King's throat. Mercifully, his eyes stopped. Unconscious of the peril through which he had just passed, he began to sing in his best manner; and the effect was like that of David's singing on Saul. Still, I cannot help thinking that it is just as well that I am not in the habit of carrying a javelin. Though now that I think of it, how musical performances would improve if all critics of fine taste carried javelins—and used them!

These afternoon concerts are odd affairs. The tickets are half-a-guinea apiece; and nine-tenths of the audience are obviously deadheads. The artists sing to oblige one another: about 70 guineas' worth of them turned up on this particular occasion, and helped Mr Phillips to entertain a few of his friends and a host of strangers who never did and never will contribute a farthing to the gate money upon which Music depends for her living. When I arrived the attendants were strictly carrying out a regulation which I have often insisted on as indispensable to the comfort of artists and audience, but which I now denounce as intolerable. I allude to the practice of closing the doors during each piece. I should not have objected had I been on the right side of the door; but I came late, and so was on the wrong side during the performance of the first movement of Grieg's violin sonata (Op. 13) by Miss Sasse and Henri Seiffert. I was utterly disgusted with the selfishness of the people who, to save themselves a momentary discomfort, kept me on the stairs for nearly three minutes.

When I got in I found Miss Sasse playing Grieg in a hopelessly un-Grieg-like fashion, and Mr Seiffert, who had apparently lost interest in the transaction, absently playing the violin part. Even when he reappeared to give us Wieniawski's Legende, he once or twice took down his instrument and looked perplexedly at it as one communing with himself thus: "What on earth is this thing under my chin? Looks like a fiddle. Gad! this must be a concert; and I expect I've been put up to do something at it. Wonder what she's playing! It sounds like Wieniawski. Yes, by Jove! it's the Legende. I must wake up; here goes!" And in these brief intervals of wakefulness he played very finely, though he seemed to master the polyphonic difficulties as easily asleep as awake.

I am always inclined to believe in a violinist who can play Wieniawski. Beethoven and Mendelssohn were great composers of music for the violin; but Wieniawski was a great composer of violin music. There is all the difference in the world between the two.

I have no space to tell of the rest of this typical concert —of how Mr Herbert Sims Reeves, whose determination never to force his voice has been rewarded by a considerable growth in its power and beauty, sang a couple of those Italian songs which are the ultimate perfection of utter brainlessness; of how Madame Patey, with ruthless affectation and exaggeration, used a fine song of Handel's merely to give a thundering display of her voice and power; of how Miss Pauline Cramer astonished everybody by her majestic stature and the brightness and impetuosity which make her genuine German sentiment so acceptable; and of how cleverly and expressively Miss Rosina Filippi recited Henry the Fifth's wooing (Henry V was an insufferable Jingo snob; but that is not Miss Filippi's fault), besides leaving all the other ladies nowhere in the point of artistic dressing. I say I have no space to tell of these things; nor for Signor di Giambattista's concert in the evening, except that I should recommend the application of vinegar and brown paper to the pianoforte on which he played, especially to the bass.

The Spanish Students at the Café Monaco seem to have made a poor job of their academic studies, as most of them carry wooden spoons in their hats as trophies of their performances under competitive examination. When I entered I was the fortieth arrival; and about a hundred more came in before I left: chiefly Spaniards, though some English people were there to study the thing from an ethnological point of view. In one of the Henry VI chronicle plays which Shakespear had a hand in, there is a ghost who abruptly closes a conversation by saying, "Have done; for more I hardly can endure." It was with much the same feeling that I withdrew at the end of the first part, leaving the Spanish part of the audience to sit out the second, and astonish the natives by stamping and shouting after the Iberian manner. The guitar and mandoline band, with its tum-tum melodies and simple-minded contrasts of forte and piano, is pretty; but I had heard the sort of thing before, and a little of it went far with me. Señor Cano played on himself very smartly with a tambourine; Señorita Reyes sang exactly as an Irish fish-wife cries "Dublin Bay Herrings!" two Andalusians danced as the Carmens of real life dance; the guitarist accompanied very quaintly and skilfully; and—and, in short, I came away.

20 *May* 1889

To lovers of poetry the pearl fisher is known as one who "held his breath, and went all naked to the hungry shark." To the patrons of the Opera he is now familiar as an expensively got-up Oriental, with an elaborate ritual conducted in temples not unlike Parisian newspaper kiosks, the precincts whereof are laid out, regardless of expense, in the manner of a Brussels tea garden. The chief ceremony is a ballet; and though here, if anywhere, we might expect to find our pearl fisher in the condition mentioned by Keats, such is by no means the case. He—or rather she—is clothed and, within operatic limits, in her right mind. As to holding his breath, he turns that accomplishment to account for the better execution of roulades and fioriituras. He keeps the hungry shark in order by the prayers of a virgin priestess, who remains veiled and secluded from all human intercourse on a rocky promontory during the oyster season.

Out of these simple and plausible conditions we get a pretty poem. Leila is the priestess. Nadir and Zenith—no: I find on looking at the libretto that the name is Zurga— fall in love with her. Nadir sacrilegiously serenades her on the promontory. She responds; and the two, amid a hideous tempest, are seized and condemned to the stake. Zurga effects a diversion, and enables them to escape by setting Ceylon on fire: an extreme measure; but then, as he doubtless reflects, you cannot have an omelette without breaking eggs. The natives then burn him; and really, under the circumstances, it is hard to blame them. That is all.

Of the choral music, the dance music, the procession music, and the melodramatic music, by all of which the dainty little poem of the two friends in love with the veiled priestess has been stuffed and padded into a big Covent Garden opera, it is needless to speak. It is effective and workmanlike enough; but a dozen composers could have done it to order as well as Bizet. The best of it is the choral unison in the first act—*Colui, che noi vogliam, per duce*, which has something of the swing and frankness of Donizetti's choruses. (These, by the bye, have been discovered by the Salvation Army: I heard one of their bands playing *Per te immenso giubilo* capitally one Sunday morning last year down at Merton.) The leading motive which runs through the opera is very beautiful, but no more Bizet's than the chorale in Les Huguenots is Meyerbeer's: it is simply that wonderful old Dies Iræ which has fascinated generations of musicians and worshippers. Bizet is only himself—his immature self—in the love music, which has that touch of divine rapture which a young poet's love music should have, and which has the distinction and charm of the Carmen music without the firmness of its style. In the first act, the conventional amorous cavatina for the tenor is replaced by a duet in which the two rivals recall the romantic atmosphere of that evening at the gate of an eastern city when they caught their first glimpse of Leila. The duet, and all those parts of the opera which are in the same vein, are enchanting. He who has no indulgence for their want of solidity is fit for treasons, stratagems, and spoils.

The cast was only four strong. M. Talazac, whose figure offered a terrible temptation to the hungry shark, has a pretty and fairly steady mezza voce, besides some sweet head notes; but the tremolo with which he uses his chest register will prevent him from attaining popularity here. M. F. D'Andrade is a useful artist, free from conspicuous faults, and in earnest about his work. Miss Ella Russell is an accomplished singer of the Patti school, with a fine ear, and a voice of enviable quality, range, and flexibility. Her shortcomings are lack of distinction and bad pronunciation. She has not the intense dramatic instinct which has enabled some singers to take a foremost place as by natural right without the acquired culture and habits of thought which are becoming more and more necessary for success on the lyric stage; but a lady of Miss Russell's energy and confidence can do much for herself in this direction if she shuns the seductive illusion that no more remains for her to do. At all events, she should at once take a set of lessons in Italian so as to avoid such achievements as

> Bentosto una barbarar gentay
> Accor minacciantay, furentay.

It may be said that this is one of the consequences of operas performed in a language which is not that of the country, not that of the singer, and not that in which the opera was written.

Signor Mancinelli conducted, as he always does, like a man of character and energy, and the orchestra minded their business accordingly. With such players as there are at Covent Garden, nothing more is needed to secure satisfactory results in such work as the score of the Pearl Fishers. Tonight, Faust, with Miss Macintyre and M. Montariol. M. Winogradow, the sole success of the ill-fated Russian troupe, will be the Valentine; and Mephistopheles will be played by Signor Castelmary, who used to make the part curiously fantastic and interesting, not by his wolflike singing, but by his peculiar realization of the grotesque aspect of the character.

21 *May* 1889

LAST night's performance at the Royal Italian Opera, Covent Garden, was rather of the subscription kind: that is

Jean de Reszke was not the Faust, nor Edouard the Mephistopheles. The success of the evening was Winogradow's Valentine. At first the savage fervor and rich tone which made such an effect at the Albert Hall were missing, but they speedily returned. *Dio Possente* aroused a cold and listless house to an encore, which was declined. His share of the sword chorale and duel trio were given magnificently. The Faust, M. Montariol, did not make a favorable impression at starting. His declamation in the first act was forced and unskilful. Later on it appeared that he was not without his merits. He took his high notes, which are slightly veiled, quietly, and was comparatively guiltless of tremolo; so, on the whole, there was much to be thankful for. As Miss Macintyre's Margaret unquestionably delighted the audience it is nobody's business to demur to her performance; but I must add that she perpetrated a shocking Vandalism in ending the final trio on the high B natural. Castelmary is less slim and sudden than of yore: he has got an additional chin, too, and has become a Mephistopheles of the Rabelaisian variety, rather short of wind. He retains his old diabolical enjoyment of the part, and annoys the house, as he always did, by his occasional abandonment of all artistic method and self-control. The soldiers' chorus went with thundering vigor. The orchestra left something to be desired in point of delicacy and balance; but they will probably improve as the season goes on, as they did all last year. Excuse these perfunctory notes scrawled between the acts.

24 May 1889

Now that the season is in full swing, I am afraid I shall have to drag in the subject of music rather often in this column. I know that it is my King Charles's head; and I can assure my readers that I do what I can to avoid it. But when there are several concerts every afternoon, and an opera in the evening, I cannot, in spite of my diligence in not going to them, quite keep them out of my memoranda. Nobody knows better than I do that a musical critic who is always talking about music is quite as odious as an ordinary man who is always talking about himself. I venture to hope that I have never been guilty of the latter vice; and I shall try to steer clear of the former. Therefore, it is with no desire to talk shop that I proceed to confess that I did not go to the Tonic Sol-fa meeting at Exeter Hall on Monday, though The Star was duly represented there.

My chief reason for not going was that one of the items in the program was a collection, a form of musical composition to which I have an incurable repugnance, except when I am myself the performer. A subordinate reason existed in the necessity for my being elsewhere: at Covent Garden, in fact. But I wish carefully to disclaim any hostility whatever to the Tonic Sol-fa. I will go further, and declare my suspicion (my experience is not sufficiently wide to justify me in calling it a conviction) that the Tonic Sol-faists do undoubtedly teach people to read music. That the staff notationists, as a rule, don't, I take as granted on all sides.

An ordinary choir generally contains a few people naturally gifted with the power of recollecting the absolute pitch of notes. If you met them in the middle of the Sahara and said, "How do you do? Will you kindly give me A flat?" they would give it to you promptly. John Hullah seems to have supposed that because he could do this all the world could do it. Teach such people the symbols which, in the staff or any other notation, denote the sounds used in music, and they can read whatever you put into their hands. Almost all the champion sight-reading pupils who are brought forward as samples of the efficacy of the staff system, the Chevé system, the Tonic Sol-fa system, or any other system, are persons with this sense of absolute pitch, their proficiency proving nothing except the mere literary legibility of the notation they have before them. They have in their heads not only a fixed *"Doh,"* but the other 11 notes in the octave fixed as well, and they use the Tonic Sol-fa as a "fixed *Doh*" system, just as many staff-notation readers use the staff as a move-

129

able *Doh* system, and would not be in the least put out if all their parts were written in the key of C, like horn parts in an orchestral score.

The system is undoubtedly the di Bassetto system, as practised by me and by the great majority of sight readers throughout the world. I should explain that I cannot remember the absolute pitch of notes, and that though I can imitate an interval instantaneously, by ear, I cannot calculate it with sufficient presence of mind to carry me through a *presto con fuoco* movement at sight. For instance, if you asked me for A flat in the Sahara, I should borrow a tuning fork and listen to its note. Then, if I saw C stamped on the handle, I should, after some minutes' careful calculation warble the minor sixth above, which would of course be A flat (more or less). But my practical choir method renders reference to a tuning fork unnecessary, and entirely dispenses with mental arithmetic. At the first rehearsal I depend mainly on my natural power of improvising what is called "a second." By keeping my eyes and ears open, I soon identify the few who are really able to read at sight. These are generally, of course, absolute pitchers. The rest is easy. I simply get beside one of them, and sing what he sings until I have picked up my part. The merits of this method are proved by its almost universal adoption. I have no hesitation in saying that for one person who reads music on the Curwen system or the Hullah system, there are fifty who read it on mine.

In confessing to a deficiency in the sense of absolute pitch: a deficiency which prevents me from detecting a transposition of one of the numbers in an opera, except when (as in the case of *Dio dell'or*, as sung by Castelmary the other night in Faust) the wrong key is attained by a flagrantly burglarious transition without any alteration of the previous modulating cadence, I may as well say that I wish Mr F. Galton would open a criticometric laboratory to test scientifically the pretensions of those who have perfect faith in the infallibility of their ears. I daresay that you, exacting reader, would not give twopence for a critic who, hearing a note out of tune, could not say whether it was sharp or flat. Well, have you seen, in the New Gallery, Mr Phil Burne-Jones's portrait of Lord Rayleigh in his laboratory, seeking the philosopher's stone with the aid of a retort, a few test tubes, and a second-hand kettledrum?

Lord Rayleigh once lured some eminent musicians into that laboratory, and proceeded with cold-blooded physicist's scepticism to test their pretensions. He began by putting pairs of notes just sufficiently out of unison for the eminent ones to recognize that there was a difference in pitch. Then he asked them which was the higher of the two. They answered confidently; and, lo! they were just as often wrong as right. And when he varied the quality of the notes, making the lower one shrill and the higher one dull and veiled, he had them every time. I do not defend Lord Rayleigh's conduct in playing it thus upon men before whom he should have been awestricken, and whose ears were diviner instruments than his soulless mechanical reeds. Still, there is food for reflection in the matter.

I could write quite a treatise on the imaginary powers which musicians have attributed to themselves in perfect good faith, and in the absence of any scientific verification; but it is time to pass on to other matters. I think it must have been on some evening last week that I found myself celebrating the silver wedding of Mr Lansdowne-Cottell, at a recklessly overcrowded concert in St James's Hall. Here I paid sixpence—people seem to think I am made of sixpences —for a program about eight inches by ten, containing a dozen pages of advertisements and two of program. If everybody bought one and got a ticket for nothing, the silver wedding cannot have been wholly in vain. However, the sensation of that part of the evening which I spent there was a performance by Miss Anna Teresa Berger on the cornet. I do not know why a lady should play the cornet: indeed, I do not know why anybody should play it; but her right is as valid as a man's. Miss Berger's double-tonguing verges on the unattainable; and in keenness of blare she

131

rivals Mr Howard Reynolds at his loudest.

Sarasate, whose first concert I missed, played Mendelssohn's concerto last Saturday. But I had as lief hear him play Pop goes the Weasel as any classic masterpiece; and what is more, I believe he would himself just as soon play one as the other. They say he runs through a new composition once with his pianist, and then has it by heart for ever afterwards; and I can believe it; for he often produces tedious affairs that no artist of his reputation would find it worth while to learn if it cost any trouble. I have never been able to detect any preference on his part for Mendelssohn over Dr Mackenzie, Bernard, Lalo, Max Bruch, or anyone else. He never interprets anything: he plays it beautifully, and that is all. He is always alert, swift, clear, refined, certain, scrupulously attentive and quite unaffected. This last adjective will surprise people who see him as a black-haired romantic young Spaniard, full of fascinating tricks and mannerisms. It will surprise them still more to hear that the person they so idealize produces the whole illusion with his fine eyes alone, being for the rest a man of undistinguished stature, with hair very liberally sprinkled with grey, and a plain square face with more than a fair forty-one years' allowance of marks from Time's graver. There is no trace of affectation about him: the picturesqueness of that pluck of the string and stroke of the bow that never fails to bring down the house is the natural effect of an action performed with perfect accuracy in an extraordinarily short time and strict measure.

29 May 1889

FAUST, no matter who writes the music to it, will remain the most popular opera story of the century until some great musician takes Henrik Ibsen's Peer Gynt as a libretto. Boito's version seems almost as popular as Gounod's, though Gounod's is a true musical creation, whereas Boito has only adapted the existing resources of orchestration and harmony very ably to his libretto. In short, Gounod has set music to Faust, and Boito has set Faust to music.

The house likes Boito's prologue, in spite of the empty stage and the two ragged holes in a cloth which realize Mr Harris's modest conception of hell and heaven. The great rolling crashes and echoes of brazen sound in the prelude transport us into illimitable space at once; and the tremendous sonority of the instrumentation at the end, with the defiant devil's whistle recklessly mocking each climax of its grandeur, literally makes us all sit up. Perhaps I am reading into the score what the composer never intended: Boito may have meant no more by the piccolo here than Beethoven meant by it in the last bars of the Egmont overture. If so, that does not invalidate my remark: it only shews how much the critic can add to the work of the composer.

There is a great deal in Mefistofele that is mere impressionism; and like impressionism in painting it is enchanting when it is successful, and nonsensically incoherent when it is the reverse. In the unrestrained colloquialism of private conversation I should not hesitate to describe a good deal of the Brocken scene and some of the rampart scene as ingenious tiddy-fol-lol. The witches' revel, with the spurious fugato at the end, is stuff for a pantomime, not for serious opera. But at innumerable points the music is full of suggestive strokes and colors in sound, happiest sometimes when they are mere inchoate instrumentation. The whole work is a curious example of what can be done in opera by an accomplished literary man without original musical gifts, but with ten times the taste and culture of a musician of only ordinary extraordinariness.

There was little novelty in the representation last night. Miss Macintyre doubled Helen and Margaret for the first time at Covent Garden, and sang the duet in the classical interlude in the most exaggerated vein of romanticism. She did not wholly resist the temptation to force her chest voice up in the prison scene, which is likely to prove a terrible engine of voice destruction among dramatic sopranos in this

particular and most fatal way. She relied largely for her acting on the exploitation of what is nothing but a bag of tricks;
and it is quite true, as a ruthless critic tells her this week,
that she walks badly and twists her mouth to one side. But,
with all these drawbacks, her natural talent and refinement,
and the charm of her unspoiled young voice, carried her triumphantly through the two parts. Signor Massini cannot
act; but his throatiness and his aptitude for singing flat were
established beyond question in the first act. He improved
greatly afterwards, getting quite into tune in the garden
scene, and coming off with some credit in the final act; but
he is, on the whole, rather useful than distinguished as a
primo tenore. Signor Castelmary was announced for Mefisto.
He would have been hopelessly out of breath after three bars
or so had he appeared; so nobody was disappointed at his replacement by Signor Novara, who played the part with unexpected success, delivering the text with clearness and purpose, and acting without any senseless posturing and point-
making. The part exactly suits his voice. Madame Scalchi
was good as Martha—not so good as Pantalis.

Signor Mancinelli conducted. He again dragged that irresistible hysterical quartet in the garden scene; and again
it missed the effect it never failed to produce when Christine
Nilsson was the Margaret. In the prologue, on the contrary,
he took the choruses too fast; they were gabbled in a way
that suggested anything but the ethereal whisper intended
by the composer. The stage management and scene shifting
were occasionally needlessly careless and destructive of stage
illusion. An oath or two from Mr Harris will no doubt improve matters in this respect.

31 May 1889

It is a sign of the shallow musical culture of the classes that
they come late for Lohengrin merely because it begins at
eight instead of half-past. A set that will not sacrifice its
cheese and ice pudding to hear the Lohengrin prelude—the

first work of Wagner's that really conquered the world and changed the face of music for us—may be a smart set for dancing; it is the reverse at music. When the élite of the beau monde did come they found that Mr McGuckin had sprained his ankle badly, and had refused all proposals to go through his part in a Bath chair. His place was accordingly taken by Signor A. d'Andrade, who phrased his narrative in the last act very nicely. Miss Nordica turned Elsa of Brabant into Elsa of Bond-street, by appearing in a corset. She produces her voice so skilfully that its want of color, and her inability to fill up with expressive action the long periods left by Wagner for that purpose, were the more to be regretted. Madame Fürsch-Madi, who has been subject to Italian opera for many years, got severe attacks of spasms and staggers at the emotional crises of her part. Her music, however, was not ill sung. Signor F. d'Andrade rather distinguished himself as Telramond; but on the whole, the principal singers lacked the weight, breadth of style, richness of voice, and sincerity of expression needed for Lohengrin. Signor Mancinelli's Italian temperament came repeatedly into conflict with the German temperament of the composer. Where the music should have risen to its noblest and broadest sweep he hurried on in the impetuous, self-assertive, emphatic Southern way that is less compatible than any other manner on earth with the grand calm of the ideal Germany. He perpetrates, too, that abominable butcherly cut in the prelude to the second act, which is an odious inheritance from the bad old times. I confess that I cannot speak amiably of performances at which I am subjected to wanton outrages of this sort. There are reasons for the other cuts: bad reasons, but ones which must be let pass under the circumstances. But this particular cut is without excuse. Under its exasperating influence I proceed to complain that the choristers shouted instead of singing. This is an improvement on the old choristers, who could not even shout; but shouting should not be the goal of even an operatic choir's ambition, and I do not see why, if Mr Mansfield has trumpets on the stage in Richard III, the Royal Italian Opera should be unable to get anything better than four vile cornets. And I wish those ladies of the chorus whom Mr Harris has provided with train-bearers and splendid dresses, would learn to walk in the true *grande dame* manner, and not make the bridal procession ridiculous by their bearing. And I should have liked more precision and delicacy from the orchestra. And, generally speaking, I do not think they can do Lohengrin worth a cent at Coventgarden; and that is the long and short of it. This is the sort of temper you get a critic into when you carry your eternal Cut! Cut! Cut! a bar too far.

ELSEWHERE you will find a letter on The Music of the People, by Mr Marshall-Hall, a young composer who is much spoken of among the young lions of Mr Hamish McCunn's generation. At one of Mr Henschel's concerts Mr Santley sang some portions of an opera, the poem and music of which were by Mr Marshall-Hall. I was not at that concert, so I am quite out of it as far as Mr Marshall-Hall's music is concerned; but I am delighted to find him, as a representative of young genius, denouncing the stalls, trusting to the gallery, waving the democratic flag, and tearing round generally.

Young genius has rather a habit, by the way, of writing to my editor to denounce me as flippant and unenlightened, and to demand that I also shall tear round and proclaim the working man as the true knower and seer in Art. If I did, the working man would not think any the better of me; for he knows well enough that society is not divided into "animated clothes-pegs" on the one hand and lovers of Beethoven in ligatured corduroys on the other. For Beethoven purposes society is divided into people who can afford to keep a piano and go to operas and concerts, and people who cannot. Mr Marshall-Hall's idea that the people who cannot are nevertheless screwed up to concert pitch by honest, thorough, manly toil, shews that, though he be an expert in the music question, in the labor question he is a greenhorn.

Take a laborer's son; let him do his board-schooling

mostly on an empty stomach; bring him up in a rookery tenement; take him away from school at thirteen; offer him the alternative of starvation or 12 to 16 hours work a day at jerry building, adulterated manufactures, coupling railway waggons, collecting tramway fares, field labor, or what not, in return for food and lodging which no "animated clothes-peg" would offer to his hunter; bully him; slave-drive him; teach him by every word and look that he is not wanted among respectable people, and that his children are not fit to be spoken to by their children. This is a pretty receipt for making an appreciator of Beethoven.

The truth is, that in the innumerable grades of culture and comfort between the millionaire on the one hand, and the casual laborer on the other, there is a maximum of relish for art somewhere. That somewhere is certainly not among the idle rich, whose appetites for enjoyment are not sharpened by work, nor is it among those who, worn out by heavy muscular toil, fall asleep if they sit quiet and silent for five minutes of an evening. Professional and business men of musical tastes who work hard, and whose brains are of such a quality that a Beethoven symphony is a recreation to them instead of an increased strain on their mental powers, are keen patrons of music, though, in outward seeming, they belong to the animated clothes-peg section. Middle-class young ladies, to whom there is no path to glory except that of the pianist or prima donna, frequent St. James's Hall with astonishing persistence, and eventually form musical habits which outlast their musical hopes.

The musical public is the shilling public, by which I mean the people who can afford to pay not more than a shilling once a week or so for a concert without going short of more immediately necessary things. Music can be better nourished on shilling, sixpenny, and threepenny seats than on the St James's Hall scale. The laborers are so enormously numerous that the absolute number of their exceptional men— men who will buy books out of 13s. a week in the country and 18 in a town, and find time to read them while working

12 hours a day—is considerable. The more comfortable members of the artisan class can often afford a shilling much better than the poorer middle-class families; but it has a certain customary and traditional scale of expenditure, in which concerts stand at threepence or sixpence, shillings being reserved for the gallery of a West-end theatre, and half-crowns for Sunday trips to Epping Forest and for extra refreshments.

After these come the innumerable "poor devils" of the middle class, always craving in an unaccountable way for music, and crowding the Promenade Concerts on classical nights, the Albert Hall gallery, and wherever else decent music is to be heard cheaply. To these three classes Mr Marshall-Hall must look for the little that is now possible in the way of a musical public. Even when we have supplied all three with as much music as they can stomach, the laborer in ligatured corduroys will still open his eyes to darkness, and the vapid snob grub like a blind puppy in the light. What we want is not music for the people, but bread for the people, rest for the people, immunity from robbery and scorn for the people, hope for them, enjoyment, equal respect and consideration, life and aspiration, instead of drudgery and despair. When we get that I imagine the people will make tolerable music for themselves, even if all Beethoven's scores perish in the interim.

Pending these millennial but perfectly practical measures, I must beg my readers not to blame me if the progress of the race makes it more and more apparent that the middle-class musical critic is the most ridiculous of human institutions. I do not take my function seriously, because it is impossible for an intelligent man to do so; and I am an eminently intelligent man. I often yield to quite romantic impulses. For instance, when Miss Adrienne Verity sent me a ticket for her concert at Collard's the other day, I went because Adrienne Verity struck me as being a pretty name. And I must own that I found her a pleasant-faced, well-grown lass, with refreshingly unceremonious ways and a healthy boisterousness which would make her the life and soul of a haymaking. But a singer! an artist! not yet. The way in which that young lady plunged into *Saper vorreste*, and rampaged through Be wise in time, and fired off Cherry Ripe at us, was bewildering. When ladies and children came forward with trophies of flowers, and did her floral homage as a Queen of Song, my brain reeled. And now I suppose that Miss Verity, having invited me to hear her sing, expects me to give her my opinion. My opinion is that she will either study hard with a competent teacher for a couple of years to come, learning to sing, to speak, to walk, to bow, and to abjure premature concerts and flower offerings, or else she will find a place in Mr D'Oyly Carte's or Mr Leslie's chorus, and there unskilfully scream her voice away in less than six months. And whoever gives her a more flattering opinion will do her a very cruel kindness.

Of the numerous concerts which I unavoidably missed, none caused me any particular regret, except the performance by pupils of the Royal Normal College for the Blind at the Crystal Palace, and a Board School contest at Hampstead, which the head master was quite right in bringing under my notice. It was, for example, much more important than Miss McKenzie's concert at Dudley House, which has been much written about, and concerning which I have nothing whatever to say except that it went off very successfully; that Mr Giddings amused me by his recitation; that the Dudley pictures interested me more than the music; and that the Dudley livery of black and yellow continually reminded me of the contrast between the gildings in Park-lane and the gloom of the coal pits wherein that gilding is made.

I need hardly say that my remarks about the Tonic Sol-Fa have brought letters upon me insisting on the attractive simplicity of the notation, and even inviting me to learn it myself forthwith. This reminds me of a sage whom I consulted in my youth as to how I might achieve the formation of a perfect character. "Young man," he said, "are you a vegetarian?" I promptly said "Yes" which took him aback. (I subsequently discovered that he had a weakness for oysters.) "Young man," he resumed, "have you mastered Pitman's shorthand?" I told him I could write it very nearly as fast as longhand, but that I could not read it; and he admitted that this was about the maximum of human attainment in phonography. "Young man," he went on, "do you understand phrenology?"

This was a facer, as I knew nothing about it; but I was determined not to be beaten, so I declared that it was my favorite pursuit, and that I had been attracted to him by the noble character of his bumps. "Young man," he continued, "you are indeed high on the Mount of Wisdom. There remains but one accomplishment to the perfection of your character. Are you an adept at the Tonic Sol-Fa system?" This was too much. I got up in a rage, and said: "Oh, dash the Tonic Sol-Fa system!" Then we came to high words; and our relations have been more or less strained ever since. I have always resolutely refused to learn the Tonic Sol-Fa, as I am determined to prove that it is possible to form a perfect character without it.

7 *June* 1889

I AM indebted to Mr. Fisher Unwin for a volume of essays by an American critic, Mr Henry T. Finck, author of Romantic Love and Personal Beauty. I am not sure that I should not have preferred a copy of Romantic Love and Personal Beauty, as these are subjects of enthralling interest to me; but perhaps Mr Unwin has not published that work, and so could only send me Chopin, and other Musical Essays. It is not for me to criticize Mr Finck further than to say that his speciality among musical essayists of the lighter sort arises from his unusual grip of the fact that we, having reached the eighteen-eighties, are well out of the eighteen-forties. This enables him to tell us a good deal that is interesting about the rise of German opera in New York, and to repeat some very old stories from a fresh point of view. For instance, he has shared the common lot in giving way to the

temptation to narrate how Porpora kept Caffarelli singing
the same sheet of exercises for five years (it used to be six),
and then said, "You have no more to learn. You are the
greatest singer in the world." But instead of glorifying Porpora therefor, and lamenting that we have no such teachers
as he nowadays (the truth being that we have far too many
of them), he sensibly cites the anecdote as a proof that
Porpora was a foolish pedant and Caffarelli a mere vocal
acrobat.

However, my object in mentioning Mr Finck's book was
to make an excuse for quoting the following sentence from
it. "The danger is," writes Mr Finck, "that the custom of
delaying dinner till eight, which is coming into vogue among
the English, who care neither for music nor the theatre, will
be followed in New York." Last week I pointed out that
Lohengrin, in spite of outrageous cutting down, lasted until
midnight, though it began at eight instead of half-past. But
the stalls and boxes remained half empty until nearly nine
o'clock. Mr Mapleson accordingly has fixed the hour for beginning at a quarter to nine. The people for whose conven-
ience this is done also insist on long waits between the acts,
in order to get through rounds of visits to one another's
boxes, conversations in the crushrooms, promenades round
the corridors, and cigarettes on the balcony over the portico. To many of them, in short, the act is the interval, and
the interval is the act.

Personally, I am not very grievously affected by these
matters. Having attained the dignity of an habitual deadhead at the opera, I am soothed by the comparative comfort
and coolness of a stall; and the long intervals enable me to
scrawl my notices before I leave the theatre. Fifteen minutes
after the curtain falls I am at home; in fifteen more the notice is posted, and I am in bed. But if I had paid half a crown
to swelter in the gallery; if the long intervals brought no possibilities of movement or change of air; if my last train home
were the five minutes to twelve from King's Cross, the
twelve from Waterloo, or even the ten past twelve from

Liverpool Street then I think I should execrate the habits
of the people downstairs, and take it rather ill of the management to ignore my circumstances in making their arrangements.

Under present circumstances, however, it is not only impossible to please everybody: it is actually impossible to
please anybody. Aristocratic audiences and wage-workers
are exactly alike in respect of loafing in at a quarter to nine,
no matter what the appointed hour may be. But then the
wage-worker wants to get to bed at midnight, whereas the
aristocrat, who can afford to lie late in the morning, holds
that the best of all ways to lengthen his days is to steal a few
hours from the night. The suburban middle-class amateur
either stays in town on the occasion of his visit to the opera
and takes his tea at an aerated bread shop, in which case
half-past seven would not be at all too early for him; or else
he goes home for his wife and sister-in-law, and cannot get
back to Covent Garden much before eight. It is to be borne
in mind throughout all these calculations that the patron of
the gallery, if he wants a good seat, has to go at least half an
hour sooner than the man with the numbered stall. And for
this class the opera must finish at twenty-five minutes past
eleven at latest. Finally, some of the greatest modern operas
require not less than five hours for their complete representation, to which should be added, in common humanity, one
interval long enough to admit of the whole audience turning
out for a walk or a light meal. The social conditions for stalls
and gallery are, therefore, irreconcilable, and both are in
conflict with the artistic conditions.

What, then, you ask, can I propose for the better adjust-
ment of these affairs? Well, if I were a manager, I should do
as Mr Harris does with the long operas: begin at eight, as
being on the whole the best arrangement. But if I were a
dictator I should settle the matter by enacting a seven hours'
working day, taxing the incomes of the stall and box-holders
twenty shillings in the pound, and subsidising a National
Opera out of the proceeds of the tax, using convict labor for
142

the chorus and minor rôles, as well as for the sceneshifting. As to the two unfortunate soldiers who are now placed for show purposes in the vestibule—and I hold that it is an insult and a dishonor to a soldier to make any such use of him —I should transfer them to the stalls, where they could enjoy the opera and turn their rifles to account by occasionally picking off the people who disturb the performance by talking loudly in their boxes. Even under existing circumstances, it is my firm belief that if something is not done to relieve these unfortunate grenadiers they will use their bayonets some evening out of sheer aggravation.

It will be observed that I have said nothing specifically about the performances at Her Majesty's Theatre. Is any explanation necessary? Suppose Mr John Coleman were to take the Haymarket Theatre, reconstruct it on the Buckstone model, double and treble the ordinary prices, and begin playing a round of Green Bushes, The Wreck Ashore, Black-eyed Susan, and The Duke's Motto, with a provincial company, helped out by a few old stagers! Would any dramatic critic in London be expected to criticize these plays gravely, and describe how they were done? Would he not be deemed generous enough if, for the sake of old times, he gave his tickets away to people able and willing to fill up places that would otherwise be empty, and then write a few lines of commonplace, recording the occurrence which he had not witnessed? Well, frankly, I regard Mr Mapleson's case as exactly parallel; and I shall do nothing to encourage his delusion that Il Barbiere, Lucia, and La Sonnambula can do anything for him now except ruin him.

If I had time to go into the fashionable opera business in competition with Mr Harris, I should try German opera, with Seidl or Hans Richter as conductor. I should then hammer away at the Nibelungen tetralogy until all was blue. If Mr Mapleson had the gumption to go to Mr Armbruster even now, and tell him to put up Siegfried or Tristan, with Miss Pauline Cramer and any cast, amateur or professional, that he could scrape together to support her, the whole

Wagner-Richter connection would go to Her Majesty's, and be followed by hundreds of outsiders from mere curiosity. I should, for one. But wild horses shall not drag me to Lucia.

Tchaikovsky's symphonic poem Romeo and Juliet at Sarasate's concert on Saturday proved impressive enough to keep Mr Cusins's orchestra thoroughly alive and alert. The usual thing is for Mr Cusins, looking every inch a fine old English gentleman, to make astounding faces at the band, of which they are too well-bred to take the slightest notice. He is conscious that they are doing nothing right; and they are conscious that they are doing nothing wrong; and between the two one learns how it was that the Philharmonic so narrowly escaped coming completely to grief in Mr Cusins's time, in spite of the rare degree of skill on both sides. Sarasate's tone was wiry and his pitch sharp when he began; but after a few minutes he left criticism gasping miles behind him.

7 June 1889

I HAVE been to *Il Barbiere*, *La Sonnambula*, and *Lucia*; but do not quail, reader: I am not going to inflict on you a single word of criticism concerning these antiquities. I know your opinion; and you know mine. As you say, there are pretty things in the dear old Barber. Perhaps you remember Mario in *Ecco ridente?* No? Of course not; you are too young, I ought to have seen that. You used to sing *Dunque io son?* Well, so used I when my voice was more flexible than it is now. Only think of that! And then, talking of *La Sonnambula*, most conciliatory of operas, is not *D'un pensiero* still acceptable even after Wagner; and can you have a finer test of true vocal expression in a singer than the pathetic *Ah non credea*, and the rapturous *Ah non giunge*, one after the other? Lucia, as you very pointedly observe, is a vulgar beast of an opera; and yet what passion and what melody there is in every act of it; and what memories cluster for some of us about those melodies! No, with all my experience I cannot tell you why Edgardo never comes on the stage without throwing his cloak on the floor, much as Mr Pickwick cast his spectacles into the middle of the kitchen at Dingley Dell. Sims Reeves used to do it on his great entrance before *Chi mi frena*, but whether he was the inventor of this choice effect I know not. But enough! these are the reminiscences of old fogies. Suffice it to say that Mr Mapleson is hammering away again at Her Majesty's with Il Barbiere, La Sonnambula, Lucia; Lucia, La Sonnambula, Il Barbiere; and some of us fogies are going—mostly on complimentary tickets.

For the sake of old times, I will let Mr Mapleson's enterprise alone. I know how it must end; how it ended before; how we must all, in the highest interests of the lyric stage, be content that it shall end again. There is something pathetic in Mr Mapleson's conviction that at all hazards he must be an impresario. There is something cruel in the reply of the world, *Je n'en vois pas la necessité*. Yet there is no reason why Mr Harris should have the field to himself, though Mr Mapleson, in opposing him with his present repertory, is pitting a wooden frigate against a modern Minotaur. What about German opera, conducted by Richter, Seidl, or Levy? What about opera in English? What about even Italian opera at popular prices? Alas! Mr Mapleson will not learn from me what he refuses to learn from experience. I can only shake my head over the good money he is throwing after bad, and wish him better success than I can honestly pretend to expect for him.

14 *June* 1889

LET me recur for a moment to certain observations recently let fall by Spectator in these columns. Spectator, it will be remembered, went to the Opera, and saw Madame Albani as La Traviata. Far from being impressed by his visit to the temple in which all the arts meet, he spoke of the whole performance with unqualified contempt, and positively refused to take our eminent lyric *tragédienne* seriously as an actress.

What is more—and I recommend this point to all who are interested in opera—Spectator was right. Whatever may be his failings—however deficient he may be in a natural and becoming awe when he alludes to persons whose age and attainments should command his respect—there is no denying that the sort of thing that Madame Albani and her colleagues do at the Opera is beneath the notice of any intelligent student of dramatic art, and that the critics who gravely write about it in terms which would be rather overstrained if applied to Ristori, Sarah Bernhardt, Ellen Terry, Ada Rehan, Janet Achurch, or Mrs Kendal, richly deserve to be waved aside as foolish amateurs by such competent dramatic critics as Spectator, Mr William Archer, Mr —— well, the list is not so long as I thought, so I had perhaps better not continue it.

On Saturday we are to have at Covent Garden Gounod's setting of Romeo and Juliet. It is solemnly announced in the advertisements that Signor Montariol is in a high state of condescension towards Tybalt, which "he has kindly consented to play, although not a leading part (*sic*) in order to assist in making a perfect ensemble." Really handsome of Signor Montariol, is it not? Let us hope that he *will* make the ensemble perfect, as he so modestly promises.

14 *June* 1889

"Good old Don Giovanni!" said some vulgar and disrespectful ruffian in the stalls last night. "Good old Arditi!" he continued, as the conductor took his seat. "Good old Robert Elsmere!" he added presently, as Mrs Humphry Ward wandered into his neighborhood in search of her number. "Good old Lady Colin!" he resumed, as the most divinely tall of the art critics took her place in front of me and extinguished my view of the stage. Standing up, he took out his opera-glass and said, "Where's good old Gus?" He then proceeded to musical criticism. "There's little Van Zandt: aint she a joy? Who's the tenor? Lestellier! Aint he a terror?" And so on. If

146

this should meet the eye of that man, I ask him, as a personal favor to myself, to commit suicide. Nothing in life can become him like the leaving it.

I cannot say that the performance was an adequate one. A musical critic does not write that often in a lifetime about Don Giovanni—unless, indeed, he is given to writing the thing that is not, as many excellent critics do. M. F. d'Andrade made a passable libertine; but all libertines are not Don Giovannis, though all Don Giovannis are libertines. And on the whole, I think Signor d'Andrade might as well sing *Viva la liberta!* and *Via, buffone!* and other numbers as they are written. At any rate, Mozart's version is good enough for me. Madame Fursch-Madi, in *Or sai chi l'onore*, mistook the second section for the first, and during one madly anxious moment, Arditi's fringe of hair stood straight out on end. But she picked up the thread again; a smile mantled the back of Arditi's head; and a minute later I had the pleasure of making a note to the effect that Madame Fursch-Madi had sung the *scena* very well indeed, and richly deserved her double recall. She omitted *Non mi dir*!!! Miss Van Zandt made a quaint and pretty Zerlina. Madame Valda should bear in mind that the fashion of providing gratuitous B flats in Mozart's operas, though it may be coming in in Australia, is going out here. For the rest, she was not the noble and pious Elvira of Molière and Mozart; and she sang with more spirit and spontaneity than classic grace; but she looked superb. M. Lestellier left out *Dalla sua pace*, and will, I hope, leave out *Il mio tesoro* next time, unless he will take the trouble to learn the song in the interim. Of the Leporello let it suffice to say that it was mainly to his exertions that we owed the turning of the incomparably strange and solemn scene of the invitation to the statue into a profane and ridiculous burlesque which severely taxed the patience of the gallery. Masetto was a failure. The Commendatore distinguished himself at the climax of the supper scene by a wrong note that made our very souls recoil. In short—and here is the truth of the matter—the opera had been insufficiently rehearsed; and the last three scenes can scarcely have been rehearsed at all. Even the stage business went all astray. Let us assume that Romeo and Juliet has absorbed all the energy of the establishment.

17 June 1889

IT was instructive to compare the effect of the thoroughly prepared representation of Gounod's Romeo and Juliet on Saturday with that of the scratch performance of Don Giovanni two nights before. In every sort of merit that an opera can have, Don Giovanni is as superior to Romeo as a sonnet by Shakespear to a sonnet by Adelaide Proctor; yet on Thursday the house was bored and distraught, whereas on Saturday it was alert and interested. Everything on the stage had been thought about and practised: everybody there was in earnest and anxious. The result was that an opera with an established reputation for tedium became engrossing where another opera, with an established reputation for inexhaustible variety and vivacity, had just fallen flat. Many persons went about asking why Romeo had never been a success before. The question implied too much; for, after all, the opera has had its measure of success in the past. Further, it is quite true that the work is monotonous in its mood. One greatly misses the relief which Mephistopheles gives to Faust. No doubt when you first fall under the spell of the heavenly melody, of the exquisite orchestral web of sound colors, of the unfailing dignity and delicacy of accent and rhythm, you certainly do feel inclined to ask whether the people who disparaged the work were deaf. Not until you have had your fill of these, and have realized that there is nothing more coming, do you begin to look at your watch. On Saturday the watch would have come out sooner and oftener but for M. Jean de Reszke. He is an artist who cannot be described in a few words. Though a highly intelligent one at his best, he has moments of *naïveté*—not to say stupidity—which seem to run in his gifted family. Again, though
148

he does everything with a distinction peculiar to himself, there is an exasperatingly conventional side to his posing and playing across the footlights. And though he has the true dramatic instinct, and does really throw himself into his part, yet he is not consistently an actor: for instance, no human being—except perhaps a sexton—ever entered a tomb at midnight in the fashion illustrated by him in the fifth act on Saturday night. I do not believe in ghosts; but if I had occasion to visit a mausoleum, even in the daytime, I should not come bounding into it. Under such circumstances one refrains from gambolling until one's eyes get accustomed to the dim light. The charm of De Reszke lies in the beauty of his voice, his sensitively good pronunciation, and the native grace and refinement of his bearing, all of which make his manliness, his energy, and his fire quite irresistible. The charm of the man may be separated from the interest in his performance, which is created almost entirely by his declamation. In the pretty duet, the Madrigal which practically begins Romeo's part, he did not make much effect; but when he exclaimed, "O douleur! Capulet est son père; et je l'aime!" the effect was electric. At the end of the balcony scene his half-whispered "Adieu, jusqu'à demain—jusqu'à demain," will surely be remembered by many a woman in the audience. His acting in the duel scene, uneven as it was, was convincing; and he rose to eloquence in the scene which follows the sentence of exile from the Duke: a scene newly written by Gounod. Madame Melba may thank her stars that she had so good a Romeo to help her out in the last two acts. At one or two points in the balcony scene she sang with genuine feeling; and in the tragic scenes she was at least serious and anxious to do her best. In the first act, however, she was shrill and forward, the waltz ariette coming out with great confidence and facility, which I think Madame Melba mistook for art. Her fresh bright voice and generally safe intonation are all in her favor at present. Mdlle. Jeanne de Vigne phrased *Que fais-tu, blanche tourterelle* nicely, and would have got an encore—which she evidently wanted badly—had she been content with the simple run up to C and down again of which Gounod made such a perfect ornament. But she *would* try to improve the final phrase; and as her taste is not quite as fine as Gounod's, the encore was nipped in the bud, which I think served her right. Madame Lablache had, of course, no trouble with the part of the nurse. Mr Winogradow, as Mercutio, shewed all the symptoms of a short life and a merry one as a singer. No man can, without wrecking his voice, sing on the plan of delivering every note with the utmost possible intensity and vehemence. Unless Mr Winogradow pulls in at once, and learns to get at least nine out of ten of his effects quietly, Covent Garden will soon know him no more. M. Montariol (Tybalt) was as good as his word, as far as improving the ensemble went, though he should have done this without saying anything about it. He played his second-rate part like a first-rate artist, just as he has occasionally played first-rate parts like a second-rate artist. Also he fenced so perfectly that Romeo was able to go for him quite recklessly; and this, of course, is the explanation of the nonsense about his condescending to play Tybalt. If he had not, Brer Jean would now be awaiting his trial for manslaughter. M. Séguin also helped materially by playing Capulet. But the honors among the basses went, of course, to Edouard de Reszke, who had a tremendous time of it as Friar Laurence. The family *naïveté* already hinted at peeped out in such brilliant readings as *Dieu, qui fis l'homme à ton image*, delivered in the stentorian manner of master-builders when they seek the ear of a bricklayer on a very high scaffold, and the magic word *femme* marked by sudden subsidence to a tenderly respectful *pianissimo*. But the marriage service and the potion scene delighted the audience; and a special cheer was always received for Frère Edouard when the rest, having passed before the curtain, left him—he coming last—for a moment in sole possession of the proscenium.

LONDON MUSIC IN 1888–89

AFTER the success of the Romeo and Juliet experiment, the substitution of Scribe's original libretto of Les Huguenots for the Italian version, or rather for the mixture of two Italian versions which now does duty at Covent Garden, is only a matter of a little rehearsal—chiefly for Madame Scalchi. Last night we had Brer Jean as Raoul and Brer Edouard as Marcel, who looked remarkably like Sir John Falstaff reformed and teetotalized. Brer Jean altered the ending of his first song because it was too high; and Brer Edouard presently altered the ending of his Lutheran chorale because it was too low. When Piff Paff was duly disposed of, the twain went off for a walk, and—Brer Jean being presently wanted—kept the stage waiting for some time before they returned. On the whole Brer Jean would have been better if he had not been obviously afraid of his part. For some bars before the C sharp in the duel septet, which he did not attempt to sustain, he suffered from something like stage fright; but when it was over he cheered up considerably, though he remained more or less preoccupied and unhappy all through the evening. Yet he sang delightfully in spite of his mood. Marcel is a part that does not suit Brer Edouard. The music is too low for him; and the character is one for a clever actor. Now Brer Edouard's endowment is mainly vocal: if the De Reszkes had been an English country family, he would certainly have gone into the Church. Madame Toni Schläger, the new prima donna from Vienna, began badly by a most discouraging display of tremolo, and an even more alarming composure, which did not give way in the least when her lover unexpectedly called her names before the whole cast. The calm way in which she arranged herself on M. Lassalle's arm for a comfortable stage faint as the curtain descended presented a spectacle of matronly decorum before which the house quailed. But if Madame Schläger is matronly, she is also extraordinarily comely. Her long dark hair is wonderful. Her voice, too, unsteady and uncertain as it is, asserts itself every now and then with striking power and penetration. Her acting consists in an exhibition of intense sorrowfulness which is oddly impressive. The house, which rebelled against her at first, ended by accepting her. Her final effect, when, on seeing Raoul spring through the window, she uttered a heartrending cry and fell supine into a wavy river of her own hair, won her a demonstrative curtain call. Madame Scalchi, as Urbain, made an astonishing deal of as much of her part as she could manage, and slipped over the rest very cleverly. Miss Russell achieved so many gratuitous vocal feats to propitiate us for not singing exactly what Meyerbeer wrote that I have no doubt she will achieve that feat too some day. Mr Harris provided her with a beautiful milk-white steed in the third act; but it began to waltz the moment she began to sing; and at last Brer Edouard had to lift her down and leave the animal free to return to its native hippodrome. M. D'Andrade's intonation in the part of De Nevers became very faulty after the first two acts. M. Lassalle was the San Bris. Signor Mancinelli is at his best in interpreting Meyerbeer; but his generalship last night was seriously at fault: more than once he got excited, and failed to keep his forces together. I fear I shall shortly have a rather bad fit of plain speaking on the subject of the band. There are among the first violins some half a dozen or so gentlemen who play with a flow of undisciplined animal spirits which, gratifying as it is to everyone who likes to see young people enjoying themselves, has the incidental disadvantage of destroying all the delicacy, dignity, and grace of the orchestra. The stage business again shewed want of rehearsal and want of thought. In the Pré aux Clercs scene the moon rose most naturally, but it shone brightly enough to make ridiculous all that part of the dialogue which derives its point from Marcel's groping after Valentine's voice in the darkness. During vespers the Catholics kept their hats on; and several of the Protestants took them off. Have these choristers no religious feeling that they cannot grasp so simple a situation? The substitution in the gipsy ballet of a *pas seul* for the old business with the soldiers is not, in my opinion, an improvement.

The performance began about twelve minutes past eight. At the end of the fourth act it only wanted five minutes of twelve. The band accordingly cut the entertainment short by going home. Signor Mancinelli, after a moment's hesitation, followed their example. I left several of the audience waiting for the fifth act. I wonder whether they are there still.

21 June 1889

I HOPE the Royal Italian Opera will not grow conceited on the strength of my general approval of Romeo and Juliet. Lest it should, I hasten to find fault with one or two points in the performance. The unaccompanied prologue, which was sung as Gounod directs, by the principal singers, ought to have been an invaluable lesson to the chorus in distinctness of enunciation, crispness of attack, beautiful tone formation, pure intonation, and finesse in managing the delicate *nuances*. As a matter of fact, it was unintelligible; it buzzed and dragged; the pitch fell during each line so that the harp made us squirm when it came in; and there was much less gradation than a well educated horse shows in his paces. I imagine that the chorus were vaguely trying to help from the wings. If so, they had much better not have interfered. Here, then, is one opportunity for that constant improvement which Mr Harris's artists doubtless thirst for.

Signor Mancinelli misjudged one or two movements so widely that I strongly suspect him of a conscientious attempt to follow the composer's metronome marks: the surest way, need I add, of violating the composer's intentions. In a theatre of reasonable size a very skilful singer, daintily accompanied, could no doubt point all the vagaries of Queen Mab as rapidly as poor M. Winogradow was haled through them on Monday; but, under the circumstances, the result was that the song missed fire. The great duet in the fourth

153

act was taken so fast that the *molto sostenuto* indicated by Gounod, which is the characteristic effect of the movement, was quite lost. And again, the *allegretto agitato* "Il faut partir, hélas!" was overdone in the same way. What with Jean de Reszke's impetuosity, and Signor Mancinelli's tendency to rush strong numbers, one sometimes yearns for the advent of Richter, the unhasting, the unresting.

I cannot understand why some account of the very interesting Doll's House dinner last Sunday at the Novelty Theatre has not crept into print. It was distinctly understood that the affair was to be kept quiet, and from that I naturally concluded that the Press would be full of it on Monday. I hasten to remedy the tactless discretion of my fellow guests.

It was an odd affair, because, as every discoverable Norwegian in London had been recklessly invited, the company was a queer mixture of people whom everybody knew and people whom nobody knew. Among the latter was a very quiet lady of forty or thereabouts, with some indescribable sort of refinement about her that made her seem to have lost her way and found herself in a very questionable circle. Nobody was taking any notice of her; so I charitably introduced myself (she pretended to know who I was) and tried to make her feel more at home. You shall hear more of her presently.

Then we had supper and toasts and so forth. William Archer led off the speechmaking by toasting Ibsen, with special insistence on the great dramas in verse which preceded the Doll's House order of play. (How often have I not informed composers that the next great opera will not be a setting of Faust over again, but of Peer Gynt?)

Two famous actresses from Christiania, Fru Gundersen and Fröken Reimers, represented the Norwegian stage. Miss Reimers was asked to recite, but said she could not declaim without statuesque drapery. No garment that could by any stretch of imagination be deemed statuesque could be discovered; and we should have lost the recitation had not somebody produced a couple of yards of common white tape.

154

Miss Reimers at once beamed her gratitude; flung the tape over her shoulder; and shewed us what real stage declamation is like, to the manifest depression of the British actors present, who had all picked up their profession anyhow. Their discomfiture was completed by a young Danish actor, whose *maintien* and delivery were so perfect that we frankly threw in our hands and returned to the savage pursuit of British speechmaking. The whole cast of the Doll's House were present, except Mr Royce Carleton and the three youngest members, who had been put to bed. There was also present a Herr Nansen, who was described to me as the brother of the discoverer of Greenland; but I imagine there is some mistake about this, for I have been familiar with Greenland and its icy mountains since my childhood. Then there was Mr Herman Vezin, at the head of the board. Herr Barth answered for painting, and Dr Hagerup answered for everything else. Mr H. L. Brœkstad, who has at last succeeded in planting the Norwegian standard firmly in London, was immensely in evidence. Mr Charrington, in a disconsolate manner, made the best speech of the evening, and sat down obviously convinced that he had made the worst. Miss Achurch made two speeches in a brief and fearless manner, which at once exposed the awkwardness and pusillanimity of the unfortunate persons who were trying to look like the stronger sex. "A woman making a speech," said Dr Johnson, "is like a dog standing on its hind legs. It is not well done; but the wonder is that it should be done at all." Now mark my words. The time is approaching when that story will reverse its genders, and be attributed to some female sage. What is more, *it will not lose its point in the process.* I foresaw this long ago; and, with a manly determination to uphold the superiority of my sex, at once adopted the view that public speaking is a despicable art, only fit for women. I declare, in spite of the editor's teeth, that I enjoyed Miss Achurch's speeches far more than I have ever enjoyed Mr Gladstone's; but let Miss Achurch just try her hand at musical criticism and you will soon acknowledge the unassailable pre-eminence of Creation's masterpiece: Man. I am a man myself, and ought to know.

After dinner we all went down to the stage and finished the evening in the doll's house, where the snow on the window-sill, which I had always supposed to be real (knowing Mr Archer's conscientious devotion to naturalism in art) turned out to be a wretched cotton-wool imposture which came off on my clothes. The first thing everybody did was to go straight to the stove, open it, and stare into the interior. Then they tried the famous letter-box, and slammed the famous door. Then Mr Vezin plucked up a postprandial courage and recited all the most blood-curdling poems he could think of. Miss Reimers, who had very nearly upset even my gravity at dinner by asking me with perfect sincerity why the splendid, the intellectual, the free English people had no national theatre, recited Tennyson's Rizpah and the first speech from Schiller's Maid of Orleans in Norwegian. Miss Achurch, rashly called on for a recitation, and being totally unacquainted with that art, adventured desperately on Kingsley's Three Fishers, and first conveyed to us that she did not know her business at all, and then, in a curiously original way, and not without a touch of extravagance, left us impressed and astonished.

When our resources were at last exhausted and the entertainment was on the point of petering out, our hosts had to play their last card. Could anybody play the Helmer piano and oblige us with a tune. There was general shaking of heads until it appeared that the quiet lady, neglected and unknown, could play some pieces. As she went to the little piano we prepared ourselves for the worst and stopped talking, more or less. To encourage the poor lady I went to the piano and sat beside her to turn over for her, expecting The Maiden's Prayer or an oldfashioned set of variations on The Carnival of Venice. I felt I was being very good to her.

After the first two bars I sat up. At the end of the piece (one of her own composition) I said, "Has anyone ever told you that you are one of the greatest pianists in Europe?"

Evidently a good many people had; for without turning a
hair she said, "It is my profession. But this is a bad instrument. Perhaps you will hear me at the Philharmonic. I am
to play Beethoven's E flat concerto there."

Her name is Agatha Ursula Backer-Gröndahl. She played
upon Helmer's pianoforte as it was never played upon before, and perhaps never will be again. A great artist—a serious artist—a beautiful, incomparable, unique artist! She
morally regenerated us all; and we remained at our highest
level until we were dragged down by the shrieks and groans
of two Italian waiters who started quarrelling among the
knives in the saloon. Fraternity having been re-established
by Mr Charrington, Mr Archer was requested to improvise
a *World* article for the entertainment of the company. He
blushingly declined. Later on it was felt that the evening
would be incomplete without a song from me; and after some
pressing I reluctantly consented. The guests then left pre-
cipitately; and the scene, a historic one in the annals of the
theatre, closed.

2 July 1889

THE Handel orchestra at the Crystal Palace is not the right
place for work so delicately and finely concentrated as Mendelssohn's Athalie. Nor is it, as many people seem to think,
a favorable arena for the display of choral excellence. The
more fiddlers you have in your orchestra and the more singers you have in any section of your chorus, the less likeli-
hood is there of any defects being noticed, since at any given
moment there will be enough performers right to drown a
considerable minority who may be wrong. The proportion of
error can only be guessed at by the magnitude of the mere
indeterminate noise—the buzz and rattle—that comes along
with the definite vocal tone. From this the tonic sol-faists on
Saturday were commendably free: the tone was clean and
the intonation very good indeed: much better, I venture to
assert, than is usual in staff-notation choirs, where practice

mostly begins by taking the reading powers of the members for granted. In volume and penetration the vocal mass was fully up to the ordinary standard; but then the ordinary standard is absurdly low. Considering what a formidable sound can be produced by a single properly trained man or woman of ordinary physique, the mildness of the result of combining 2500 of them on an orchestra is almost ridiculous. It is not too much to say that nine-tenths of the potential efficiency of our choirs is wasted through the diffidence that comes from conscious want of individual skill. The way in which the tone from the sopranos dwindled at every G and A shewed that a large number of these healthy young Englishwomen were deliberately shirking every note above F. Now a soprano, or even a mezzo-soprano, who is afraid of an occasional A simply does not know how to sing; and I would respectfully put it to these fair sol-faists whether it is of much public use to know how to read if you cannot sing what you read. If a soprano breaks down over Mendelssohn, what sort of a figure would she cut if she were put at, say, the Choral Symphony?

As an exhibition of choral singing the concert was interesting enough: as a performance of Athalie it was neither here nor there. The work is one of Mendelssohn's finest; and it can only be mastered by a conductor who studies his part as seriously as he might study the part of Hamlet if he were an actor. Mr Venables confined himself to beating time for the choir with steadiness, spirit, and—except in one number—with judgment. That number, unfortunately, was the duet with chorus, "Ever blessed child," an inspired composition, standing with "I waited for the Lord" among the most beautiful and touching utterances of Mendelssohn. But, alas! it is in six-eight time; and whenever an English conductor sees six-eight, he exclaims: "Ha! Sir Roger de Coverley!" and scampers off up the middle and down again, reckless whether it is "Ever blessed child" or "O thou that tellest" that he is murdering. When Mr Venables had duly dragged the duet through by the hair, he changed his mood just in time to quench the fire of the fiercely impetuous "Behold, Zion, behold." Otherwise I have nothing to reproach him with. The orchestral effects, notably those striking *fortissimo* chords in "The sinner's joys decay," were feeble and scattered in the vast space. The unpublished fugue, which was performed for the first time at the end, is just like any other fugue by a master of Mendelssohn's calibre. The subject begins with the usual skip, and the parts solemnly trudge along to the pedal, after which climax of insanity the welcome end comes with due gravity of cadence. Then Madame Antoinette Sterling, loudly applauded, came on the platform to give away prizes. A huge ribbon, inscribed "Honorable mention" was held up by two respectable citizens. A third citizen then exhibited a placard bearing the name Bayswater, whereat the audience, fugally demoralized, roared with laughter. Further placarding conveyed the gratifying intelligence that Nottingham had borne off the first prize, which Madame Sterling accordingly handed to Mr J. S. Derbyshire, the Nottingham conductor, amid enthusiasm. I then dashed away to catch a low-level train, which I just saved by the desperate expedient of doing the last third of the journey by toboggan, a fearful method of progression. I owe an apology to Mr T. Newton, who was announced to sing a song "in twelve distinctly different voices" at half-past five. Why are not the musical critics invited to hear this gifted polyphonist?

5 July 1889

I must apologize to the Shah for my failure to appear at Covent Garden on Tuesday. He will cut rather a foolish figure in Persia when he confesses—if he has the moral courage to admit it—that he saw the opera without Corno di Bassetto; but if Mr Harris chooses recklessly to select the night of the Hyndman-George debate for the reception of Persian majesty, he has himself to thank for my absence. Possibly, however, Mr Harris acted out of consideration for me.

Of the program I can only faintly convey the truth by

saying that it was the most extravagantly Bedlamite hotch-potch on record, even in the annals of State concerts. It was evidently the work of a committee on which conflicting views had to be reconciled. Thus, view No. 1 was that the Shah is a gentleman of ordinary and somewhat vulgar European musical taste; therefore let him hear the overture to William Tell. View No. 2: the Shah is an idiot; therefore ply him with the mad scene from Lucia. View No. 3: The Shah's artistic culture is deep, earnest, severe, and German; there-fore strike up the great Leonora overture by Beethoven. View No. 4: It does not matter what the Shah is: we are going to let him see what Covent Garden can do; therefore let us put on the fourth act of Faust, which is one of our big things. View No. 5: the Shah is a savage and a voluptuary; therefore treat him to the Brocken corroboree from Boito's Mefistofele, as the most unseemly thing we can very well do under the circumstances. How beautifully the Pall Mall's own visitor summed it up as "a scene of brilliancy, *tempered by ladies.*"

In dealing with the performance of Les Huguenots lately, I felt strongly tempted to warn Signor Mancinelli that the band parts in use at Covent Garden are inaccurate at the most striking point in the whole score. In the fourth act, when Raoul, in the transport of discovering that Valentine loves him, forgets the impending massacre and the duty of instantly warning his friends, he is suddenly struck dumb by the distant sound of the bell which is the signal for the car-nage. The bell strikes the keynote F, and takes a veiled, sinister color from a dull accompanying chord in the lowest register of the clarinets. Almost immediately a clear, terrible C is delivered in unison by the brass; and never, not even in Wagner's Flying Dutchman, has the peculiar character of the fifth of the scale been more dramatically employed. But what happens at Covent Garden? Why, they actually bring out a prosaic F with an effect which is perfectly senseless.

I therefore appeal to Signor Mancinelli to look at the horn, trombone, and bassoon parts in the first dozen bars of the *maestoso* movement following the famous *andante amoroso*, and see whether the C's are right in every second bar. Also to exhort the first trombone and the third and fourth horns to give the necessary prominence to that C, which is above the F of the bell. I further appeal to Mr Harris to incur the trouble and expense of placing a first-rate drum player behind the scenes, and providing him with two clangorous bells, accurately tuned to F and C, so that we may hear the scene as Meyerbeer planned it. However, I fear my appeal will be in vain. If it were a new patent moon, or an extra horse, or half-a-dozen new dresses, or any other unmusical vanity, there would be a rush to meet my views. But a part in the score that nobody bothers about or misses —what stuff! Fulfilment of the composer's intention is not, like evening dress, indispensable.

9 July 1889

CALL no conductor sensitive in the highest degree to musical impressions until you have heard him in Berlioz and Mozart. I never unreservedly took off my hat to Richter until I saw him conduct Mozart's great symphony in E flat. Now, having heard him conduct Berlioz's Faust, I repeat the salutation. I never go to hear that work without fearing that, instead of exquisite threads of melody, wonderful in their tenuity and delicacy, and the surpassingly strange and curious sounds and measures, ghostly in touch and quaint in tread, unearthly, unexpected, unaccountable, and full of pictures and stories, I shall hear a medley of thumps and bumps and whistles and commonplaces: one, two, three, four: one, two, three, four; and for Heaven's sake dont stop to think about what you are doing, gentlemen, or we shall never keep the thing together. Last night there was no such disappointment. The Hungarian March I pass over, though I felt towards the end that if it were to last another minute I must charge out and capture Trafalgar Square singlehanded. But when the scene on the banks of the Elbe began

161

—more slowly than any but a great conductor would have dared to take it—then I knew that I might dream the scene without fear of awakening a disenchanted man. As to the dance of will-o'-the-wisps in the third part, Richter's interpretation of that most supernatural minuet was a masterpiece of conducting. I need say no more. The man who succeeds with these numbers does not make the usual failure with the Easter Hymn or the Ride to Hell.

The four principal singers were, in order of praiseworthiness, Mr Max Heinrich, Mr Bantock Pierpont, Miss Mary Davies, and Mr Edward Lloyd. I put Mr Lloyd fourth only because, there being but three others, I cannot put him fifth or sixth. I do not mind his shirking the C sharps and even the B natural in the duet with Margaret; but I indignantly demand what he meant by wantonly tampering with the Invocation at its finest point, the burst into C sharp major, on the words "My soul thrills with delight." If Mr Lloyd had suspected what my soul thrilled with when he made the most annoyingly vulgar alteration I ever heard an artist of his eminence perpetrate, he would, I hope, have refrained. I also object to his ending the beautiful episode in F, "Oh, will ye come again," on the higher octave of the note written by Berlioz. Miss Davies is so hampered by the remains of her Academy method that she never seems quite certain of what her voice will do; but if she does not sing safely and happily, she at least sings with taste and feeling, sometimes very sweetly. Mr Pierpoint is always efficient; and Mr Max Heinrich acquitted himself like a fine artist, though the person who told him to pronounce "linings" as "lennix" is unworthy of his confidence.

The chorus did everything to perfection except sing. Their time, their tone, their enunciation, their observance of light and shade, testified to the pains taken with them by the conductor. But not even he could get any considerable volume of sound out of them. As the roaring drunkards of Auerbach's cellar they were polite and subdued; as bragging soldiers they were decent and restrained; as convivial stu-

dents chanting *Jam nox stellata*, etc., they did not forget
that there might be a sick person in the neighborhood; and
as devils in Pandemonium their voices were sweet and low.
The decorum of these warblers would have done honor to
the choir of the Chapel Royal.

12 July 1889

In my youth I used to speculate upon the curious but almost invariable failure of public music schools—Royal
Academies, Conservatoires, and the like—to turn out good
singers. The case was even worse than this: the voices were
not only undeveloped, they were crippled and sometimes
utterly destroyed by the process of training to which they
were subjected. The moral seemed to be that private teachers were the safest; but I soon observed that private teachers
were fully as destructive as public ones. I wonder whether
this state of things prevails to any extent at present.

The odd thing was that when I read the treatises penned
by the teachers, or conversed with them, I found that they
were eloquent in their denunciation of the very faults which
their own pupils most flagrantly exemplified. They would
insist that the voice should be produced without the slightest
effort or constriction of the throat, and with an expiration
so steady, gentle, and perfectly controlled that a candle-flame
would not flicker before the singer's lips. Then they would
proudly produce their champion pupil, who, after setting
every muscle of the neck and jaws as if she (it was generally
she) wanted to crack a walnut with her glottis, would turn
on a blast from her lungs sufficient to whirl a windmill, much
less flicker a candle. The result generally was that the family
doctor interfered when the damage to the student's health
had gone too far; and the medical profession soon adopted
the notion that singing is a dangerous exercise, only suitable
for persons of exceptionally robust lungs and heart.

I assure you it is not pleasant to live next door to a young
lady who, from the very common accident of having a loud

voice and an aptitude for picking up tunes, has resolved to become a prima donna, and, with that view, has engaged Signor Fizzelli, or Fizzini, or Fizzoni to train her for the ordeal of a first appearance at La Scala, Milan, where he broke his voice some years ago on the occasion of his début as Arturo in Lucia di Lammermoor, thanks—as he avers—to the intrigues of the jealous nincompoop who, though unable to sing *Fra poco* in the original key, supplanted him in his rightful part of Edgardo. Fitz's training system is the walnut system, scientifically known as "tension of cords and force of blast."

When Fitz tells his pupil to sing on the vowel *a*, she either rolls her tongue up into a ball at the back of her mouth and brings up an *awr*, or else she bleats out the flattest of *ha-a-a-a-h's*. Fitz rages at her until she finds some intermediate sound that suits his taste. Then, on that sound, and on the walnut system, he makes her sing scales in one unvarying slow, deadly grind that would wear the soul and health out of a millstone. You—next door—hear the process getting more difficult, the effort more exhausting, the voice more inhuman every day, until at last a morning comes when Fitz does not appear, and the doctor's brougham does. In the meantime you are desperately tempted to rush out some day as Fitz comes down the front garden after applying the torture, and remonstrate with him on the chance of his assaulting you, and thereby giving you an excuse for killing him in self-defence.

If you actually did remonstrate, he would not hit you. I never knew a hitting voice trainer except one, who declared quite seriously that the only method to make a man produce the vowel *o* in Nature's way was to get him to hold a full breath for fifteen seconds, and then punch him smartly in the thorax. There can be no doubt of the effectiveness and certainty of this plan; but, except when the teacher can punch hard enough to incapacitate the pupil from hasty reprisals, it should be practised only on women and invalids; and even with them it is apt during future lessons to engender a certain mistrust of the professor's intentions which spoils the harmony essential to the relation between master and pupil. But Fitz is not that sort of man. You will sometimes find him unexpectedly intelligent and even sensible as a talker, though you cannot safely depend on this. What you *can* depend on is that he will defend his method on the ground that it is the true Italian method of Porpora, rediscovered and patented by himself; and that every other teacher in the universe is a notorious humbug and quack, the mainspring of whose activity is a despicable jealousy of the same Fitz.

Let me say, however, that I think Fitz's vogue is waning. His failures have been too flagrant and too fearful to pass unnoticed. The young English girls, with sweet and promising voices, who went to Paris to be "finished" in grim earnest by the final attempt to grind them into savagely dramatic Viardot Garcias have invariably disappointed the hopes formed of them. The wobbling, screaming crew, with three horrible high notes and three Richardson's show gestures, who infested the operatic stage twenty years ago—the ignoble Fernandos and Manricos, Lucias and Leonoras—had to retreat before Wagner, since they could no more sing his music than they could sing Handel's. The increase in the number of people who now keep a pianoforte, and amuse themselves at it with cheap vocal scores of operas, is producing a common knowledge of the defects of our standard performers, which enables the critic to attack the inaccuracies, the vulgarities, the innumerable petty artistic dishonesties of the operatic stage with a sense of having the public at his back, which is a new, powerful, and most noteworthy factor in musical criticism. The effect of it on me occasionally moves concert givers and managers (otherwise of sound mind) to demand whether it is not obvious that I must be in the pay of their enemies or else maliciously mad.

Just as cheap literature is restoring Shakespear to the stage and banishing gag, Garrick, and Cibber, so cheap music will banish cuts, interpolations, alterations, and perversions from the opera house. It will not teach the people to sing; but it will teach them to miss the qualities which are never forthcoming with bad singers and to value those which are always forthcoming with good ones.

And now, what on earth did I begin all this about? I must have intended to lead up to something; and now I have hardly any room left for it. Ha! I recollect. The performance of Goetz's Taming of the Shrew, by the students of the Royal College of Music on Wednesday afternoon at the Prince of Wales's Theatre.

It struck me that though the students who sang had not received any specially valuable positive instruction in the art of producing the voice, they had been abundantly warned against Fitz and the walnut system. If a man could become a great tenor by dint of doing nothing that could possibly injure his vocal cords, then Mr Pringle, who played Hortensio, would be the Tamagno of the twentieth century; and doubtless Mr Herbert Sims Reeves would be the De Reszke. Mr David Evans, as Lucentio, certainly knocked up his voice and lost his way in the delightful gamut solo, from sheer want of skill; but he did not seem to have been deliberately taught to sing badly: he has not been taught to sing well: that is all. The opera is such an excessively troublesome one to commit to memory that only students with unlimited opportunities of rehearsal could have afforded to get it up for the sake of one performance as perfectly as it was got up at the Royal College. The rich finale to the wedding scene, a sort of comic version of the great ballroom finale in *Don Giovanni*, was not so steady or crisp as it might have been: indeed, at one moment it wavered perilously; but on the whole the slips were very few and far between. The solo singing was of course jejune, lacking variety and sincerity of expression; and the acting ran into mock heroics on the serious side, and into tomfoolery on the comic; but if experience had not taught me the desperate risk of praising young amateurs, I should be tempted to compliment Miss Emily Davies on her plucky and intelligent effort to play Katherine,

and to slap Mr Sandbrook on the back for his hard work as
Petruchio. The orchestra acquitted itself admirably, the
violins, played exclusively by students, being distinctly
above the professional average. The first oboe, one trombone, two of the horns, and the first cornet were manned by
professional players from outside. I am sorry to say that the
bad custom of bouquet-throwing was permitted; and need I
add that an American prima donna was the offender. What
do you mean, Madame Nordica, by teaching the young idea
how to get bouquets shied? One consolation is, that if the
critics cannot control the stars, they can at least administer
the stripes.

P.S. I have just paid my first visit to Otello at the
Lyceum. The voices can all be beaten at Covent Garden:
Tamagno's shrill and nasal, Maurel's woolly and tremulous,
Signora Cataneo's shattered, wavering, stagy, not to be
compared to the worst of Mr Harris's prima donnas. On the
other hand, Maurel acts quite as well as a good provincial
tragedian, mouthing and ranting a little, but often producing striking pictorial effects; Tamagno is original and real,
showing you Othello in vivid flashes; and the interpretation
of Verdi's score, the artistic homogeneity of performance,
the wonderful balance of orchestra, chorus, and principals,
stamp Faccio as a masterly conductor. The work of the
orchestra and chorus far surpasses anything yet achieved
under Signor Mancinelli at Covent Garden. The opera is
powerful and interesting: immeasurably superior to Aida:
do not miss it on any account. But if you go to the five-
shilling pit, as I did, remember that there are four rows of
stalls under the balcony, and that the pit therefore consists
almost entirely of that square hole in the wall at the back
which is one of Mr Irving's most diabolical innovations.

13 July 1889

"BASSETTO," said the editor of The Star, "you say that
Madame Backer-Gröndahl is a great pianoforte player?"

"Commander of the Faithful," I replied, "one of the very greatest in Europe." "Then what about an interview?" cried my chief. "Commander of the Faithful," I said, "this lady is so truly fine and noble an artist that I am afraid and ashamed to intrude on her in the ribald character of a journalist." "Your modesty is well known to me; and your feelings do you credit, O Bassetto," he answered; "but if you dont go I will send someone else." So I could not choose but go; and on Tuesday evening my hansom jolted slowly along the Marylebone Road, bound for Madame Gröndahl's apartments in Blandford Square. You remember when I first found out Madame Gröndahl. It was at a Philharmonic concert, in Beethoven's great concerto in E flat. You know the long passage in octaves beginning *fortissimo*, with the *diminuendo* at the end. Well, I never heard anything quite so rough and strange as the beginning of those octaves under Madame Gröndahl's fingers. I did with my ears what I do with my eyes when I stare. What followed was no more a mere *diminuendo* of sound than a beautiful sunset is a mere *diminuendo* of light. It was a series of transfigurations—a letting loose of voices imprisoned in the passage—a wonderful suffusion of its steadily beating heart—a delicate lifting of it gradually out of the region of audible sound. A critic can no more express these things in words than he can describe his sensations when an artist of genius appears suddenly in front of the crowd of performers whose varying skills and tastes it is his ordinary business to sort out, patting one on the back and rapping another over the knuckles, like a schoolmaster. On such occasions his feeling for really great playing, which so seldom gets exercised that he sometimes doubts whether he possesses it, awakes like the Sleeping Beauty; and the critic knows that he is not wholly a vain thing.

But what I wanted to find out from Madame Gröndahl was how London had continued to remain for seventeen years unacquainted with a public player whose position is as exceptional, and whose talent is as rare and exquisite, as that of Madame Schumann. For Madame Gröndahl is, in round numbers, forty; that is, she is in the full maturity of her genius. And here you become curious about her personal appearance: you would like a little description. Well, she is what you would call—observe, what *you* would call—a perfectly plain woman. Her hair is not golden like yours: it is, I think, almost ashen: you would call it grey. Her figure and style are— well, quiet, slender, nothing in particular, nothing superb or Junonian: what can I say? Complexion? Quite Norwegian: no cream or coral, nothing to be afraid of there. Eyes? Well, eyes are a matter of opinion: I should rather like you to see them for yourself: they are *memorable*. A noble brow; but then, as you say, how unbecoming to a woman to have a noble brow! Would anybody look at you if you were in the same room with her? Ah, there you have me. Frankly, they would forget your very existence, even if there were no such thing in the world as a piano. For there is a grace beside which your beauty is vulgar and your youth inadequate; and that grace is the secret of Madame Gröndahl's charm.

At Blanford Square I find the invaluable, the ubiquitous H. L. Brœkstad, who explains my errand to our hostess, and at intervals corrects my propensity to neglect my business and talk eloquently about myself. In excellent English Madame Gröndahl tells me how, when she was three or four years old, she used to make music for the stories her father told her; how, later on, Halfdan Kjerulf gave her lessons and taught her what expression in playing meant; how she was struck by hearing the late Edmund Neupert play Beethoven; how she was sent to Berlin and studied under Kullak for three years, working six and sometimes nine hours a day; and how she made her first appearance there seventeen years ago. She composes, she says, in the quiet of the evening, when the day's work is done: chiefly, indeed, in the evenings of December, when the year's work is done.

"What work?" I ask, astounded.

"Oh, all the things one has to do," she replies; "the house-

keeping, the children, the playing, the three lessons I give
every day to pupils." I rise up in wrath to protest against
this house, these children, these pupils swallowing up the
ministrations that were meant for mankind; but she adds,
with a certain diffidence as to her power of expressing so
delicate a point in English, that it is as wife and mother that
she gets the experience that makes her an artist. I collapse.
Bassetto is silenced. He can only bow to the eternal truth,
and think how different his column would be if all artists
were like this one. Here, then, is the reason why she never
came to England before. She was too busy in her own house!

Presently she begins to speak with earnest admiration of
some of her compatriots—of Svensden, for instance, and
"Mr Grieg." Her respect for Grieg infuriated me; for she is
a thousand times a finer player than he; and I got quite beside myself at the idea of his presuming to teach her how to
play this and that instead of going down on his knees and
begging her to deliver him from his occasional vulgarity,
and to impart to him some of her Mendelssohnic sense of
form in composition. In spite of her perfectly becoming consciousness of her gift and her reverence for it she is aggra-
vatingly modest. If I could play like her there would be
simply no standing me. But she seems quite as gratefully
surprised at her instantaneous success in London as she was
when, on her return to Christiania after it, she was presented
with a Steinway Grand, which stands in the same relation
to the finances of Norway as half a dozen men-of-war to the
finances of Mayfair. The presentation had been brewing for
a long time, but her London triumph precipitated it.

As it grows dark in the sitting room in Blandford Square
I prepare to withdraw; and we have some parting words
about her recital on Saturday afternoon at Prince's Hall,
where you can hear whether I have at all exaggerated her
gifts. She will play Grieg's violin sonata with Johannes
Wolff, who, it will be remembered, played it at St James's
Hall with Grieg himself. She will not play a Beethoven
sonata—thinks it would be too much to ask the public to

listen to two sonatas. *Sancta simplicitas!* too much! However, she will play Chopin, of whom she is a famous exponent, and some of her own compositions, of which I shall have a word to say some other day. Today week she leaves us to rejoin Herr Gröndahl in Paris. He has trained a choir, and brought it to the Exhibition, his genius lying in the conducting direction. I venture to prophesy that she will come back, and eventually become as regular a visitor as Joachim or Madame Schumann.

P.S. I asked her about the octave passage in the concerto. She replied, "That is the *heroic* point in the work. Von Bulow once drew my special attention to it."

15 July 1889

THE spectacle of Mr Augustus Harris making for righteousness with a whole mob of aristocratic patrons hanging on to his coat-tails is one which deserves to be hailed with three times three. It is difficult to conceive a more desperate undertaking than an attempt to make Die Meistersinger a success at Covent Garden. As well try to make wild flowers spring from the upholstery by dint of engaging tremendously expensive gardeners. There are many things needed for Die Meistersinger: scenery, dresses, persons with voices of a certain strength and compass, a conductor, a band, etc., etc., etc.; but there is one pre-eminent condition, without which all the others are in vain, and that one is the true Wagner-Nuremberg atmosphere: the poetic essence of the medieval life wherein man, instead of serenading, duelling, crying, "T'amo, t'amo," and finally suiciding (mostly in B flat or G), went his mortal round as apprentice, journeyman, and master; and habitually demeaned himself by doing useful work. Of this atmosphere there is hardly a breath at Covent Garden; and that is the first and last word of the higher criticism on Saturday's performance. But the practical criticism has to consider not whether the performance was perfectly satisfying, but whether it was better worth doing than letting alone; and on this point there must be a unanimous verdict in Mr Harris's favor.

The first step taken was to secure a large sale for the two-shilling librettos by substituting a colorless translation of the German poem not into English, because the audience would understand that, nor into Polish, French, or Russian, because then one or two of the singers could have declaimed it with native familiarity, but into Italian, the least congenial language in Europe for the purpose. How Johannistag sounds as "solenne di," and Wahn! Wahn! as "Si, si," may be imagined. In order to make quite sure of the librettos going off well, the usual opera bills were carefully removed from the stalls, probably not by Mr Harris's orders; for it is due to him to say that petty dodges of this stamp, characteristic as they are of fashionable entertainments in general and of opera house tradition in particular, are just those of which he has striven to rid Covent Garden. It is greatly to his credit that, in order to do as much of Die Meistersinger as possible, he dared on this occasion to begin at half-past seven, with the encouraging result that the attendance was more punctual than it usually is at eight, or even half-past eight. Yet, though the curtain did not fall until eighteen minutes past twelve on Sunday morning, chunks—absolutely whole chunks—had to be cut out of the very vitals of the work to get it over in time. The first half of Sachs's *Wahn! wahn!* Walter's denunciation of the master's pedantry in the second act, a section of the trial song, a section of the prize song, Beckmesser's scolding of Sachs in the third act, may be taken as samples of the excisions. This could have been avoided only by some such heroic measure as dispensing with the first act altogether: a fearful expedient; but then a single honest murder is better than half a dozen furtive mutilations.

So much for what was not done: now for what was. The honors of the evening went to Lassalle, whose singing was grand, especially in the third act. If he could only learn the part in German, cultivate a cobbler-like deportment about the elbows, and cure himself of his stage walk and his one perpetual gesture with the right hand, he would have very few dangerous rivals in Europe as Hans Sachs. Jean de Reszke, who wandered about the stage as if he had given Die Meistersinger up as a hopeless conundrum, but was always anxious to oblige as far as a tenor part or a spell of love-making was concerned, sang charmingly in the last two scenes. The ever condescending Montariol, as David (which he played with much spirit and evident relish), again sacrificed his dignity as *primo tenore assoluto* on the altar of devotion to the management. Abramoff gave due weight to the music of Pogner. Madame Albani is always at her sincerest —that is, her best—in playing Wagner. In the first scene of the third act she got so carried into her part that for the moment she quite looked it; and the quintet at the end was one of the happiest passages of the evening. Mdlle Bauermeister, the invaluable, whom I have heard oftener than any other living artist (I once saw her as Astriffiamante) was Magdalen.

Signor Mancinelli, who was literally dragged twice across the stage in agonies of dorsaflexion, had evidently taken great pains. With fresh impressions of Richter and Faccio rife in the house, his limitations inevitably made themselves felt, especially in the overture and first act, where the orchestra, being in a continual bustle, requires the smoothest and most sympathetic handling to prevent it getting on one's nerves. And the waltz and procession music in the last scene were much too slow: a grave fault at midnight, with watches popping in and out all over the house and the end still distant. The staging of this last scene, by the way, was excellent. The chorus, if the substitution of women for boys must be accepted without a murmur, acquitted themselves very well; but the riot in the second act would have been better if it had either been sung note for note as written, or, as usual, frankly abandoned as impossible and filled up according to the vociferative fancy of the choristers. A combination of the two plans resulted in a failure, both in accuracy and *laisser-aller*. Such misplaced nocturnal buffooneries as the emptying of vessels from the windows on the crowd, and the subsequent clowning of the nothing-if-not-stolid watchman, should be at once stopped. M. Isnardon as Beckmesser set a bad example in this way; and his chief opportunity of really funny acting—the exhibition of the miseries of acute nervousness before the public in the last scene—was entirely missed.

The audience kept together wonderfully at the end, considering the lateness of the hour; and their conduct in suppressing ill-timed applause and insisting on silence after the fall of the curtain until the very last chord was played, was quite delightful. The proceedings ended with a tremendous ovation to Mr Harris, who fished out of the wing a stout gentleman generally but erroneously supposed to be Wagner. The assembly then broke up in high good humor.

19 July 1889

I SEE that Lord Dunraven has undertaken to move in the House of Lords the rejection of the amendment forbidding children under ten years of age to be used for the purpose of making money for their parents and for the proprietors of theatres. The House of Lords is exactly the place for such a heartless piece of mischief. Those who are on the side of social responsibility and of the children in this matter are undoubtedly reinforced for the moment by the party which would abolish the theatre altogether if it could. But that does not blind me to the fact that even Mr Winterbotham's stuff about the children going from the ballet to the streets is more sincere than the speeches of the Infants' Exploitation deputations. If Mrs John Wood can form no higher conception of the duty of the community towards the children whose parents' poverty makes them practically helpless, than that it should leave her free to buy them at so much a week for her pantomime, and ask no questions so long as she is personally—if not socially—kind in her dealings with

174

them, then, it is to be hoped for the credit of the time that Mrs John Wood is fifty years behind it. As to Mr Beerbohm Tree's naïve complaint that the clause would prevent his producing A Midsummer Night's Dream, that, at any rate, was honest. Indeed, all the straightforward opponents of the clause make it pretty plain that the chance of occasionally seeing Pizarro, East Lynne, The Bohemian Girl, and A Doll's House (which I shall not be suspected of undervaluing) is of sufficient importance to justify us in keeping infants working for money between half-past eight and eleven every night for months at a time.

However, there is a way out of the difficulty. The Bill says nothing about amateur help from the nursery. If, then, children are so educated, elevated, and delighted by their exertions in the bracing atmosphere of the gas battens, the parents who are convinced of this will surely not hesitate to send their own olive branches without money or price, to become healthy, wealthy, and wise by staying up late, and to drive home the moral lessons of Ibsen and Shakespear. Until they are prepared to give that simple proof of their sincerity, the managerial cry of "Suffer little children to come unto me" will be set by all sensible and humane persons to the tune of "Will you walk into my parlor?" The reply in either case will, I hope, be a resolute "No."

I must say that I feel somewhat jealous as I read Mr Harris's magnificent half column of Meistersinger testimonials in the daily papers. An acute and critical letter from Mr Kühe is given *in extenso*. A dispassionate and grave tribute to the "simple perfection" of the performance at Covent Garden, is signed by the "representatives of Wagner's works in England," meaning the publishers, who will probably gain much more by the popularity of the opera than Mr Harris without having incurred his risk. The Morning Post is unjustifiably severe: It says that "the whole production was worthy of the house and its associations." Considering that Mr Harris has succeeded, and deserved to succeed, just in so far as he has turned his back on the associations of the house, it was magnanimous of him to insert this. Perhaps he only did it as a set-off to the heroic eulogies of The Times critic. But what I want to know is why *my* criticisms and letters are never reproduced as advertisements. I protest against this undeserved neglect, which I can only ascribe to a gross insensibility to the merits of my style and the extent of my influence.

On Saturday afternoon, at Prince's Hall, Madame Backer-Gröndahl not only bore out all that I have said in her praise, but left me considerably her debtor to boot. I adhere to my opinion that she should have played a Beethoven sonata instead of Grieg's violin sonata in C minor; but if we had no Beethoven we had at least Schumann and Chopin. The day has gone by when it was possible for us to get out of our depth in Schumann's pianoforte music: an artist like Madame Gröndahl gets to the bottom of such a composition as the novelette in F, and leaves us wishing that it, and not she, were deeper. But the Traumeswirren satisfied us ineffably.

There is, however, a special pianistic form of musical genius which Schumann had not, but which Chopin had, and which Madame Gröndahl has. Thus it was Chopin's nocturne in F, bracketed with the fantasia in F minor at the end of the program, that constituted the chief and final test of the occasion. Madame Gröndahl sustained it triumphantly. She was delicate, splendid, everything that an interpreter of Chopin should be; and she leaves England—surely only until next season—with a London reputation as a great Beethoven player, a great Schumann player, a great Chopin player, and, consequently, a great pianoforte player.

I must not leave this subject without a word concerning Madame Gröndahl's compositions. Those for the pianoforte reminded me strongly of Mendelssohn by their sensitiveness, their clear symmetrical form, and their perfect artistic economy. The peculiar Norwegian feeling comes out most in the songs, some half-dozen of which were sung by Miss Louise Philips with a skill and taste which agreeably surprised me; for, as it happened, I had not heard her before; and I instinctively prepare for the worst at a recital when the singer appears. Johannes Wolff played the Grieg sonata with a finish which shewed even more than his usual address. The genial audacity and technical skill with which he made the audience wax rapturous over a detestable polonaise by Lauf (called Lamb in the program) were immense.

I heard the Grieg sonata again on Wednesday at a concert given by Mdlle de Hoerschelmann somewhere in the wild west of the Old Brompton Road. I was fascinated beyond measure by a Miss Nellie Levey, a young lady with a guitar, an exquisite ear, a quaint vein of humor, and an irresistible smile, who threw such subtle appeal into the words, *Perche tradirmi? perche fuggirmi?* that I could hardly refrain from rising and earnestly protesting that nothing was further from my intentions. I should like to hear that young lady again.

Mademoiselle de Hoerschelmann—who is, I understand, a Russian—did not sing nor play. She recited in four languages, none of which she pronounced with any special virtuosity. She is, however, a very graphic reciter; and her idea of reading a canto from the *Inferno* is the right one in the right place. Recitation, as ordinarily practised, is about as entertaining as royalty-song singing. If I ever go into the business I shall simply read Homer or Dante or the Arabian Nights to the audience for an hour or two at a stretch. Mdlle de Hoerschelmann's delivery of the third canto would have been a great success had the audience understood Italian. As for me, I never have any difficulty in understanding a play or poem in a foreign language when I know what it is all about beforehand; and I enjoyed Dante much more than I had enjoyed Ostler Joe earlier in the afternoon, when Mrs Kendal favored us with it at the Opera Comique to the utter stupefaction of an audience which had fallen under the strange spell of Ibsen, a spell of which Mrs Kendal, who had just dropped it for her recitation, was happily unconscious.

Note that the Wagner performances at Bayreuth com-

mence on Sunday next. It is well to see Parsifal twice, with
Tristan and the Meistersinger in between. Each performance
costs a pound for admission alone. It is eminently possible
to spend £20 on the trip without exceptional extravagance.
But I never met anyone who complained of not having had
value for his money.

26 *July* 1889

THE season is over. By the end of next week there will be
hardly four millions of persons left in London, mostly riff-
raff, mere working people, for whom nobody thinks of
running an opera house or a series of St James's Hall concerts. And what a season it has been! Take the opera alone,
and consider what wonderful things have happened. Tamagno
was promised, as he has been repeatedly promised before;
but this time, in defiance of all precedent, he has actually
come, and his magnificent screaming is henceforth among
the *sante memorie* of London amateurs. The Covent Garden
management promised, above all things, Die Meistersinger
and Romeo and Juliet; and both have been carefully produced. These things take away the breath of the old stager.
Once upon a time it seemed a law of Nature that a London
impresario should begin the season with a column of announcements of singers whom he had not engaged, of new
works which he had not the smallest intention of producing,
of eminent tenors, the undoubted successors of Mario, who
were in fact the refuse of the Italian stage. Only a few years
have elapsed since then; and yet even Mr Mapleson, who
still believes in the irresistible attractiveness of Donizetti
(and may therefore be supposed capable of believing in anything), does not venture to resuscitate the old-fashioned
prospectus. As to Mr Harris, he thinks nothing of simply
saying what he intends to do, and doing it.

When Mr Mapleson made his annual effort with Lucia,
Il Barbiere, and La Sonnambula, etc., I flatly refused to
waste my own time and The Star's space on an experiment
178

which was of no public interest, and which was certain to fail. In vain the weeping staff held out stall tickets for Her Majesty's Theatre to me with imploring gestures. I folded my arms and said that if the name of Lucia di Lammermoor were mentioned in my presence again my resignation would follow instantaneously. This threat never fails to bring Stonecutter Street to its knees; though, lest too frequent repetition should blunt it, I am careful not to employ it more than three times in any one week. It was effectual on this occasion; and I did not once set foot in Her Majesty's during the season.

To Mr Harris I have paid much more attention. He is a man with a future: there is something to be got by pitching into him. To let him alone, or to lavish indiscriminating praise on him whilst London is as ill-provided in the matter of opera as at present, is to trifle with the situation. It must never be forgotten that the Royal Italian Opera, far from paying its way, depends on a subvention as much as any Continental opera house. Unfortunately, this subvention is not yet forcibly levied on excessive West-End incomes by the London County Council, and by them entrusted to Mr Harris for the purpose of maintaining a serious and pro-gressive artistic institution for the performance of the best dramatic music. Instead, it has to be extracted by him from excessively rich people for the purpose of maintaining a fashionable post-prandial resort for them during the season.

The following are the steps by which these munificent patrons make their plutocratic power felt at Covent Garden. They delay the rise of the curtain until half-past eight, and then come late. They insist on intervals of twenty minutes between the acts for what is to them the real business of the evening: visiting and chatting. They waste invaluable space with their comfortless dens of boxes. The percentage of in-considerate persons among them is so high that there are always at least three parties disturbing the audience by talking and laughing at full pitch during the performance. The prices which their riches enable them to bid for admission drive ordinary amateurs to swelter among the gods, whilst box after box is thrown away on inveterate dead-heads whose mission in life is to pester impresarios for free admissions. And they impose on the management impertinent sumptuary regulations by which I, for instance, am compelled to attend the opera in the cheapest, ugliest, and least wholesome suit of clothes I possess: regulations which are supposed to afford me a guarantee of the high personal character and perfect propriety in appearance, manners, and conversation of my neighbors. The guarantee is worth nothing. I shall not pretend that the average opera stall-holder is in any of these respects a specially offensive person; but I unhesitatingly affirm that the average pittite is at no disadvantage whatever compared to him and is, on the whole, better company. The enthusiastic young students, male and female, whose last half-crown has been dedicated to Wagner, and who, flushed with triumph after a devoted wait at the doors and a long push, a strong push, and a push all together on the stairs, await the rising of the curtain with delightful eagerness, are, of course, hopelessly lost to the stalls, though they are the most amusing and interesting of neighbors. As soon as women are educated to understand, as a minority already does, that it is grossly rude to keep on one's headgear in a theatre, the last rag of excuse for "evening dress indispensable" will vanish.

Yet I would forgive Mr Harris's fashionable patrons their class mumbo jumbo if only they would insist also on having the best of everything on the stage and in the orchestra—if they would rise up against those dreary deadly subscription-night Traviatas and Trovatores—if they would ask why more fuss has been made over the production of one Wagner opera in rich London than about the complete cycle of them which was given between the middle of May and the middle of June in comparatively needy Berlin—if they would ask why they are expected to put up with clever accompanists and bandmasters whilst great conductors like Richter, Levi, and Faccio are extant, and presumably open to sufficient offers—if they would ask why the eighteenth century fashions in scenic art should be maintained at Covent Garden any more than at the Lyceum—if——

This is getting insufferably long: let me get back to the point. Before Mr Harris can procure money to perfect his opera house, there must be a pressure and a clamor behind him. Before he can effectually humble and terrify his artists (an operatic artist is by nature the most arrogant worm in existence) he must have more criticisms like mine to read to them in the greenroom. Before he can appear in the official gold chain and cocked hat of Chief Superintendent of Operatic and Dramatic Performances to the County Council of London (as Sir Augustus Harris, with a salary of ever so much a year) the Opera must be brought into much closer relation to the life of the people and the progress of dramatic music. As a beginning for next year, I suggest the production of one quite new opera, by a composer under forty; freshly studied and carefully rehearsed performances of Don Giovanni and Le Nozze di Figaro; and the shelving of the old Bellini-Donizetti-Verdi stopgaps to make room for The Taming of the Shrew, Tannhäuser, Tristan, at least one of the four works from the Nibelungen tetralogy, and an old work of some merit called Fidelio, of which Mr Harris may have heard in his youth, though of late years it seems to have escaped his memory. Faust, Mefistofele, Les Huguenots, and Lohengrin can be exploited as usual; but I confess I should not regret seeing Carmen, Les Pécheurs de Perles, and even Roméo et Juliette handed over to the smaller theatres. Berlioz's Benvenuto Cellini would also excite great interest now that his Faust has become so popular.

Bless my soul! it is later than I thought: I must be off to Bayreuth at once, or I shall be late for Parsifal on Sunday afternoon. *Auf wiederschreiben!*

LONDON MUSIC IN 1888-89

IMAGINE yourself in a state of high indignation at having paid a pound for admission to a theatre, and finding yourself in a dim freestone-colored auditorium, reminding you strongly of a lecture theatre by the steepness of the bank of seats and the absence of a gallery. But whereas most lecture theatres are fan-shaped or circular, with a rostrum at the pivot or centre, this one is wedge-shaped, with a shabby striped curtain cutting off the thin end of the wedge, the difference being that the parallel benches are straight instead of curved. Partition walls jut out at right angles to the wall of the building at intervals along the side, and break off short just in time to avoid getting between the people in the end seats and the stage. These walls, which do not quite reach the ceiling, are surmounted by branches of lamps in round globes, which shed a dun-colored light over the dun-colored house. You come prepared by countless photographs and engravings for the shape of the place; but this prevailing dun tone, and the prevailing absence of cushion, curtain, fringe, gilding, or any gay theatrical garniture, with the steepness of the bank of seats (no pictures give you an adequate idea of this), make you inclined to think that the manager might really have touched up the place a little for you. But you have nothing else to complain of; for your hinged seat, though of uncushioned cane, is comfortably wide and broad, and your view of the striped curtain perfect. The highly esteemed ladies are requested by public notice obligingly their hats to remove, and those who have innocent little bonnets, which would not obstruct a child's view, carefully remove them. The ladies with the Eiffel hats, regarding them as objects of public interest not second to any work of Wagner's, steadfastly disregard the notice; and Germany, with all its martinets, dare not enforce discipline. You open your libretto, your score, your synopsis of *leitmotifs*, or other idiotic device for distracting your attention from the performance; and immediately the lights go out and leave you

in what for the moment seems all but total darkness. There
is a clatter of cane seats turned down; a great rustle, as of
wind through a forest, caused by 1300 skirts and coat tails
coming into contact with the cane; followed by an angry
hushing and hissing from overstrained Wagnerians who resent every noise by adding to it with an irritability much
more trying to healthy nerves than the occasional inevitable
dropping of a stick or opera-glass. Then the prelude is heard;
and you at once recognize that you are in the most perfect
theatre in the world for comfort, effect, and concentration
of attention. You inwardly exclaim that you are hearing the
prelude played for the first time as it ought to be played.
And here, leaving you to enjoy yourself as a member of the
analytical public, I strike in with the remark that the perfection is not in the performance, which does not touch the
excellence of one which Richter conducted at the Albert
Hall, but in the conditions of the performance. And I may
say here, once for all, that the undiscriminating praise that
is lavished on the Bayreuth representations is due to the
effect of these conditions before the curtain and not behind
it. The much boasted staging is marred by obsolete contrivances which would astonish us at the Lyceum as much as a
return to candle-lighting or half price at nine o'clock. Mr
Mansfield playing Richard III in the dress of Garrick, or
Mr Irving Hamlet in that of Kemble, would seem modern
and original compared with the unspeakable ballroom costume which Madame Materna dons to fascinate Parsifal
in the second act. The magic flower garden would be simply
the most horribly vulgar and foolish transformation scene
ever allowed to escape from a provincial pantomime, were
it not recommended to mercy by a certain enormous *naïveté*
and a pleasantly childish love of magnified red blossoms and
trailing creepers. As to the canvas set piece and Gower St.
sofa visibly pulled on to the stage with Madame Materna
seductively reposing on it, the steam from a copper under
the boards which filled the house with a smell of laundry and
melted axillary gutta-percha linings, the indescribable im-

possibility of the wigs and beards, the characterless histori-
cal-school draperies of the knights, the obvious wire connection of the electric light which glowed in the ruby bowl
of the Holy Grail, and the senseless violation of Wagner's
directions by allowing Gurnemanz and Parsifal to walk off
the stage whilst the panoramic change of scene was taking
place in the first act (obviously the absence of the two men
who are supposed to be traversing the landscape reduces the
exhibition to the alternative absurdities of the trees taking
a walk or the auditorium turning round): all these faults
shew the danger of allowing to any theatre, however imposing its associations, the ruinous privilege of exemption from
vigilant and implacable criticism. The performance of Parsifal on Sunday last suffered additionally from Herr Grüning
executing a hornpipe on the appearance of Klingsor with
the sacred spear; but this was introduced not as an act of
whimsical defiance, but under pressure of the desperate necessity of disentangling Parsifal's ankle from the snapped
string on which the spear was presently to have flown at
him.

Now if you, my Wagnerian friends, wonder how I can
scoff thus at so impressive a celebration, I reply that Wagner
is dead, and that the evil of deliberately making the Bayreuth Festival Playhouse a temple of dead traditions, instead of an arena for live impulses, has begun already. It is
because I, too, am an enthusiastic Wagnerite that the Bayreuth management cannot deceive me by dressing itself in
the skin of the dead lion. The life has not quite gone out of
the thing yet: there are moments when the spirit of the master inspires the puppets, and the whole scene glows into real
life. From the beginning of the Good Friday music in the
last act, after the scene where the woman washes Parsifal's
feet and dries them with her hair—the moment at which
Parsifal's true character of Redeemer becomes unmistakeably obvious to the crassest Philistine globe-trotter present
—the sacred fire descended, and the close of the representation was deeply impressive. Before that, a point had been

brought out strongly here and there by individual artists; but nothing more. I shall return to the subject and deal more particularly with the two casts later on, when I see the work again on Thursday. For the present I need only warn readers that my censure of some of the scenic arrangements must not be allowed to obscure the fact that the Grail scene is unsurpassed as a stage picture; that the first scene, though conventional, is finely painted; and that the Spanish landscape, from which the magic garden suddenly withers (this is a capital effect), and the Good Friday landscape in the last act, are fine pieces of stage scenery.

2 August 1889

I WRITE under difficulties this week. I am not a good sailor. After being rocked in the cradle of the deep all night, I am at present being rocked in a Dutch railway carriage. I have been in it for five hours, and I assure you that if an express were to come in the opposite direction on the same line of rails and smash the whole affair, Bassetto included, into pulp, I should make no unmanly complaints. After all, there is something grand in being able to look death in the face with a smile of welcome; but I should enjoy it more if I could look life in the face without feeling so poorly.

It is later in the day; and I think life is, perhaps, worth living after all. To drive up the Rhine from Bonn to Coblenz, whilst the hours advance from afternoon to night, is better than a dozen press views of different schools of landscape. Cologne Cathedral, too, has affected me. I am extremely susceptible to stained glass, and the old glass there transports me, whilst the new glass makes me long to transport it—with bricks. Yes, I confess I am enjoying the evening. I wish I were undressed and in bed, with twelve hours' sleep before me; I wish that when that terrific shower caught me in Cologne my mackintosh had not split up the back like a trick coat in a farce, throwing the younger posterity of the Three Kings into derisive convulsions. I wish I knew whether

that very genial market woman really gave me, as she implied, an enormous bargain for the sake of my *beaux yeux*
(one and elevenpence for half a pound of grapes and six little
hard pears), or whether she swindled me; and I wish I could
go back by Channel Tunnel. But still, for the moment, I do
not regret having been born.

Some hours have elapsed, and I now distinctly *do* regret
having been born. Imagine reaching Wurzburg at two in the
morning, and being told to wait two and a half hours for a
train to Bamberg. Imagine a wilderness of a German waiting room—a place like a café running to seed for want of a
little paint—crowded with people in various grades of wakefulness. The young what's-their-names wearing badges, and
carrying military paraphernalia wrapped up in umbrella
cases, are very wideawake indeed: they are continually
breaking into Lorelei, or some other popular air, only to
break out of it in quite British fashion the next moment.
The men who are stretched on the two broad forms in the
middle of the room, and on rows of chairs in the background,
might be supposed asleep if a man could really sleep with
the back of his neck pillowed on the handle of a travelling-
bag, and his occiput taking an impression of the catch. The
seated slumberers, with their arms folded on the table and
their faces hidden upon them, are probably less miserable,
especially those who are not at marble tables. I tried this
plan for a moment myself; but it was a failure: after killing
ten minutes by the familiar process of making them appear
ten hours, I have taken to writing as the best way I know of
making time seem too short (*ars longa, vita brevis*, you understand). The fearfully weary woman with the fretful child
has just got up and tried a walk, after addressing to me a
remark which I do not understand, but which I accept as a
commission to see that nobody steals her luggage during her
promenade.

Pshaw! describing a scene like this is like trying to draw
one of the faces you see in a cloud. Already the noisy young-
sters are gone, and the horizontal figures have transferred

themselves, during their vertical intervals, to the trains
which an official with a brutal bell and an undistinguished
delivery enters to announce from time to time. There are
but twelve of us now, including the two waiters, myself, and
the child, who has, I am happy to say, left off worrying its
mother to stare at the tremendous spectacle of Corno di
Bassetto writing his sparkling Star column, and looking
more melancholy and jaded over it than any infant's mind
could have conceived. But hark! methinks I scent the morning air. The shunter's horn—a silly child's affair with a harmonium reed in it—takes a bustling tone as if it were paid
so much a week to call the lark in time. A passing engine
shews against the sky no longer as a bright gleaming mass
of metal against a dead darkness, but as a black shadow on
a dim grey galanty-sheet. And it is beginning to strike cold
and raw! Ugh! What an idiot I was not to go on to Nuremberg; and what stupids they were to give me tickets via
Bamberg! I feel that I shall slate something presently—
Parsifal, probably.

After all, Bamberg has its merits. It was worth coming
round to see: that affable young German gentleman at
Cook's who sold me my tickets evidently knew a thing or
two. How Bamberg manages to have so many rivers and
bridges and yet to be on top of a group of hills I do not know:
it is only another proof of the worthlessness of the commonplace that water will find its own level. The town has such
an odd air of being built by persons with artistic instincts,
but with the temperament which usually earns for its possessor the title of rum customer, that the climb up from the
vegetable market, strong in marrows and carrots, under the
Bridge House, decorated with frescoes exactly like the ones
I used to produce on whitewashed walls with penny paints
when I was a boy, and up to the Cathedral, freshened me
more than all the naps I had snatched in the train from
Wurzburg: more even than the delightfully musical German
of the two young ladies *en route* for Kissingen, who were my
fellow-travellers to Schweinfurth. Really a perfect ante-

Gothic cathedral of the plainest and most reasonable beauty, looking its best in the morning light.

Glancing through Baedeker as I bowl along Bayreuth-wards I perceive that the chief feature of the Wagner district is a great lunatic asylum. At Neumarkt an official railway colporteur thrusts into my hand a great red placard inscribed with a WARNUNG! (German spelling is worse than indifferent) against pickpockets at Bayreuth. This is a nice outcome of Parsifal. In the town an enterprising tradesman offers "the Parsifal slippers" at 2m. 50 the pair as "the height of novelty." It is a desperately stupid little town, this Bayreuth. I was never in Bath but once; and then they were trying to make it exciting by a meeting of the British Association which I addressed for a solid hour in spite of the secretary's urging me to be brief. Trying to make Bayreuth lively by a Wagner Festspiel is much the same thing.

However, there are hills with fine woods to wander through, and blackberries, raspberries, and other sorts of edible berries, about the names of which no two persons agree, to be had for the picking. On the top of the hill on which the theatre stands is a tower erected to the brave sons of Bayreuth who fell in 1870-71. Except that the tower is round, and that there is no courtly old lady to take toll and sell ginger-beer, you might, by a vigorous contraction of the imagination, fancy yourself on Leith Hill. The town contains a bust of Mr John Cobden Sanderson, with somebody else's name under it; also the most extravagantly and outrageously absurd fountain and equestrian statue in the world (of Margrave Somebody). Jean Paul Richter is much commemorated in the neighborhood. I am surprised to find how few faces I know here. Charles Dowdeswell, William Archer, Antoinette Sterling, Stavenhagen, Richter, Carl Armbruster, Pauline Cramer, Rimbault Dibdin, and Benjamin R. Tucker of Boston, are all I can identify. It is desperately hard work, this daily scrutiny of the details of an elaborate performance from four to past ten. Yet there are people who imagine I am taking a holiday.

LONDON MUSIC IN 1888-89

TRISTAN AND ISOLDA comes off better than Parsifal by just so much as the impulse to play it is more genuine and the power to understand it more common. To enjoy Parsifal, either as a listener or an executant, one must be either a fanatic or a philosopher. To enjoy Tristan it is only necessary to have had one serious love affair; and though the number of persons possessing this qualification is popularly exaggerated, yet there are enough to keep the work alive and vigorous. In England it is not yet familiar: we contentedly lap dose after dose of such pap as the garden scene in Gounod's Faust, and think we are draining the cup of stage passion to the dregs. The truth is that all the merely romantic love scenes ever turned into music are pallid beside the second act of Tristan. It is an ocean of sentiment, immensely German, and yet universal in its appeal to human sympathy. At eight o'clock yesterday (Monday) I wondered that people fresh from such an experience did not rashly declare that all other music is leather and prunella; shrug their shoulders at the triviality of *La ci darem*; and denounce a proposal to try the effect of the fourth act of Les Huguenots as a direct incitement to crime.

The performance on Monday was an admirable one. After the scratch representations we are accustomed to in London, at which half the attention of the singers is given to the prompter, half to the conductor, and the rest to the character impersonated, the Bayreuth plays seem miracles of perfect preparedness. Nothing is forgotten; nothing is slurred; nothing on the stage contradicts its expression in the orchestra. At Covent Garden, where you cannot get an artist even to open a letter or make a sword thrust within four bars of the chord by which the band expresses his surprise or his rage, a tithe of the thought and trouble taken here would work wonders. The orchestra, too, by certain methods of treating the instruments, produce many effects of which the tradition must be handed down orally; for most of them defy such directions as a composer can write into his score with any prospect of being rightly understood. Everything that can be done by educated men thoroughly in earnest is done: the shortcomings are those which only individual gifts can overcome.

That shortcomings do exist may be inferred from the fact that, except at those supreme moments at which the Wagnerian power sweeps everything before it, it is possible for an ungrateful visitor to feel heavily bored. The reason is that the singers, in spite of their formidable physique, thick powerful voices, and intelligent and energetic declamation, are not all interesting. They lack subtlety, grace, finesse, magnetism, versatility, delicacy of attack, freedom, individuality: in a word, genius. I remember how Carl Hill sang the part of Mark when I first heard that second act: how we were made to understand the simple dignity, the quiet feeling, the noble restraint, the subdued but penetrating reproach of the old king's address to the hero whom he had loved as a son, and in whose arms he surprises his virgin wife. Herr Betz gave us hardly any of this. He turned his head away, and lifted his hands, and sang most dolefully: nobody was sorry when he had said his say and was done with it. Only a few months ago, at the Portman Rooms, I heard Mr Grove, who makes no pretension to the eminence of Herr Betz, sing this scene with much truer expression. But when Hill sang the part Wagner was conducting; so perhaps the comparison is hardly fair to Betz. In the third act again Vogl surpassed Charles II in point of being an unconscionably long time dying. Wagner's heroes have so much to say that if they have not several ways of saying it (Vogl has exactly two—a sentimental way and a vehement way) the audience is apt to get into that temper which, at English public meetings, finds vent in cries of "Time!" For the fuller a poem is, the duller is an empty recitation of it.

The honors of the occasion were carried off by the women. The men shewed that they had been heavily drilled and were under orders; but Frau Sucher and Fraulein

Staudigl played as if the initiative were their own. Frau Sucher, indeed, is not a good subject for leading-strings. Her Isolda is self-assertive and even explosive from beginning to end: impetuous in love, violent in remorse, strong in despair. Frau Sucher has the singer's instinct in a degree exceptionally keen for Bayreuth: she, like Frau Materna, can fall back sometimes on methods of expression solely musical. Fraulein Staudigl's Brangaena was excellent. If I were asked to point to the page of music in which the most perfect purity of tone would produce the greatest effect I think I should select the warning of Brangaena from the tower top to the lovers in the garden. I cannot say that Fraulein Staudigl quite satisfied me in this indescribable episode; but I can praise her warmly for not having fallen much further short of perfection than she actually did. The orchestra, conducted by Felix Mottl, played with an absolute precision and a touch of austerity which reminded me of Costa, who, obsolete as his tastes were, and quickly as he has been forgotten, deserves this reminiscence for having kept his foot down so long on slovenly and vulgar orchestral work. So much so that I sometimes wish he were alive again; though there was a time when—musically speaking, you understand —I heartily wished him dead. Curious, that Tristan and Isolda in Bayreuth should have set me talking about Costa, of all men that ever were!

Perhaps the reason why these Bayreuth artists interest me so much less than they ought to, is that they make no mistakes, and I am consequently deprived of an irritant to which I have become accustomed in London. Whatever it is, I sighed more than once for ten minutes of Covent Garden. Not, of course, for the Covent Garden orchestra, or the conductor, or the cuts, or the stalls and boxes, or the late hours, or the superficialities, or the general cloudiness as to the meaning of the stage business, or the pointless Italian verse. But I could have borne a stave or two from Jean de Reszke and Lassalle with a tranquil mind. It is true that Herr Gudehus understands the part of Walther much better than

De Reszke: he acts with humour and intelligence, and sings by no means without fervor and power. Moreover, he is venerable; whereas our Polish favorite is a mere sprig of forty or thereabouts. Again, Reichmann gives a more characteristic portrait of the cobbler master-singer of Nuremberg than Lassalle: one, too, much fuller of suggestive detail. And though his voice is much the worse for wear, there is, here and there in his compass, still a rich note or two; and he was able to finish the part bravely, though the last hundred bars or so evidently cost him a severe effort. But in musical charm neither Gudehus nor Reichmann touched De Reszke and Lassalle, though at every other point they far surpassed them. I wish some man of science would provide critics with a psychology capable of explaining how the same man may sing through an opera like a genius and act through it like a country gentleman; or, conversely, why he may interpret the book like a student and philosopher, and sing through the score like an improved foghorn. The first case prevails in London and makes Covent Garden frivolous: the other monopolises Bayreuth and makes the Festival Plays heavy. The performance was an arduous one, the third act lasting two hours. Richter conducted; and this is as good a place as another to say that he is by far the freest, strongest, and most gifted conductor of the three, though he left Parsifal to Levi (it is an open secret that Wagner at first offered the work to the Gentile conductor), and does not always take the trouble to secure the faultless precision attained by Möttl in Tristan. I have heard nothing played here with such an effect as the prelude to the third act; and the judgment, the good husbandry, and—at the right moment—the massive force with which Richter got the maximum of effect in the scenes of crowd and tumult were great feats of generalship. The stage management was above praise: how much it did to make the situations intelligible could only be adequately felt by those who had seen Die Meistersinger in theatres where nothing but a few of the simpler incidents seem to be thoroughly understood by anybody concerned.

The final scene was one of the most imposing I have ever
seen on the stage; and here, as in the previous acts, the effect
produced was not the result of money freely lavished, but of
care conscientiously taken. The waltz was charming because
it was a dance and not a ballet (I wish I could persuade
Stewart Headlam that ballet is the death of dancing). Anyhow, the scene at Bayreuth was no more like that at Covent
Garden than a picture by Teniers is like an *aquarelle* by
Dubufe. Of the principal artists, besides those of whom I
have already spoken, the most distinguished was Friedricks,
who played Beckmesser like a finished comedian. Fraulein
Staudigl again showed considerable intelligence as an actress
in the part of Magdalena; and Fraulein Dressler's Eva was
a good Eva as Evas go, though she crowned Walther at the
end with an appallingly flat imitation shake. Hofmüller was
comparatively bright as David. The remarkable completeness and depth of the impression produced shewed the wisdom of performing great works without mutilation, at whatever tax on the time and endurance of the audience. The
flood of melody throughout the work astonished the few
survivors of the sceptics who originated the brilliant theory
that Wagner devoted his existence to avoiding anything of
a musical nature in his compositions.

The place is by this time full of English. I shall retreat
to Nuremberg after Parsifal.

7 August 1889

THIS Parsifal is a wonderful experience: not a doubt of it.
The impression it makes is quite independent of liking the
music or understanding the poem. Hardly anybody has the
slightest idea of what it all means; many people are severely
fatigued by it; and there must be at least some who retain
enough of the old habit of regarding the theatre as an exception to the doctrine of Omnipresence, to feel some qualms
concerning the propriety of an elaborate make-believe of
Holy Communion, culminating in the descent of a stuffed

dove through a flood of electric radiance. Yet Parsifal is the magnet that draws people to Bayreuth and disturbs their journey thence with sudden fits of desperate desire to go back again. When you leave the theatre after your first Parsifal you may not be conscious of having brought away more than a phrase or two of *leit motif* mingled with your burden of weariness and disappointment. Yet before long the music begins to stir within you and haunt you with a growing urgency that in a few days makes another hearing seem a necessity of life. By that time,too, you will have been converted to the Church and Stage Guilds' view that the theatre is as holy a place as the church and the function of the actor no less sacred than that of the priest.

The second performance given during my stay at Bayreuth was much better than the first. It is sometimes difficult for a critic to feel sure that an improvement of this sort is not in his own temper rather than in what he is listening to; but as I found Klingsor decidedly worse than before and was conscious of one or two points at which Fraulein Malten as Kundry fell short of Frau Materna the difference must have been objective, since, had it been merely subjective, the apparent changes would all have been, like my mood, from worse to better. Malten has several advantages over Materna in playing Kundry. Not only is she passably slim, but her long thin lips and finely-turned chin, with her wild eyes, give her a certain air of *beauté de diable*. Only an air, it is true, but enough for a willing audience. Her voice, though a little worn, is bright; and her delivery is swift and telling. Altogether, one may say that her individuality, though it would not startle London, is quite magnetic in Bayreuth. Frau Materna, the rival Kundry, is not perceptibly lighter than she was when she sang at the Albert Hall in 1877. She is comely, but matronly. Still, as Kundry is as old as the hills no complaint need be made on this score; indeed, the part is one which a very young woman would play worse than a mature one, unless she were a young woman of extraordinary genius and precocity. At moments Materna's sing-

194

ing is grand, and her acting powerful: at other moments she holds up the corner of an absurd scarf as if it had descended to her from a provincial Mrs Siddons. Fraulein Malten also clings to a scarf rather more than is good for the sobriety of spectators with an untimely sense of fun. But nobody laughs. It is a point of honor not to laugh in the Wagner Theatre, where the chances offered to ribalds are innumerable: take as instances the solemn death and funeral of the stuffed swan; the letting out of Parsifal's tucks when his mailed shirt is taken off and his white robe pulled down; and the vagaries of the sacred spear, which either refuses to fly at Parsifal at all or else wraps its fixings round his ankles like an unnaturally thin boa constrictor. Nevertheless, nobody behaves otherwise than they would in church. The performance is regarded on all hands as a rite. Miss Pauline Cramer, if she had no deeper feeling than a desire to oblige the management, like Montariol at Covent Garden, would hardly have volunteered for the silent part of the youth whose whole duty it is to uncover the Grail. As to Frau Materna, it is impossible to believe that when she goes up nearly the whole depth of the Grail scene on her knees, she is only aiming at a stage effect. As such, it is not worth the physical exertion it costs. Van Dyck, though not so steady a singer as Grüning, has a certain impulsive *naïveté* which, with his engaging physical exuberance, makes him the better Parsifal. The part is a unique one, full of never-to-be-forgotten situations. Impressive as the first Grail scene is, nine-tenths of its effect would be lost without the "innocent fool" gazing dumbly at it in the corner, only to be hustled out as a goose when it is over. His appearance on the rampart of Klingsor's castle, looking down in wonder at the flower maidens in the enchanted garden, is also a memorable point. And that long kiss of Kundry's from which he learns so much is one of those pregnant simplicities which stare the world in the face for centuries and yet are never pointed out except by great men.

LONDON MUSIC IN 1888-89

I SEE that Dr Morell Mackenzie has again explained the physiology of song, this time in the Contemporary Review. I notice that he describes abdominal breathing as "pushing down the diaphragm and protruding the stomach." Many people—including myself—have always taken it for granted that abdominal breathing means the trick of retracting and depressing the diaphragm as an alternative to lifting the ribs, as a woman or an opening umbrella does. But after a few experiments I find that I can breathe in a manner answering to Dr Morell Mackenzie's description by pushing what I suppose to be my diaphragm forwards and downwards, instead of pulling it inwards and downwards. I quite agree with the doctor that it is a bad plan; but the other variety does not seem to me to be open to the objections he urges. However, I speak with diffidence on a matter which involves a knowledge of the whereabouts of the stomach, because I entirely forget where that organ is situate. It is a long time since I dipped into Huxley and Foster; and all that comes back to me of their teaching is that they disabused me of my original impression that my stomach was a sort of hollow kernel, situated exactly in the centre of my body. On consideration I recollect that it is shaped like the bellows of a bagpipe, and is all to one side; but which side, or how high up or how low down, I cannot for the life of me remember. Hence the caution with which I offer my opinion.

Dr Morell Mackenzie returns to his old and apparently reasonable contention that children should be taught to sing early, and that the training of the voice need not be discontinued whilst the voice of the boy is breaking into that of a man. He also righteously protests against the height of the English pitch; but in doing so he makes a slip. "Nearly all singers," he says, "are in favor of lowering the pitch. The sole exceptions are, I believe, the contraltos, whom a high pitch does not affect so much as it does others. I know of one justly celebrated contralto who produces an extraordinary effect by her low E. If the pitch were altered this vocal feat would no longer be so wonderful; and it is natural, therefore, that this lady should wish the present state of things to continue." Dr Morell Mackenzie, to say the least, has not decomposed much brain tissue over this point. Obviously a lowering of the pitch, which eases the high B's and C's of the sopranos, makes the low E's and F's of the contraltos and bassos more difficult. Astriffiamante can only be relieved at the expense of Sarastro. If Dr Mackenzie had written that the lady objected because the change would render her favourite vocal feat impossible he would have been nearer the mark.

The Musical Times has had the happy idea of extracting from Edward Fitzgerald's letters his notes upon music. On the whole, Fitz was a sound critic; by which you will please understand not that his likings and dislikings in music were the same as yours, but that he knew one sort of music from another, and was incapable of speaking of the overtures to Mozart's Zauberflöte, Beethoven's Leonora, and Rossini's William Tell as if they were merely three pieces cut off the same roll of stuff by three different tailors. His walking out of the house after the first act of Les Huguenots because it was "noisy and ugly" was rash but perfectly consistent with his remark on the C minor symphony: "I like Mozart better: Beethoven is gloomy." The two criticisms bring to light the whole secret of the extraordinary sensation made by such men as Byron, Beethoven, and Meyerbeer in the first half of the century. Beethoven was the first to write gloomy music for its own sake. Meyerbeer was the first opera composer who had the courage to write persistently lugubrious music for its own sake. This was quite a different thing from writing a funeral march because Saul was dead, tromboning a terrible invocation to the *divinités du Styx* because a heroine had to descend into the shades, or in any of the old tragic ways purifying the soul with pity or terror. Mozart's Don Giovanni was the first Byronic hero in music; but the shadows cast by him were so full of strange reflections and beautiful colors that such lovers of beauty as Fitz were not alarmed. But when Beethoven came, the shadows were black and gigantic; the forms were rough and bold; the Mozartian enchantment was gone. Instead of it there came a sense of deep import in the music—of, as Fitzgerald says, "a Holy of Holies far withdrawn; conceived in the depth of a mind, and only to be received into the depth of ours after much attention." The translator of Omar Khayyám did not like the black shadows; and though he recognized that Beethoven had "a depth not to be reached all at once," and was "original, majestic, and profound," yet he liked the no less deep and more luminous Mozart better. As to Meyerbeer, who had the lugubriosity of the new school without its profundity, Fitz simply walked out of the house at the end of the first act, and thereby missed the discovery that the arch trifler could rise magnificently to the occasion when his librettist offered it to him.

His worst shot at the music of later days is his description of Carmen as "an opera on the Wagner plan," a description which shews that his notion of "the Wagner plan" was entirely superficial. But his dismissal of Bizet's opera as containing "excellent instrumentation, but not one new or melodious idea through the whole," though it seems absurdly severe, is the natural deliverance of a man who speaks from that zone of Parnassus in which Handel has his place. Fitz appears to have lived on Handel; and Carmen is the very smallest of small beer to a palate accustomed to even Acis and Galatea, much more Samson, Messiah, Israel in Egypt, or Jephtha. But it would never do for Press critics to contemn in this fashion every farce for not being a tragedy. By the way, Fitz saw Carmen at Her Majesty's in 1880; and of the singers he says that "only one of them could sing at all; and she sang very well indeed: Trebelli her name." This shews that he knew good singing from bad, in spite of his fogeyish habit of comparing every singer with Pasta. From the purely musical point of view, Trebelli was certainly the best of all the Carmens.

LONDON MUSIC IN 1888-89

Tomorrow the Promenade Concerts at Covent Garden begin. Arditi is to conduct. Glancing at the first program: *Ernani involami, Il segreto, Un di se ben,* and so on, I feel that Arditi will be in his element. But what about the classical nights, on which the prestige of these concerts always depends? I do not mean to imply that Arditi cannot conduct a symphony: he can conduct anything, and come off without defeat, thanks to his address, his experience, and his musical instinct. But symphony is not his department. He knows the Leonora overture, which he has so often conducted at the opera; and I give him credit for the deepest respect for Mozart's Jupiter symphony, to which he is by this time pretty well accustomed. But Beethoven's symphonies are not his affair. I remember once seeing him conduct the slow movement of the Ninth symphony. He smiled; he beat away genially; he checked the entries of the instruments vigilantly; occasionally he ecstatically rose and sank in his characteristic manner like an animated concertina set on end; but a skilled reader of faces could see that he was profoundly puzzled, and could not for the life of him catch the swing of the movement. This was not to be wondered at, since he had begun the first section by briskly beating four in a bar, whereas eight in a bar, at a moderate pace, would just about have got him right. The second section, in three-four time, a ravishing strain which should go much more ardently than the first section, he conducted with funereal solemnity. Since then his acquaintance with the later works of Beethoven may have ripened; but I doubt it. His temperament is so Italian, and his training has so confined him in the mid-century operatic habit of mind, that I cannot believe that the classical nights will be the strong points in the forthcoming season. If, however, he will follow up *Un di se ben* by plenty of Italian concerted music, I shall applaud him to the echo. Are we never again to hear *Guai se ti sfugge un moto, E rimasto, Chi mi frena, E scherzo di follia, O sommo Carlo,* and half a dozen other delightful concerted pieces which will occur to Arditi at once in this connection? The singers, it seems, will have sufficiently frequent engagements together to make it reasonable to ask them to get up these beautiful and simple numbers, and so to relieve us from the perpetual solo, solo, solo, varied only by encores.

12 *August* 1889

WHEN I reached Covent Garden on Saturday at eight I found it crowded to the ceiling. Business had begun at half-past seven; and when I entered the orchestra was employed, absurdly enough, upon the ballet music from Ponchielli's Gioconda. For why, in the name of reason, should the accompaniment to a dance be played in public without the dance itself, any more than the accompaniment to a song? I grant you that there are a few dance tunes that are worth listening to for their own sakes, but they are to be found neither in the Gioconda nor any other grand opera ballet. I gathered from the program that the band had already disported itself with the overture to Zampa, the allegretto from the Eighth Symphony, and other not too severe orchestral compositions. After Gioconda Mdlle. Tremelli sang Il Segreto in an undisciplined manner, running very short in the matter of breath, but achieving an effective shake which sounded as if it were a double-voiced one in thirds. Miss Nettie Carpenter played Svendsen's Romance for Violin, and played it very well, though her tone is just a little soapy, if I may be permitted to use such an expression. Signor Foli followed with I Fear no Foe; and I had just made a note that his voice was entirely gone, when, in singing The Millwheel for an encore (everybody was encored), it came back again and relieved him of the arduous task of interpreting the ballad by facial expression alone. Eloquence of feature is one of Signor Foli's strong points. In the waltz from Die Meistersinger I heard no glockenspiel. However, as I was not just then very favorably situated it is barely possible that it may have been tinkling beyond my hearing. Nikita—the young lady spurns a prefix—gave us *Ernani involami*, which she

sang well. Yet if good teaching were common, and an artistic
atmosphere prevalent in British homes, every third girl in
England would be able to do nearly as much. Nikita has
been well taught: she does not scream her high notes nor
make shots at them; and she can imitate feeling sympathetically. She is too young, I hope, for her expression to be more
than imitation. I was astonished to hear so sensible an artist
as Mr John Radcliffe play a ridiculously old-fashioned set of
variations for the flute on Irish airs. Surely he does not seriously believe that any human being nowadays cares for such
nonsense as the first variation on The Minstrel Boy. The
composer named in the bill was Sauvelet. I wonder is this a
flautist named Sauvelet whom I heard more than 20 years
ago on a concert tour with Madame de Meric Lablache and
a tenor then comparatively unknown, named Edward Lloyd.
The last thing I heard was the quartet from Rigoletto, the
success of which proved the wisdom of my advice the other
day to the managers to make a feature of concerted music.
I came away as the orchestra, abetted by the Coldstream
Guards, began a tremendous assault and battery on Carmen.
Arditi was in high feather, and shewed his histrionic ability
by the cleverness with which he put on that touch of the
ringmaster which has been expected from conductors at
promenade concerts since Jullien's time. He was expansive,
paternal, enthusiastic, and liberal with the most extravagantly superfluous leads to his veterans, most of whom could
have done their work equally well in the dark.

16 *August* 1889

THIS dead season, at least, enables the unfortunate Londoner to hear orchestral music every night for a shilling, and
brings into use two-thirds of our stock of opera houses. We
have three of them: Covent Garden, Her Majesty's, and
Drury Lane. The space occupied by them is of enormous
value; and I presume somebody pays the rent of that space
to the ground landlord. Yet the theatrical work done by the

three could be done equally well at any one of them. When melodrama is raging at Drury Lane, Covent Garden is idle. When Mr Harris goes to Covent Garden for the opera season, Drury Lane closes. Her Majesty's remains closed all the time, except when somebody is seized with an insane impulse to lose a few thousand pounds by providing the deadheads of London with a fortnight or so of bad opera. Will some actuarial or mathematical reader kindly add up the square feet of space occupied by the three big houses, and divide the result by the total number of performances given in them during the year? If the result does not prove that we are far more extravagant in the matter of space than they are at Bayreuth, I will eat the paper or even the slate on which the calculation is made. Be it remembered, too, that the extravagance in space is nothing as compared to the extravagance in value; for the site of Her Majesty's alone must be worth half a dozen streets in Bayreuth. Yet when we complain of the inferiority of our theatres, we are always told that the necessity for economy of space makes a reasonable model impossible.

The calculation might be carried on to include all the prominent places of entertainment in London: the Albert Hall, the Globe, Olympic, Opera Comique, Shaftesbury, Novelty, and St James's theatres would of course be in the list. Here again it would certainly be found that a much smaller number of houses, and consequently of square feet of valuable space, would suffice for the work actually done. This is sheer waste of money produced by competition. Now, every intelligent man of business hates competitive waste. He longs to abolish the superfluous expenditure (carefully keeping up prices lest the public should be pauperized) and put the saving into his own pocket. Why should not this be attempted in the case of the theatres? All that is necessary is to substitute competition for combination, American fashion, by forming a Public Entertainments Trust to buy up all the theatres in London and throw them into a common stock. The superfluous ones could then be

demolished, and the sites sold or let on building leases. All
the older theatres might be demolished and replaced to the
necessary extent by new ones, possibly on more favorable
sites. The Trust would then have a monopoly of the London
theatres: a monopoly which, astutely managed, might make
any fresh attempt at competition unprofitable.

I may as well say beforehand that my position as critic
would make it impossible for me to accept the position of
chairman of the Trust; and the discouragement created by
this difficulty may delay the project for some time. But in
the meantime, combination is advancing. Mr Harris, for instance, is no longer competing at Drury Lane against the
Alhambra, the Royal Italian Opera, and the Carl Rosa Company. He is interested in all three. This makes him powerful
as against the race of artists. Suppose you are a lady of the
ballet engaged at the opera, and you feel aggrieved at some
act of the manager. Once upon a time you could say, "Tyrant, I shake the dust of your theatre off my feet" (a dancer
can do this very prettily) or, "I go to obtain an engagement
at the Drury Lane pantomime, where, perhaps, I shall be
columbine." And if they annoyed her at Drury Lane, she
could say, "I will not stand this, I will go to the Alhambra."
Nowadays, the three are practically all one establishment.
When, after a few more years of competing syndicates, we
have a great "combine" of the Harris, Leslie, D'Oyly Carte,
and all the other interests, the spread of artistic culture in
the meantime continually making pleasant young singers
and actors more plentiful, and consequently cheaper, we
shall have an agitation for a Factory Act applicable not
merely to children under ten, but to all women over seventeen and men over eighteen.

Talking of the children under ten, I see that my friend
Archer, in this week's World, returns to the Protection of
Children Act by printing a dialogue which took place at
Bayreuth between himself and some inconceivable idiot who
defended the Act on the ground that Miss Mabel Love was
a victim of mental over-pressure, and generally served him-

self up on toast for immediate consumption by the eminent
critic, who is unfortunately in favor of infant exploitation.
Archer, in fact, has become a sort of theatrical Dr Barnardo,
eager to snatch children from the gutter and raise them to the
culture and affluence of tinsel fairyland. The choice, he says,
is "between the sty and the stage." The homes of the children are such that the stage pittance "converts misery into
comparative comfort." Withdraw it, and "Back and side go
bare, go bare: Foot and hand go cold." Archer thinks that
the demand for theatre children is so immense, and so small
the supply of comparatively respectable children whose parents are quite willing to make a few extra shillings by them,
that managers have to undertake the education of "sty children!"

But, even if it were so, what would be the effect on the
earnings of the family? Archer is confident that the employer
would not cut down the father's wage; and he is right: the
employer might, on the contrary, have to raise the proffered
wage in order to tempt the father to work at all. If I lived in
misery in a sty, with my children naked as to their back,
their sides, and their feet—that is, dressed in aprons alone—
I should have formed a habit of living on, say, from nothing
a week to eight or nine shillings, according to luck. And I
should earn those shillings by brutalizing drudgery. Now, if
some liberal-minded householder, overlooking the probability of my partner in the sty being by force of circumstances
an uncleanly and dishonest person, were to offer her half-a-
crown a week for charing, I would certainly not thereupon
offer to accept a lower wage from my employer: rather
would I take out the half-crown in six or seven hours' relief
from my detested toil. And if by any extraordinary accident
I had a pretty or shapely child, and that that child put on
its apron and called on Mrs John Wood to explain that it
was in want of an engagement, and that that lady benevo-
lently clothed it, fine-tooth-combed it, introduced it to Miss
Morleena Kenwigs and the rest, and gave it five shillings a
week, I should promptly retire from active industry alto-

gether, feeling that I was improving myself by withdrawing from degrading and ruinous toil, and at the same time elevating my child in the manner so eloquently set forth by William Archer.

Archer would of course still be able to say quite logically that this was at least better than the former conditions, in which the child never escaped from the sty. The manager, he would argue, will take care that the child is well and happy. Is he not "directly interested in keeping his little troop physically fit?" Must they not "be bright, alert, and well disposed if they are to do their work properly and please the public?" Just like the child acrobat of the circus, with his well brushed hair, his physically fit muscles, his rosy complexion, and his cultivated mind! Just like the charming barmaid, who must be bright, alert, and well disposed for fourteen hours a day, if she wishes to keep her place! How much better than being on the streets! The beauty of this sort of logic is that if the system went on unchecked to the point of making children bear the whole burden of breadwinning in the proletarian community, Archer would always be forced to cry "Go on" and to oppose those who cried "Stop." You first put your children between the devil and the deep sea; and then, on philanthropic grounds, you push them to the devil to save them from drowning.

Briefly put, Archer's argument in favor of infant exploitation is that it is a remedy for poverty. Briefly put, the reply is that it isnt. Slightly amplified, the reply goes on to say that even if it were a remedy it would be a surpassingly dastardly one. Specially applied to the mistaken assumption that the theatre children are "sty" children, the reply is that the income of a sty never rises, because the head of it never works one hour more than absolute necessity compels him to. Specially applied to the correct assumption that the children are of the Kenwigs class, the reply is that the assertion that their board school education and drill and their home life are less healthy for them than theatrical training and night work, is an interested one, the commonsense objections to which have been evaded by the "sty" theory. Comprehensively applied to the contention that the managers' interests are identical with those of the children, the reply casts off its logical form and expresses itself through a symbol formed by applying the thumb to the tip of the nose and throwing the extended fingers into graceful action.

19 August 1889

I WAS greatly grieved on Saturday at Her Majesty's to see that out of the 100 orchestral players announced, only 76—even including 20 Scots Guards—were in their places. The other 24 are, I fear, seriously ill, or they would hardly have failed Mr Leslie on so important an occasion. I trust we shall see the poor fellows back at their posts before the season is over.

The house looked better than I expected; for, if the truth must out, I was at the private view on Thursday, and the reason I said nothing about it here was that the "Old London" decoration seemed to me to destroy the gaiety of the house, and to turn an imposing interior into a ghastly, zinc-colored travesty of an open-air scene. However, on Saturday, with the finishing touches added, with the floor and the muddy sandbanks under the orchestra hidden by a crowd of promenaders too closely packed to promenade, and with powerful lights everywhere, matters were greatly improved; and I am now prepared to admit that the decorations serve their turn well enough. Signor Bevignani looked much pleased with himself, and got on fairly well until he attempted the shepherds' dance, the storm, and the thanksgiving finale from the Pastoral Symphony (compendiously described in the program as "scherzo"), when, I am sorry to say, he covered himself, and the orchestra, with humiliation. The band, instead of holding the harmonies, attacked them anyhow, and let the tone tail off at once; and Signor Bevignani, under the erroneous impression that this sort of kid-glove trifling with music still passes for orchestral playing in London, 206 tried to cover up the thin spots by hurrying on, which, of course, made matters worse. I must say that if Signor Bevignani is so hopelessly out of it as not to have learnt that we do things differently nowadays, the band, at least, know better, and ought, for their own credit, to astonish him with some of the sustained tone that Richter would expect—and would get—from them. Mr Howard Reynolds sets a capital example in this respect: indeed, the Waldteufel waltz, which was his *cheval de bataille*, was the only piece in which I heard twopenn'orth of tone from the strings; but I wish Mr Reynolds would not make a point of forcing at least two notes in each solo to the point of splitting the ears of everyone, groundling or other, within range of his cornet. And if he would delicately hint to his two colleagues that they get half the intervals in the opening phrase of Tchaikovsky's Italian Caprice most detestably out of tune, he will greatly oblige me. M. Vladmir de Pachmann gave his well-known pantomimic performance, with accompaniments by Chopin, a composer whose music I could listen to M. de Pachmann playing for ever if the works were first carefully removed from the pianoforte. During the Doris selection I wandered about the house inattentively; but I was struck by the beauty of tone and accuracy of intonation of a euphonium soloist—Mr Guilmartin, I presume—who was not mentioned in the program. Mr Edward Lloyd, wildly encored, gave us When other lips, Come into the garden, Maud, and so forth. Miss Alice Gomez sang *Porgi amor* not so effectively as on other occasions, but still attractively. After Mr Lloyd's second appearance I fled, M. de Pachmann being imminent; and I have only to add that the place has a successful air, and that the ventilation is much better upstairs than down.

23 August 1889

ONE cannot be always chronicling promenade concerts, even in August and September. As there is nothing else to chronicle just now, I am thrown back for matter on the letters of my correspondents, and on the general resources of my intellect. In busy times I often wonder whether the gentlemen who take the trouble to write to me about musical affairs ever have their breath taken away by the calmness with which their information is, without the slightest acknowledgment, appropriated and retailed in this column as an original product of the vast factory in which my brain machinery works up the raw material of my experience. Let me explain to them, however, that when their information arrives, I sometimes know already, and sometimes know better.

One epistolarian who went to the "classical night" at Covent Garden on Wednesday, found that the audience liked Herr Friedheim's pianizing better than Mozart's G minor symphony. Indignant thereat, he waited in the hope that the thunders of The Star would avenge Mozart. But he was disappointed; for I did not go to that concert. Why? Because I foresaw that the symphony would, in the words of my correspondent, be "hardly cheered at all." A Mozart symphony at a promenade concert never is cheered except by a few mistaken devotees, who are jealous for the supremacy of the classical masterpieces. But your even Christian wisely declines to cheer, voting the thing as vapid as flat soda water. Give him, he says, something rousing, something warm and alive, something with substance and entrails in it: a rattling selection from Doris, or a solo by Mr Howard Reynolds that makes his diaphragm vibrate. And he is quite right. His is honest love of music sincerely seeking a genuine gratification. As such it is far more respectable and hopeful than the "culture" that pretends to relish the insipid classic it thinks it ought to like, and with which it is inwardly utterly disappointed.

So then, cries Culture, the low nature of the creature is confessed at last. Corno di Bassetto is a Philistine: he thinks classical music insipid, and prefers cornet solos! Good Mr Culture, be honest. It is you and such as you with your hypocrisies and affectations that keep sham classical performances in countenance. Do you suppose that when the orchestral parts of a Mozart symphony are placed before a body of players who can fiddle off the notes without hesitating, there is nothing more to be done than to set up somebody to beat one-two-three-four, and then let every player rip ahead? Apparently you do; for you pay for it and pretend to like it. What is more, you turn up your nose at the people whom you take for novices because they will not join in your humbug, and who, for all you know, may be experts, aware that the random shots of the orchestra are flying as wide of Mozart's intention as a school-girl's shot at the Pathetic Sonata flies wide of Beethoven. Do you really believe that the verdict of a hundred years on Mozart has come from a packed jury of pretenders to culture? If you do, then nothing can be done except leave you to your chance of some day hearing a Mozart symphony played as Mozart meant it to be played. You will applaud with a will then; and you will find plenty of others to help you. In the meantime, kindly recollect that applauding what you dont like is only one out of a great many ways of telling a lie.

By the way, my correspondent must not take these scathing rebukes to himself unless he deserves them. I have no reason to class him with the race of culture humbugs. But this subject of Mozart circuitously reminds me of a viper who has bitten me in a weekly paper—a Sunday paper too. Last Sabbath morning a relative threw me into a paroxysm of fury by reading aloud a paragraph in which the writer asked would I be surprised to learn something. This is an insult—an intentional insult. No matter what it is that I would be surprised to learn, that way of putting it breathes envy, disparagement, rancour, belittlement, and intolerable assumption of superior knowledge. No, sir: I am not surprised to learn that you are quite satisfied that everything that was done at the Bayreuth Festival playhouse when Wagner was alive was done exactly according to his intentions. That is just what I should have expected from a man capable of so injuriously reflecting on a colleague who never injured him.

I ask—addressing myself to the intelligent and well-disposed *alone*—I ask what mortal reason there is for assuming that Wagner ever succeeded in getting one single detail of Parsifal done at Bayreuth to his entire satisfaction? When a lyric dramatist carefully writes a stage direction which clearly suggests a very happy effect, and the attempt to carry it out on the stage utterly fails to realize that effect, am I to be told that the failure is exactly what the composer meant, because he, too, had to put up with it?

Wagner was in a dilemma at Bayreuth. Early in his career he had been disheartened by the inanity of the conventional performances of Mozart's instrumental works; and he had been hugely delighted with the way in which the orchestra of the Paris Conservatoire executed Beethoven's last and greatest symphony. In Mozart's case nothing had come down concerning the composer's own manner of conducting except a tradition that he was extraordinarily exacting in point of expression, and that the orchestras of his time found it hard to play some of his allegros fast enough to please him. Furthermore, his scores contain very scanty indications of how they are to be dealt with. In Paris, on the other hand, the Conservatoire orchestra kept alive an exhaustive treatment of the Ninth Symphony, formed, in the first instance, by three seasons' dogged rehearsal under Habeneck. Warned by these striking instances, negative and and positive, of the value of tradition, he naturally set great store by the establishment of an exceptionally authoritative one for his own works. He not only filled his scores with marks of expression, but contrived at last to build a special theatre for typical performances of his lyric dramas. At that theatre accordingly the artists are in possession of a mass of authentic tradition, the value of which is considerable in the prevalent scarcity of original interpretative talent. But the difficulty is that the tradition includes all the shortcomings as well as the excellencies of the representations personally superintended by Wagner. Every practical artist knows that such shortcomings are, under existing circumstances, inevitable, even when cash does not run short, as it did at the first Bayreuth Festival in 1876. It is therefore perfectly legitimate to appeal to the directions in Wagner's score as against the Bayreuth traditional practice, and perfectly unreasonable to call my omniscience in question for doing so.

Reverting for a moment to the question of cornet performances, I wish the musical ambition which that instrument undeniably inspires in the breast of amateurs were better guided than at present. I am not now speaking of the drawing-room amateur, who ought promptly to be converted into a lethal chamber amateur, but to the members of the brass bands of the volunteer corps, Salvation Army, the police force, and the musicians who play in the clubs of working men, or accompany them in demonstrations. There is no artistic limit to the ambition of a wind band: it may discourse as fine music as any orchestra, and in as worthy a manner. I do not see why we should not in time have in each of our parks a wind band at least a hundred and twenty strong, playing transcriptions of the works of the greatest masters, and educating the people out of their present meek submission to trashy quicksteps and music-hall tunes.

I imagine that the difficulty of getting good bandmasters is a more formidable obstacle to improvement than the costliness of good instruments; for I notice that even in pretentious volunteer bands the men do not seem to have been shewn how to make the most of such instruments as they have. The notes produced by the pistons are often horribly out of tune, because the tuning slides have not been adjusted, the guilty performer not knowing the use of them. In processioning and demonstrating bands, execrable villians with brass instruments are allowed to "vamp": that is, improvise their parts by feeling for a few of the simplest diatonic harmonies, and grunting them out on the off-chance of their fitting in. During a march in the key of G they play F natural and C in alternate bars, occasionally hastily trying B flat when seized with a momentary misgiving that all is

not well. I have not space to enlarge on the subject this
week; but I think I shall return to it some of these days; for
the brass band is really the music of the masses. I remember
once making an impassioned speech from the balustrade of
Trafalgar Square with a band playing the Marseillaise in
four different keys close behind me. That is the sort of thing
that makes a critic thoroughly in earnest about his work.

24 August 1889

THE managers at Her Majesty's kindly sent me a ticket for
Thursday night to hear a young lady of nine play the violin.
I prefer not to be an accomplice in the exploitation of young
ladies of nine, so I did not go until the following night, when
classical doings were afoot. Signor Bevignani's orchestra has
settled down into the most charming drawing-room orchestra
conceivable at a promenade concert. It has no force; but it
is polite and delicate, and can put in the touches for wood
wind and horns into a Mendelssohn symphony or a Mozart
accompaniment with the gentlest of breaths. It was, of
course, not within ten tons of the weight of the Zauberflöte
overture; but not at Bayreuth itself was the Meistersinger
prize song more sweetly accompanied. M. de Pachmann also
played very prettily. The whole atmosphere was pre-Wagner,
reminding one of Mendelssohn and Spohr and the Prince
Consort. Also, perhaps, of Poole and Lincoln and Bennett.
I was glad, for the honor of a once famous name, when Miss
Marie Tietjens, whom I had not heard before, sang *Vedrai
carino* quite unexceptionally, with a voice still fragile, and
hardly quite formed yet in the middle, but of remarkably
pure and pleasant tone and perfect intonation. To Mr
Holman Black, who attempted the serenade from Don Giovanni, and came off rather nervously, I will just say that he
has learnt the song from an edition in which the words are
wrongly set, a very easy thing to do; for none of the English
editions, as far as I know, except Novello's, contain the
restorations of Mozart's phrasing to be found in Breitkopf

and Hartel's great edition. The lines *"Tu che il zucchero porte in mezzo core,"* are now really out of the question as Mr Black sings them. He will find, too, that the effect of the last bar of the song is not in the B, C, D which he makes so much of, but in the lower D. Fashionable baritones can make nothing of the song, because they sacrifice the middle of their voice to the top. When a composer uses the contrast between the upper and lower D—one of the most effective of vocal contrasts with a completely cultivated bass voice—they are at a loss. However, it is better to fail on the low note written by Mozart than to try for a high F sharp, as the fashion once was. Mr Black afterwards rashly sang a new setting of The Minstrel Boy by somebody bearing the illustrious name of Shelley. The audience took this rather in bad part, not unjustifiably; for the new tune was a commonplace march, much inferior to the old one. On the other hand, they encored Mr Lloyd rapturously in the Preislied from Die Meistersinger and in Alice, where art thou? and behaved handsomely to M. Tivadar Nachez, who fiddled, and to Mr Howard Reynolds. Among the announcements for this evening is "Mrs Shaw, the American Lady Whistler." I cannot make this out: if she is Mrs Shaw, how can she be Lady Whistler? Senor Albeniz takes the place of Mr de Pachmann as solo pianist.

30 August 1889

STILL promenading! I went to Covent Garden on Wednesday to hear the classical program, and to Her Majesty's on the previous Saturday to hear Mrs Shaw, who is not, after all, the American Lady Whistler, but an American lady whistler, which is not exactly the same thing. Mrs Shaw is a tall, dark, pleasantly-favored woman, with a good deal of cheek, not too chubby, but just slack enough to allow plenty of play to her lips. After the manner of her countrywomen, she travels with enormous wreaths and baskets of flowers, which are handed to her at the conclusion of her pieces. And no matter how often this happens, she is never a whit the less astonished to see the flowers come up.

They say that the only artist who never gets accustomed to his part, is the performing flea who fires a cannon, and who is no less dismayed and confounded by the three-hundredth report than by the first. Now it may be ungallant, coarse, brutal even; but whenever I see a fair American thrown into raptures by her own flower-basket, I always think of the flea thrown into convulsions by its own cannon. And so, dear but silly American ladies, be persuaded, and drop it. Nobody except the very greenest of greenhorns is taken in; and the injury you do to your artistic self-respect by condescending to take him in is incalculable. Just consider for a moment how insanely impossible it is that a wreath as big as a cart-wheel could be the spontaneous offering of an admiring stranger.

If these persuasions do not avail, sterner methods must be taken. The public can protect themselves by organization. There is—or was—an institution called the Playgoers' Club. Some day I shall get up an affiliated Society of Hissers and Hooters, whose mission it will be to attend "first appearances" in force, and hiss all bogus demonstrations until the sight of a basket of flowers becomes more dreadful to a debutante than any fear of a cold reception could possibly be. However, I shall not leave my Society plunged for ever in the barbarism from which hissing and hooting survive. It is a savage thing to assail a possibly nervous artist with fierce sibillations and booings. At a well-conducted public meeting a gentle, but very expressive murmur of "Oh! oh!" is quite sufficient to bring to his senses a speaker who says or does anything unbecoming. My club shall be trained to "Oh! Oh!" like cooing doves at a first offence. Only persistent wrong-doing will be dealt with by hissing, or, in the last extremity, by brickbats.

But to return to Mrs Shaw. I cannot say that her performance astonished me. Indeed, when I had conquered my first impulse to laugh at the oddity of this novel prima donna gravely whistling Arditi's Il Bacio to the orchestral accompaniment, I began to entertain serious thoughts of going into the business myself. I am by no means an exceptionally gifted whistler; but at the very first trial I found that I could get within a sixteenth of a semitone of B natural, which is apparently Mrs Shaw's highest note. As to *Il Bacio*, with its pretty but easy and trumpery bravura, who could not whistle that? Now if Mrs Shaw had whistled the waltz from Gounod's Romeo, or the Shadow Song from Dinorah, there would have been something in the feat. The audience seemed hugely amused and delighted; but unless Mrs Shaw can greatly surpass her performance of Saturday, any demand her success may create for lady whistlers is sure to bring forward a dozen equally brilliant performers.

As far as my knowledge of whistling goes there are two methods open to the virtuoso. One, Mrs Shaw's method and mine, is to whistle with the lips and tongue. This produces the best results as far as purity and flexibility are concerned. The other, which totally baffles me, but which comes naturally to a talented friend of mine, is to open a corner of the mouth, tuck it under the ear, and whistle through the back teeth. The tone produced is penetrating in quality, and will attract the attention of a disengaged cabman at a great distance. Mrs Shaw makes no use of this method even in *forte* passages, perhaps because it is somewhat lacking in facial beauty. On the whole, my verdict upon her is that she lacks sustaining power and volume of tone, and that Il Bacio is not a sufficiently arduous test to entitle her to claim a first-class as a florid whistler. As a further test, I should suggest the performance by some competent singer of the final air from L'Etoile du Nord, with the double flute obbligato by Mr Barretti and Mrs Shaw. But in order to make the comparison fair, Mr Barrett must wear a corset sufficiently powerful to deprive him of at least half his natural lung capacity.

I invite the attention of the Covent Garden orchestra to the fact that they are completely beaten at Her Majesty's in point of style and discipline. The spirit of Costa is still abroad there. On this particular whistling Saturday I heard hardly any blunders: a more alert and conscientious band could not have been desired at a promenade concert. Their performance of the Masaniello overture was brilliant—so brilliant, in fact, that Signor Bevignani lost his head over it and spoiled the coda by first letting it run away with him, and then running away with it. The audience recognized the success at once; for, stupidly as the mere bar loafers at these concerts keep up a foolish and mechanical round of applause and encores for everything, good or bad, you hear the difference at once when the clapping is taken up by the people who only applaud when they know why.

At Covent Garden on Wednesday I heard the Lost Chord with the orchestral accompaniment which Madame Antoinette Sterling eschewed after her first experience of it at the Crystal Palace. The scoring of the last verse wants grandeur of tread: it does not march; and much of the effect is lost in consequence. Madame Belle Cole—well, I hardly like to say why Madame Belle Cole's voice is less free and resonant than it was. But how is the importance of physical training for singers to be duly insisted on if critics shrink from personalities? The training of a champion wrestler, who is nothing if not eighteen stone, is one thing: the training of a vocalist is another; but both have, within certain limits, power to choose their own weight. For instance, no human being need weigh more than fourteen stone at most unless he or she pleases. I remember Tietjens as Fidelio and as Margaret; and I cannot help asking myself whether mischief such as she did to the poetry of the lyric drama by for years associating its heroines with monstrous obesity, is never to be rebuked or even noticed by a suffering public. Loth as I am to condemn a lady to drink nothing for two months except six gallons of boiling water per diem, yet there are circumstances which justify this extremity. I venture desperately to blurt out to Madame Belle Cole that if she continues to grow as she has grown since the middle of the

season, she will, in a few years, be quite fat. And fat spoils
artists. Look at Hans Richter, the greatest orchestral conductor we know. When he first came here with Wagner,
twelve years or so ago, he was only half as wide as he is now,
but he was twice as effective. Everybody whispers that
there is a falling off of late years. Alas! there is, on the contrary, a putting on, and that is the secret of the growing
impatience and incompleteness of his achievements. Macadam designed a little ring, through which he declared that a
stone must be small enough to pass before it was fit for
paving. The entrance to our concert platforms should be
guarded by a hoop of standard diameter—say six feet to
begin with—through which all the artists should be compelled to pass successively before taking part in the performance.

A new-comer at this Wednesday concert was the pianist,
Madame Roger-Miclos, who played Beethoven's comparatively youthful C minor concerto: a curious selection for
such an occasion. She is a swift, accurate, steely fingered
player, who can make a scale passage sound as if it were
made by a dexterous whipcut along the keyboard. I admire
Madame Roger-Miclos much as I admire the clever people
who write a hundred and eighty words a minute with a
typewriter. Her classic Madame de Stael draperies suited
her slim figure, Egyptian profile, and cold style. She was the
only artist who came off without a mishap. When Madame
Belle Cole repeated the last two verses of the Lost Chord,
in response to an encore, the wood wind got a bar before her
at the start. When Mr Barrington Foote came forth to sing
Nazareth, the band, insufficiently instructed as to the transposition required, began simultaneously in two different
keys. Mdlle. Colombati, attempting to sing *Batti, batti* on
the most superficial acquaintance with it, strayed into the
second verse during the first, and caused Signor Arditi to
turn with a shiver of agony and rage and prompt her by
bursting into song himself. His voice, a counter tenor, has
a gooselike quality which is startlingly effective. Mr Foote

tried to drown the trombone, but was easily overcrowed by Mr Hadfield.

6 September 1889

I NOTICE that my respected colleagues speak with humble submission, and even with approval, of the intention attributed to Madame Wagner, of reserving the right of performing Parsifal for Bayreuth exclusively. In other words, the whole world is to be robbed of one of its most precious heirlooms for the glorification of a stupid little Bavarian town about as large as Notting Hill-gate and its neighborhood. Such a report, if I believed it, would almost reconcile me to the custom of suttee. As it happens, I do not believe it; but I am none the less amazed at the frame of mind which can accept it as tamely as if such a monstrous exercise of the rights of property were perfectly natural and proper. It is bad enough that such rights should, under any circumstances, be vested in an irresponsible private person; but the mere suggestion of enclosing Parsifal for the autumnal sport of a few thousand tourists and journalists ought to elicit a vehement protest from the exponents of musical opinion from one end of Europe to the other. It is not for Madame Wagner to say where or by whom any of Wagner's works shall be performed, except that she may reasonably insist on having, besides her royalties, some guarantee that the performances will be of sufficient merit to maintain the commercial prestige of the copyright. The rest is between us and our artistic consciences.

The whole tendency to make Beyreuth an occidental Mecca ought to be resisted tooth and nail in England. The English people have little enough part in fashionable opera in London, with its guinea stalls; but Covent Garden is a people's palace compared with Bayreuth, to witness a single performance at which costs a Londoner at least five days' absence and £12 out of pocket. Such luxuries concern the ordinary Englishman about as much as the Criterion five-shilling dinner concerns the docker on strike. Madame Wagner ought to disestablish Bayreuth, and urge all the Wagner societies to get Parsifal performed in their own countries.

I see by a stray paragraph that Blondin has an orchestrion, or high-class automatic barrel organ, to which he loves to listen whilst it grinds out hundreds of operatic selections. Once upon a time I looked on these machines with a placid contempt which, like that of a Low Church divine for the theatre, excluded even the curiosity necessary to stimulate me to take steps to hear one play. At last I happened to dine with a man who, after dinner, asked me would I like some music. I secretly mistrusted his intentions (the most unlikely sort of men will sometimes pull out a cornet or concertina, or call upon you for the accompaniment to When other lips), but, of course, I politely said Yes, as he expected me to. "Will you have Dinorah, or national airs?" said he. I hastily declared for Dinorah. Then he took what looked like a thick roll of wall paper into the next room. Presently Dinorah started, and he came back with an air of modest elation. The machine really performed very handsomely. It phrased with almost affected elegance, and made pauses and ritardandos and accelerandos in the most natural manner. The tone was sweet and low: an excellent thing in orchestrions after dinner; but it occasionally asserted itself with strenuous majesty. Since then I have had much more respect for music machines; and I no longer wonder at Madame Patti delighting in one at her burglar-proof castle in Wales.

I wonder why our theatre managers do not get their music done by machinery. Usually the high-class theatre orchestra is like a threadbare garment, full of holes, parts left out, harmonies incomplete, the thread of melody thin and ineffectual, the whole impression paltry and timid. The inferior theatre orchestra is music-hally, blatant, thumping, out of tune. If I were an actor-manager I would announce an "invisible orchestra," as at Bayreuth and the Criterion, and invest in an orchestrion. In melodramas I would start the accompanying slow music myself by a button placed under

my foot on the stage, exactly as the captains of penny steam-
boats have worked the engine-room signals since the abolition of riparian call-boys. Of course, if the suggestion were
generally adopted some thousands of instrumentalists would
have to go down to the docks for a living; but then that is
our established way of making progress: always over somebody's body.

An obbligato to a song is rather a questionable advantage
to a singer. On Monday last I happened to look in at Her
Majesty's. Presently out came Mr Howard Reynolds, looking so like the champion of England, and Mr Reginald
Groome, looking so like the master of the ceremonies, that I
half expected an exhibition of gold belts and an invitation to
buy one of Mr Reynolds's handkerchiefs for a sovereign.
However, what actually ensued was Balfe's ancient, absurd,
and charming "In this old chair my father sat," with cornet
obbligato. It was rather a pretty performance: Mr Groome
was soft and sentimental, and Mr Reynolds merciful. But
it happened that the cornet had the last word in the little
ritornel which ends the song; and when Mr Reynolds came
to the penultimate note he lifted up his cornet and blew two
of the most terrific blasts that have been heard on earth since
Jericho fell. His pent-up opinion of the human voice and of
Balfe thus let loose, he retired with the greatest gravity, followed by the deafened tenor, who kept his countenance admirably, and looked quite pleased and amiable.

Besides Mr Reynolds, no less than three virtuosi performed. There was Mrs Shaw, who again gave us Il Bacio,
with fuller tone than on the first occasion. Mrs Shaw's main
secret is that she whistles in tune. It is true that there are
not many public performers who habitually sing and play
falsely enough to justify one in saying that they are out of
tune; but between that and being in tune lies generally the
whole difference between a very ordinary singer and a very
successful one. I remember once going to a music hall to see
a very clever juggler. Before the juggler came a gentleman
who sang a song which made brutal fun of a particularly

painful divorce case then proceeding. But he sang in tune, and with a quick sense of the lilt and swing of the refrain. After the juggler came a lady who ridiculed the higher education of women by presenting herself in a chintz sunbonnet and spectacles, and singing an inane composition entitled Dr Mary Walker. She, too, could sing in tune in a high ringing voice, with engaging impetuosity of rhythmic movement. Her name, if my memory serves me aright, was Bellwood, and the gentleman was hight Macdermott. They were the only two artists whose songs did not bore my neighbors, by whom, strange to say, their success seemed to be attributed to their vulgarity. This was obviously a mistake: they had no monopoly of vulgarity. They *had* a monopoly of singing musically (comparatively speaking), and that was the true secret of their success.

M. Tivadar Nachez, the violinist at Her Majesty's, has gained his success in quite the opposite way to Miss Bellwood. He plays some easy affair like Raff's cavatina with the air of a man who is making a masterly conquest of untold difficulties, the members of the orchestra, who know better, looking on the while with mingled feelings. An encore follows, and he thereupon plays a bravura piece as fast as he can bow it. He has, of course, very little time to spend in aiming at the exact pitch of the notes; but he seems well satisfied when he gets within half a semitone of the bull's eye. But in my opinion a miss is as good as a mile at work of this sort; and I do not see why M. Nachez should come all the way from Spain to do what plenty of our native violinists can, if they try in earnest, do quite as badly. Senor Albeniz, the pianist, though a finer artist, is content to achieve similar feats under the easier conditions of an instrument which takes care of the intonation for him. His playing of harpsichord music is prodigiously swift and dainty; but it gives no gauge of his capacity for serious playing.

LONDON MUSIC IN 1888–89

LAST Saturday evening, feeling the worse for want of change and country air, I happened to voyage in the company of Mr William Archer as far as Greenwich. Hardly had we inhaled the refreshing ozone of that place for ninety seconds when, suddenly finding ourselves opposite a palatial theatre, gorgeous with a million gaslights, we felt that it was idiotic to have been to Wagner's Theatre at Bayreuth and yet be utterly ignorant concerning Morton's Theatre at Greenwich. So we rushed into the struggling crowd at the doors, only to be informed that the theatre was full. Stalls full; dress circle full; pit, standing room only. As Archer, in self-defence, habitually sleeps during performances, and is subject to nightmare when he sleeps standing, the pit was out of the question. Was there room anywhere, we asked. Yes, in a private box or in the gallery. Which was the cheaper? The gallery, decidedly. So up we went to the gallery, where we found two precarious perches vacant at the side. It was rather like trying to see Trafalgar Square from the knifeboard of an omnibus half-way up St Martin's Lane; but by hanging on to a stanchion, and occasionally standing with one foot on the seat and the other on the backs of the people in the front row, we succeeded in seeing as much of the entertainment as we could stand.

The first thing we did was to purchase a bill, which informed us that we were in for "the entirely original pastoral comedy-opera in three acts, by B. C. Stephenson and Alfred Cellier, entitled Dorothy, which has been played to crowded houses at the Lyric Theatre, London, 950 and (still playing) in the provinces 788 times." This playbill, I should add, was thoughtfully decorated with a view of the theatre showing all the exits, for use in the event of the performance proving unbearable. From it we further learnt that we should be regaled by an augmented and powerful orchestra; that the company was "Leslie's No. 1"; that C. J. Francis believes he is now the only HATTER in the county of Kent who exists on the profits arising solely from the sale of HATS and CAPS; and so on. Need I add that Archer and I sat bursting with expectation until the overture began.

I cannot truthfully say that the augmented and powerful orchestra proved quite so augmented or so powerful as the composer could have wished; but let that pass: I disdain the cheap sport of breaking a daddy-long-legs on a wheel (butterfly is out of the question, it was such a dingy band). My object is rather to call attention to the condition to which 788 nights of Dorothying have reduced the unfortunate wanderers known as "Leslie's No. 1." I submit to Mr Leslie that in his own interest he should take better care of No. 1. Here are several young persons doomed to spend the flower of their years in mechanically repeating the silliest libretto in modern theatrical literature, set to music which, pretty as it is, must pall somewhat on the seven hundred and eighty-eighth performance.

As might have been expected, a settled weariness of life, an utter perfunctoriness, an unfathomable inanity pervaded the very souls of "No. 1." The tenor, originally, I have no doubt, a fine young man, but now cherubically adipose, was evidently counting the days until death should release him from the part of Wilder. He had a pleasant speaking voice; and his affability and forbearance were highly creditable to him under the circumstances; but Nature rebelled in him against the loathed strains of a seven hundred-times repeated rôle. He omitted the song in the first act, and sang Though Born a Man of High Degree as if with the last rally of an energy decayed and a willing spirit crushed. The G at the end was a vocal earthquake. And yet methought he was not displeased when the inhabitants of Greenwich, coming fresh to the slaughter, encored him.

The baritone had been affected the other way: he was thin and worn; and his clothes had lost their lustre. He sang Queen of My Heart twice in a hardened manner, as one who was prepared to sing it a thousand times in a thousand quarter hours for a sufficient wager. The comic part, being simply that of a circus clown transferred to the lyric stage, is better suited for infinite repetition; and the gentleman who undertook it addressed a comic lady called Priscilla as Sarsaparilla during his interludes between the haute-école acts of the prima donna and tenor, with a delight in the rare aroma of the joke, and in the roars of laughter it elicited, which will probably never pall. But anything that he himself escaped in the way of tedium was added tenfold to his unlucky colleagues, who sat out his buffooneries with an expression of deadly malignity. I trust the gentleman may die in his bed; but he would be unwise to build too much on doing so. There is a point at which tedium becomes homicidal mania.

The ladies fared best. The female of the human species has not yet developed a conscience: she will apparently spend her life in artistic self-murder by induced Dorothitis without a pang of remorse, provided she be praised and paid regularly. Dorothy herself, a beauteous young lady of distinguished mien, with an immense variety of accents ranging from the finest Tunbridge Wells English (for genteel comedy) to the broadest Irish (for repartee and low comedy), sang without the slightest effort and without the slightest point, and was all the more desperately vapid because she suggested artistic gifts wasting in complacent abeyance. Lydia's voice, a hollow and spectral contralto, alone betrayed the desolating effect of perpetual Dorothy: her figure retains a pleasing plumpness akin to that of the tenor; and her spirits were wonderful, all things considered. The chorus, too, seemed happy; but that was obviously because they did not know any better. The pack of hounds darted in at the end of the second act evidently full of the mad hope of finding something new going on; and their depression, when they discovered it was Dorothy again, was pitiable. The S.P.C.A. should interfere. If there is no law to protect men and women from Dorothy, there is at least one that can be strained to protect dogs.

I did not wait for the third act. My companion had

several times all but fallen into the pit from sleep and heaviness of spirit combined; and I felt as if I were playing Geoffrey Wilder for the millionth night. As we moped homeward in the moonlight we brooded over what we had seen. Even now I cannot think with composure of the fact that they are playing Dorothy tonight again—will play it tomorrow—next year—next decade—next century. I do not know what the average lifetime of a member of "No. 1" may be; but I do not think it can exceed five years from the date of joining; so there is no question here of old men and old women playing it with white hair beneath their wigs and deep furrows underlying their make-up. Doubtless they do not die on the stage: they first become mad and are removed to an asylum, where they incessantly sing, One, two, three: one, two, three: one, two, three: one, two, be wi-eyes in, ti-I'm oh, Ph-ill is, mine, etc., until the King of Terrors (who ought to marry Dorothy) mercifully seals their tortured ears for ever.

I have always denounced the old-fashioned stock company, and laughed to scorn the theorists who fancy that they saw in them a training school for actors; but I never bargained for such a thing as this 789th performance of Dorothy. No: it is a criminal waste of young lives and young talents; and though it may for a time make more money for Mr Leslie, yet in the end it leaves him with a worn-out opera and a parcel of untrained novices on his hands when he might have a repertory of at least half a dozen works and a company of fairly-skilled artists able to play them at a day's notice. We exclaim at the dock directors' disregard of laborers' bodies; but what shall we say of the managers' disregard of artists' souls. Ti, rum ti ty, rum ti ty, rum ti ty, rum m m: tiddy tum tiddy tum tiddity, tum! Heavens! what hum I? Be wi-eyes in—Malediction!

LONDON MUSIC IN 1888-89

20 *September* 1889

SINCE Monday, when I saw Offenbach's Brigands at the
Avenue Theatre, I have been trying to make up my mind
whether I run any serious risk of being damned for preferring
the profligacy of Offenbach, Meilhac, and Halévy to the
decorum of Cellier and the dulness of Stephenson. Perhaps
an item more or less in the account can make no very great
difference to me personally; but I warn others solemnly that
Offenbach's music is wicked. It is abandoned stuff: every
accent in it is a snap of the fingers in the face of moral
responsibility: every ripple and sparkle on its surface twits
me for my teetotalism, and mocks at the early rising of
which I fully intend to make a habit some day.

In Mr Cellier's scores, music is still the chastest of the
Muses. In Offenbach's she is—what shall I say?—I am
ashamed of her. I no longer wonder that the Germans came
to Paris and suppressed her with fire and thunder. Here in
England how respectable she is! Virtuous and rustically
innocent her 6-8 measures are, even when Dorothy sings
"Come, fill up your glass to the brim!" She learnt her morals
from Handel, her ladylike manners from Mendelssohn, her
sentiment from the Bailiff's Daughter of Islington. But
listen to her in Paris, with Offenbach. Talk of 6-8 time:
why, she stumbles at the second quaver, only to race off
again in a wild Bacchanalian, Saturnalian, petticoat spurn-
ing, irreclaimable, shocking cancan. Nothing but the wit of
a Frenchman shining through the chinks in the materialism
of English comic opera artists could make such music endurable and presentable at the same time.

When Mr Gilbert translated Les Brigands for Messrs
Boosey, years ago, he must have said to himself: "This
Meilhac-Halévy stuff is very funny; but I could do it just as
well in English; and so I would too, if only I could find an
English Offenbach." In due time he did find his Offenbach
in Sir Arthur Sullivan. Accordingly, when Falsacappa the
brigand chief exclaims: "Marry my daughter to an honest

226

man! NEVER!" we are not surprised to recognize in him a missing link in the ancestry of the Pirate King of Penzance. The relationship of the carbineers to the policemen is too obvious to be worth dwelling on; but there are other ties between the two phases of musical farce. The extremely funny song in the second act, *Nous avons, ce matin, tous deux,* is closely allied to When I First put this Uniform on in Patience; and the opening chorus *Deux par deux ou bien par trois* is first cousin to Carefully on Tiptoe Stealing in H.M.S. Pinafore.

I cannot, however, suppose that Mr Gilbert's objection to the use of his libretto was founded on an idiotic desire to appear "original." The people who regard the function of a writer as "creative" must surely be the most illiterate of dupes. The province of the fictionist is a common which no man has a right to enclose. I cultivate that common myself; and when someone claims to have grown a new plant there, different from all the rest, I smile sardonically, knowing that the selfsame plant grows in all our plots, and grew there before he was born. And when he discovers in my plot a plant which he has raised in his own or seen in his neighbor's, and thereupon cries out, "Stop, thief! Stop, plagiarist! Stop, picker of other men's brains!" I only smile the widelier. What are brains for, if not to be picked by me and the rest of the world? In my business I know *me* and *te*, but not *meum* and *tuum*.

Mr Gilbert's book as played at the Avenue is much nearer in spirit to the original than Henry Leigh's. Leigh's lyrics sometimes flowed more smoothly than Mr Gilbert's; but his libretti were silly and raffish: the fun too often degenerated into tedious tomfoolery: his feeble and fleshy whimsicalities are inferior in grit and sparkle to even the most perfunctory paradoxes of Mr Gilbert. His Royal Horse Marines, commanded by Marshal Murphi, and his brigands Jacksheppardo, Dickturpino, and Clauduvallo, only shew how French wit of no very high order can yet be degraded by translation into English fun. The horse-collar bar-loafing buffoonery is not in the least like the genuine Meilhac and Halévy *opera bouffe*, in which the characters, primarily persons of engaging culture, reasonableness, amiability, and address, are made irresistibly ridiculous by an exquisite folly, an impossible frivolity of motive, which exhibit them as at once miracles of wit and sensibility and monsters of moral obtuseness. Mr Gilbert has given us the English equivalent of this in his own operas; and a curiously brutalized, embittered, stolidified, middle-classical, mechanical equivalent it is; but the essential wit and incongruity are preserved. In translating Les Brigands, he naturally did not wholly miss these qualities; though, oddly enough, his version makes hardly anything of a couple of points which might have been expected to appeal specially to him: to wit, the family sentiment of Falsacappa, and the conscientious scruples of Fiorella on the subject of robbing handsome young men (just as the Pirates of Penzance drew the line at orphans).

As to the performance at the Avenue, I do not grudge the admission that Messrs Van Biene and Lingard's company is a good one as provincial companies go. But as companies for the performance of Offenbach's operas *ought* to go, in the provinces and elsewhere, its members are as babes and sucklings playing at Meilhac and Halévy in the nursery. The orchestra is not large enough, not dainty enough, not immoral enough to supply that inimitable effervescence which is the great achievement of Offenbach in orchestration. In the second act, the Princess of Grenada, entering with Gloria-Cassis and her suite, should look like the court in Ruy Blas, grave, punctilious, an assembly of etiquette ridden grandees, with their appearance in the wildest contradiction to the Spanish dance rhythm movement of *Jadis vous n'avez qu'un patrie* (transferred at the Avenue from Gloria-Cassis to the Princess, Miss Marie Luella, who caught the musical intention of the song perfectly and brought down the house with it). The only point attempted was by Mr Maurice de Solla, who made himself up as Gloria-Cassis into an exact likeness of Mr Robert

Browning! In the name of Sordello, why?

The third act depends altogether on Antonio, the ancient treasurer of the Duke of Mantua, who has squandered the contents of the treasury on his love-affairs. His song, *O mes amours, O mes maitresses!* with its refrain, *Vi'a-a! Vl'a-a! Vl' a mon caractère*, ending in falsetto on high D, is the most important number in the act. At the Avenue it is omitted, the part being taken by a gentleman who presumably cannot sing, and who seems to have derived his ideas of character acting from the antics of Lurcher in Dorothy. Undaunted by Mr Gilbert, he "gagged" the line about the sundries in his accounts, and gagged it so senselessly that Mr Gilbert would only have pitied him and passed on. Under these circumstances the act was even less worth waiting for than the third act of a farcical performance usually is. Years ago, somewhere or other, I saw Mr Edward Royce, of Gaiety fame, double a brigand's part with that of Antonio very cleverly indeed. I wish he had been at the Avenue on Monday.

Falsacappa was gigantically impersonated by a Mr Hallen Mostyn, who sings so noisily that he cannot hear what key the orchestra is playing in, and so, though his ear is sound enough, occasionally sings in a different one. The whole company did this at one place (where a cut had been newly restored) for about 15 bars in the first act. Serve them right, say I, for scamping their work in the provinces with their cuts! The vocal forces were economized by knocking the parts of Campotasso and the carbineer captain into one; but as a set-off the Princess's part was made worthy of a prima donna by the aforesaid transfer of Gloria-Cassis's song to her. Fragoletto was originally a woman's part: such lines as *Nous avons pris ce petit homme: Il est tout petit, mais en somme*, etc., refer to the feminine proportions of the hero. However, the opera is all the better for the substitution of Mr Frank Wensley, who lilts *Falsacappa! voici ma prise* very prettily. Miss Delaporte is, I have no doubt, a capital Fiorella, now that she has had time to recover from the fatigue which a little oppressed her and veiled her voice on the first night. Fiorella, by the way, should not be announced in the bill as the sister of Falsacappa. Young women do not present their portraits to their brothers.

27 September 1889

THE 16th November will be a dreadful afternoon at the Crystal Palace Saturday concerts. It is to be devoted to Mendelssohn's St Paul. I suppose this would not occur unless there were people capable of enjoying such musical atavisms as nineteenth-century scriptural oratorios. There is no accounting for taste. In the last century people used to like sham Shakespear: tragedies in five acts and in blank verse, in which the hero, usually a compound of Macbeth, Richard III, and Iago, used to die declaiming "Whip me, ye grinning fiends" at the ghosts of his murdered victims. In the same way legions of organists and academy professors have turned out sham Handel for the use of festival committees anxious to vindicate themselves from the charge of neglecting English art. Now I grant that Mendelssohn is better than the organist, the professor, the Mus.Bac., and the Mus.Doc.; just as Tennyson is better than Cumberland or Colman. But compared with Handel he is what Tennyson is compared with Shakespear. If you are shocked at these sentiments, I challenge you to go to the Crystal Palace on 16th November; to set all that dreary fugue manufacture, with its Sunday-school sentimentalities and its Music-school ornamentalities, against your recollection of the expressive and vigorous choruses of Handel; and to ask yourself on your honor whether there is the slightest difference in kind between "Stone him to death" and "Under the pump, with a kick and a thump," in Dorothy. Then blame me, if you can, for objecting to the Palace people pestering mankind with Mendelssohnic St Pauls and Gounodic Redemptions and Parrysiac Judiths and the like, when one hardly ever hears Jephtha or a Bach cantata. But of what use is it to complain? If my cry were heeded, the Palace directors

230

would simply say: "Oh, he likes Handel, does he? How nice! We rather think we can meet his views in that direction." And they would straightway kidnap five or six thousand choristers; put Israel in Egypt into rehearsal; and treat me to a dose of machine thunder on the Handel orchestra. It would be utterly in vain: I should complain worse than ever: the machine thunder is as unimpressive as the noise of the thousand footsteps in Oxford St.

4 October 1889

IT is all but thirteen years since I went to the Lyceum Theatre one November evening to hear the Carl Rosa Company perform for the first time an opera by Mr Fred Cowen entitled Pauline (surnamed Deschapelles, of course). I was not then the lenient, almost foolishly goodnatured critic I have since become; and I am afraid I rather dropped into Mr Cowen over his opera. At that time it was the fashion to say that History repeats itself. At present it is the fashion to point out that it does not; but, however that may be, the fact remains that on Tuesday I received an invitation from Major Cockle to attend the dress rehearsal of his new opera The Castle of Como at the Opera Comique the same evening at half-past seven. Happening to have engagements of an unmusical nature for the first night, I eagerly seized the opportunity of escaping it, and so took care to be in the theatre punctually at a quarter to eight.

When I entered, I was much puzzled to find a huge orchestra thinly scraping through a minuet, which the composer was conducting in a state of the wildest excitement, occasionally stopping for a frantic altercation with the stage manager, who declared—as managers will—that it would be "all right tomorrow," an assurance with which the composer-conductor, mindful of the great truth that "tomorrow never comes," altogether declined to be satisfied. Claude Melnotte and Pauline were dancing the minuet conscientiously in a dingy apartment, whilst Monsieur Deschapelles slept on a

231

sofa. Presently, to my utter confusion, Pauline said she was going to marry her father; and Claude reproached her on the ground of a prior attachment, contracted when they were children together. M. Deschapelles then rose, and, declaring that he had overheard every word of their conversation, said, "You are a noble fellow" to Claude, and magnanimously withdrew in his favor and blessed the union of the young people. These transactions, conducted in language of wasting dreariness, drove me to appeal to my neighbor as to whether the opera was over, or whether they were taking the last act first. He told me it had not yet begun; that this was only a curtain-raiser; and that the excited conductor was Mr Milton Wellings. I gazed with inexpressible awe at the illustrious composer of Some Day; for I know as well as M. Dumas *fils* how much merit it takes to make even a small success. And I admire a man who is as desperately anxious about a hopelessly dull little piece to which he has written a dance tune as Wagner was about the 1876 Nibelungen performance at Bayreuth. *Sang froid* can be acquired: earnestness is the gift of the gods.

Here let me respectfully offer Mr Milton Wellings and the management a piece of advice which they will probably not take. Let them cut out the dialogue and the old man, and turn the curtain-raiser into a masque consisting either of the minuet alone or of a set of dances which Mr Milton Wellings can add. In the Jubilee year a masque was performed at Gray's Inn, with a success from which no manager has yet taken a hint. The dancers were amateurs, but the performance was interesting and pretty: much more so than the pedantries of the modern ballet, which presents the art of dancing at the very deepest depths of degradation. Pious people who are not ashamed to confess that they have never been to a theatre think the ballet indecent. Would it were! Just as a burglar, having some sort of rational human purpose in him, is a more hopeful subject than an idiot; so indecency is better than the blind stupidity which substitutes proficiency in a set of technical forms and feats for the attainment of beauty and significance, which are the true life of all art forms that really are alive. The ballet indecent! Why, it is the most formal, the most punctilious, ceremonious, professor-ridden, pig-headed solemnity that exists. Talk of your fugues, canons, key relationships, single and double counterpoint, fifty orthodox resolutions of the chord of the minor ninth and the rest of it! What are they to the *entrechats*, *battements*, *ronds de jambes*, *arabesques*, *élévations*, that are the stock-in-trade of the art of theatrical dancing? The man who said that the British bishop is unique had never met a ballet master or the president of an academy of music. I have often wondered that the essential identity of mental attitude presented by them has not opened Stewart Headlam's eyes to the fact that an ordinary ballet is no more a true dance than an ordinary Church of England service is a true act of worship.

Fortunately, public opinion is sound upon this matter. At one period of my chequered career I made a point of seeing every ballet produced at the Alhambra in order to study one of the most remarkable artistic institutions of the time. The virtuosity of the principal dancers was the result of a training of a severity and duration unknown among singers since Porpora taught Caffarelli. Even the rank and file were skilled to a degree unknown in opera choruses, and by no means common in orchestras. The grouping and coloring were thought out by real artists. A ballet called Yolande, produced about twelve years ago, when Aurelia Pertoldi was dancing her best, reached a standard of technical perfection which would have been received with astonished acclamation in any other art. Yet nobody of any intelligence cared two straws about the Alhambra. The brainless artificiality of the ballets was too much for the public. People went and stared; but the quality of the applause was always poor. I gave it up at last as a hopeless affair; and though it was not I who set fire to the old Alhambra, I stayed in Leicester Square nearly all night watching it burn without a pang of regret. Then, in 1885, came Excelsior at Her Maj-

esty's, the delightful dance in Mary Anderson's revival of A
Winter's Tale, and the Gray's Inn masque, all successful in
waking up the public love of dancing. In Excelsior two
dances caught the public: one executed by men in heavy
boots and spurs; the other a simple piece of shawl waving
and handkerchief fluttering (I could have done it myself) by
Miss Kate Vaughan, at whose success the unappreciated
pirouettists and entrechatists looked on as indignantly as an
organist who can write tonal fugues looks on at the success
of Mr Milton Well—. Bless my soul! that reminds me: I
have forgotten all about The Castle of Como. To business!

Well, as I was saying, Mr Cowen had to make Claude
Melnotte a baritone for the accommodation of Mr Santley,
who was then Carl Rosa's trump card. The tenor in Pauline
was Glavis. Major Cockle makes Glavis a contralto, and so
adds another woman-man monstrosity to the Maffio Orsinis,
Urbains, Siebels, Oscars, and Adrianos of the past. There are
duets, solos, declamatory recitatives instead of dialogue, choruses, ballets, wedding processions, visions, bells, orchestral
effects, and so on. Have I not often enough declared that these
things can be as easily manufactured by an intelligent man
with a musical turn as a shilling shocker by an idiot with a
literary turn? Major Cockle blazes away most courageously
with horse, foot, and artillery: strings, wind and drums,
taking his effects where he can get them, in the school of experience (of other people's works) after the eclectic fashion
of Max Bruch and M. Massenet. But the plan of listening to
twenty operas and then saying, "Go to: let us make a twenty-
first," though it may make a beginning for a composer, will
never make a reputation for him. And The Castle of Como
is such a beginning and nothing more. The orchestration,
handled in the coarsest Italian manner under Signor Coro-
naro, who forgot that the Opera Comique is not quite as
large as La Scala, and that his men are very rough performers indeed compared to those of Signor Faccio, is spirited
but not very adroit, the wood wind parts especially being
piled up in a heap in the most undistinguished fashion. The

notion of illustrating Claude's description of the "palace lifting to eternal summer" by an ill-contrived vision of a Mediterranean gambling hell, is a folly that will probably not survive the laughter of the first few representations. The principals are fairly competent as far as singing goes, which is as much as one can say at present for the raw levies of English opera.

Leaving The Castle of Como at the end of the second act, I was able to look in at the Avenue Theatre in time for Mr Solomon's musical version of The Area Belle. I do not know whether they measure and number a policeman like a hat, by adding his length to his breadth and halving the result; but unless they do, Mr Penley is not credible as a member of the police force. However, it is traditionally correct to have a very short policeman and a very tall soldier. Mr Solomon's tunes are neat, fluent, and lively; and when he interpolates a stave of The Girl I left behind me, the dramatic critics recognize it and hail it as a high contrapuntal achievement. But when Mr Penley, in the middle of a concerted piece, ridiculously warbled a line to the tune of Come into the garden, Maud, the allusion was, I noticed, too subtle: nobody laughed. I was sorry to see how new methods of education are sweeping old jokes into oblivion. The girl in the piece was called Penelope solely to give the soldier an opportunity of saying, "I love Penelope," and so provoking the policeman to retort, in the words of Lindley Murray, "Penelope is loved by me." Will it be believed that Mr Penley actually says, "*She* is loved by me"? I should have demanded my money back on the spot had I not been fascinated by Miss Alma Stanley's perfect intonation, excellent delivery of her words when singing, and the thorough and hearty care she took of her part. The ghost business—always a weak point in this funny old-fashioned farce—is much too long.

I have left myself too little space to speak of my trip to Camberwell on Monday to hear the South London Choral Association songfully illustrating a lecture on Mendelssohn by Mr F. G. Edwardes, organist of the St John's Wood Presbyterian Church. I cannot say that the part-songs had any relevance to the lecture beyond the fact that Mendelssohn composed them; and I should like to ask Mr Edwardes rather pointedly whether it is not time to leave off that Mendelssohn petting which is as essentially inappreciative as it is childishly uncritical and unintelligent. Surely we have suffered enough of it at the hands of Mr Bennett in the Daily Telegraph and Musical Times without having it perpetuated by younger men. But my main purpose in mentioning the occasion was to proclaim the excellence of Mr Venable's choir. The quality of sound produced was admirable: all tone and no noise; and its volume was so well under control that Mr Venables showed some disposition to shew it off, like an organist with a new swell shutter. I have no doubt, from the way Mr Gatehouse played part of the violin concerto, that he is a very capable leader for the Institute orchestra.

11 *October* 1889

On Thursday evening last week, something drew away my attention from the fact that I am The Star musical critic. I have recollected it only this moment, when it is too late to go anywhere in search of a performance to write about. Therefore there will be no column this week, as I have made up my mind resolutely to check my tendency to discursiveness, and confine myself to a simple direct account of current musical events. It is plain that people do not buy The Star to read about my private affairs and opinions; and since I have missed the Leeds Festival, whither I unquestionably ought to have gone, I had better hold my tongue until I have something to say. I really regret Leeds, not so much on account of the music as of the improving influence of all the oratorios and cantatas.

Just a word before I affix my signature. The gentleman who wrote to The Daily News insisting that tenors should sing in the register called falsetto (or "short reed," as Dr Morell Mackenzie calls it) has been promptly assailed by another gentleman, who reminds him that Mario and Jean de Reszke began as baritones. As Mario began without the advantage of my critical super-audition, I cannot say anything about him, except that he certainly ended as a baritone, and a bad one, at an age which left Mr Sims Reeves's voice pure and undiminished. De Reszke's baritone days I remember very well. He was by no means the deep powerful *basso cantante* his brother Edouard now is. Don Giovanni and Valentine in Faust were his best parts (though he was, of course, quite an immature Don): his voice was light, delicate, and of a charming quality; he was slim, and the handsomest young man I ever saw on the stage; and out of a score of Don Juans and Valentines he is the only one I specially remember. Nowadays he is a tenor, robust in person and method, still good-looking and distinguished, but, except when something wakes him up, comparatively —well, I do not like to say inane. Let us call it disillusioned.

And now, will Mr Palmer or Dr Morell Mackenzie, or some other expert, tell us what has happened, physiologically, to De Reszke's voice? The aerial upper register of the baritone is now the thick middle register of the tenor; and the change has been from less to greater power and vigor, and not the converse, as the change from baritone to tenor seems to have suggested to Mr Palmer's critic. Was the gain of an extra fourth at the top of his compass an incident in his physical growth, like the appearance of an eye tooth? Did the middle of his tenor voice, which was so much lighter and purer when it was the top of his baritone voice, change from a short reed or falsetto register to a long reed or chest one? Finally, can anyone explain how the trick is done? I am a baritone myself; but my disposition is so romantic that I have kept off the lyric stage because nearly all the romantic parts are written for tenors. Still, if De Reszke and Mario raised themselves from baritones to tenors, why should not I?

Though I loathe nothing more than the commonplace

that the truth always lies between the two extremes (truth being quite the most extreme thing I know of), I venture to suggest that the balance of advantage lies with singers who can use both registers effectively, and who have intelligent instincts of self-preservation to prevent them from forcing the long reed production above its safe limit. Mr Sims Reeves and his son, and Maas in his later days, are samples of Mr Palmer's system. So, in speaking, was Charles Mathews. They all saved their voices from coarsening, and from wear and tear; but they also sacrificed dramatic vigor to coddle their falsettos, and were insufferably lackadaisical except where the appropriate expression of the music fell within the limits of their method.

I heard Mathews play Used Up when he was so old that his throat was externally like wrinkled parchment; and I was struck with the perfect lightness and preservation of his voice. But in the last act, where Sir Charles Coldstream lifts up the cellar trap and sees the man whom he has, as he thinks, murdered, a vehement exclamation is required; and this Mathews could not manage, just as Maas, when playing Don Cæsar de Bazan, could not challenge the captain of the guard like a man, but warbled at him like a querulous dove. On the other hand, the plan of using the long reed production all over the voice destroys, first, the quality of the voice, then the power of adjusting the overstrained vocal cords to the right pitch, and finally the voice itself. Tietjens once warned a friend of mine against this in terms which shewed how keenly she felt its danger. Yet within a year or so she took up the contralto part of Leonora in La Favorita, and became such a slave to the practice she had denounced that she speedily became a mere wreck. Not long before her death I heard her in Fidelio. At the end of *Komm Hoffnung, lass den letzten Stern*, she, by a frantic effort, sang the B natural with her chest voice, or, at least—to use the Mackenzie terminology—with as long a reed as she could humanly bring to bear on it. During the rest of the opera she failed to get a single note in tune—and failed con-

238

sciously. A tragic hearing!

These terms, "long reed" and "short reed," are an improvement on the old "chest voice, head voice, falsetto," etc. Perhaps I should explain what "registers" are. Well, inquiring reader, your windpipe is furnished at the top with a pair of lips; and when you whistle with these lips instead of with your facial ones, the result is: singing. When you are whistling through their whole length and altering the pitch by lengthening or shortening the organ pipe formed by the back of your throat—a process involving only very slight modifications in the tension of these inner lips—you are singing with your chest voice, or *voce di petto*, or long reed register, whichever you please to call it. When you want to get up to notes which could be better produced if the lips were shorter and thinner, you perform a curious operation called changing the register: that is, you shut the lips at one end far enough to leave only the convenient length open, and with the "short reed" so left, you start again on a new plane, adjusting the length of the organ pipe as before. Then you are singing falsetto, or in *voce di gola*, or throat voice, or short reed register. The most striking example of change of register is when a man sings a low note in his natural voice and then another high up in imitation of a woman. This high voice is what used to be called *voce di testa* or head voice, before the names got so appallingly confused as they are at present. A more agreeable and subtle, but still very distinct contrast of registers may be heard whenever Madame Patey sings Beethoven's Creation's Hymn. The laryngoscope has proved that the old tradition of three voices, giving the sensation of coming from the chest, the throat, and the head respectively, had, in the registering mechanism, a foundation of physiological fact; but as to how many registers can be made, how many *should* be made, whether any at all ought to be made, whether the old names should be retained, which was which, and what practical conclusions the singing master should draw: on all these points there exist not only differences of opinion, but feuds—deadly, implacable vendettas—in which each party regards all the others as impostors, quacks, voice smashers, ignoramuses, rascals, and liars.

Somehow, musicians are amazingly ill-conditioned controversialists. They are almost as bad as scientific men: not quite so dogmatic or so insolent perhaps, but still equally void of good humor and sense of social solidarity with their opponents. Just as, in my boyish days, I hardly ever met a schoolmaster who seemed to know that he was as much bound to be polite to me as long as I behaved myself as to my father as long as he paid the bill, I seldom read a musical paper now without wondering whether the writers are as unmannerly in private life as they are in print. It is my schoolmaster over again. He had a notion that his whole duty was to know, or pretend to know, more about Euclid or Virgil than I; and the result was that his obvious limitation, incompleteness, and lack of social charm made me resolve to shun the mathematical and classical influences which had apparently made him what he was. And the musical papers seem to think that *their* whole duty is to know more about music than anybody else. If some unfortunate amateur calls a tuba a bassoon, or a sonata a symphony, they write of and to him as Colonel Newcombe (a pestilential humbug) spoke of and to the Hindoos.

Mr William O'Brien obeyed a right instinct when he told the people of Dublin to demand "that Irish music shall be heard and honored on Irish soil before the music of Italy or Germany." But the thing is impossible at present. The best modern music is the fruit of a complex culture which no Irishman can enjoy today in his own country. To honor Professor Villiers Stanford more than Wagner, or Balfe more than Mozart, is as impossible as to place Moore above Shelley, or Lever above Ibsen. If Ireland were to set about honoring Irish musicians tomorrow, what would she do? Would she go to the only class that is nationally alive: the peasantry, and give a wreath to the countryside lilter, or whistler, or piper, whose unwritten tunes made the best real music? Not a bit of it: she would go to the educated class—a class nationally dead, and artistically as sterile as Sodom and Gomorrah; pick out some plausible imitator of the hated foreigner; and then desperately pretend to think him a great Irish composer. Why, Mr O'Brien delivered this very speech in support of a concert-giver who made his reputation, not as an Irish singer under his real name of Ledwidge, but as an imitation Italian opera singer calling himself Mr Ludwig. It was not Ireland, but a lucky chance of escaping from Ireland under a foreign impresario (Carl Rosa), that made Mr Ludwig. Nations, like individuals, put off opera writing until they have got out of prison. Ireland has not reached the Wagnerian stage yet. I have been there; and I know.

18 *October* 1889

I NOTICE with alarm that the parties to the great music hall discussion are talking about "the want" of a censor for comic songs, as if that were something to be deplored. This is encouraging, hopeful, helpful, quite delightful. Reader: can you not hear my teeth gnash as I pen these sarcasms? But I will be calm. Listen. We have got a censor of plays at present. We have had him for a considerable time. He will, I hope, excuse me if, in the exercise of my duty as a critic, I describe his function as an unmitigated nuisance. I repeat, an unmitigated nuisance. It prevents serious plays from being acted, and consequently prevents them from being written. And according to the uncontradicted statement made by Mr George Conquest the other day to the Pall Mall Gazette, it has led him to force East End managers to cook their plays to suit his social prejudices and class interests by inducing them to alter plays in which the villain of the piece is represented as a gentleman by condition.

If he prohibited bad plays as well as good ones, and impartially reduced stage dialogue to the inanity of drawing-room conversation, there might be some excuse made by shortsighted and conventional people for his censorship, on the ground that in depriving the thoughtful of their theatre he also deprived the vicious of theirs. But he never objects to a thoroughly immoral play. Mind: I do not say that I should approve of a censorship if it did forbid immoral plays. But since such prohibition is the sole ground on which the advocates of "official licensing" defend it and declare its necessity, I hasten to point out once more what has been already pointed out again and again; *i.e.*, that you can perform any number of farcical comedies which from beginning to end turn upon the stage humors of adultery and prostitution; but you cannot perform Shelley's Cenci; and if you were to spend a considerable capital in preparing one of Ibsen's great works, you would do so at the risk of being forbidden to proceed at the last moment by the licenser.

This state of things is not the fault of Mr Pigott: it is inherent in the institution of censorship. On the whole, if Mr Pigott were not a little better than his function, he would hardly have been tolerated so long. But at best he must either virtually abolish his office (except as to salary) by licensing everything indiscriminately, which would be neither honest nor, considering the moral responsibility improperly put upon him, reasonably possible; or else he must, to the best of his judgment, license the plays which seem to him tolerable and forbid those which he deems objectionable. Certainly, if I were censor, this is what I should do, short of abdicating in favor of someone who would be no less a nuisance than I. And the result would be that whilst I should never dream of objecting to the Cenci or Ibsen, I should prohibit such plays as Still Waters Run Deep, Impulse, and The Profligate, as being, to my way of thinking, false in sentiment and therefore essentially depraving to the spectators.

Obviously I should at once be recognized as an insufferable tyrant by Mr Robert Buchanan, and by that large section of the British middle class which he typifies as far as his view of the morals of dramatic fiction is concerned. But I should not care a snap of my fingers for him. The

242

question of the censorship has not yet reached Parliament; my salary could not be dwelt on for hours in Committee of Supply, like that of the Chief Secretary for Ireland. It would be necessary of course to keep the public in good humor by keeping my hands carefully off the farcical comedies; but, for the rest, my contention would be that since I had been appointed as Pope of the playhouse to decide by my own inner light what was good for the English people and what not, I could do no less than assume my own infallibility, and despotize away to the top of my bent.

I submit then, that the result of establishing a new censor for the music halls is foreknown by all persons who have watched the institution at work over our theatres. It will not stop the indecency, the frivolity, the inanity; and it will stop all progress upward from them. If we can think of no more effective machine than a censor for making music halls better than the people who go to them, we may as well try *laisser-faire* for a while. Mr McDougall himself saw the futility of suggesting a censorship of the lines sung; for the indecency, innocent Mr Juggins, is always between the lines, where nothing but virgin paper would meet the eye of a licenser. He was quite right in concluding that the only way to bring the music halls into accord with his ideas of what they should be, was to force on them the alternative of that or peremptory closure.

As to the general question of the quality of music-hall entertainment, I have nothing to say about that: I am not a representative of the true music-hall public, which consists partly of people whose powers of imaginative apprehension and attention are too limited to follow even the most incoherent melodrama, and partly of people who like to sit smoking and soaking in lazy contemplation of something that does not greatly matter. What astonishes a theatre-goer at a music hall, or an educated woman when she realises one of her most cherished dreams by at last persuading either her husband or the man-about-towniest of his friends to take her to the London Pavilion or the

Empire, is the indifference of the audience to the performance. Five out of six of the "turns" are of the deadliest
dulness: ten minutes of it would seal the fate of any drama;
but the people do not mind: they drink and smoke. Under
these circumstances the standard of interest, much less of
art, is low, the strain on the management or the artists to
keep it up being of the slightest. It is rising slowly, in spite
of the influence of that detestable product of civilization,
the rich man's son, who now represents a distinct class,
technically described as "masher," and growing with the
accumulation of riches in idle hands produced by our idiotic
industrial system. If left to develop freely, our best music
halls would in course of time present a combination of
promenade concert, theatre, and circus (minus the horses):
that is, you would have a good band, decent concert singers,
acrobats, jugglers, ballets, and dramatic sketches, all in the
same evening. And the refreshment department will probably develop also, as 'Arry develops into the noble Juggins,
and begins to prefer the aerated bread shop to the public-
house.

Of course the theatre monopolists fear that this would
ruin most of them. But it does not follow; though if it did
we should allow them to be ruined just as complacently as
we allowed the stage coach proprietors to be ruined by the
introduction of railways. The manager whose patrons prefer
a variety entertainment, can give them what they want by
turning music-hall manager. The houses whose patrons prefer the drama, have simply to stick to the drama, and they
will not be ruined. When a theatre has been playing down as
nearly as possible to the music-hall level, it will lose the tail
of its audience when the music halls are set free from their
present mediæval shackles; but it can, and ought to, recruit
its thinned benches by playing up to the level of the
thoughtful people who now avoid the theatre because the
life and morals of the stage are a century behind those of
the educated world. All these results are at present hindered
by absurd monopolies, censorships, and protective regula-

tions which are enough to make Adam Smith turn in his grave, so completely do they defeat their professed public ends.

Just consider this one fact. A newspaper or book containing lewd matter can do a thousand times more harm than any indecent song or dance. Yet there is no censor of the Press. Nothing but a sense of public responsibility, and the prospect of being called to account before a jury, prevents the proprietors of The Star from turning it into a broadsheet of obscene anecdotes. Yet the editor would never dream of allowing such pleasantries into his columns as the official licenser of plays hall-marks for public use on the stages of the Avenue, the Criterion, the Gaiety, and the Comedy Theatres. I shall not insult the public intelligence by again drawing the moral.

1 November 1889

THIS week, dear reader, we shall have some nice little reviews of recent musical publications. But do not on that account resolve too hastily to skip me: the subject has its lively side, unless you happen to be on the premises whilst the reviewer is trying them over. Publishing enterprise must have recognition and encouragement—when it deserves them. For I must add that one or two eminent firms have seen in the simplicity of my character only something to practise upon with lays that they would not impose on a City Father after a heavy dinner.

Here are a couple of samples of the sort of thing sent to me on the off—the exceedingly off—chance of my having been born recently enough to describe them respectively as "a graceful and effective drawing room song, compass F to G," and "a dashing nautical ballad, with swinging chorus, suitable for a smoking concert, and within the resources of a robust baritone."

Are they all forgotten?
Moments that are past?

245

Have they fled for ever?
　Moments that are past.
　　A-a-a-a-a-a-a-a-ah!

Only come again
　As you came to me that day
When the sun was on the river
　And the scent was in the hay.
　　A-a-a-a-a-a-a-a-a-ah!

Only come again
　As you came to me that day
When we sat and talked together
　As true lovers only may.

Here is the other—

Dead! Men! No! secrets tell
　Mer! Cy! But! scant we shew
Young or old we seize their gold
　Then up the plank they go
Jolly good luck to our flag so grim
　Emblem of deeds we do
Millions of wealth, long life and health
　To the Vam-Pire's crew.

The last verse explains that "England, hearing rumors of
bloodshed and marauding, dispatched a cruiser ably armed
and manned, commanded by a Briton (by danger nothing
daunted) to mete out vengeance with relentless hand. They
fell in with the schooner and brought her soon to action.
The combat raged with fury fierce and long. The pirates,
taken captive, were hanged beside their leader, who never
more will sing his gruesome

Dead men no, etc., etc., etc."

My readers will hardly believe that such things have been
thrust upon my notice; but they have. I do not think I have
deserved it. At any rate I decline to put myself in danger of

hell fire by calling the people who admire such trash by their proper name.

Messrs Novello have treated me far more handsomely. And yet there is one thing in their contribution which I must declare inferior to the Vam-Pire's Crew, because there are unquestionably idiots in the world who like the Vampire; but no human being ever liked a Church Cantata written to order for one of our provincial Festivals. Here it is, in the familiar Novello buff and brown cover, price two shillings. The words, I blush to say, are by a brother critic. Listen!

Rest thee, my Saviour, rest Thy head meetly.
Angels watch over Thee sleeping so sweetly.
    No dream alarm
    With thought of harm
Till night and its shadows have vanished completely.

Take it away, Messrs Novello, take it away. Burn the whole edition, lest any choral society should waste its time on rhyme-jingling that never once rises to the level of blasphemy, and on music-mongering that is enough to make every intelligent student in England forswear counterpoint. I suppose the stewards of the —— Musical Festival thought they were encouraging English music by ordering a cantata; and I am bound to assume that my colleague of the largest circulation in the world is honestly and infatuatedly unconscious of how detestable his verses are from a literary point of view, and how their essential triviality must jar on all sincere Christians. But there are limits to the allowances I am prepared to make. In future it will be necessary to square The Star if the truth about these matters is to remain untold any longer. Either I must have my share of the libretto-making or I blow the gaff.

8 *November* 1889

HERE is a gentleman from Somersetshire wishing to know how I can "reconcile the statement that working men care not for oratorios on account of their sacred or religious character to the fact that at the People's Palace Elijah, Messiah, etc., draw enormous audiences." Now I tell the gentleman from Somersetshire once for all that it wont do. I never speak of "working men" as if they were a consignment of regulation boots, all alike except as to assorted sizes.

There are working men who delight in piety—who join the Salvation Army, or drag their unfortunate children evening after evening to dismal chapels, where their poor little imaginations are filled with eternal torment, vengeance, sin and the devil. Others there be who go to secular halls, and revel in demonstrations that Moses thought the earth flat, and that if any of the four evangelists told the truth the other three necessarily told lies. Of the two extremes, that of extracting nothing from Hebrew literature but discrepancies and absurdities is on the whole more religious than extracting nothing but wrath and terror from it. Both practices, regarded as rites, are essentially savage; but the prevalence of one gives a certain humor to the other, and indeed grows inevitably out of it.

The majority of church-going workmen, probably, are heathens like the rest of us, going as a matter of habit, just as they wear neckties, because their respectability would be doubted if they omitted the observance. Some abstainers who are lazy or prefer their club, approve of churchgoing as an institution, and make their children go. Others, again, go because they like it or are used to it, but dont attach sufficient importance to it to insist on their families coming with them. Hundreds go because they have a vague sense of higher duties owed somewhere, and can find no other means of payment. And the reasons for abstention are quite as various and inconsequent as those for attendance.

Hence, in speaking of the working men who go to hear Berlioz's Faust, but are repelled by Scriptural oratorios, I was careful to speak of them as a section only, though I mentioned certain reasons for regarding them as a section important to cater for: numerous, curious, aspiring, intelligent, and comparatively independent in their judgment. It is not necessary for me to repeat here what I then said; but I desire to impress on my Somersetshire correspondent that oratorio performances at prices within the means of working men are so few relatively to the huge bulk of the working class that if there were twice as many of them, and these twice as crowded, they would be as dust in the balance against the general presumption that the average laborer knows and cares no more about Elijah than he does about the Thirty-nine Articles. It is true that wherever human life is there also is music, and a belief in the supernatural; and probably no slum in Europe is without denizens who will sing or dance or send at point of death for a priest. But that does not make every slum contribute to the congregation of St Paul's or the audiences at the Albert Hall. The unlucky majority still want bread and butter much more than they want Bach and Beethoven.

Another correspondent asks me to decide a wager for him. The question at issue is whether alto parts are not frequently sung in our churches by men as well as by boys. I am hardly the man to settle such a point. In my small boyhood I was a victim of the inhuman and absurd custom of compelling young children to sit out morning service every Sunday. To sit motionless and speechless in your best suit in a dark stuffy church on a morning that is fine outside the building, with your young limbs aching with unnatural quiet, your restless imagination tired of speculating about the same grown-up people in the same pews every Sunday, your conscience heavy with the illusion that you are the only reprobate present sufficiently wicked to long for the benediction, and to wish that they would sing something out of an opera instead of Jackson in F, not to mention hating the clergyman as a sanctimonious bore, and dreading the sexton as a man likely to turn bad boys out and possibly to know them at sight by official inspiration: all this is enough to lead any sensitive youth to resolve that when he grows up and can do as he likes, the first use he will make of his liberty will be to stay away from church. Anyhow, I have not attended a service seven times in the last twenty-five years, nor do I propose to stir up gloomy memories and wrathful passions by altering my practice in this respect. Therefore, all I can say on the subject of my correspondent's wager is that adult male alto and counter tenor singers, though no longer as common as they once were, are still to be heard in all directions singing the parts specially written for their kind of voice by the composers of the great English school: not the second-hand Handels and Mendelssohns of the past century and a half, but the writers of the glees, madrigals, and motets and services which are the true English musical classics. Nowadays, however, since the opera and the concert platform offer golden opportunities to a tenor or a baritone, whereas an alto or counter tenor is confined to the choir or the glee quartet all his life, a promising choir boy gets rid of his treble as soon as Nature permits him. The effect of this in diminishing the number of adult altos must be considerable.

Thackeray students will remember that when Colonel Newcome returned from India, and obliged a convivial circle by singing a ballad in a counter-tenor voice with florid ornaments in the taste of his own heyday, he was astonished to find everybody laughing at him. But I myself have seen a singer—a young man—appear before an audience of "the classes" in a blue evening coat with brass buttons, and gravely sing a song by Mendelssohn in an alto voice. The effect was by no means disagreeable; but it was so strange and unexpected that the room positively vibrated with suppressed laughter. The same thing would happen at one of Messrs Boosey's ballad concerts if an alto were engaged; though downstairs, at the Christy Minstrels, an alto, black with burnt cork, might at the same moment be piping away as a matter of course to an audience quite familiar with his voice. Thus to some people the man alto is an everyday phenomenon, whilst to others he is either a Thackerayan tradition or an extravagant novelty. Hence wagers!

LONDON MUSIC IN 1888-89

Before quitting the subject of church music, I may mention that an exciting discussion has been raging in the Musical World on the proper accentuation of the Nicene Creed. Archbishops have joined the fray; and their letters, mostly in Greek, form a pleasing variety to portraits of Madame Patti. This is all to the good: any discussion which brings into relief the inadequacy of mere musical grammar to qualify a Mus.Bac. or Mus.Doc. to raise human speech to the eloquence which Purcell and Handel gave it will help music. I observe with immense approval that the Musical World now makes room for criticism of all the arts. Nothing more unmusical can be imagined than a musical paper all about music.

The students of the Royal Academy of Music had a concert of chamber music all to themselves at St James's Hall last Monday afternoon. It was a very creditable performance, especially the Mendelssohn pianoforte trio, the first three movements of which were excellently played, in spite of an accompaniment from somebody on the roof with a hammer, who produced exactly the effect of Hans Sachs in Beckmesser's serenade. Pupils' work cannot be criticised except from a merely technical point of view, as the performers are carefully doing what they have been taught instead of following their own original impulse. The choir of young ladies, in unnecessarily ugly arrangements of white dress and red sash, sang correctly; and there was less than I had feared of that baneful grinding of the voice which has always been the curse of Academy and Conservatoire teaching. But the diction was bad throughout. As far as I could distinguish the words sung, the articulation was distinct but not pure; and the vowels were often as corrupt as they could be. A professor of really fine elocution is needed in Tenterden-street.

THERE is no harm in saying now that when Madame Falk-Mehlig was Miss Anna Mehlig she was not my favorite pianist. She was well taught, diligent, and accurate; but she used to leave me in the frostiest and most forlorn condition, because she was still in the school-girl phase of being troubled with a conscience. Now you cannot be a great artist until you have outgrown your conscience—until in playing the right way you are doing exactly what you like because you like it. When the news came that Miss Mehlig had married, and retired—in other words, had sacrificed her sonata playing for love—I counted it as the first genuine artistic act in her career. Accordingly, nothing can be more natural than her return to her art after some years in full possession of a ripened talent expressing itself freely and sympathetically with a warmth and charm that were lacking in the old days. She was cordially welcomed at the Crystal Palace on Saturday, when she sat down to the famous Beethoven concerto in E flat; and she played it for the greater part very prettily. I say for the greater part, because the last movement, the peculiar accentuation of which requires the finest rhythmical management, baffled her; only a few bits of graceful passage-playing in it being really worth listening to. Madame Nordica, with her capital method, light vocal touch, and bright tone, all in complete working order, gave us a song of Marschner's—one so German as to be nothing if not sentimental—with a surprising want of feeling. As to the ballad by Gomez, which was her second contribution, it sounded like the very last sweepings of the refuse of the Rossini school. Liszt's Campanella, a piece of rank drawing-room rubbish, sounded serious and original in comparison. I appreciate Madame Nordica, I hope; but there are two things about her that I cannot get over: the transparent superficiality of her artistic feeling; and her bonnets, which may be excellently confected from the bonnettist's point of view, but which give her an air of not being at home in the very

252

place where an artist should feel and look most at home. They make us feel as if we had interrupted her on the point of going out for a walk. The orchestra gave an appetising taste of its quality in the concerto, the horn parts in particular coming out quite beautifully, though I must add that these instruments met with reverses later on, in the intermezzo to the Goetz symphony. Concerning which noble work by a great composer, I would ask Sir George Grove whether he has become at all conscious of the obvious absurdity of the patronizing tone which he and Macfarren adopted when Goetz's works were first produced here. Sir George was not so bad as Macfarren, who could find nothing more sensible to say about the joyous Spring overture than that it contained consecutive sevenths; but he programmed in a pat-the-young-man-on-the-back style which was a very unworthy response to such an inmost confidence; for the symphony is of no less sacred a nature. But, now that I think of it, Sir George patronized everyone in his programming days: even Beethoven. The new rhapsody by Lalo has a second movement which would make a suitable and spirited *entr'acte* for a Norweign play; but from the dignified standard of the Crystal Palace concerts I must describe it compendiously as tiddy-fol-lol.

St Paul next Saturday. I shall go expressly to abuse it.

15 *November* 1889

I MUST apologise to the Musical Guild of ex-scholars and ex-students of the Royal College of Music for having missed their first concert at the Kensington Town Hall on Tuesday. Last season, appreciating the importance of such a society, I was one of the first to call attention to it and to recommend its opening concerts to the public. The Guild showed its sense of my foresight and magnanimity by not inviting me even once. This time I forgot all about it; and the result is, of course, an invitation to the whole series of concerts. Such is musical life. However, I did not introduce the subject to complain of the slights and ingratitudes to which my zeal in the public service and my too indulgent attitude as a critic expose me, nor even to make it known that the second concert will be given on next Wednesday week, and will include the Kreutzer sonata and Brahms' trio in E flat for pianoforte, violin, and horn, Op. 40. I simply wish to explain my absence on Tuesday.

The fact is, I was at Leicester delivering to the midlanders an impassioned appeal for a remodelling of their municipal institutions on Bassettoist principles. Now it happened whilst I was in the greenroom of the Co-operative Hall, contemplatively enjoying the "Bayreuth hush" which preceded my bodily appearance on the platform, my eye fell on a writing upon the wall. Curiosity is one of my finest traits; and I at once began to read the document. It was a list of the songs which can only be sung subject to performing rights held by a certain Mr Harry Wall, who made himself famous in the eighteen-seventies by the persistence with which he mulcted in penalties singers of all degrees who had unsuspectingly warbled his property. The difficulty always lay in finding out what songs were Mr Wall's and what were not. The London Figaro, which pursued him throughout with relentless disapproval, noted the songs which he had made the subject of legal proceedings, and published a list for the guidance of singers. The writing on the wall at Leicester is probably a copy of this list.

The list had no direct interest for me at the moment, as I did not propose to entertain the audience with minstrelsy. But it reminded me that there is at present in the field a formidable and more dignified representative of performing rights in the person of Mr Alfred Moul, whom bandmasters and arrangers and "selection" makers of all sorts, accustomed to free communism in musical compositions, are now vigorously denouncing as a blackmailer. This means that he has been making people pay for something which they have hitherto pirated for nothing. Before I say anything as to the merits of such a proceeding I may mention that the denunciations of Mr Moul specially amused me, because he is an old acquaintance of mine; and I derive the usual entertainment from seeing people whom I privately know in a vigorous row of any kind.

When I first came across Mr Alfred Moul some twenty years or so ago, I took him to be a young man of about eighteen, unnaturally self-sufficient and finished for his age, and a very clever pianist, though not then a professional one. When I last saw him, at the "private view" of Her Majesty's Theatre as decorated for Mr Leslie's recent promenade concerts, the lapse of two decades had made the gravest alterations, not to say ravages, in my own aspect; but Mr Moul (I lapse for the moment into the familiarity of private intercourse) was still eighteen. The effect of this curious phenomenon was totally to destroy my faith in my original estimate of his years. He may have been threescore all along: he may be the Wandering Gentile, if there is such a person. Certain it is that age cannot wither him; and as to custom staling his infinite variety, I can only say that I have had glimpses of him through the smoke of the battle of life during the twenty years in question, as pianoforte virtuoso, conductor, voice trainer, composer, publisher, artist, professor, and man of business. But he has always been elegant, and always eighteen.

As a composer I never could elude him for long. As he invariably gave up an enterprise the moment he succeeded in it, and so was never the same thing for long; so he never composed under the same name for more than a month. When I got a bundle of music to review, it was sure to contain a song, or a waltz, or a pianoforte piece by Cyril This, or Prosper That, or Stephen the Other (he was particularly fond of Stephen); but the first six bars would reveal the style of Moul; for *le style c'est l'homme*. At first I used to hail these discoveries with pleased surprise. Later on I received them with imprecations, having exhausted every form of words that logrolling amenity could take.

Then he disappeared for a long time; and I was mourning him as dead or married or otherwise extinguished when a colonial prima donna told me of a great pianist named Alfred Moul who had given concerts at the Antipodes. Some time after this I began, from the tops of omnibuses, to catch glimpses in passing hansoms of a figure which I supposed must be that of a son of Moul's, wonderfully like his father. Later on the figure accosted me, and convinced me that he was Alfred Moul himself, looking perhaps six months younger, but, save for a certain added mellowness of manner, otherwise the same. In his latest incarnation he is Agent-General for the British Empire of the French Society of Authors, Composers, and Music Publishers; and his business is to enforce the rights created by copyright legislation as interpreted by the articles of the International Convention held at Berne in 1887. And in my opinion the society is to be congratulated on having got hold of a very capable representative.

If I could gather from current complaints that the new Agent-General had enforced these rights offensively, or made unreasonable and extortionate demands, or aggrieved the complainants in any other way than in making them pay for what they had been accustomed to lay hands upon freely, I should have hurried to 40 Old Bond Street, and called upon him to explain or amend his life before I alluded to the subject in print. But there is no case against him. There is a case against the law—against its ambiguity in the abstract —against the difficulty of ascertaining its bearing on any particular emergency—against the uselessness of the Stationers' Hall register—against the impossibility of finding whether the law's bite is as bad as its bark by any other process than the risky one of putting your head into its mouth. But these are not the fault of any Agent-General: they are the fault of our legal machinery. There is also a case —a very strong case—in favor of Communism as against Private Property; but the implied suggestion that Communism should be the rule as to works of art whilst Private Property remains the rule for everything else is unworkable.

We cannot reasonably deny to the author or composer those rights (or wrongs) against others which others have against him. Copyrights and patent rights are as a matter of fact the least objectionable forms of private property in permanent sources of wealth and pleasure; because, unlike the analogous property rights in land and capital, they are limited in duration, and their reversion to the entire community is eventually secured. Shorten their duration by all means if expedient—I have always urged that copyrights should be shortened as they extend internationally—but whilst they last they are the means by which the author or composer gets paid for his labor. If Mr Moul is a blackmailer for enforcing them, then so is any agent who enforces the payment of a patentee's royalty; so equally is the concert-giver who enforces payment of a shilling at the turnstile; and so doubly is the agent who enforces payment of a landlord's rent or a shareholder's dividend. I might as well complain of blackmail whenever I pay for admissions to musical entertainments, because, forsooth, I am often invited to attend such entertainments freely as "a gentleman of the Press."

Therefore, I advise conductors who make potpourris and selections from the works of living composers to pay their shot without abusing the collector, except in cases where they admit the audience either for nothing or at a cost barely sufficient to cover the rent of the room and the gas bill, in which case they would, of course, have some ground for an appeal to the generosity and public spirit of the composer. But when they are simply trading in music for profit I am at a loss to see why the composer should allow them to exploit a single semiquaver of his without getting his share of the money it attracts. Moral therefore: Agitate (as a Communist) for the repeal of the Copyright Acts if you will; point out the inconveniences of its operation as much as you please; but in the name of common sense let the innocent and useful Mr Alfred Moul alone.

I have quite a mass of other subjects to deal with this week; but I find that this copyright question has mopped up all the ink I have space for. I must, however, call attention to one real grievance. A remarkable drawing has arrived here representing a young lady who has cast herself despairingly on the floor amid the ruins of what seems to be a voluminous manuscript. Underneath is written, "When your heart is rent at sight of this, P.T.O." Turning over as requested, I find that the subject of the picture is my correspondent (resident at Brook Green) after Mr Barnum's steam organ has begun its fourteenth repetition of its repertory of a waltz, a polka, and variations on the National Anthem. "I need not describe the sound," she says: "you can hear it at Stonecutter-Street if you open the window." I have opened the window and can hear it quite distinctly. I appeal to Mr Barnum's chivalry. Can he not either stop it or play *con sordino?*"

18 *November* 1889

To sit on hard chairs listening to oratorios from three to half-past ten, with a few intervals of train and tramcar, is not the liveliest way of spending a Saturday half-holiday, especially when one of the oratorios is St Paul. But since the other was Judas Maccabeus there were compensations in my lot on Saturday: at any rate, my last state was not worse than my first. St Paul, you will understand, was done on Saturday afternoon at the Crystal Palace concert; and Judas followed in the evening at the People's Palace. Of the first of the two performances, I need not renew my weariness by writing much. After all, Mendelssohn was Mendelssohn, who, even in his emptiest *tours de force* where he had no message to deliver and nothing to feel deeply about, yet felt deeply about nothing, and wrote beautifully, if not pregnantly, because he could not endure to write otherwise. But even beauty does not make subjectless music interesting; and I had as lief talk Sunday-school for two hours and a half to a beautiful woman with no brains as listen to St Paul over again. As to the performance, the orchestra was good;

the choir was odious—simply odious; Mr Lloyd was in his best vein; and Mr Brereton, I must charitably hope, in his worst. If Miss Anna Williams's intonation were as pure as her voice, what distance would I not travel to hear her? I do not mean that she habitually sings out of tune, but she has to take conscious aim at the pitch, and some intervals never get quite on the centre of the bull's eye. I see that some critic complains of Miss Marion Mackenzie as not up to her usual mark in the contralto music. I thought she sang But the Lord is Mindful of His Own, particularly well. You really cannot believe what critics say.

The exchange value of the difference between the Crystal Palace oratorio and that at the People's Palace was exactly six and fivepence, including travelling expenses. It was a great occasion at Bow—their first oratorio—and I looked round expectantly for a great muster of critics. But I looked in vain. If it had been St James's Hall with Joachim playing the Mendelssohn concerto, or Mr Edward Lloyd singing, Lend me Your Aid for the hundredth time, they would have been there by dozens. In my solitude I was enjoying a sense of superior virtue, when in walked Mr Fuller Maitland, of the Times. You might have knocked me down with a feather. The performance began with great spirit, the strings, in full harmony, giving delusive promise of excellence. When the fugue broke them into parts, it became evident that though the second violins meant quite as well as their rivals under Mr Manns, yet they were not equally able to give effect to their intentions. However, they got through with an occasional lift from the organ, and one or two pauses for tuning, during which each fiddler scraped his A string, found that it was about an eighth flat; and left it so with apparent satisfaction. The choir got on capitally, putting to utter shame the multitudinous dolts who are the bane of Mr Mann's artistic life. They sang with admirable spirit and earnestness, and there was not a dull moment in the oratorio, which, to be sure, was slightly curtailed. As to the principals, the only one who was not equal to the occasion was the tenor, who was heavily overweighted by his part, and not in the best of voice to attempt it. Miss Margaret Hoare astonished the natives with From Mighty Kings, and a young lady named Miss Hoskins, whose fine contralto voice has the first bloom still on it, brought down the house with Father of Heaven: to Thy Eternal Throne. I do not think Miss Hoskins quite knew that she was singing one of the most beautiful songs ever written, even by Handel; but she would at her present stage have sung it all the worse if she had sung it more consciously. Mr Bertram Latter sang the baritone music without a fault: the comparative ineffectiveness of his songs was the fault of the conductor, who took both of them too slowly. Arm, arm, ye brave, in particular, went at exactly half the proper speed. On the whole, I enjoyed the concert, which is more than I can truthfully say of the Sydenham performance. And the crowd which filled the great hall seemed to be of my opinion.

19 November 1889

At the Avenue Theatre, at half-past two every day, an "opera" is sung by children. At least, they are all guaranteed under fourteen. But some people are not children at fourteen: they are hobbledehoys; and there is no charm in hobbledehoyhood. A child should have a child's ways, a child's stature, above all a child's voice. The giantess at the Aquarium, for instance, is not, artistically considered, a child. And the young ladies of the ballet in the first act of Belles of the Village are as unchildlike as the ballet itself, which is no less inane and artificial than genuine children's dances are interesting and pretty. The rest is pleasant enough. Nothing could be more naïve than the rustic drama by Hugh Foster, or more innocent than the music by John Fitzgerald. Master Fred Allwood takes himself with commendable seriousness as Will Green, the Jack Tar. His dancing of the sailor's hornpipe is beyond belief: it brought down the house. But Master Allwood sings precociously in the voice, not of the passing boy, but of the coming man; and I am greatly afraid that he will some day find that voice considerably the worse for his present efforts. Master Alfred Bovill, as the beadle, shewed himself a comedian of genius. He is the first operatic vocalist I ever saw leap into popularity by a *couac*, as the French call it. There was one note in his song upon which his voice broke every time with irresistibly comic effect; and the audience encored him again and again for it, going into convulsions at each repetition of the catastrophe. Of what the effect on a sensitive child would have been I shudder to think; but Signor Bovill had no more delicacy about making comic capital of his precarious upper notes than Coquelin has in exploiting the curled tip of his nose. Master Frank Mettrop, as the oldest inhabitant, also brought off a small part with some comic talent. Of the girls, only two are really child singers and actresses, namely, Miss Bessie Graves, a little artist ready made by nature, who sings very sweetly, and Miss Lizzie Primmer, who has doubtless had to study rather harder, her fairy godmothers having been stingier than Bessie's. Miss Annie Fieber and Miss Bessie Colman are only spoiling their adult voices by using them prematurely; and Miss Fieber's coquetries will sit better on her when she is older. Miss Lizzie Dungate, a little more grown that the others, is staid, but pleasing. When Master Allwood was resting, flushed with triumph, after his miraculous hornpipe, she said, as if it were one of her lines (which can hardly have been the case) "You will be encored again for that, tomorrow," whereat the house laughed indulgently. On the whole, the grown-up people were decidedly amused; and as people generally bring their children to the plays, and buy them the toys that amuse themselves, I take it that the Belles of the Village is likely enough to serve its turn through the winter.

OF all the thousands of Star readers who have delighted in Mendelssohn and loved him only one has cared enough to hurl a postcard at me for what I said about St Paul. Here it is.

"AN IGNORANT SELF-CONCEITED ASS is the Star musical critic (!) who scribbles on Mendelssohn and the Oratorio of St Paul at the Crystal Palace on Saturday!!!

"He should be put under a glass case and exhibited at Barnum's menagerie; for SURELY he has the LONGEST PAIR OF EARS IN ALL LONDON.

"The animal!

"Who was his father?—and who his mother? The breed should be perpetuated as a curiosity!!!"

My heart warms to this anonymous correspondent. The postcard is an outburst of genuine feeling about music, somewhat unsocially expressed, perhaps, but still heartfelt. Yet I shall probably often again wound that feeling, because, for the musical critic in England, Mendelssohn is The Enemy. Until we have got far enough to recoil from Elijah flippantly rattling off his atrocious "God is angry with the wicked every day" we shall never fathom the depths of truly great music. Mendelssohn, who was shocked at Auber's writing an opera in which a girl sang *Oui, c'est demain* (meaning "Tomorrow I shall be a bride") at her looking-glass before going to bed, was himself ready to serve up the chopping to pieces of the prophets of the grove with his richest musical spice to suit the compound of sanctimonious cruelty and base materialism which his patrons, the British Pharisees, called their religion. If my correspondent will compare such work as his with Parsifal, and his career with that of the man who produced Parsifal, he (or she; for the handwriting is of uncertain sex) will understand why Wagner once said, speaking of an occasion when Mendelssohn invited him to applaud an orchestral full gallop through the

262

beautiful slow trio of Beethoven's eighth symphony, "I thought I saw before me an abyss of superficiality." The Philharmonic orchestra scampers through its work in the same elegantly superficial manner to this day, thanks to Mendelssohn. Probably all my correspondent really means is that Mendelssohn composed music of exquisite grace and tenderness. I am no more insensible to that than was Wagner, who used to ask his pianist friends to play Mendelssohn's overtures for him. But when I am asked to spend an afternoon listening to oratorios that must stand or fall, not by the grace or tenderness of their prettiest strains, but by the depth and moral dignity of their conception, then Mendelssohn gets roughly handled; and it serves him abundantly right.

Here is another communication marked "Private," which I shall answer publicly, as there may be others interested in my reply.

"Dear Sir,—As I believe your opinion to be one of the best in London [this is a man of sense], would you, as a great favor, be kind enough to give me information about the following matter:

"I think of taking singing lessons from Professor —— of ——, and I wish to know if you consider him competent to teach in opera and oratorio—provided that in course of time I found I had sufficient voice and ability to lead me to hope that by hard study and perseverance I had a chance of rising so high.

"I have never had any singing lessons; but my voice has been tried and found to be rather powerful.—Yours faithfully,
X Y Z."

Now observe here how much more vaguely a musical career is conceived than one in any other art. Had X Y Z wished to go on the stage he would hardly have asked whether Mr Herman Vezin is "competent to teach *drama*." Just as there is no such thing as teaching drama, so there is no such thing as teaching opera or oratorio. Mr Herman

Vezin can, of course, take a novice and coach her in the part of Juliet to the point of enabling her to go through it with verbal accuracy and with a certain propriety of gesture and deportment: even that depending, however, on the extent to which the pupil's natural gifts make her capable of understanding the teacher's instructions. Similarly Professor —— is no doubt competent to coach a pupil in the part of Jephtha or Manoah, Faust or Mephistopheles. But if artists could be turned out in this fashion, Mr Herman Vezin and Professor —— could at once open shops, and supply Juliets and Gennaros to the managers as Mr Clarkson supplies wigs. The truth is that the artist must be at once his own master and everybody's pupil. If he cannot learn from all that he sees and hears, and then teach himself the practical application of what he has learnt, art is not his affair, and he had better remain an amateur. Mr Joseph Jefferson, as indisputably the most finished comedian among English-speaking actors as M. Coquelin is among French-speaking ones, years ago repudiated the notion that any part of an actor's business could be learnt off the stage. And my own art of literary composition, much the most difficult in the world, was certainly not taught me by a master, nor do I propose to take apprentices.

I can, however, tell X Y Z some of the things he must learn in order to become a fine artist—things which he will never learn by shutting himself up twice a week for an hour with the same man and the same pianoforte in the same drawing room. First, he must learn to sing: that is, to touch or sustain any note within his compass with certainty of pitch and beauty of tone, and withal with an unembarrassed management of it, so that it may be lightly or vigorously touched or sustained, just as he wishes. Second, he must learn to pronounce with purity the syllables *do, re, mi, fa,* so that his more or less genteel variations on the original cockney *dow, roy, meey, fawr* may become utterly repugnant to him, and that he may no longer ignorantly laugh at Mr Irving for saying simply "gold" instead of the customary "gah-oold." He must also learn foreign vowels, so as to be able to sing *re* both as *ré* or *rè*, and sustain them without ever closing, English fashion, into an *ee* at the end. All this must be checked by his own ear, not his master's. There is no use in getting other people to listen to him: he must listen to himself with his whole soul until his ear has grown exquisitely sensitive to minute shades of intonation and pronunciation—until he cannot go wrong without literally hurting himself.

This cultivation of the ear never stops. The fine artist improves until age unmakes more progress in the year than culture can make. But how is X Y Z to set about cultivating his ear? Alas! how indeed? in this British world of ugliness and noise! But he can, according to his means, keep good music sounding in his ears. He can go to concerts—to the Crystal Palace on Saturday afternoons, at least sometimes (always is too dear); to the Saturday and Monday Pops; to the Philharmonic; to the Richter concerts; to the best of the numerous suburban oratorio performances; to the opera occasionally; and to the theatres. Let him make studies of inferior, good, and first-rate artists in point of intonation and pronunciation. Any friend will oblige him with a song in the first capacity. Then let him try how much better in these points he finds Mr Edward Lloyd, Mr Henschel, or Mr Max Heinrich. Finally, let him try Madame Patti in Within a Mile, or Home, Sweet Home.

A fresh course can be gone through on pronunciation. Look through Mr Alexander J. Ellis's little book on Speech in Song (I think Messrs Novello published it some years ago), in order to get some idea of what to watch for; and then call in a friend again—a vulgar friend, if you have one. Study his vowels, and how loud he thinks it necessary to speak. Then go to the theatre and compare with his the speech of a mediocre actor. Then try an actor of the rank of Mr Kendal. Finally, go and hear Mr Irving; and also the masterly Coquelin in Les Precieuses Ridicules if possible; for in that you will hear how beautifully in tune he can sing.

Then begin over again with the women, thus—1. Vulgar lady
friend. 2. Actress of good position, not specially famous as a
speaker: say, Miss Amy Roselle. 3. An actress who is famous
for clever but not for beautiful speaking: say, Mrs Kendal. 4.
An actress who speaks very cleverly and most beautifully—
there is only one—Miss Ada Rehan. 5. An intentionally
musical speaker of the highest class: Sarah Bernhardt. A
course of violinists culminating in Sarasate, would also be
useful; but once the habit of studying has been established
there is something to be picked up from the whistle of every
locomotive and the hail of every bus conductor.

Pray note, however, that although Mr Irving and Miss
Rehan speak so admirably, their personal mannerism is so
strong that an attempt to imitate them would be the surest
way to court overwhelming ridicule. The problem is to speak
as beautifully as possible, and not for a moment to speak like
this or that person who speaks beautifully. And further,
there must always—what! no more space this week. Then it
shall be continued in our next. I will have my say out if I
fill The Star with it until Christmas.

25 November 1889

UNTIL Mr Leslie gets rid of the Dorothy tradition at his
theatre, there will be little to record there except the waste
of three excellent artists and a tolerable comedian. Mr H. P.
Stephens, author of The Red Hussar, is a Molière, a Sheridan,
a Congreve, a very Shakespear compared to the author of
Dorothy and Doris; but even he has done nothing except
put a smart face on the inanities of his forerunner. Miss
Tempest is still a masquerading heiress; Mr Ben Davies still
a spendthrift in difficulties; Mr Hayden Coffin still one of
Mr Davies's acquaintances with a song; and Mr Arthur
Williams is not regenerated by the change from a comic
sheriff's officer to a comic corporal. There is the usual second
young lady (Miss Dysart) to pair off with Mr Coffin; and
there is an old lady to attempt to repeat the dreary tom-

foolery of the Priscilla scenes in Dorothy. Towards this part of the affair, however, the attitude of the audience on Saturday night was distinctly threatening. Squire Bantam, though transformed to Colonel Sir Marmaduke Mashem, remains essentially an unmitigated bore, Mr Christian, who impersonates him, being unable to make bricks without straw, as Mr Williams can. Some variety is obtained by sending all the characters campaigning for a while; but the military music of the second act, in which this occurs, is the most mechanical trash imaginable, with noisy, tiresome orchestration, in which a crowd of trivial conceits and contrivances jostle one another in the most impertinent and irritating fashion. Something of the same fault appears in the stage management: the soldiers are too often doing pointless scraps of business that were better left out. In fact, there are moments when, what with Mr Solomon fidgeting with the instruments, and Mr Charles Harris fidgeting with the supers, it is hard for a nervous spectator to sit still and refrain from objurgation. The first act is by far the most effective of the three: partly because the audience are unwearied: partly because Miss Tempest sings some bright, if not particularly novel, numbers with that care and feeling for the musical part of her work by which she has made her mark from her first appearance on the stage. Mr Davies also has a capital song, A Guinea here, a Guinea there, which he sang with his eyes shut, but otherwise admirably. The first of Miss Tempest's songs, by the way, has tagged on to it a worn-out scrap of conventional ornament, which Mr Solomon might as well cut off and throw on the musical dustheap. Mr Coffin's voice, as anyone might have foreseen, has been displaced and damaged in quality by the unsuitable work it had to do in Doris. In the concerted music of the first act, his tone was hard and aggressive, and would not blend with the others on any terms. His song, My Castle in Spain, in the second act, was not much better. I almost began to suspect him of deliberately sacrificing the beauty of his voice to its power: the surest way of losing both in the long run. But in the third act he sang a song in his old fashion, and was heartily encored, though it was past eleven, and a suburban god very sensibly called out that it was too late for encores. The audience throughout received the work very handsomely.

At the Crystal Palace concert in the afternoon Miss Nettie Carpenter played Saint-Saëns' violin concerto and a few solos in the manner of her master Sarasate, who, had he been present, would have had no reasonable fault to find; for she played very well indeed, and will take high rank as a player if her style matures and her tone amplifies by further experience. The rest of the concert was hopelessly dismal. The muggy, muddy weather had got into the very souls of the audience and performers alike. Mr Manns doggedly went through the program like a brave man fighting a broadsword combat against overwhelming odds. The Flying Dutchman overture would not come right; and the seventh symphony was a mockery. Liszt's Festklänge (sounds of rejoicing!) completed our discomfiture; and we trudged off sadly through the rain, feebly hoping for better luck next time. I forgot to mention that Miss Fillunger sang Schubert's Auflösung nicely; but Mendelssohn's *Infelice* requires a voice which is as good all over as in the upper register, outside which Miss Fillunger seems quite lost.

29 November 1889

ONE more book, The Story of Music, by W. J. Henderson, an American critic. It is concisely and intelligently written; but I can find little criticism in it that goes beyond a repetition of opinions which have been printed over and over again, and which were formed from the point of view common in 1850 and now obsolete. A critic who at this time of day cannot follow Wagner's harmony, and talks of "false relations" in it, is as hopelessly out of date as he himself would consider the professors who, on the ground that "*mi contra fa* diabolus est," object to a chord containing B natural following a chord containing F. When he goes on to inform us that Wagner "did not give sufficient attention to the powers of the human voice," it is time to shut the book. And yet he is by no means an anti-Wagnerite, this Mr Henderson; only his modesty—the critic who is modest is lost—is such that he feels bound to accept as gospel all the stale rubbish of the musical book makers who have been preying on popular ignorance of art since Lord Mount Edgecumbe's time. He even declares that Donizetti "wrote tunes simply and solely for their own sake, caring nothing for dramatic significance." Far be it from me to stand between Donizetti and his righteous doom; but whenever there was any dramatic significance to care for he cared for it to considerable purpose, although he was not one of those great masters who, refusing to make the best of hopeless old forms, create new ones for themselves. As to Lucia's scena, I have ridiculed its absurd flute tootling and fioriture often enough; but I never objected to it, as Mr Henderson does, on the ground that it is a waltz. Why should it not be? Handel's famous *Lascia ch'io pianga* is a saraband; but is it any the worse for that? What are all our song forms but evolved dance measures?

Here is a letter elicited by last week's column:

Sir,—With reference to your article of today, may I be allowed to point out that M. Coquelin and Mme Bernhardt both pronounce French as French is spoken by educated Frenchmen, whereas Mr Irving and Miss Terry pronounce English as no Englishman or Englishwoman has ever, whether educated or not, spoken the language since the world began. Also that the glorious voice of Madame Patti in Home, Sweet Home is but a melancholy study at best of the demand for music in this "musical people," and supply in a potentially great artist.—Yours faithfully,

H. Ashworth Taylor.

Hereupon I would observe that Mr Taylor, in so far as his statement about educated French people is true, has put the boot on the wrong leg. It is not M. Coquelin who speaks like the educated Frenchman: it is the educated Frenchman who tries to speak like M. Coquelin, because the diction of the Comedie Française is a standard diction in Paris. Here in England we have no standard (though Miss Glyn once assured me that Mr Gladstone had taken Charles Kean for his model as a speaker). In order to arrive at one, which course would Mr Taylor prefer? the adoption of average colloquial pronunciation by Mr Irving, or the adoption of Mr Irving's pronunciation by the average man? Mind, I say his pronunciation, and not his personal peculiarities: his undershot jaw, for instance, or the shape of the oral and nasal cavities which give his voice quite a different timbre from that of Mr Taylor. As to Miss Terry, the dry, husky quality of her voice is not her pronunciation: neither is the staccato articulation which her imitators catch at. To take another example, Mr Thomas Thorne's trick of pumping up every word with a separate sob is not *his* pronunciation. Mr Taylor does not seem to distinguish these differences; therefore I am at a loss to know whether he means anything more than that Miss Terry and Mr Irving have not got exact doubles anywhere among educated English people.

As to Madame Patti, I think she is never better employed than when she is singing her stock ballads. If she were a great dramatic artist, I should say by all means let her devote herself to Donna Anna, Leonora, and Isolde. But she is not, never was, and never will be. There has not yet been witnessed a dramatic situation so tragic that Madame Patti would not get up in the middle of it to bow and smile if somebody accidentally sprung his opera hat. She is simply a marvellous Christy Minstrel; and when you have heard her sing Within a Mile in the Albert Hall so perfectly that not a syllable or a whisper of it is lost, you have heard the best she can do. And this best of hers is not to be despised; nor is the demand for it any discredit to the taste of the people; for between it and the very highest sort of music (which no sane critic ever supposed to be Madame Patti's affair) there is only a chaos of artificiality, a demand for which would be only a sign of that musical curiosity which people acquire from reading about the subject, and which is very different from the true love of music.

29 November 1889

MOST of the people who went to hear Mr Andrew Lang's lecture on How to Fail in Literature at the South Kensington Museum yesterday afternoon were quite capable of doing it without his instruction. It was very cold out of doors; and the museum corridors looked dismal enough with here and there a solitary light throwing all sorts of grotesque shadows, in which lurked depressed policemen. Mr Lang himself lost his way, and was rescued by an exploring expedition just in time to save a stage wait. The lecture was, of course, only a Daily News article drawn out to an hour's duration. The ladies giggled resolutely all through, knowing Mr Lang to be a reputed wit of the first water; but there was not much laughter. The fact is that, though it may require a surgical operation to get a joke into the head of a Scotsman (Mr Lang is a Scotsman), it requires a sledge-hammer to knock one into an English audience. Mr Lang's play was too light for platform work; and it was only when he expressly announced that he was going to be funny, and served up burlesque poems with such chestnut sauce as calling the aesthetic ones "Grosvenor Gallery poetry," that there was anything like a general rise to the occasion. These good people have not yet found out that for the last two years the Grosvenor Gallery has been as Philistine as Madame Tussaud's; and Mr Lang practised on their innocence without a blush.

Mr Lang, like all literary men of slim build and languid bearing, wears an old-fashioned silk-faced frock coat, wrinkling and buttoning at angles that would prevent any self-respecting tailor's dummy from acknowledging a bow from him in Bond Street. He has the figure and air of a young man; but his worn face, with the chin, cheekbones, and nose projecting under the drawn skin, almost reminds one of the veteran Professor Owen. His black hair is streaked with grey, and the front row of it is silver white. The weakest part of the head is outside the eyes, where the temples are cut scantily away. Like Sarasate's, his remarkable appearance is due to his large, striking eyes. His tongue does not betray the Caledonian except by a certain prolongation of the "oo" in "book," and an occasional locution like "pairallel" for "parallel." His voice is high pitched and a little *criarde*; his delivery is recklessly colloquial; his best "holt" is on sly gibing; and he punctuates his speech always in the wrong place, by abrupt pauses after every two or three words, the effect being irresistibly suggestive of Matthew Bagnet in Bleak House. "Took me in. With a second-hand violin-seller. For a friend. That money was no object to. And said he played the fife. When a boy." Mr Lang cuts it quite as small as that; but he peppers in his pauses much more arbitrarily.

2 December 1889

LAST week, when my colleagues were filling in their stereotyped "magnificent rendering of the Seventh Symphony by Mr Mann's famous orchestra," I was sorrowfully recording my opinion that the famous ones did not on that occasion play worth a cent. On Saturday they had evidently, to a man, made up their minds to let me know whether they could play or not. This is interesting, by the bye, as proving that Mr J. A. Smith, the eminent drum player (I would give anything to play the drum), is not the only orchestral artist who studies the press (he, I may remark, does so with such diligence that when I compose a symphony for the Palace, or for Herr Richter, I shall not write in the old style, "the drums count" but simply "Mr Smith reads the paper"). He does not mean to annoy me, I am sure; but if he only knew how desperately I long for something to read myself during a tedious movement, he would rightly ascribe my feelings to mere envy. However, whether it was the sharp, crisp weather, or my disparagement of the previous concert, certain it is that the band was on the alert, strings keen and impetuous, wood wind and horns full of soft color, brass noble and splendid. The Euryanthe overture had "a magnificent rendering," if you like; and Brahms' symphony in D delighted me, though I try to turn up my nose at Brahms. Individual, or rather dual, virtuosity was represented by Mr and Mrs Henschel, who, after making a genuinely valuable contribution to the concert by their Euryanthe selections, in every bar of which Wagner casts his shadow before, unexpectedly relapsed into a feeble drawing-room duet entertainment, in which Mrs Henschel sang in tune, and thereby took the part of the pianoforte against her own husband, which was hardly acting up to her vows. I wonder whether Mr Henschel is conscious of his trick of forcing the intonation just the fiftieth part of a comma to the bad. Let him beware: such habits grow; and there is the spoiling of a good singer in him. As to Sir Arthur Sullivan's Macbeth music, I am eagerly in favor of such performances at standard orchestral concerts, as the anticipation of them causes composers to take their theatrical commissions for incidental music in a much more earnest and lofty spirit, with a view to their subsequent enlargement to the full scale of grand orchestra. By making such events customary, we should at least get a good overture occasionally. This music of Sir Arthur's, clever, skilful, brilliantly scored, catchingly runs the round of the most paying modulations; and there are some ha'porths of true Celtic melody and feeling to boot. Mr Hamish MacCunn's Ship o' the Fiend, which, as it happened, I had never heard before, did not supplant Lord Ullin's Daughter in my affections. The ship is certainly a river steamer in a desperate hurry. I have listened to the sea in all weathers for months together; and whenever I heard four in a bar going, that was a steamer, reader, usually a screw-steamer. Neither oar, wave, nor sailing ship ever made

273

that dread Harwich-Rotterdam Dover-Calais rum-tum accompaniment to the only wishes for death that are really
sincere. The big drum is fine; but methinks I have heard the
effect before—in Les Francs Juges, was it not? Not, of
course, that it is any the worse for that.

5 December 1889

THERE must be a stop put to this sort of thing. Sterndale
Bennett, when asked to write an opera, is said to have stipulated that there should be no soldiers' chorus in it. On
receiving the libretto, the first thing he saw was: "Act I:
The *Pré aux Clercs*, Soldiers drinking." He promptly rolled
it up, returned it, and never wrote an opera. I warn composers that in future, if the curtain goes up on "Act I:
Village inn, with sign, benches, and practicable door L; village lasses and lads discovered singing," I shall presently be
discovered making my way home.

I have already hinted that I do not consider Dorothy
one of the summits of operatic art; and the last dozen imitations I have been invited to witness have left me slightly
restive on the subject. Gretna Green is Dorothy complicated
by Erminie. It will be recollected that the appalling dulness
of the beginning of Erminie was dispelled by the introduction of our old friends Robert Macaire and Bertrand. The
melancholy of the first act of Gretna Green is in like manner
relieved by the appearance of Lurcher in the character of
the Sleeper Awakened, otherwise Abou Hassan, otherwise
Christopher Sly, and on this occasion Robin Bates, a strolling player. But the upshot is that in the second act the
inevitable three men arrive at the inevitable Bramble Hall,
in the inevitable disguise, and there dance the inevitable
minuet, with the inevitable ladies in powder and patches.
What happens in the third act is as dark a mystery to me as
are the closing incidents of Dorothy and Doris. Men have
died, and worms have eaten 'em, but not for love; and I
have gone to theatres and sat out third acts, but not for

Dorothy, not for Doris, not for Gretna Green.

There is an important difference between Dorothies at the Lyric and Dorothies at highly experimental matinées. At the Lyric they are forced into success by persistently concentrating upon them the efforts of far better and more popular artists than they deserve. At the matinées the little merits they may possess are hidden by defective execution. Mr John Storer, the composer of Gretna Green, is a Mus. Doc., and therefore knows his musical grammar, and I imagine, arranges his score with a view rather to the resources of St James's Hall and Crystal Palace than of the Comedy Theatre. He rings the changes on the ordinary trade patterns in music with some fluency and spirit; but too many of the numbers come in just where they interrupt the action instead of advancing it; and the finales are without force or interest. The representation was so imperfect that I can hardly believe that the preparation had got as far as a single complete rehearsal. A few of the principals knew their parts; but the band was evidently playing at sight; and the general business of the stage was pushed through at random, not without occasional profane remonstrances from the wings. Miss Leonora Braham and Mr Richard Temple played like experienced hands; and Mr L. Cadwalader, late Claude Melnotte in Major Cockle's opera, was much in earnest over the tenor part. But Mr Cadwalader must do what his countryman Mr Barton M'Guckin manfully did before him: face the fact that the nose given him by Nature is out of the question for any part except that of Jack Sheppard; and that until he builds up a new one, Phyllis's exclamation when she catches sight of him, "Oh, I hope the Squire [her unknown betrothed] may be like *him!*" will make even the most considerate audience laugh. And even that will avail him nothing until he learns to sing evenly instead of in a squeezed *mezza voce* broken by an irregular series of shouts on all the ascending intervals. Miss Maude Vena is a plump and pleasing person, but no vocalist. As to Miss Velmi, the heroine, I shall defer criticism until she has had a

more favorable opportunity than she had yesterday afternoon.

6 December 1889

I REMEMBER once coming to loggerheads with the late Dr
Francis Hueffer, about fifteen seconds after the opening of
our first conversation, on the subject of musical culture in
English society. Whenever the subject arose between us, I
declared that English society did not care about music—did
not know good music from bad. He replied, with great force,
that I knew nothing about it; that nobody had ever seen me
in really decent society; that I moved amidst cranks, Bohe-
mians, unbelievers, agitators, and—generally speaking—
riff-raff of all sorts; and that I was merely theorising emptily
about the people whom I called bloated aristocrats. He
described, by way of example, an evening at Lord Derby's
house, where he had greatly enjoyed some excellent music;
and he asked me whether I knew that such music was, in a
quiet way, a constant grace of the best sort of English social
life. I suggested that he should give me an opportunity to
judge for myself by introducing me to these circles; but this
he entirely declined to do; having no confidence whatever
in my power of behaving myself in a seemly manner for five
consecutive minutes.

On the first occasion it so happened, fortunately for me,
that a firm of music publishers, having resolved to venture
on the desperate step of publishing six new pianoforte
sonatas, had just sent out a circular containing an appeal
ad misericordiam that at least a few people would, either in
public spirit or charity, take the unprecedented step of buying these compositions. I promptly hurled this at Hueffer's
head, and asked whether that looked like evidence of a constant and enlightened patronage such as the upper classes
accord to racing, millinery, confectionery, and in a minor
degree to literature and painting (for, hang it all! even if the
sonatas were not as good as Beethoven's, they were at any
276

rate no duller than the average three-volume novel or Academy picture). There the subject dropped, my method of controversy being at that time crudely unscrupulous and extravagant. Hueffer, I fancy, regarded me as an unschooled dangerous character; but once, when I was perched on the gunwale of a wagon in Hyde Park, filling up some ten minutes of a "demonstration" with the insufferable oratorizing which is the only sort feasible on such occasions, I was astonished to see his long golden beard and massive brow well to the front among the millions of "friends and fellow citizens." He never told me what he thought about the contrast between the new musical criticism demonstrating on wagons in the sunlight, and the old, groping in perpetual evening dress from St James's Hall to Covent Garden Opera House and back again.

One point I might have put to him, but didn't, is that when you get up a musical entertainment for the exclusive delectation of the nobs, you must either be content with a very scanty audience, in which case the nobs will not think it good enough to come again, or else pack the room with a contingent of musical deadheads, who are not nobs, nor even respectable Philistine snobs, but rank outsiders—though you would be surprised at the costly entertainments, operatic and otherwise, that are run solely for their sake, and that of the jaded pressmen. Last Friday, happening to have an invitation from the Grosvenor Club to their "ladies' night" at the Grosvenor Gallery, I thought I would go and see whether things were altering at all. For the Grosvenor Club, you must know, is no vulgar free-and-easy; and its concerts, from 9.30 to midnight, are never wholly nobless.

On entering that Bond Street portal which was brought here bodily all the way from Italy, and approaching the stairs which I have so often worn with the weary feet of an art critic, I found on one side a descending stream of sad and hollow people, and on the other an ascending one, flushed and swollen. By this I perceived that the refreshments were downstairs; and I hurried up with all convenient speed.

Here I found a nob or two, a deadhead or two, and a vast majority of solid snobs. No celebrities, no literary lot, no journalistic lot, no artistic lot, no Bohemian lot, nothing (to speak of) except plain snobbery, more or less choice. In short, there were—professionally engaged musicians excepted—not above twelve people in the room known to me; and I should have congratulated Mr Prange on such an entirely satisfactory result if I had been quite certain that he would have appreciated the full force of this final proof of the respectability of the gathering, and of the success of his elimination of the great army of "private view" people.

I could not get a program; and when Signor Ducci went to the piano, and Mr Radcliffe took his flute, Mr Mann his horn, and the fiddlers four their fiddles, I wondered what was coming. It proved to be resurrection pie of the dustiest flavor. For a long time I was at a loss. I thought vaguely of Clementi, of Dussek, of Field, of all the Sir Arthur Sullivans that existed before Mendelssohn's time. Not until several elegantly empty movements had worn themselves out did I hit on the right man: on Hummel, the genteel, the talented, the tastefully barren. Here are serenades by Mozart, chamber music with wind parts by Schubert, by Weber, by Schumann, by Mendelssohn, by Brahms, all ready to Signor Ducci's hand; and he goes and digs up Jean Nepomuk Hummel! One unfortunate gentleman said to me: "These things are very nice, of course; but they are very long." Forgetting that I was for once among respectable people, I morosely expressed an opinion that this particular thing was strongly qualified rubbish. "Oh," said he, "you are so very critical: I daresay it does not come up to *your* standard. But it was certainly too long for a place like this." Thus does music get into disrepute. If my friend had heard Beethoven's septet, he would have been delighted. Hearing Hummel instead, he concluded that it was in the nature of classical music to be dull; and he will probably think so to his dying day.

However, the choicer spirits sat in the front of the room

and faithfully listened. The others sat at the back and talked. How they talked! One young lady, who must, I should think, be the champion chatterbox of the universe, so out-did with her tongue the most rapid flights of Signor Ducci's fingers that I stole round three times through the east gallery merely to see whether she had stopped from exhaustion; but she was as fresh as an aviary each time. Another lady, who coaches me in the ways of good society, and makes certain pre-arranged warning signals to me when I eat with my knife or help myself to potatoes with my fingers, was very severe with me because I took sides with the front of the room and listened to the unimpeachable Jean Nepomuk. "You were a failure there," she said next day. "Everybody was noticing your disgraceful behaviour. You will never be a gentleman." "What should I have done?" I demanded. "I say nothing," she replied, "about your not bringing us down to the refreshment room, and your furtively leaving before you had seen us off in a cab. But you should at least have come and *talked* to us." "But that would have disturbed the music," I pleaded. "Music!" she retorted, with scorn. "The Grosvenor is a private club where some rather crack people go: not a concert room. People go there to talk. Besides, you *scowled*." On reflection, I daresay I did. I would suggest to Mr Prange that in future a curtain should shut off the east gallery from the west, and that the fireman should be employed to keep the musical section and the loquacious section in different rooms.

On Wednesday, I at last got to Kensington to hear the Musical Guild. By the bye, I recently stated here that the Guild had ungratefully omitted to invite me to their concerts last season. The secretary writes to say that this was a lie. I do not mean that he expressed it exactly in that way: he is far too polite; but there can be no doubt that it actually was a lie. The invitation was sent; but the Stonecutter Street staff, who have an unquenchable thirst for classical music, boned the ticket, and it never reached me. When I got to the Town Hall on Wednesday, I found that Kensing-

ton society, which combines the Philistinism of old Blooms-
bury with the frivolity of old Brompton, has left this
excellent little Guild in the lurch. A ball at the Kensington
Town Hall is always full: a chamber music concert, it appears, is empty. I and Mr du Maurier and about a hundred
other people had the room to ourselves. Item the first, a
string octet by Mr Holmes, a violinist whom I have had the
misfortune to have heard hardly at all since he used to lead
the quartet at the Popular Concerts some twelve or thirteen
years ago, between the engagements of Madame Néruda,
Joachim, or sometimes Herr Strauss. As Mr Holmes is a
professor, the octet was in regulation form, with four movements, first and second subjects, development, recapitulation, and so on. At first we were all on the alert to hear what
the eight fiddles playing all together would sound like; but
gradually the orthodoxy of the octet numbed us, and we sat
mutely reminding one another of the eve of the battle of
Agincourt.

> The poor condemnéd English
> Like sacrifices, by their watchful fires,
> Sit patiently, and inly ruminate.

The worst of it was that Mr Holmes was there, and could
see us all; so that we had to applaud like mad. And no doubt
his music would have been enjoyable enough had he kept
his ideas off the rack of the sonata form, and stopped when
he had said his say. As it was, the only people who relished
it thoroughly were the experts on my left who had a copy
of the score, and so could feast their *eyes* on the construction of the work. The execution was highly creditable: the
Kensingtonians are fools to neglect these concerts.

After a Schumann duet on two pianofortes by Miss
Annie Fry and Miss Maggie Moore (I do not know which
was which) I walked in the teeth of the east wind all the way
to the Institute over Princes' Hall, in Piccadilly, where the
members of the Wagner Society were having their conversazione. There I got for the first time close enough to Miss

Fillunger to perceive that the reason her voice is all top and no middle is that her method may be summed up in two words: sheer violence. It is a pity; for she sings certain songs with much taste and feeling. Isolde's Liebestod was a failure; but the fault was partly that of the accompanist. Mr Max Heinrich sang *Anrede*, also to a rather trying accompaniment, very well; Mr Shakespeare warbled in his prettiest toy tenor fashion; and Senor Albeniz, after playing Brassin's transcriptions of the rainbow scene from Das Rheingold and the fire charm from Die Walküre, had a final tremendous wrestle with the Walkürenritt. The dead silence produced by his playing, particularly during the second piece, was the highest compliment he could have desired.

To Herr Rudolph Liebich, who gave a concert at Barnsbury Hall on Wednesday, I could only say, "Had I three ears, I'd hear thee." But I have only two, and these cannot be in different postal districts on the same evening. In short, my apologies: I really could not come. In reply to an inquiry why I said nothing about the concert given by the Hallé Manchester orchestra at St James's Hall some time ago, I can only say that I never heard a word of it until it was over; and then I was not surprised to hear that a concert so carefully concealed from me had also apparently been concealed from the general public. At least, this seems the likeliest reason for the thin attendance complained of. I presume that Sir Charles Hallé's concert agent has not yet heard of The Star, and is carefully sending two stalls for every concert to all the crop of sixpenny weeklies which came out in the seventies and died at the half-dozenth number. (You would not credit the stupidities of this sort that go on.) Now, I dont want your tickets, gentlemen agents; but do, in the name of common sense, send me your prospectuses. If not, you will have your own behind-the-timeness to thank for "a rather thin attendance."

LONDON MUSIC IN 1888-89

THE past week has, I believe, been a busy one for the musical critics. It has certainly been a busy one for me, but not musically: I have not even been to the Savoy opera. The first night I have to spare, I shall—but stop! I have not seen The Dead Heart yet, nor La Tosca, nor A Man's Shadow. So let us fix the fourth night I have to spare for The Gondoliers. It will probably come about Easter, or if not then, towards the end of August.

Do not be disappointed at this, eager reader. A new Savoy opera is an event of no greater artistic significance than—to take the most flattering comparison—a new oratorio by Gounod. We know the exact limits of Mr Gilbert's and Sir Arthur Sullivan's talents by this time, as well as we know the width of the Thames at Waterloo Bridge; and I am just as likely to find Somerset House under water next Easter or autumn, as to find The Gondoliers one hair's-breadth better than The Mikado, or Gounod's promised Mass a step in advance of Mors et Vita. The Savoy has a certain artistic position, like the German Reed entertainment; but it is not a movable position. The Red Hussar might have been a new departure at the Lyric; Gretna Green might have been anything; but I am already as absolutely certain of what The Gondoliers is as I shall be when I have witnessed the performance.

One result of this is that I have no real curiosity on the subject. Indeed, I may as well confess that I have no real conviction that I shall ever fulfil my promise to go. Would you be surprised to learn that I have never seen The Sorcerer, Iolanthe, Princess Ida, and Ruddigore at all, nor even Patience, except from behind the scenes at an amateur performance. I have a sorrowfully minute acquaintance with the music of them all; but it has been imposed upon me by circumstances over which I have no control. And as I have seen Trial by Jury only as an afterpiece by a provincial company when it first appeared ever so many years ago; as I saw The

282

Pirates at the Opera Comique, and H.M.S. Pinafore by the secessionists at the Imperial, I begin to realize the fact that I have been only once inside the Savoy Theatre. On that occasion I was haled thither forcibly by a friend who had a spare stall for a Mikado matinée. The conclusion is irresistible that the attraction of Gilbert-Sullivan opera is not sufficient to overcome my inertia. The reason is not far to seek. Mr Gilbert's paradoxical wit, astonishing to the ordinary Englishman, is nothing to me. Nature has cursed me with a facility for the same trick; and I could paradox Mr Gilbert's head off were I not convinced that such trifling is morally unjustifiable. As to Sir Arthur's scores, they form an easy introduction to dramatic music and picturesque or topical orchestration for perfect novices; but as I had learned it all from Meyerbeer (not to profane the great name of Mozart in such a connection), and was pretty well tired of Offenbach before Trial by Jury was born, there was no musical novelty in the affair for me. Besides, Sir Arthur's school is an exploded one. Neatly and cleverly as he exploits it, he cannot get a progression or a melody out of it that is not the worse for wear. It smells mustily of Dr Day and his sham science of harmony, beloved of the Royal Academy of Music. Give me unaffected melodies consisting chiefly of augmented intervals, a natural harmony progressing by consecutive fifths and sevenths, plenty of healthy unprepared tonic discords and major ninths, elevenths, and thirteenths, without any pedantic dread of "false relations"; and then I will listen with some interest. But no more of Dr Day for me.

By the way, the question of learning harmony reminds me that I never finished the reply I began some weeks ago to the gentleman who asked my advice as to how he should proceed in the matter of taking singing lessons. But I do not know that I have anything to add, except that if he succeeds in finding in one and the same person a master able to teach him to produce his voice and pronounce well, besides helping him with really valuable artistic advice and criticism, I shall be glad to learn that gifted one's address.

Here are a few samples of the teachers who are quite willing to undertake the entire instruction of a public singer, from his first scale to his first ovation at La Scala, Milan, or at the Handel Festival. 1. Competent teacher of voice production. Can speak English with an Irish accent, and pronounce Italian with the same. Pretends to know French and German, but doesnt. Considers Rossini the most famous and popular of contemporary composers; but confesses to have been much struck with the modern innovations in Les Huguenots, Il Trovatore, and Gounod's Faust. Has rediscovered Porpora's method, as taught for six years from a single sheet of exercises to Caffarelli. 2. Frenchman. Great master of pronunciation, style, deportment, and dramatic expression, all, except the pronunciation, of the most artificial, unnatural, and impossible order. Sublimely egotistical, overbearing, but timid if resolutely bullied. Has originated all he knows himself. Considers all other teachers quacks. Relates all the anecdotes of Delsarte as having happened to himself. Has smashed his own voice, and is at present busy smashing everybody's else. Intends to come out at the Grand Opera in Paris some day, and bring the world to his feet, like Farinelli, by singing one note—just one—which will be the revelation of a new era. Shews you how Talma (whom he never saw) declaimed. Also gives imitations of Rachel. Regards the French nation as the most degraded on the face of the earth. Is under the impression (erroneous) that he has composed a great Mass. Teaches Gluck's *Divinités du Styx* to lady pupils, and Schubert's *Erlkönig* to gentlemen. 3. Englishman. Organist, Mus.Bac. Unaffectedly colloquial delivery. Suburban accent. Thinks he ought to know something about singing, considering the number of choirboys he has trained. Was a choirboy himself. Member of the Church of England, except for the eighteen months when he was an Irvingite, having taken an organ of that persuasion. Was at the opera once, but is not much of a theatre-goer. Understands fugue and canon, and wrote a Nunc dimittis in five real parts for his degree. Successfully "analyzed" the last movement of Mozart's Jupiter symphony on the same occasion. Favorite classics, Handel and Mendelssohn. Favorite moderns, Jackson and Goss. Dislikes foreigners. Can teach the staff notation, and does not see what more a man can do with a pupil who only wants to sing. 4. Alsatian. Native tongue a patois, which he has forgotten. Cannot speak any language, but communicates with his fellow-creatures in bad French. Composes fantasias, berceuses, serenades, etc., with great facility. Can play the guitar, roll twenty-four cigarets in a minute, and do Badeali's trick of singing a note and swallowing a glass of wine at the same time. Capital critic of cookery. Can shew you exactly how Malibran sang La Sonnambula, Schröder Devrient Fidelio, and Cabel Dinorah. Has known every musician and celebrity of the century, and can tell you discreditable things about most of them. Heard Rossini say that the overture to Tannhäuser would sound just as well played backwards, and, with all due deference to you, prefers Rossini's opinion to yours. Considers that Wagner shewed his evil disposition by drinking coffee out of a golden cup, wearing velvet dressing-gowns, and being ungrateful to Meyerbeer. Knows good singing and music from bad in all the old-fashioned styles, and can work introductions, engagements, and press notices for you. 5. German. Enthusiast. Thorough musician. Well read, well educated, fully up to the modern standard of musical culture. Despises the ignorant dolts and dastards who drag music through the mud in England. Tells them so whenever he meets them. Finds that everybody quarrels with him, and asks whether it is not obvious that this conspiracy against an eminently reasonable and well-disposed man is not the work of the Jews, who are the curse of modern civilization. Will unmask them some day; and in the meantime will let them know what he thinks of them whilst he has breath in his body. Has no sense of humor; cannot see from anybody's point of view but his own; cannot understand that any other person should, except from corrupt motives or mental incapacity, have any other point of view; and would infallibly ruin himself by

mere incompatibility but for the indispensability of his professional skill, knowledge, and devotion.

20 December 1889

WHEN I went down to the Crystal Palace last Saturday I
knew that I was not going to have a treat. Mr Manns was
over the hills and far away; and Mr Cowen was installed instead with a cantata. Still, it might have been worse. It
might have been an oratorio. So, though straitened, I was
not utterly cast down; and I should have reached the Palace
in a fairly serene temper had not the train which brought me
from Charing Cross to Victoria stuck in the tunnel and lost
me the quarter past two express. The next time it happens I
will have the law of them, if there is law in England.

Just as a considerate dentist warms his forceps in hot
water, and hides it behind his back as he approaches you, so
Mr Cowen disguised his cantata as "an old English idyll."
But he could not conceal the ominous fact that the libretto
is by Mr Joseph Bennett, who also supplies an "analysis" of
the music, said analysis being about as difficult as an experienced chemist would find that of a cup of tea. If Mr Cowen
had only written an analysis of Mr Bennett's poem, the two
authors would have been even with one another. As it is, Mr
Cowen has all the praise; and Mr Bennett has to be content
with a slice of the pudding.

Here are some extracts from the "analysis." Easy rhythmic flow and natural harmonies—effective change of key and
tempo—light and sparkling accompaniment—thoroughly
appropriate simplicity—the composer reflects the spirit of
old English music in almost every phrase—simple sugges-
tiveness of the hushed accompaniment—animated and vigorously written number—frank and straightforward music
—very effective return of the first part of the chorus—unaffected beauty of the song—unadorned eloquence of which
Mr Cowen's music now presents so many examples—strong
and earnest feeling, etc., etc., etc. Here is a final gem. "As
286

for the vocal melody, it is simple and simply melodious, be-speaking, moreover, a manly and healthy sentiment entirely appropriate to the circumstances under which it is intro-duced."

The reflections suggested to me by Mr Cowen's simple and simply melodious melodies ran upon the irony of the ar-rangements of that musical Providence which ordains that blunt English professors shall be set to write about Judith and Jael and Deborah, whilst subtle descendants of the race of these heroines are imitating old English ballad music. St John's Eve is just as like The Vicar of Bray or Down Among the Dead Men as Mr Goschen is like Lord Brassey or Mr W. H. Smith. It is the drawing room music of Maida Vale in an "old English" fancy costume. Mr Bennett has played up to the fancy costume, hardily but vainly, by flavoring his verse with such Augustan spices as "gentle Zephyr," and describ-ing his heroine as "the fair." Which only reminded my ir-reverence of Mrs Simkins in the ballad of The Resurrection Man.

Then came the Resurrection Man, the corpse resolved to
    raise:
He broke the coffin with his axe, and at the fair did gaze.
Up started Mrs Simkins. Says she, "My gracious Me!
What are you with that axe about?" "Why, axe about,"
    says he,
With my fol the diddle, ol the diddle, hi fiddle dee.

What a capital subject and title for a cantata, by the way, The Resurrection Man would make!

I do not propose to add an analysis of my own to Mr Bennett's. I doubt if I was as attentive to the music as I ought to have been. The opening St John theme set me thinking about a stave of David's in Die Meistersinger. Then Mr Geard began to play it as a solo on the second trombone; and it immediately struck me as a pity that Mr Manns never gets Mr Geard, with Mr Hadfield and Mr Phasey, to play one of those quaint mediaeval pieces for organ and three or four trombones, which are so much more pleasant to listen to once in a way than Cherubini's overture to Anacreon played for the fiftieth time.

Happening, as I mused thus, to look down at my program, in a sudden wave of speculation as to why its price should have been doubled in honor of Mr Bennett's verses, my eye caught the heading

ARABELLA GODDARD

"Arabella Goddard stands in need of help. Her health, failing for some time past, is now so impaired that she can no longer follow her profession as a teacher; and this appeal is issued by her friends and admirers in the confident expectation that it will not be vainly put forth." Address, Chappell and Co., 50 New Bond Street, W.

The writer of the appeal is wrong in his dates as far as Madame Goddard's retirement is concerned. She may not have played at the Popular Concerts after 1873; but she did not retire then: I heard her play Beethoven's E flat concerto, and one by Sterndale Bennett at the Crystal Palace as lately as 1876, if not 1877; and at about the same period she was playing some of her old Thalberg pieces at Messrs Boosey's ballad concerts. She was an extraordinary pianist: nothing seemed to give her any trouble. There was something almost heartless in the indifference with which she played whatever the occasion required: medleys, fantasias, and potpourris for "popular" audiences, sonatas for Monday Popular ones, concertos for classical ones; as if the execution of the most difficult of them were too easy and certain to greatly interest her. I have a notion—which may be pure fancy—that she wore wide hanging sleeves long after everybody else had given them up, and that they gave a certain winged grace to the travelling to and fro of her elbows; for she always held her forearm at right angles to the keyboard, never perceptibly turning it out. She was more like the Lady of Shalott working away at her loom than a musician at a piano-

288

forte. I can see her now as she played; but I confess I cannot hear her, though I can vouch for the fact of her wonderful manipulative skill. Professional jealousy ascribed her success to the influence of her husband, who was musical critic to The Times; but no influence could have kept her in the front rank for nearly a quarter of a century without great ability on her part. I hope her old admirers will be generous. She must either have spent a fortune or lost it. I hope she has spent it and enjoyed it; and if she had spent ten, her position as the most famous of English pianists entitles her to ask for the means of enjoying dignity and comfort in her retirement.

I do not know what young women are coming to nowadays. You should see the artful letters with which they practise on the weakest side of my nature when they want to get me to a concert. I very nearly succumbed to the wiles of two concert givers on Wednesday; but I hardened my heart for three reasons. 1. They called me a "musical *critique*," a term which lacerated my literary sensibilities. 2. They sent me a half-crown ticket, though their program mentioned high places at half a guinea and five shillings. They little know how small-minded "critiques" are, if they habitually wound their dignity in this greedy fashion. 3. I was performing myself at Westminster, and could not have come anyhow.

27 *December* 1889

THE only music I have heard this week is waits. To sit up working until two or three in the morning, and then, just as I am losing myself in my first sleep, to hear *Venite adoremus*, more generally known as Ow, cam let Huz adore Im, welling forth from a cornet (English pitch), a saxhorn (Society of Arts pitch, or thereabouts), and a trombone (French pitch), is the sort of thing that breaks my peace and destroys my good will towards men. Coming on top of a very arduous month, it reduced me last Saturday to a condition of such complete addledness, that it became evident that my over-wrought brain would work itself soft in another fortnight unless an interval of complete mental vacuity could be induced.

Obviously the thing to do was to escape from the magnetic atmosphere of London, and slow down in some empty-headed place where I should be thoroughly bored. Somebody suggested Broadstairs. I had always supposed Broadstairs to be a show place at Wapping; but I found that it was half-way between Margate and Ramsgate, in neither of which famous watering-places had I ever set foot. So on Christmas Eve I made my way to Holborn Viaduct, where I found a crowd which I cannot honestly describe as a nice crowd. A blackguard crowd, in fact: a betting, loafing, rowdy crowd, with a large infusion of fighting men in it. The fighting men were much the most respectable of the company. They had quite an air of honest industry about them, being men without illusions, who will calculate your weight and earn your money by the sweat of their brow if the opportunity looks good enough—who are not courageous but fitfully hopeful, not fearful but anxious, fighting being to them not a romantic exploit but a trade venture. The question was, however, what were they doing at Holborn Viaduct?

Well, I suppose they were waiting to hail the return of the heroes from Bruges: of the prudent Smith, who is a fairly competent but by no means first-rate artist, and of the heroic Slavin, who is, it appears, a pianist, the Orpheus of the ring. Also, perhaps, of the referee, whose decision proves that he is versed in the history of the ring, and knows what has happened to referees in the past when they have incautiously declared a winner without considering that by doing so they also declared a loser, and thereby took money out of the pockets of men with wives and families. As I came along in the train I read some indignant articles on the unfairness of the Bruges prize fight, evidently written by men who do not know that the proceedings which caused Mr Slavin to demand with noble indignation whether the occupants of Mr Smith's corner were Englishmen, are in every respect typical of the prize ring, and were as familiar in every detail to our grandfathers as Handel's Messiah is to me. Of course the corner-men were English; and I am bound to say that they seem to have earned their money faithfully, which is more than can be said for the mere betting men— real gentlemen, bent on getting money anyhow except by working for it.

I have no illusions about pugilism or its professors. I advocate the placing of the laborer in such a position that a position in the ring will not be worth his acceptance, instead of, as it now is, a glorious and lucrative alternative (for a while) to drudgery and contempt. I have not the smallest respect for the people who call the prizefighter a brute, without daring to treat him like one, but who will treat him much worse than one (than their hunter, for instance) if he remains a laborer for wages. I object to gamblers of all sorts, whether they gamble with horses, fighters, greyhounds, stocks and shares, or anything else. I hate foxhunting, shooting, fishing, coursing (a most dastardly pursuit); and I would, if I had the power, make horse traction in the streets, with all its horrors, as illegal as dog traction is. Furthermore, I do not eat slaughtered animals; and I regard a man who is imposed on by the vulgar utilitarian arguments in favor of vivisection as a subject for police surveillance. No doubt, all the other journalists who disapprove of prizefighting are equally consistent.

However, this has nothing to do with Broadstairs. Let no man henceforth ever trifle with Fate so far as actually to seek boredom. Before I was ten minutes here, I was bored beyond description. The air of the place is infernal. In it I hurry about like a mouse suffocating in oxygen. The people here call it "ozone" and consider it splendid; but there is a visible crust over them, a sort of dull terra-cotta surface which they pretend to regard as a sign of robust health. As I consume in the ozone, this terrible lime-kiln crust is forming on me too; and they congratulate me already on "looking

291

quite different." As a matter of fact I can do nothing but eat: my brain refuses its accustomed work. The place smells as if someone had spilt a bottle of iodine over it. The sea is absolutely dirtier than the Thames under Blackfriars Bridge; and the cold is hideous. I have not come across a graveyard yet; and I have no doubt that sepulture is unnecessary, as the houses are perfect refrigerating chambers, capable of preserving a corpse to the remotest posterity.

I am staying in Nuckell's Place; and they tell me that Miss Nuckell was the original of Betsy Trotwood in David Copperfield, and that the strip of green outside is that from which she used to chase the donkeys. A house down to the left is called Bleak House; and I can only say that if it is any bleaker than my bedroom, it must be a nonpareil freezer. But all this Dickens-mania is only hallucination induced by the ozone. This morning a resident said to me, "Do you see that weatherbeaten old salt coming along?" "Yes," I replied; "and if you will excuse my anticipating your reply, I may say that I have no doubt that he is the original of Captain Cuttle. But, my dear madam, I myself am Corno di Bassetto; and in future Broadstairs anecdotage will begin to revolve round Me." Then, impelled to restless activity by the abominable ozone, I rushed off to the left; sped along the cliffs; passed a lighthouse, which looked as if it had been turned into a pillar of salt by the sea air; fell presently among stony ground; passed on into muddy ground; and finally reached Margate, a most dismal hole, where the iodine and ozone were flavored with lodgings.

I made at once for the railway station, and demanded the next train. "Where to?" said the official. "Anywhere," I replied, "provided it be far inland." "Train to Ramsgit at two-fifteen," he said: "nothing else till six." I could not conceive Ramsgit as being so depressing, even on Christmas Day, as Margit; so I got into that train; and, lo, the second station we came to was Broadstairs. This was the finger of Fate; for the ozone had made me so ragingly hungry that I burst from the train and ran all the way to Nuckell's Place, where, to my unspeakable horror and loathing, they triumphantly brought me up a turkey with sausages. "Surely, sir," they said, as if remonstrating with me for some exhibition of depravity, "*surely* you eat meat on *Christmas* Day." "I tell you," I screamed, "that I never eat meat." "Not even a little gravy, sir? I think it would do you good." I put a fearful constraint on myself, and politely refused. Yet they came up again, as fresh as paint, with a discolored mess of suet scorched in flaming brandy; and when I conveyed to them, as considerately as I could, that I thought the distinction between suet and meat, burnt brandy and spirits, too fine to be worth insisting on, they evidently regarded me as hardly reasonable. There can be no doubt that the people here are mentally enfeebled. The keen air causes such rapid waste of tissue that they dare not add to it by thinking. They are always recuperating—that is to say eating—mostly cows.

Nevertheless it was with some emotion that I trod sea sand for the first time for many years. When I was a boy I learnt to appreciate the sight and sound of the sea in a beautiful bay on the Irish coast. But they have no confounded ozone in Ireland, only ordinary wholesome sea air. You never see an Irishman swaggering and sniffing about with his chest expanded, mad with excessive oxygen, and assuring everybody that he feels—poor devil!—like a new man.

By the way, I did not escape the Waits by coming down here. I had not walked fifty yards from the railway station when I found them in full cry in a front garden. However, I am bound to confess that the seaside vocal Wait is enormously superior to the metropolitan instrumental one. They sang very well: were quite Waits off my mind, in fact. (This is my first pun: let who can beat it.) A couple of boys and the basso were conspicuous in the harmony. I suspect they were the church choir turning an honest penny.

3 January 1890

THE other day, mad for want of something to do, I stood on the edge of the cliff and took a last look at sea and sky before plunging head-foremost to the rocks below. The preceding week had been a deadly one. I had been to Canterbury to see what the boy in Edwin Drood called the Kinfreederl; and my attempt to look right down the building from end to end had been baffled by a modern choir screen compared to which Costa's additional accompaniments to Mozart seemed pardonable and even meritorious. Why can't they let the unfortunate Kinfreederl alone? I rushed off angrily into the wilderness, and after wandering for eighteen miles or so found myself back here at Broadstairs again. I had also gone to Ramsgate to see a melodrama; but I had to leave the theatre at the eleventh murder, feeling that my moral sense was being blunted by familiarity with crime. As a last resource, I had been to the North Foreland Lighthouse to seek employment there; but the resident illuminating artist, whose intelligent and social conversation was an inexpressible relief to me, told me that the Trinity House catches its lighthousists young, as no man with an adequate knowledge of life would voluntarily embrace so monotonous a career. "I have come to such a state of mind in a rock house," he said, "that I believed at last that we two in it were the only people in the world."

One thing that struck me about the lighthouse was that it had a certain character and a certain beauty about it, just like the old Cathedral, except in so far as it was not like it at all. The constructors, I have no doubt, did their very best to make a good lighthouse, because they understood the want of such a thing. Now when we start to put up a choir screen—a thing we should never dream of doing on our own spontaneous initiative—we dont understand the want of it. We dont want it, in short. Consequently, when the restorative architect sketches a miserable sham mediaeval obstruction, we hand the sketch over to the builder as being probably the right thing. The shape is much the same; and, after all, the fellow is an architect, and ought to know. The guide who showed me the Cathedral told me, as well as I can recollect, that the building was designed by one Thomas Ibbekket, who was killed by the Black Prince. So they made him a saint, and put his shrine near the tomb of the Prince, upon whom the pious pilgrims did poetic justice by stealing the diamonds out of his helmet. Well, if Ibbekket's ghost were set to repair the North Foreland Lighthouse, how would he regard the job? He would say, "By'r Lady, here be a bell tower, and eftsoons a gra-mercifully ill-favored one. The wight that wrought here did but foolishly to seek beauty in curiously fashioned wedges of glass, the whiles forgat he it wholly in the shape of his window; whereas every churl knoweth that the beauty of glass is but in its hue, and eke the majesty of a window in the stone arch that surroundeth it. Fain would I build these fools a new tower; but since they will neither have me do that nor disuse their silly custom of firing a beacon in the loft, I must e'en do what I faithfully can to hide their folly, and shield them from the scoffing of the passing shipmen." With such notions, Thomas, it is safe to say, would make a hash of the lighthouse, but by no means such a hash as we have made of the choir screen. To touch that for bungling, Thomas would have to set to at manufacturing dioptric lenses as a sham nineteenth century optician.

However, I am digressing. When I had exhausted the Kinfreederl and the Lighthouse and the melodrama, suicide, as I have related, seemed the only thing left. But I was loth to cast myself off the cliff; for I had just read Mr Walter Besant's sequel to Ibsen's Doll's House in the English Illustrated Magazine, and I felt that my suicide would be at once held up as the natural end of a reprobate who greatly prefers Ibsenism to Walter Besantism. Besides, it seemed to be rather Walter's place than mine to commit suicide after such a performance. Still, I felt so deadly dull that I should hardly have survived to tell the tale had not a desperate expedient to wile away the time occurred to me. Why not telegraph to

LONDON MUSIC IN 1888-89

London, I thought, *for some music to review*? Reviewing has one advantage over suicide. In suicide you take it out of yourself: in reviewing you take it out of other people. In my seaside temper that decided me. I sent to London at once; and the music came duly by parcels post.

I have tried all the songs over carefully, and am under notice to leave when my week is up.

I note that one of these compositions is dedicated by its author to his brother Edgar. Absurd as this is, it is at least pecuniarily disinterested. The point of this remark lies in the fact that dedicating a song is usually only a polite way of begging, as the dedicatee, if a private person and not a relative, is expected to buy five pounds' worth of copies in return. I take the opportunity of mentioning this custom in the hope that the innocent people who gush dedications all over their title-pages may be made aware of the construction which older hands place on such follies. If people do meaningless things, they must not complain at having meanings supplied by other hands.

In coming to the more successful efforts contained in my bundle, I feel far from sure that my standard has not been unduly lowered by trying over the failures. I know a pianoforte dealer who has an artful way of selling indifferent pianos, even to experts. When you go into his showrooms to choose an instrument, he leads you straight to a dashing, rattling, fireirony, "brilliant" atrocity, upon which he half murders your ear before you can stop him. Then, professing to understand by your protests exactly what you really want, he opens just such another, only ten per cent worse all round. By the time he has assaulted you in this manner some five or six times, you are ready, by force of contrast, to accept a very middling piano as a quite exquisite instrument. This old acquaintance of mine has more establishments in Europe and America than I care to mention.

Ha! the postman. What is this? My ticket for the Press view at the Old Masters on Friday! Hooray! Good-bye, Broadstairs.

LONDON MUSIC IN 1888–89

10 *January* 1890

PRETTY lot of fellows, these dramatic critics. Do you remember Cousin Feenix, in Dombey and Son, who spoke of Shakespear as "man not for an age but for all time, with whom your great grandfather was probably acquainted"? That is much the manner in which the dramatic critics have treated the performance of A Midsummer Night's Dream at the Globe. They have sat it out; yawned; put in a good word for Mr Benson as an Archbishop's nephew and for old William; and then set to work in earnest over their beloved penny dreadful equestrian lions and half-crown dreadful Toscas, and forty thousandth night of Sweet Simpering Lavender, and stale dramatic dog biscuit generally. However, it is an ill wind that blows nobody any good. When I entered the pit at the Globe on Monday evening, just as the overture was getting under way, I found only four rows occupied, and so had practically a choice of positions and an easy view for my hard-earned two shillings. But the stalls were full; and I noticed that several of the occupants had brought sacred-looking books, and that the men were unusually particular about removing their hats when they came in.

Now, I am loth to spoil such excellent business; but I am bound to avow that I found myself next a gentleman who is an old acquaintance of the manager's, and he assured me (and I have since verified his assurance) that the archiepiscopal connection is a pure invention of the Press, and that Mr F. R. Benson is neither an archbishop, nor an archbishop's son, nor an archbishop's nephew, nor even, so far as can be ascertained, his remotest cousin-german. My first impulse on hearing this was, I own, to demand my money back. But just then Miss Kate Rorke's draperies floated through the arcades; and when she said

O happy fair!
Your eyes are lodestars, and your tongue's sweet air
More tunable than lark to shepherd's ear

Lambeth Palace might have been dynamited across into Millbank for all I cared. Reader: do you remember Shield's three-part song; and have you ever yourself lent a hand with

> O——h! hap-pee hap-pee hap-pee hap-pee fai-air
> Your eyes, are lodestars and your tongue, sweet, air.

Which, I frankly admit, spoils the sense of the verse, but not its music. This generation, I sometimes think, has no sense of word music. They will go to the Arts and Crafts Exhibition, and admire tissues of cottons, wools, and silks; but give them a beautiful tissue of words, and they have no more sense of the art of it than if it was the Post Office Directory. For instance, William Morris has been weaving words into an article on the art and industry of the fourteenth century in Time. Now watch the reviews, and see whether one of them will draw the slightest distinction between the beauty of this article's verbal fabric and the literary kamptulicon of Mr Blank of the Sterile Club, situate in the region between Dan and Beersheba. But if William Morris had woven a carpet instead, how everybody would have pretended to admire it!

The confounded thing about it is that actors, whose business it is to be experts in word music, are nearly as deaf to it as other people. At the Globe they walk in thick darkness through Shakespear's measures. They do not seem to know that Puck may have the vivacity of a street Arab, but not his voice: his bite, but never his bark; that Theseus should know all Gluck's operas by heart, and in their spirit deliver his noble lines; that Oberon must have no Piccadilly taint in his dialect to betray him into such utterances as

> Be it ahnce, aw cat, aw bea-ah
> Pahd, aw boa-ah with b'istled hai-ah
> In thy eye that shall appea-ah
> When thou wak'st, it is thy dea-ah.

By this time I should be converted to the device of joining consecutive vowels with r's, if conversion were possible. I know that it is easy to say Mariar Ann, and cruelly hard to say Maria Ann. But the thing is possible with courage and devotion. When Mr Benson schools himself to say

> Not Hermia but Helena I love

instead of

> Not Hermia but Helenar I love

I shall be spared a pang when next thereafter I hear him play Lysander. Helenar sounds too like cockney for Eleanor.

On the whole, I fear I must declare sweepingly that Miss Kate Rorke is the only member of the company who is guiltless of verse murder. She is by no means the gentle Helena of Shakespear. The soul of that damsel was weak; but none of Miss Kate Rorke's organs, I take it, is stronger than her soul. Yet by this very strength she forces herself on the part; and I accept her with joy and gratitude. Artist in one thing, artist in all things. The sense of beauty that guides Miss Rorke through the verse, guides her movements, her draperies, her eyes, and everything about her. She has charms in her fingers and charms in her toes; and she shall have music (by Mendelssohn) wherever she goes.

Miss Maud Milton, who played Hermia, took the part at such short notice that she evidently had to learn it during the intervals; for in the first act she left out all about the simplicity of Venus' doves, and a good deal more beside. Later in the evening she was comparatively letter-perfect; and she played with intelligence and force. But she was melodramatic: the indispensable classic grace was wanting: she looked persecuted, and seemed to be struggling through the toils of some forger villain towards a reconciliation with a long lost husband in the fifth act. As to Bully Bottom, I have no doubt he was more Athenian than Shakespear made him; but his stupidity lacked the true unction, and his voice had not caught the Stratford-on-Avon diapason. The rest of the company must excuse me. I never trespass on the province of a colleague. The criticism of acting is Arthur Walkley's business.

About the music, however, I may venture on a word. Mendelssohn's score, even when eked out by Cooke's Over hill, over dale, and Horn's I Know a Bank, falls short of Mr Benson's requirements. Accordingly, not only are two "songs without words," the Spring Song and the so-called Bee's Wedding, pressed into the service, but the Fingal's Cave overture has been cheerfully annexed for the last *entr'acte*. I fully expected a selection from Elijah to crop up in the course of the fifth act. But how different this music is from the oratorio music! how original, how exquisitely happy, how radiant with pure light, absolutely without shadow! Nineteenth-century civilization had a job after its own pocket in knocking all that out of Mendelssohn, and setting him to work on Stone Him to Death and the like.

I am glad to be able to say that the nineteenth century has not utterly defeated the execution of the music at the Globe. True, the orchestra is a little shorthanded, and now and then rather rough; but it greatly enhances the pleasure of seeing the play; and, under the circumstances, I ask no more except that the wedding march should be pulled together and smartened up. At present it is slovenly. The audience behaved stupidly, talking too much during the *entr'-actes*, and encoring "I know a bank" a charming piece, but one which does not require to be heard twice over, as its melodic ideas are repeated and elaborated as much as they will bear. The singing was very fair, though here again imperfect training in diction told on the effect. For instance, Miss Townsend's voice was pretty when she was singing old-fashioned florid passages without words; but when she came to tell us about hills and dales, the excessive acuteness of her vowels made the effect grotesque. I must use a French *é* to represent the effect of the first line she sang—

Oveh heels, oveh *déllz*, etc., etc.

But if I harp too much on diction, some idiot will begin to clamor for the introduction of the French system, by which all the actors, instead of cultivating and developing each his own diction, acquire a second-hand article which is much more hateful than the honest incompetence of our British buskineers. (This phrase is at the service of any dramatic critic who would like to write The British Buskineers to the tune of British Grenadiers. For example:

On parle de Mounet Sully: on parle de Coquelin,
De Febvre, Got et Maubant, du sociétaire enfin.

And so on, ending with the dow, roy, meeh, fawr, saorl, lar, see, of the British buskineer.)

The death of Gayarré places it beyond my power to make amends for the injustice—if it really was an injustice —which I did him the first and last time I heard him sing. The occasion was his debut at Covent Garden in 1877 in the character of Raoul de Nangis. I was not then accustomed to the now happily obsolescent vocal method called goatbleat; and I thought he had a horrible voice and a horrible way of using it, whilst his bearing and acting aggravated rather than redeemed his vocal disadvantages. Not only thought so, reader, but said so; for in those days Italian opera was in the valley of the shadow; and the performances at Covent Garden were one long exasperation from the first note to the last. Mr Harris had not taken matters in hand then: he was, I rather think, playing in Pink Dominoes at the Criterion. Howbeit, I protested vehemently against Gayarré; but although I stand to my opinion of the solitary performance I witnessed, I cannot doubt that in concert rooms, in private, and in theatres too small to frighten him into forcing his voice beyond all reason, he must have been an artist of considerable charm, as his position was not one of those that are to be had for nothing. Cases are by no means uncommon of practised singers and speakers losing all confidence in their old methods in new and alarming conditions as to space. When that happens, they begin to bleat frantically, with the effect that Gayarré produced on me. Actors and singers who have small voices should remember that the problem for them is to make themselves *heard*, and by no means to make themselves *loud*. Loudness is the worst defect of quality that any voice, large or small, can have.

17 *January* 1890

THE other day, passing Her Majesty's Theatre, I saw by the placards that a Christmas pantomime was going on inside. I had not been to a pantomime for fourteen years at least. So I went in; and now I do not think I shall go to one for fourteen years more. It was terribly stupid. The investment it represented may have been anything between ten and twenty thousand pounds. Every thousand of it produces about a farthingsworth of enjoyment, net. I say net, because a balance has to be struck between positive and negative results. In estimating that the entertainment exceeds the annoyance and tedium by a tenth of a farthing per cent, I am making a generous allowance for the inferior tastes of my fellow creatures. As far as I am personally concerned, the balance is on the other side; for I am sorry I went; and wild horses could not drag me thither again.

What struck me most was the extraordinary profusion of artistic talent wasted through mere poverty of purpose. One fiftieth part of it placed at the disposal of a man with the right sort of head on his shoulders would have sufficed for a quite satisfactory pantomime. The scene painters, costumiers, property makers, armorers, and musicians are for the most part capable artists; a few of the players are actors; and the dancers do not all walk like irresolute ostriches. But they might almost as well have been walking up and down the Strand with their hands in their pockets—or in Mr Leslie's pockets—for all the use that is made of their ability in the Haymarket. In the Strand they would bore nobody but themselves: in the Haymarket they bored Me—Me, that never injured them.

The whole affair had been, according to the playbill, "invented and arranged by Charles Harris." I have no animosity towards that gentleman; but I must say I wish he would invent a little more and arrange a little less. Take the procession of beetles, for instance. When I was a small boy there was in the house a book on entomology, with colored plates. The beetles depicted in them were so gorgeous and fantastic that it was delightful to turn over ten plates or so. After that they palled, rapid and easy as the turning over of a bookleaf is; for the mind thirsted for a new idea. Now it was a capital notion of Mr Harris's, that of having a processional ballet of beetles. But he has worn the notion to death —or, to put it tropically, he turns over too many plates. The first five minutes are interesting, the second tedious, the third wearisome, the fourth exasperating, and the fifth sickening. As of old, I craved for a fresh idea, and was given a stale beetle. The character of the color scheme never varied, the drill never varied, the music never varied; so that at last I felt as if Mr Harris were brushing my hair by machinery for half an hour on the strength of my having enjoyed it for the first half minute. The fairy tale procession and the Shakespearean procession were far more successful; for here was a world of ideas annexed as cheaply as a slice of Africa by the British Empire.

Perhaps I may seem a little rough on the pantomime, in view of all the praise the papers have lavished on it. But you must remember the fourteen years which have elapsed since my last experience in this line. I have not been let down gently from Christmas to Christmas by a ladder of fourteen steps: I have come down the whole distance with a crash. I used to regret that the performers were merely ordinary actors and not pantomimists as well. Imagine my feelings on finding that they are now not ordinary actors, but "variety artists" without any dramatic training whatever. The reduction of the harlequinade to three or four scenes lasting only an hour or so seemed inevitable owing to the curious scarcity of the sort of talent required to make it really funny. I have never seen a good clown (this is without prejudice to Mr Payne, to whose clowning I am a stranger); and I have my doubts as to whether the character was not as purely idio-

syncratic with Grimaldi as Dundreary was with Sothern. I
remember one brilliant harlequin—Mr Edward Royce—who
donned the spangles one evening in an emergency. Also one
solitary pantaloon, a member of the Lauri troupe, an imposing old gentleman, punctiliously mannered and beautifully
dressed, whose indignant surprise at the reverses which over-
took him was irresistibly ludicrous.

But even in its decay, with stupid and vulgar clowning,
and harlequins and columbines who had never seen Dresden
China or Watteau pictures, the harlequinade still consisted
of a string of definite incidents, involving distinct parts for
an old woman, a masher (then known as a swell), a policeman, and a nurserymaid. The policeman still plotted, the
clown counterplotted, the pantaloon muddled everything he
attempted, and the harlequin at least danced. At Her
Majesty's I found to my astonishment that all this has
dwindled to a single scene, lasting about twenty minutes,
during which two clowns, two pantaloons, two policemen,
and a crowd, without distinct functions, improvise random
horseplay in the feeblest and most confusing way simultaneously in opposite corners of the stage.

This idea of doubling the clown and pantaloon is about
as sensible as if Mr Irving were to invite Edwin Booth to
come back to the Lyceum and revive Othello with two
Othellos and two Iagos.

The question now is, shall we leave it there, and shall I
never see a pantomime again? Such a solution is impossible.
When Mr Harris and Mr Leslie have gone on for a few years
more egging each other on to greater expenditure behind the
curtain for the sake of greater weariness before it; when even
the grown-up people who have learnt to be thankful for
small mercies begin to echo the sneers of the cynical little
children for whose sake the entertainment is professedly got
up; when the essential squalor of the whole affair becomes so
obvious that even the dramatic critics will grow tired of
writing strings of goodnatured lies about it, then some manager will suddenly strike his forehead and say, "Suppose I

try a real pantomime! Suppose I get rid of my foul-mouthed, illiterate, ignorant stage manager, who, though he dips thousands deep into my treasury, cannot with all his swearing get two supers to walk across the stage in step, much less tread the boards like self-respecting men! Suppose I take the matter in hand myself as an artist and a man of culture!"

Well, suppose he does, how could he set to work? I had better give explicit directions, since it appears that nobody else will. First, then, Mr Manager, get rid of your "literary adviser," if you have such a thing. The theatres which harbor such persons at once become conspicuous by their illiteracy. This done, think over the whole profession as far as you know it, with a view to selecting dancers, acrobats, and comedians who are good pantomimists. At Her Majesty's, for instance, there is a ballet of young ladies who are supposed to represent rabbits. You can pick out at a glance the girls who ever saw a rabbit and who have the faculty of suggesting the peculiar movement of the creature's head and paws. These are the girls to select for the new departure in pantomime. Leading artists are to be found everywhere. At a circus in Amsterdam I saw a troupe which made music out of kitchen utensils. Their leader was a capital pantomimist: his imitation of an orchestral conductor was immense; and his posturing as the ringmaster on a sham horse outdid nature itself. In *Le Voyage en Suisse* there was a Frenchman, Agouste by name if I mistake not, who was a most artistic pantomimist. When Offenbach's *Voyage dans la Lune* was produced at the old Alhambra, Madame Rose Bell, a lively French lady, distinguished herself therein, not more by the qualities which endeared her to the Alhambra audience than by the vivacity and expressiveness of her pantomime. Such examples show how a company of pantomimists could be selected by a good judge. It must finally contain a pair of young and beautiful dramatic dancers for lover and sweetheart (harlequin and columbine), a good comedian for the intriguing valet (clown), a good old man for the tyrannical father, the rich old suitor (pantaloon), or anything except

305

the detestable Ally Sloper of today. Finally, you must get a dramatic poet who is a born story teller and who knows the Arabian Nights better than Two Lovely Black Eyes. The poet will tell you the rest.

24 January 1890

WHEN I laid down my pen last week I thought I had done with pantomimes and Cinderella for ever. But who shall foreknow the ways of Destiny? On Saturday I went to Bristol to fulfil a Sunday starring engagement of an unmusical nature. In the evening, having nothing better to do, I naturally went to the theatre, where I found a packed audience listening to the strains of a comic boy in buttons, who was in sole possession of the stage. I gathered from his song some more or less valuable observations on human conduct in general; but I did not find out what the main business in hand was until the entire family came in, when a glance at the two ugly sisters and the one pretty one showed me that I had wantonly exposed myself to another Cinderella pantomime. However, I do not complain. The Bristolians, an exacting people, declared that it was not as good as last year's; but I had not seen last year's, and so could only weigh it against the pantomime at Her Majesty's, compared to which it was an entertainment for artists and philosophers.

For instance, there was a musical director, Mr G. R. Chapman, who knew his business, and subdued his orchestra to the merest whisper during the harlequinade and the clog dancing (clog dancing is pretty when the dancer does not wear clogs). At Her Majesty's, Mr Solomon keeps his band scraping and blowing its loudest throughout, until it induces distraction and madness, like the steam organ of a merry-go-round. The variety items are managed so as not to confuse or unduly interrupt the story, which was never quite lost sight of by the actors. These, as actors will in pantomimes, occasionally substituted playing the fool for comic acting, with depressing results; for nothing on earth leads more to gloomy

306

meditation than the spectacle of a grown man playing the
fool. Far be it from me to deny, too, that the fun occasionally
drooped into stale and vapid vulgarity. But there was nothing like the weariness and dreariness of the London pantomime. If I were forced to choose which of the two I should
sit out again on pain of death, I should choose death; but if
that alternative were cut off I should unhesitatingly choose
Bristol, although I cannot understand why any conceivable
railway journey should at this time of day take three mortal
hours to accomplish.

But I have not resumed the subject of pantomime merely
to heave another brick at the costly follies of our big metropolitan playhouses. Nor would I have done so solely in order
to urge most vehemently upon the Jee family, who made a
delightful clangor with The Last Rose of Summer on horse-
shoes and The Harmonious Blacksmith on anvils, that the
horseshoe which sounds the keynote is flat, a defect curable
in five minutes by any harmonious blacksmith armed with a
file. Even the suicidal determination of all the singing ladies
to get chest notes or nothing, disastrous as its results must
prove to them, would not by itself have moved me to remonstrance, hardened as I am to it by this time. As to the very
pretty dance between Mr Edmund Payne and Miss Nellie
Murray in the fourth scene, did not the audience sufficiently
justify it by an encore, as they did also a clog dance (clog-
less, as aforesaid) by a Miss Lyndale, whose rosy and shapely
limbs were unembarrassed to an extent that would have considerably embarrassed my grandmother? Mr John Watson,
the scenic artist who designed the admirable effects of light
and color in the fairy coach scene and the *Incroyable* ballet,
can probably do without any congratulations; and the pro-
prietor-manager with the historic name, Mr John Macready
Chute, would, if he is anything like a London manager, consider all the praise I might lavish on him cancelled by the
diabolical hatred and personal malice betrayed by my reflection on that single horseshoe that was out of tune. Therefore, I lay no stress on any of these matters, but proceed to

the one point that seriously requires publicity.

It was towards the end of last century that this nation, having devoted itself body and soul to the making of money and of everything that would, under pressure, sweat gold, took to making money out of children. I do not propose to make my readers sick by recapitulating the horrible villainies on parish apprentice children which led to the ineffectual Morals and Health Act of 1802, and which were continued on all sorts of poor children without much alleviation almost up to the middle of this wickedest of all the centuries. Every attempt to put these villainies down was met with by declarations that the children liked them, and were benefited by them, and that their little earnings helped to brighten and beautify the dwellings of their affectionate parents. By slow and painful steps Humanity beat back Rascality, Greed, and Hypocrisy until, last year, a point was reached at which the law forbad the employment of children under ten. Unhappily an exception was made in the case of children employed in theatres, who were still left liable by means of a magistrate's special license. This breach was made in the Act solely through the ignorance and prejudice of its supporters with respect to theatres, one gentleman declaring, in effect, that children on the stage were corrupted by association with loose women there, and so forth. The gentleman apologized afterwards; but by that time the mischief was done. The Puritan assumption that every woman on the stage is necessarily a coarse and brazen voluptuary is as offensive as the counter assumption that she is necessarily a fireside angel, supporting a deserving family out of her modest earnings, and never going out without a chaperone. The moment the opposition to the exception in favor of theatre proprietors became identified with the Puritan crusade against beauty and happiness, it was damned, and the children were sacrificed.

But even those who sacrificed them by accepting the fatal amendment never intended that magistrates should do more than, after a strict inquiry, cautiously license here and there the appearance of some indispensable child character in dramas so great that they cannot, without public loss, be banished from the stage. I invite these innocent compliers to take a turn through the theatres and see for themselves how magistrates and petty sessions have been wantonly issuing their licenses wholesale. In this Bristol pantomime, in which the employment of a child under ten was no more indispensable than the appearance of a performing lion, there were at least twenty children under ten on the stage. They were all the better for the Act, which had secured for them a separate room with a fire in it, a restriction of their time at the theatre to two hours, and the vigilance of people of my way of thinking before the curtain, backed by the chance of a visit from the factory inspector behind it. Consequently they romped through and piped out Mr Farmer's Singing Quadrilles much more happily and freely than they would have done in the bad old times. Further, there were only twenty of them as against thirty before the passing of the Act. But the fact remains that they should not have been there at all.

There is some consolation in the reflection that the Bill for the further extension of the Factory Acts—a measure to which the Liberal party is pledged—will contain a clause raising the age under which children may not be employed from ten to twelve, as in Germany and Hungary. No doubt an attempt will be made to renew the present special license clause. But the way in which it is being abused to drive a coach and six through the Act of 1889 will come up in judgment and secure for the children the protection of total and unconditional prohibition. If the comfortable middle-class people are so ready to be persuaded that work on the stage is a harmless pleasure for children, let them send their own young ones gratuitously to enjoy and improve themselves there. The Acts prohibit only employment for hire. In the meantime, I hope that some member of Parliament will seize the earliest opportunity to get from the Secretary of State a return of all the cases in which licenses have been granted.

Such a return will open the eyes of the verdant dupes who thought that the licensing clause was passed solely in order to provide Richard III with a little Duke of York, or The Doll's House with three little Helmers.

31 *January* 1890

JUST listen to this:

"Star Building, Stonecutter Street, E.C.,
"27th January, 1890.

"Dear Signor di Bassetto,

"May I respectfully and deferentially invite your attention to the fact that it is about six weeks since we had anything about music in your column, and that the Popular Concerts have been running for the last fortnight in the vain hope of securing a fraction of the time that can be spared from the enlightenment of humanity at Bristol and elsewhere."

These people seem to think that I have nothing else to do than go to concerts for them. Observe, too, how severe, how classic, their taste. No vulgar pantomime music for them. Monday Popular Concerts or nothing: that is their ultimatum.

It is evident that if I am to maintain my independence as a critic, this spirit of insubordination at headquarters must be checked. But how check it? A vulgar critic would refuse ever again to enter St James's Hall—would perhaps threaten to resign. Not thus do I enforce my authority. I am no despot: when the editorial staff, madly fancying that it knows better than I, revolts against me, I immediately let it have its own way, knowing that before three columns have elapsed it will implore me to resume my sceptre and rescue The Star from the consequences of its presumptuous ignorance. The moment I got that letter I went straight off to a Monday Pop. The following notice of it will, I trust, be found to conform in all respects to the best regulation pattern.

310

LONDON MUSIC IN 1888-89

On Monday, the 27th inst., at St James's Hall, Piccadilly, a large audience assembled to enjoy the eleven hundred and fifth of Messrs Chappell's Popular Concerts, an excellent institution, now in its thirty-second season, which has contributed, more than any other cause, perhaps, to the spread and enlightenment of musical taste and culture in England. Lady Hallé, better known to our readers as Madame Norman Neruda, occupied, not for the first time, the responsible post of first violin; and the violoncello was in the capable hands of the veteran Piatti. It is hardly necessary to say that such artists as these, assisted by Herr L. Ries (second violin) and Herr Strauss (viola), gave a perfectly satisfactory rendering of Schumann's quartet in A minor, which, curiously enough, is written in the key of F major, and which, as all know, is the first of the set of three dedicated by Schumann to his friend Mendelssohn. Nor did the share of the programme allotted to the once contemned Zwickau composer end here. It is true that Schumann's *Papillons* can hardly be viewed as an adequate example of his maturest powers; but it furnished Herr Stavenhagen with ample opportunities for displaying the combined delicacy and strength of his execution, which was duly appreciated, and secured for him a merited, but—considering the character of these concerts—inappropriate encore. However, it is vain to expect artists to resist these flattering compliments: the initiative in reform must come from the public. The concert concluded with the ever fresh and perennially welcome septet of Beethoven, played—we need not say how well—by Madame Neruda and MM. Ries, Lazarus, Wotton, Paersch, Reynolds, and Piatti, who, if we except Mr Paersch, a comparatively new comer in the place formerly occupied by Mr Harper, have for so many decades charmed us with their unapproachable rendition of this delightful work, of which the composer in his old age pretended to be ashamed. But such are ever the waywardnesses of great geniuses. The vocalist was that promising young singer, Miss Marguerite Hall, who was heard to advantage in songs by Schubert and

311

Brahms, besides seizing the occasion to introduce an unpretentious but thoroughly musicianly setting of O My Love is like a Red Red Rose, by Herr Henschel.

There! How do you like it, O men of Stonecutter Street, and silly friends all who are wont to say of this column that it is "amusing, of course, but not musical criticism"? Now that bitter experience has taught you that no want of capacity, but only sheer mercy for you, restrains me from earning my income cheaply by what you in your abysmal gullibility call "musical criticism," perhaps some sense of shame may penetrate your ungrateful hearts. Idiots! I could teach a parrot to twaddle like that if I could catch a sufficiently empty-headed one. To speak more gently, it is mere beginner's work; and no critic should pretend to undertake a *feuilleton* until he has far outgrown it. However, I shall relapse into it some day. When I shall have got on terms of private intimacy with all the artists and impresarios in London— when my obligations to them in the way of tickets and scraps of information shall have made it impossible for me to say anything that would make the morrow's meeting disagreeable—when I begin to do a little business in the libretto and analytical program line—when, in short, I am thoroughly nobbled and gagged, then I, too, shall relapse into the beginner's style; and you, if you are wise, will stop reading my column.

Meanwhile, let me say, since I have had the trouble of going to that concert, that the Schumann quartet, though an excellent piece of chamber music, cuts but a feeble figure in a large concert hall; and that I cannot understand why the septet was played with all the old-fashioned repeats. The septet is just fresh enough to make it delightful without the repeats, and just old and hackneyed enough to make it wearisome with them, especially after half-past ten at night. Madame Neruda, by the way, led off the allegro about half a mile sharp, and set my ears and Mr Lazarus's on edge to such an extent that when the clarionet took up the theme, neither he nor I could tell whether it was in tune or not. As

to Herr Henschel's futile little setting of "My Love is like,"
etc., I can only hope that its very cool reception will help to
bring him to his senses when next he gets an attack of providing paltry new tunes for good old words. Brahms' *Guten
Abend, mein Schatz*, I had never heard before. It is a quaintly
pleasant little duologue in song; and Miss Marguerite Hall
hit it off very nicely.

At the Hallé orchestral concert this day week I was inhumanly tormented by a quadrille band which the proprietors of St James's Hall (who really ought to be examined by
two doctors) had stationed within earshot of the concert-
hall. The heavy tum-tum of the basses throbbed obscurely
against the rhythms of Spohr and Berlioz all the evening,
like a toothache through a troubled dream; and occasionally,
during a *pianissimo*, or in one of Lady Hallé's eloquent
pauses, the cornet would burst into vulgar melody in a remote key, and set us all flinching, squirming, shuddering,
and grimacing hideously. Under these circumstances I became morose, and could see nothing but faults. The Euryanthe overture was hurried, and so missed by a hair's breadth
the full grandeur of its march and passion of its flight. When
shall we be delivered from this Mendelssohnic curse of speed
for speed's sake? The Spohr concerto, in spite of its shapely
plausibility, is lifeless and artificial; and if Lady Hallé made
the best of the solo part, the orchestra certainly made the
worst of the dull empty accompaniments. The intermezzo by
Svensden turned out to be an inferior imitation of Glinka's
Komarinskaja; and there was no sense in encoring Grieg's
pretty Spring melody, admirably as it showed off the qualities of the string band. The interest rose considerably when
Berlioz's Romeo and Juliet music, without the vocal numbers, came on. The orgie at Capulet's was very well played:
the balance of tone between the dance measure and the
broad jubilant chant of the brass was struck to perfection.
In several passages the ringing brightness of the tone from
the wind came with exactly the effect Berlioz, one feels,
must have aimed at. The mass of violins, all executing a pro-

313

longed shake in harmonics, fluttered the audience as usual in the Queen Mab scherzo; but I cannot say that I see much beneath the *bizarrerie* of that celebrated movement except a distorted echo of Beethoven's much more beautiful Eroica scherzo.

P.S. I have just been to La Tosca; and the public will undoubtedly expect to know whether I felt like M. Lemaître, who wanted to get up and say, *"Pas cela: c'est lâche"*; or like Mr William Archer, who took it as a pessimist's tonic and felt braced by it. I felt nothing but unmitigated disgust. The French well made play was never respectable even in its prime; but now, in its dotage and delirium tremens, it is a disgrace to the theatre. Such an old-fashioned, shiftless, clumsily constructed, empty-headed turnip ghost of a cheap shocker as this Tosca should never have been let pass the stage door of the Garrick. I do not know which are the more pitiable, the vapid two acts of obsolete comedy of intrigue, or the three acts of sham torture, rape, murder, gallows, and military execution, set to dialogue that might have been improvised by strolling players in a booth. Oh, if it had but been an opera! It is fortunate for John Hare that he has only the dramatic critics to deal with.

7 February 1890

ONE day when I was expatiating to a friend on the importance of teaching people to speak well, he asked me dubiously whether I did not find that most men became humbugs when they learnt elocution. I could not deny it. The elocutionary man is the most insufferable of human beings. But I do not want anybody to become elocutionary. If your face is not clean, wash it: dont cut your head off. If your diction is slipshod and impure, correct and purify it: dont throw it away and make shift for the rest of your life with a hideous affectation of platformy accent, false emphases, unmeaning pauses, aggravating slowness, ill-conditioned gravity, and perverse resolution to "get it from the chest" and make it sound as if you got it from the cellar. Of course, if you are a professional humbug—a bishop or a judge, for instance— then the case is different; for the salary makes it seem worth your while to dehumanize yourself and pretend to belong to a different species. But under ordinary circumstances you had better simply educate your ear until you are fairly skilful at phonetics, and leave the rest to your good sense.

The above remarks express indirectly but unmistakably that I have just been to a students' concert at the Guildhall School of Music. I claim the right to measure the Guildhall School by a high standard. Your "Royal" Academies and Colleges do not appeal to me: I am a Republican, and cannot understand how any person with an adequate sense of humor can consent to have a crown stuck on his head at this time of day. But the Guildhall School is our civic school; and the time is coming when that term will have some real significance in London. Already the young savages and Philistines of the commercial classes crowd thither, and leave the private teacher lamenting and penniless. Now, the first thing that the savages and Philistines need to be taught is the art of speech. A finely skilled professor of diction would be cheap at a thousand a year at the Guildhall School. Fancy my feelings when I found that there is no such functionary in the place.

Doubtless this will strike the teaching staff as unfair. But I did not fail to perceive that the unfortunate pupils had been drilled and drummed into articulating their consonants clearly. When they came to an Italian T or D, in forming which the tongue makes an air-tight junction with the teeth until the consonant explodes, they conscientiously tucked up their tongues against their palates in true British fashion and brought out their native T or D much as a Sheffield hydraulic piston would, with plenty of hissing. Such a sound as this, followed by a racy Brixton or Bradford diphthong, produces an effect in an Italian song of the old school that would make a vivisector's mouth water. Imagine a young lady sent out by her master to sing Handel's

Lascia ch'io pianga without a word to warn her that the reiterated "e che sospire" is not pronounced "Ayee Kayee Soaspearayee." I forbear further illustration. The subject is too painful. Suffice it to say, that if Mr Tito Pagliardini were to hear an air by Stradella or Pergolesi uttered by a Guildhall pupil, he would rush from the building across the Embankment, and bury the horrid memory in the Lethean Thames.

Yet diction is not one of the lost arts. Coquelin does not speak in the Guildhall manner; nor Salvini, nor Joseph Jefferson, nor Henry Irving, nor Ada Rehan, nor Antoinette Sterling, nor Mrs Weldon, nor dozens of other speakers and singers. And remember that, though the public is not an expert, and cannot place its finger on the exact details in which the Guildhall novices differ from these finished artists, yet it hears a difference, though it mercilessly ascribes it to native vulgarity on the one hand and native distinction on the other. But it is absurd to brand young singers as vulgar because they, having spent their lives between the City and Holloway, know no other mode of speech than that which is vernacular in those regions. Half a dozen early lessons in phonetics from someone who knew at least a little about them—not necessarily a Mus.Bac. or Mus.Doc.—would set them in the right way.

Such teachers are to be found, if the Guildhall authorities care to find them. On Saturday last I received an invitation to the Albert Hall from a Mr P. J. Kirwan, who is doubtless a well-known reciter, but of whom I had never heard until that day. I found him to be an artistic speaker with a cultivated voice and a tact in comedy that enabled him to pass off all his humorous selections at about six times their literary value. His delivery of Drayton's Agincourt was most musical, though here and there the legitimate mark of the school of Mr Irving intensified into illegitimate Irvingism. One of Mr Irving's objectionable peculiarities is a trick of spoiling a vowel occurring between m and n, by continuing the humming sound of these letters through it instead of letting it flash out clearly between them. Thus his "man" or "men" becomes a monstrosity, which Mr Kirwan has picked up. Again, Mr Irving's "oo" varies from French "eu" to English "aw"; and Mr Kirwan, in pronouncing "fury" as "fieurie" or "fyawry" clearly slips into a mere imitation. Nor is he wholly guiltless of unmeaning pauses. "Along that wild and weatherbeaten coast" cannot reasonably be read as "Along that wild and weatherbeaten. Coast." Similarly, the difference between "And did the deed for ever to be sung" and "And did the deed for ever to be. Sung" is the difference between sense and nonsense.

Whilst I am in the way of faultfinding, I may as well say that I protest altogether against the Reciter's theory that verse should be disguised as prose in its oral delivery. All poets read their verses sing-song, which is the right way: else why the deuce should they be at the trouble of writing in verse at all? Mr Kirwan recognizes this to some extent; indeed he treated Agincourt quite fairly, and Hood's Equestrian Courtship exquisitely, in this respect; but when he came to Tennyson and Morris the waves of verse were flattened into ripples, and at a few points into dry flat tablecloth prose. I hardly blamed him in Enoch Arden, the desperate commonplace of which would flatten out anybody or anything; but Atalanta's Race is quite another sort of poetic commodity; and it rather got the better of Mr Kirwan. Since it was much the most difficult piece in the program, he should have placed it earlier in the afternoon. As it was, its difficulties seemed to flurry him a little; and his attempt to make the description of the race sensational by hurrying it was the one error of taste he committed—by which, of course, I mean the one point at which his taste clashed with mine. Anyhow, I heartily wish that Mr Weist Hill would appoint him professor of English diction at the Guildhall School.

Harking back for a moment to that concert, I may say that the terrible old voice-grinding which used to constitute the staple teaching at academies and conservatoires seems much mitigated in these days. The only young vocalist about whom I felt any particular anxiety was a lady who sang Gounod's Worker with the too familiar Academy pressure kept steadily on the middle of the voice. The last note but one was the conventional high note to finish with. She made an unskilful shot at it, and, being young, just saved it. I cannot pretend to think that that young lady is in the right path; but I speak with no better warrant than that of a mere critic. Doubtless her master differs from me with authority.

Mr Richard Shipman, like Mr Kirwan, recites; and as he does his best in a very good-humored way, I have no objection to offer, although I, somehow, did not sit out his recital as I sat out Mr Kirwan's. I should not mention the matter except to tell Miss Marjorie Field Fisher that many young ladies have done very well in the world as singers with less talent and charm than she possesses. But here again I must point out that the excessive acuteness of her enunciation of vowels turns "rage" into "reeje" and "wave" into "weeve": also that "Mizzahreery Dommynee" is not a fair equivalent for "Miserere Domine." This concert, by the way, began by a young gentleman trying a musical joke on the audience. He first played Home, Sweet Home. Then, in a series of insane variations, he mixed it up with the Tannhäuser march, Gounod's marionette march, The Harmonious Blacksmith, and the prayer from Moses in Egypt. Not a soul laughed; and a man near me voiced the impression of the audience by hoarsely whispering, "He aint got it off right." Britons are gey ill to joke with on a pianoforte.

Madame Sara Palma, from La Scala, Milan, is, as one would naturally suppose, a young English lady. I did not hear her in Signor Mattei's Prima Donna; and even at her concert yesterday week I did not hear her attempt anything that she could sing. Believe me, oh aspiring and comely young songstresses all: I am not hard to please or chary of praise; but what is the use of trying *Caro nome* on me when you cant phrase, and cant shake, and dont know when or how to breathe, and have no inner impulse to express your-

318

self in that sort of music at all? For the concert was a very creditable one of its kind. On the same evening I went to Mr Henry Holiday's studio at Hampstead, to hear the Musical Guild at work; and capitally they played a Beethoven trio and a Schumann quintet, brilliantly, spiritedly, and yet with an outrageous thoughtlessness proper to their youth and innocence. There was a concert at Prince's Hall on Tuesday night; but I would not go because somebody sent me a visiting card instead of a ticket; and I positively decline to negotiate *billets-doux* or private documents of any description at concert-room doors.

8 *February* 1890

WHAT shall I do to make Sir Charles Hallé take steps to abate the scandalous nuisance which I vainly pressed upon his notice in the ordinary course last Friday week? This time I took special care to get out of earshot of the quadrille band which plays in the St James's Restaurant, and which can be heard at one end of the concert room over an area quite as large as that occupied by the orchestra at the other. By looking at the agonized faces of the unfortunate people in the half-crown seats I could see what they were suffering; but I could not hear it—at first. But the quadrille band was not to be baffled in that way. It bided its time until we came to those eloquent pauses between the last broken strains of the funeral march in the Eroica symphony—pauses during which you can usually hear a pin drop. But last night it would have been necessary to let Cleopatra's Needle drop to overpower the wild strain of brazen minstrelsy that rushed through the room and doubled me up in my place of fancied safety. It was too much. When, after the march, the applause from the front of the room subsided, a voice was heard raised at the back in impassioned oratory. The stir and sensation which ensued prevented me from catching his speech in full; but the concluding sentence was "We all pledge ourselves to complain, either in writing or by word of mouth." The half-

crowners energetically cried "Hear, hear"; and the ladies
stood up to see this gentleman who ventured for the common
weal to assume the rôle of Masaniello or William Tell at a
moment's notice, and whom I take this opportunity of publicly thanking for his spirited and proper protest. Then Sir
Charles, who betrayed no consciousness of these strange proceedings, started the scherzo; and the insurrection quieted
down into dumb discontent, which found vent afterwards in
wild suggestions that it was done on purpose out of jealousy
of the Manchester band; that a rival conductor was at the
bottom of it; that the police ought to put a stop to it; that
the papers ought to take it up, etc., etc. But the papers—
save one—do not seem to care much what happens to the
people who pay a shilling or half-a-crown, so long as those
who pay either half-a-guinea or nothing (especially nothing)
go undisturbed.

14 *February* 1890

I DEVOTED myself to the encouragement of English music at
the first Crystal Palace concert of the year on Saturday
afternoon by patiently listening to a concert overture "to
the memory of a hero." The particular hero was not named;
but there was some doubt about the consecutiveness of his
memory; for I took him to be a musical amateur in whose
head the finale of Brahms's violin concerto had got mixed
with the overture to William Tell, and whose reminiscences
of Mendelssohn were adulterated with incongruous scraps
of La Favorita. Sir George Grove declares that the overture
is "apparently written on a program, though a program
which does not obtrude itself." My opinion of it is also written on a program, which I, too, refrain from obtruding. Such
overtures should be contracted for at so much the dozen.

I do not quite know why some of the audience raged so
frantically at Liszt's variations on Dies Irae. The old hymn
makes a tremendous theme; and most of the variations are
either pretty or fantastic enough to make an occasional per-

formance interesting, though I can by no means endorse Mr
Barry's assurance that "Liszt has treated his subject in a
thoroughly earnest, serious, and elevating manner." I grant
the earnestness: Liszt was always earnest; but I question
the seriousness and the elevation. A composer may treat a
subject about which he is desperately in earnest in a manner
which is neither serious nor elevating, whilst another will
set some piece of imposing humbug to most majestic music.
It is only your first-rate composer who is both earnest and
elevating (seriousness is only a small man's affectation of
bigness). Nothing was too artificial for Meyerbeer, or too
conventional for Rossini, who nevertheless gave their music
exactly the sort of passion and grandeur which Liszt strove
so desperately and expensively to force out of an expensive
accumulation of the mere materials of music. Like Berlioz,
he was rich in every quality of a great composer except
musical fertility; and when for a moment some stray breath
of inspiration relieved him of this poverty, he was triumphantly successful. But men who had hardly any quality of
a great composer except this one that he lacked, may dispute
precedence with him with almost as much public support as
the giants, from Bach to Wagner, whose superiority goes
without saying. You may respect Liszt, vainly struggling
with Dante's Divine Comedy, more than Offenbach featly
vanquishing Meilhac and Halévy's Grand Duchess; but you
can hardly deny that the Dante symphony is a failure, and
The Grand Duchess a success. It does not follow that you
would always rather hear the success than the failure. The
success is simply enjoyable for the moment: the failure is
interesting, suggestive, instructive, stimulating. Sometimes,
when listening to Berlioz's cleverest work, its very cleverness
forces us to compare its proud poverty with the unassuming
affluence of La Sonnambula; but we never doubt for a
moment that the world could have spared Bellini much better
than Berlioz, or that Offenbach's life, compared to Liszt's,
was a wasted one. Hence such Lisztian hero-worshippers as
Herr Stavenhagen and the late Walter Bache are to be en-

couraged and supported: it is good for the public and the
players and the conductor to do some hard brain work over
a symphonic poem instead of accompanying Madame Patti
in *Ah, non giunge*, or fathoming the Sunday-school profun-
dities of the pilgrims' march from Mendelssohn's Italian
symphony.

This, by the way, does not apply to the Crystal Palace
band, which sticks to serious work. They took the Dance of
Death in dudgeon, methought; and I tell them to Mr Manns's
face that their playing of the intensely fresh and energetic
syncopated passages in the first movement of the Fourth
Symphony was not worth listening to. And though the slow
movement finished admirably, yet that trochaic measure in
the drum figure which pervades it began with the customary
slovenliness which marks it as the most difficult of all measures to get rightly with an orchestra. It seems as simple as
skipping; but somehow when it comes to the point you have
the Euryanthe overture sounding vulgar, and the slow movement of Mozart's E flat symphony (a pure dialogue, like the
introduction to Weber's Invitation, though wonderfully
more elaborate), made the despair of fine conductors. For
the rest, the symphony went well; and so did the prelude to
Iphigenia in Aulis as edited by Wagner, which Mr Manns
read with admirable dignity.

The Hallé concert this day week brought out Sir Charles's
deficiencies as a conductor in a striking way. It began with
Cherubini's overture to Anacreon, an absolutely meaningless piece of pure music. I never heard it better played: I
doubt if it could be better played; and I do not greatly care
whether it could or not. From that we went on to Grieg's
entr'actes and dance music for Ibsen's great play Peer Gynt.
Grieg has done nothing more pathetic and natural than the
little prelude to the scene in which Peer's mother, lonely on
her deathbed, lies waiting and longing and listening to the
silence before Peer steals down from the mountain and beguiles her into believing that the bitter end of her earthly
journey is a glorious ride through the air to the castle east

of the sun and west of the moon (at the gate of which God Himself orders St Peter to entertain her with coffee and biscuits, which is to her a high and heavenly honor). The way in which Sir Charles Hallé contrived to make us feel before the end of the first bar that all this was a blank to him was quite wonderful. The prelude is nothing if not a tone poem; and nothing it was, accordingly—or less than nothing. I was amazed at the completeness of the failure. The Eroica symphony is something besides a tone poem: much of it is excellent abstract music from the Cherubini-Anacreon point of view; and so it went along to the strains of its own funeral march, a very handsome corpse. The truth is that no man can conduct a Beethoven symphony unless his instincts are not only musical, but poetic and dramatic as well. Consequently, as Sir Charles is only a musician, the Manchester orchestra has yet to experience the delight of really learning a Beethoven symphony. Bach's concerto in D minor for two violins was refreshing; but Lady Hallé's refinements sort ill with Bach's grand style; and I thought Mr Willy Hess had much the better of it.

I have in my hands the report of the London branch of the Wagner Society, which I peruse with mingled feelings. It is satisfactory that the 52 members of 1884 are now 309; but the balance-sheet is enough to drive any sensible Englishman mad. In German-speaking cities at present Wagner's operas are paying enormously. In Dresden, for instance, the announcement of an opera by any other composer empties the house. Even the Bayreuth performances were a financial success last year. In this miserable country a man who has seen Die Walküre on the stage is a much greater curiosity than one who has explored the Congo. Clearly, then, the business of an International Wagner Society is to transfer money from the prosperous Wagnerism of Germany to the languishing Wagnerism of Britain. Yet the London Wagner Society actually sent £46: 12 : 6 to Berlin (of which city, London, it appears, is a suburb) out of its income of £271 : 19s. In return they got sixty-four free tickets for the Bayreuth performances, which were balloted for by gentlemen in a position to spend £20 on a fortnight's holiday, to the unspeakable edification and Wagnerian enlightenment of the English nation at large. Having accomplished this masterly consignment of coals to Newcastle, the London branch proceeded to waste £60 odd, under pretext of an orchestral concert, by simply handing that sum over to Mr Vert, in return for which a scratch performance of a bit of Parsifal was thrust into an ordinary Wagner program at an ordinary Richter concert, for which the members received "free" tickets (at four and sixpence a head). The climax of folly was a conversazione, or evening party, which had as much to do with "The Meister's" cause as any evening party in Mayfair has, and which cost £43 : 11 : 4. Total money wasted, £150 : 13 : 4. As against this, there was £51 : 16s. well spent on the quarterly journal called The Meister, and some £17 on a recital of Tristan, which was, on the whole, well worth the money. But if I, instead of subscribing my guinea, had paid a shilling apiece for the four Meisters across the counter, and half-a-crown for the Richter concert as one of the public, I should have turned the odd fourteen and sixpence to much better account than the branch has turned it for me. On Wednesday last I went to one of the branch's meetings for the first time, and found, as might have been expected, that nobody present seemed to have the least idea of how such meetings should be conducted. There was no chairman, no discussion, no orderly procedure, no opportunity whatever of raising any question connected with the subject of the evening or with the society. Mr Ellis, the secretary, simply came out; fed us with lecture as if we were a row of animals in the Zoo; and walked off and left us there. The more I think of it, the more I am convinced that now that this German Wagner Society can take care of itself, we want an independent English one. Who shares that opinion?

LONDON MUSIC IN 1888-89

21 *February* 1890

I SEE that somebody in the Pall Mall Gazette wants to have Mr August Manns knighted. The suggestion will be taken up by the comic journals for the sake of saying that "a Manns a man for a' that." As for me, who am no punster, I ask why Mr Manns should be bothered about it. He knows how we manage these things here. We keep a couple of musical knights (in addition to clerical organist chivalry) in order to make knighthood a little respectable, just as we keep a couple of mounted sentries at Whitehall so as to give the War Office a military air. There is no question of selecting the man who has done most for music: Costa, who had no respect for the past, no help for the present, and no aspiration towards the future—who was equally ready to murder anything old with "additional accompaniments" and cuts, or to strangle anything new by refusing to have anything to do with it—who allowed the opera to die in his grasp whilst it was renewing its youth and strength all over Germany: Costa was made Sir Michael. The gentleman selected by Mr W. S. Gilbert to set his burlesques of grand opera to music is Sir Arthur Sullivan, though music in England would not be one inch further behind-hand than she is if he had never existed. Charles Hallé, who endowed England with a second orchestra (Rule, Britannia!), and who is therefore the only man whose services are for a moment comparable to those of Mr Manns, was given a knighthood when he was seventy. No doubt Mr Manns' position is such that he can, if he chooses, confer (at sixty-five) on a worthless order an honor that it cannot confer on him. But if he receives any such offer, I hope he will politely pass it over to Mr Barnby or Mr Cusins, and go on quietly with his work. I respect him so much that I am always half ashamed to call him Mister. If he became Sir August I should blush every time I penned that cherished distinction of successful brewers and oratorio mongers.

This reminds me that I have a word to say about the last

325

Crystal Palace concert. Mr Manns was immensely in the vein; and the Egmont overture, which at first could only be *seen* in the movement of his baton, at last got into the heads of the band, who finished it as keenly and powerfully as they had begun it sleepily and irrelevantly. There was quite an ovation to the conductor after the Scotch symphony, a work which would be great if it were not so confoundedly genteel. Miss Fanny Davies was full of speed, lilt, life, and energy. She scampered through a fugue of Bach's with a cleverness and jollity that forced us to condone her utter irreverence. The concerto by Rosenhain turned out to be a pleasant and ingenious piece of "absolute music" in the mid-century manner. I had never heard of Rosenhain; and I am surprised at the disingenuousness of other critics in the same predicament, who have hastily read him up, and are pretending that they knew him from boyhood's hour.

Upon Miss Amelia Sinico's first appearance I wish to offer a few general and impersonal observations. If ever you get behind the scenes at the opera, or into musical Bohemia, you will here and there come across some dark-eyed little imp of eight or ten, who can sing every opera from cover to cover without missing a note or a word; who can improvise cadenzas much more readily than you could invent an alias at a police-station; who knows Il Trovatore from Don Giovanni without in the least knowing Verdi from Mozart; who speaks all Western languages and knows none; who is equally used to smacks and kisses, indoor errands and comfits; and whose mother is a prima donna. However expensively you educate your daughter for the operatic stage; however many gold medals she may take at the Royal College of Music; when she reaches the opera house (if she ever does) she will be as rank a greenhorn in the eyes of the dark-eyed imp as a senior wrangler who takes to the city is in the eyes of a sharp office boy. But just as the office boy finds that the wrangler has a mysterious qualification for important duties which juvenile sharpness aspires to in vain, so the imp, when at eighteen she finds that she is only fit to be a prima donna,

sometimes finds at thirty that she was not fit even for that.
The Miss Macintyres and Madame Melbas, whom she remembers as perfect Jugginses, leave her behind almost
without an effort.

I do not wish to discourage the daughters of artists who
have, in their time, given me a good deal of pleasure; but
when I hear Miss Sinico giving her clever imitation of a
prima donna singing *Ombra leggiera*, and Miss Antoinette
Trebelli doing the same with *Non mi dir*, I cannot accept
either feat as evidence that these young ladies have as yet
ever begun the serious study of their profession. At the risk
of being impertinent, I venture to warn them that only the
most exceptional natural capacity can nowadays enable an
aspirant to dispense with the general culture and education
which nobody expected from an opera singer in London
twenty years ago. The capacity for sustained attention, the
air of purpose and self-respect that such education gives,
makes the person who has received it so much more dignified
and interesting that the public are getting more and more
intolerant of Bohemianism in art. Now I have no right to
say that Miss Sinico's education has been unsystematic; for
I know no more about her than any other member of the
public. What I have a right to say is that though her Italian
is piquant, like her mother's, it is also a little vulgar, *un*like
her mother's; and that when she next sings *Batti batti* (which
will not be for some years to come, if she is wise) she must
understand that, at the Crystal Palace at least, the day has
passed for such vulgarisms as ending an octave above the
note written by Mozart. I would also whisper to her that she
should not naively let the public see how fond she is of
applause. She obviously must be a prima donna or nothing;
but it will cost her many years' work and experience before
she can expect Mr Manns' Saturday audiences to receive
her with any feeling except one of almost paternal indulgence.

Since I do not confine this column exclusively to concerts and operas, all sorts of people suggest that I should go
to all sorts of places and give my opinion thereon. Last week,

however, one of these suggestions had a binding effect on my conscience. Among my valued friends is a clergyman—I shall not mention his name because, having been afflicted all my life with a constitutional impiety which has led the clerical profession to adopt a general attitude of expecting me to be stricken dead, I am afraid of compromising him. Let us call him the Rev. St*w**t H**dl*m, M.L.S.B. for Bethnal Green; or perhaps it will be shorter and less likely to lead to his identification if I call him simply H. Well, H. enthusiastically admires the art of dancing; and he will have it that I undervalue it—an assumption as baseless as it is injurious, for I was interested in it before he was born. However, when he wrote to me to demand why I never went to a ballet, I could not deny that I had of late years neglected the Alhambra and the Empire. So on Monday, having ascertained that "Spectator" was indulging his mania for musical criticism at Marjorie or Les Cloches, or some opera or another, I made straight for the Alhambra; saw Asmodeus there at nine; waited for M. Bruet and Madame Rivière; and got to the Empire afterwards in time to see A Dream of Wealth.

I care not a jot about the technology of the art of dancing. I do not know, and, what is more, I positively refuse to know, which particular *temps* is a *battement* and which a *ronde de jambe*. If I were equally ignorant of the technical differences between a tonal fugue and a quadrille, I should be a better musical critic than I am; for I should not so often be led astray from the essential purpose of art by mere curiosity as to the mechanical difficulties created by certain forms of it. All that concerns me is how beautifully or how expressively a dancer can dance, and how best I can stop the silly practice of ending every solo with a teetotum twirl like the old concert ending to the overture to Iphigenia in Aulis. But if you want a rule of thumb to guide you in determining the merits of two dancers comparatively, then simply see *how much of each* dances, and award the palm to the larger quantity. Let me explain. Dancing begins at the feet and progresses upwards. In some people it stops at the

328

ankles: they shine only in clog dancing, hornpipes, and the like. In others it reaches as far as to the hips: these can aspire to kicking through a Gaiety *pas de quatre*, or spurious *can-can*. When the magic fluid reaches the shoulders and invades the arms as far as the elbows, then the dancer pretends to leading business. Many a *première danseuse* holds her position in spite of a neck and wrists which are, dancingly considered, dead as doornails. But the dancer who dances to the tips of her fingers and the top of her head: that is the perfect dancer; for dancing being a sort of pulsation of grace in the limbs which dance, the perfect dancer is all grace; and if she has, to boot, a touch of tragic passion in her, it will find instant and vivid expression in her dancing. To such a nonpareil you would unhesitatingly give, if she asked for it, the head of Adelina Patti or Sarasate in a charger. So perhaps it is just as well that she is the rarest of rare birds.

At the Alhambra the best dancer is a man, Vincenti, an intelligent and cultivated artist and an admirable panti-mimist. I leave H. to chronicle the perfection of his *pirouettes* and *entrechats*, and the public to encore his amazing revolution about the centre of the stage combined with rotation on his own longitudinal axis, like an animated orrery. I should prefer to illustrate his excellence in pure dancing by an instantaneous photograph taken at the height of his bound into the air, with the crutch in his hands, at the beginning of his first solo. Nothing could be more graceful. Yet Vincenti's figure is by no means heroic; and he has a prodigious head. Signor Albertieri, at the Empire, is a prettier man; but he is comparatively no dancer at all, but only an acrobat and wrestler, who throws Madame Palladino half over his hips and holds her there in an attitude (any pugilist will show you the trick), as if that were dancing. The opulent Bessone, "première danseuse assoluta" in Asmodeus, is complete from toe to top, a superb, passionate dancer, strong, skilful, and abounding in sensuous charm. Whether she is as great a Serafina as Fanny Ellsler was in The Devil on Two Sticks I know not, since I never saw Fanny; but

with two such artists as she and Vincenti, and a happily arranged ballet by Casati, on an ever popular legend, the
Alhambra now offers between nine and ten every evening
an entertainment of high artistic rank, to which everybody
should go and bring their daughters, in spite of the abominable atmosphere of tobacco smoke.

I wanted to hear M. Bruet because I remembered his
name from a remote occasion when I somewhere heard him
give an amazingly exact imitation of a violoncellist. He and
Madame Rivière seem none the worse for wear; and I only
wish that all our would-be serious artists had half the musical talent of these two arch mockers. For the rest I cannot
deny that the Empire ballet fell flat after Asmodeus, neither
Signor Albertieri nor Madame Palladino being able to sustain the formidable and inevitable comparison with their
rivals across the square. The jewel casket scene was tawdry:
it suffered specially from the vast space of naked floor which
makes ballet scenery so hard to manage. Signorina Caval-
lazzi, however, did excellently as the miser; and some of the
pantomime was good. Possibly had I taken the two theatres
in reversed order, and seen The Paris Exhibition at the
Empire, and Our Army and Navy at the Alhambra, my
impression of the respective merits of the houses might have
been reversed also. But, as it was, I should like to see
Asmodeus again; whereas I have had quite enough of A
Dream of Wealth.

When I arrived at my door after these dissipations I
found Fitzroy Square, in which I live, deserted. It was a
clear, dry cold night; and the carriage way round the circular
railing presented such a magnificent hippodrome that I could
not resist trying to go just once round in Vincenti's fashion.
It proved frightfully difficult. After my fourteenth fall I was
picked up by a policeman. "What are you doing here?" he
said, keeping fast hold of me. "I'bin watching you for the
last five minutes." I explained, eloquently and enthusiastically. He hesitated a moment, and then said, "Would you
mind holding my helmet while I have a try. It dont look so

hard." Next moment his nose was buried in the macadam and his right knee was out through its torn garment. He got up bruised and bleeding, but resolute. "I never was beaten yet," he said; "and I wont be beaten now. It was my coat that tripped me." We both hung our coats on the railings, and went at it again. If each round of the square had been a round in a prize fight, we should have been less damaged and disfigured; but we persevered, and by four o'clock the policeman had just succeeded in getting round twice without a rest or a fall, when an inspector arrived and asked him bitterly whether that was his notion of fixed point duty. "I allow it aint fixed point," said the constable, emboldened by his new accomplishment; "but I'll lay a half sovereign *you* cant do it." The inspector could not resist the temptation to try (I was whirling round before his eyes in the most fascinating manner); and he made rapid progress after half an hour or so. We were subsequently joined by an early postman and by a milkman, who unfortunately broke his leg and had to be carried to hospital by the other three. By that time I was quite exhausted, and could barely crawl into bed. It was perhaps a foolish scene; but nobody who has witnessed Vincenti's performance will feel surprised at it.

28 *February* 1890

I WAS lucky in looking in to hear Joachim at the Popular Concert last Monday. I must first mention, however, that Joachim was never to me an Orpheus. Like all the pupils of Mendelssohn he has seldom done anything with an *allegro* except try to make speed do duty for meaning. Now that he is on the verge of sixty he keeps up the speed at the cost of quality of tone and accuracy of pitch; and the results are sometimes, to say the least, incongruous. For instance, he played Bach's sonata in C at the Bach Choir Concert at St James's Hall on Tuesday. The second movement of that work is a fugue some three or four hundred bars long. Of course you cannot really play a fugue in three continuous parts on the violin; but by dint of double stopping and dodging from one part to another, you can evoke a hideous ghost of a fugue that will pass current if guaranteed by Bach and Joachim. That was what happened on Tuesday. Joachim scraped away frantically, making a sound after which an attempt to grate a nutmeg effectively on a boot sole would have been as the strain of an Aeolian harp. The notes which were musical enough to have any discernible pitch at all were mostly out of tune. It was horrible—damnable! Had he been an unknown player, introducing an unknown composer, he would not have escaped with his life. Yet we all— I no less than the others—were interested and enthusiastic. We applauded like anything; and he bowed to us with unimpaired gravity. The dignified artistic career of Joachim and the grandeur of Bach's reputation had so hypnotized us that we took an abominable noise for the music of the spheres.

My luck at the Monday Popular Concert lay in the fact that Joachim there played very finely, especially in the Brahms sonata. Whilst I am on the subject of fiddling I may as well mention how Madame Neruda rose to the occasion at the Crystal Palace on Saturday before going off to Australia to pick up gold and silver. Madame Neruda is younger than Joachim; but only by about nine years: she is fifty, though you would hardly guess it from her bearing on the platform. But for some years past her style has been contracting a little. Her tone is less distinguished; and her old fire and eloquence are abated. In spite of the care with which she studies her playing, I find that the amateurs of yesterday are disposed to be irreverent when I fully express the admiration which survives in me from the time when her great talent was at the height of its splendor. They will admit that she is an accomplished player, but not an inspired one. That is what I should have said myself had I heard her for the first time when she played Spohr's Dramatic Concerto at the last Crystal Palace concert or the recent Hallé concert. But I heard her play it so magnificently twelve years or so ago that I will not do her reputation the injustice of pretending that it was no better then than now. Perhaps it was to shew us that it was Spohr rather than Norman Neruda who has become the worse for wear that she chose a sonata by Handel the Imperishable for her second piece. At any rate it certainly woke up the qualities which made her famous, and earned her an ovation in which the rawest recruits joined heartily.

Though each generation produces its quota of great artists, yet as the favorites of my youth succumb to inexorable Time, I never feel quite sure of their replacement until I actually see and hear their successors. Years ago I went to an afternoon concert at which no less than three eminent pianists appeared. I remember two things about it. One is, that as I entered, a gentleman turned to me trembling with anxiety and asked with the deepest earnestness "Has Cambridge won?" The other, that I heard Madame Schumann for the first time, and recognized, before she had finished the first phrase of Schubert's impromptu in C, what a nobly beautiful and poetic player she was. An artist of that sort is the Holy Grail of the critic's quest. Now, I never had the slightest fear that we should ever be at a loss for successors to Rubinstein and Von Bulow. I was once by no means so sure about Madame Schumann. Concerning one of the most gifted of her pupils, Nathalie Janotha, I reserve my opinion for a few years more, or at least until I happen to hit on a concert at which she plays: a matter in which I have been too remiss, except when I have been irresistibly attracted by an announcement that she is to play Beethoven's concerto in G. But Madame Schumann's true successor at present is Madame Backer Gröndahl, in whose perfectly original and independent style none of her predecessor's finest qualities are lacking. It will be remembered that when I first heard Madame Gröndahl last June I hailed her as a player of the highest rank. After sleeping over that judgment for a year, I am as confident as ever that events will sustain it; and I shall go to the Crystal Palace tomorrow with an uncriticlike eagerness to hear her play Grieg's con-

certo and to say "I told you so" to those who last year
thought it safer to wait another quarter century or so before
they committed themselves to an opinion.

I have rather wandered away from the Bach Choir concert, at which *Wachet auf* was sung for the second time in
public in England. This is the sort of fact that almost disables
me from writing another line. What on earth is the use of
toiling over a musical column for a nation that has waited
150 years to hear a love poem which had no peer until
Tristan und Isolde was written. However, let me not be
unjust. England has not been idle. She has produced Costa's
Eli and Macfarren's Potiphar's Wife, Dr Parry's Judith,
and Dorothy, not to mention some forty thousand performances of Elijah. *Wachet auf* is a setting of an old love
story narrated by Herodotus, which, by a misapprehension
which is perhaps the most extraordinary in literary history,
came into the Bible under the name of The Song of Solomon,
and so happily got set to music by Bach on a plane of
idealization to which Herodotus would certainly not have
raised him.

Some day, when the County Councils begin to do for
music in England what the petty courts of Germany used to
do for it, after a fashion, in Germany, I shall try to persuade
the nation that a million a year spent on Bach choirs would
be a remunerative investment. At present there is no use in
telling the people what a great man Bach was, since they
cannot help themselves. So I will only say that Mr Villiers
Stanford is too thorough an Irishman to be an ideal Bach
conductor. He is alert, clever, enthusiastic, facile; but he
lacks the oceanic depth of German sentiment that underlies
the intense expression of Bach's music.

Still, a clever Irishman is better than the usual alternative: a mediocre Englishman. Let me just suggest to him, in
passing, that whether Joachim is playing or not (he played
that D minor concerto which Madame Neruda played the
other day with Mr Willy Hess), a conductor should always
conduct. Mr Stanford modestly effaced himself whilst Joa-

334

chim and Mr Gompertz were playing the *largo*; and the result was that the basses in the orchestra lagged and got out of step with the soloists. The accompaniment I liked best that evening was the no-accompaniment of the motet; but if you must have an organ muddling matters with its tempered scales, then by all means serve it up to me with trombones in Bach's manner; for I admit that nothing in art can be compared to it except the best mediaeval building.

Then there is that Crystal Palace concert. I do not return to it to compliment Mr Manns on a capital performance of Schumann's symphony in C; for I simply do not care about Schumann's symphonies: that is the long and short of it. Nor am I going to praise the clear and confident lady who dragged in two fragments, Hear ye, Israel, and the waltz from Gounod's Roméo, into a program consisting otherwise of complete artistic wholes. But I have a word to say about Mr German's overture to Richard III, now that I have heard it under the conditions which were, of course, imperfectly fulfilled at the Globe Theatre. I advise Mr German either to rewrite the work, or else drop Richard III and simply present it as Overture in G, that is to say, as a piece of "absolute music" in overture form. For if it is to be taken as dramatic I do not see why the Richard motive should be fitted with an "answer" as if it were a "subject," there being nothing in the dramatic idea at all corresponding to such answer. Again, the fugato is flat nonsense unless Mr German wished to suggest a troop of little Richards springing up through traps and chasing one another round the stage. I hope Mr German will, on reflection, agree with me that the man who can write a dramatic overture is the man who can invent dramatic motives and develop them dramatically in music. The oftener he breaks down in this arduous task and falls back on the forms of absolute music, the worse his work will be. For instance, the most entirely foolish thing in music is an overture by a Mus.Doc. in orthodox form, written solely with a view to that form, and then sent up for concert use with the general title of Portia and Shylock, and The

335

Caskets, written in blue ink above the first and second subjects respectively. I venture to accuse Mr German of a certain degree of the confusion between "absolute" and dramatic music, of which the above is an imaginary case. Mind, I admit that he has proved his ability as a musician up to the hilt. What remains comparatively questionable is his interest in Shakespear.

The night before last I repaired to the London Institution to see The Shakespeare Reading Society recite Much Ado. I have musical associations of all sorts with these recitals. Wagner once pointed out that music would never have survived the omissions and misunderstandings of conductors and concert givers had it not been kept alive in the homes of people whose spare cash went in buying pianoforte scores and the like for private consumption. In the same way, people would know very little about Shakespear if they had no more of him than they get at the Lyceum Theatre. Therefore, as a Wagnerian, I no sooner saw that Mr William Poel was devoting himself to making ordinary people get up readings of Shakespear than I at once made a note that he was a much more important art propagandist than Mr Irving. Another musical association was formed by my seeing Mr Poel once play Beethoven to Miss Mary Rorke's Adelaide in a surpassingly unhistoric little drama. I forget when and where it was; but I have mixed Mr Poel up ever since with Beethoven as he appears in a certain sketch which represents him as wearing a Poellian collar. I have no doubt that the first-nighters who imagine that the way to be in everything in London is to keep outside everything will not condescend to encourage Mr Poel's achievements, since the human material with which he works is necessarily rather green. The more reason for an ordinary person like myself to avow that from these simple recitals, without cuts, waits or scenery, and therefore without those departures from the conditions contemplated by the poet which are inevitable in a modern theatre, I learn a good deal about the plays which I could learn in no other way. What is more, I enjoy myself, which is not invariably my experience in the more commercial atmosphere of the West-end theatre.

7 March 1890

LET me hasten to reassure those who have been terrified by certain striking examples of the destructive force of this column, and who are aghast at such power being wielded by one man. Their fears are vain: I am no more able to make or mar artistic enterprises at will than the executioner has the power of life and death. It is true that to all appearance a fourteen thousand pound pantomime, which the critics declared the best in London, collapsed at a touch of my pen. And the imagination of the public has undoubtedly been strongly seized by the spectacle of the much-written-up Tosca at the height of its prosperity, withering, like Klingsor's garden, at three lines in a postscript to my weekly article. But there is no magic in the matter. Though the east wind seems to kill the consumptive patient, he dies, not of the wind, but of phthisis. On the strong-lunged man it blows in vain. La Tosca died of disease, and not of criticism, which, indeed, did its best to keep it alive.

For my part, I have struck too many blows at the well-made play without immediate effect, to suppose that it is my strength and not its own weakness that has enabled me to double it up this time. When the critics were full of the "construction" of plays, I steadfastly maintained that a work of art is a growth, and not a construction. When the scribes and Sardous turned out neat and showy cradles, the critics said, "How exquisitely constructed!" I said, "Where's the baby?" Of course, there never was any baby; and when the cradles began to go out of fashion even the critics began to find them as dowdy as last year's bonnets. A *fantoccini* theatre, in which puppets play the parts of men and women, is amusing; but the French theatre, in which men and women play the parts of puppets, is unendurable. Yet there was a time when some persons wrote as if Adrienne Lecou-

337

vreur was a superior sort of tragedy, and Dora (alias Diplomacy) a masterpiece of comedy. Even now their artificiality passes for ingenuity. Just as a barrister in England gets an immense reputation as a criminals' advocate when a dozen of his clients have been hanged (the hanging being at once a proof and an advertisement of the importance of the cases), so when a dramatist has written five or six plays in which two hours of intrigues and telegrams are wasted in bringing about some situation which the audience would have accepted at once without any contrivance at all, he receives his diploma as a master of play construction!

I promised last Monday to return to the subject of Madame Backer-Gröndahl after her recital, the Crystal Palace concert having left me in a carping temper. But if the concert left me discontented, the recital threw me into a perfect frenzy of exasperation. Do you know that noble fantasia in C minor, in which Mozart showed what Beethoven was to do with the pianoforte sonata, just as in *Das Veilchen* he showed what Schubert was to do with the song? Imagine my feelings when Madame Backer-Gröndahl, instead of playing this fantasia (which she would have done beautifully), set Madame Haas to play it, and then sat down beside her and struck up "an original part for a second piano," in which every interpolation was an impertinence and every addition a blemish. Shocked and pained as every one who knew and loved the fantasia must have been, there was a certain grim ironic interest in the fact that the man who has had the unspeakable presumption to offer us his improvements on Mozart is the infinitesimal Grieg. The world reproaches Mozart for his inspired variation on Handel's "The people that walked in darkness." I do not know what the world will now say to Grieg; but if ever he plays that "original second part" himself to an audience equipped with adequate musical culture, I sincerely advise him to ascertain beforehand that no brickbats or other loose and suitably heavy articles have been left carelessly about the room.

338

My complaints are not at an end yet. I ask Madame Gröndahl why she has so little faith in our appetite for the classics of the pianoforte. Let her consult any of our favorite pianists (Hallé, for instance) as to whether, with all our faults, we ever swerve in our fidelity to an artist who relies on our unquenchable appetite for Bach, Handel, Beethoven, Schubert, and Schumann. What was it that at once secured for Madame Gröndahl a leading position here last year? It was the discovery that she was a great Beethoven player and a great Chopin player. Further, it was the discovery that she could bring to the execution of these composers' works a true pianist's technique, and not the sham orchestral method that breaks down when tested with two bars of an *andante* from a Mozart sonata. The audience that crowded Steinway Hall on Wednesday, and flowed over on to the platform, was deeply disappointed to find, beside the Grieg outrage and the Chopin nocturne (C minor) and ballade (A flat), nothing in the program but drawing-room music. In Norway it may be necessary to extenuate the crime of playing serious music by Neupert's studies, Lassens' crescendoes, Ole Olsen's and Grieg's dance tunes and *Bluettes en forme de Valse*, by one Ed. Schütt; but here some of us know a little better than that; and the more exquisite the virtuosity shown in the execution of these things the more we feel the absence from the program of worthier subjects for its display. And not another word will I say about Madame Gröndahl until I hear her play a Beethoven sonata in public.

It has suddenly struck me that Grieg's appendage to Mozart's fantasia must be Norway's revenge for Mr Walter Besant's appendage to Ibsen's Doll's House.

In my recent notice of the London branch of the Wagner Society, the urgent necessity for pitching into that body and waking up its committee prevented me from saying a word about the paper read by Mr Ashton Ellis on Wagner's letters to Uhlig, Fischer and Heine, published in 1888 at Leipzig by Breitkopf und Härtel (price 9 marks, or in paper cover 7m. 50). First I have to remark that the letters contain passages as to the interpretation of modern music which make the principles Wagner fought for against Mendelssohn almost plain enough to cure Sir George Grove of speaking of the distinction between "absolute" music and tone poetry as mere critics' slang. I defy any critic to attempt an intelligent classification of modern music without finding this distinction forced on him; and I further defy him to account for the difference between a Beethoven symphony as played by the Hallé and Richter orchestras without seeing exactly how Wagner found in Mendelssohn the arch enemy of progress in the orchestra. The Heine of the letters, by the bye, was not Heinrich Heine, but a costume designer and ex-comedian of the Dresden Court Theatre. An instalment of Mr Ellis's paper appears in the new number of the Meister, which also contains the first part of a really readable translation of the famous Pilgrimage to Beethoven, and a study of Die Meistersinger, in which I note only one slip: *i.e.* the description of Hans Sachs as "the lowly shoemaker." A master shoemaker in mediaeval Nuremberg was, I should imagine, anything but a lowly person.

Whilst on the subject of Wagner, let me point out to those who do not see Messrs Novello's monthly paper, the Musical Times, that Mr Bennett's papers on the life and works of "the Meister" began in the January number, and are still running. They are valuable because they are so perfectly free from Wagnerian hero-worship. Mr Bennett is one of those unhappy ones who, having shied all the bricks they could pick up at Wagner whilst he lived, have now reluctantly to build their missiles into a monument for him. In reading them I cannot refrain from chuckling at the conflict between Mr Bennett's old habits and his new and rueful conviction that the game is up. But he is a quite honest Philistine, still convinced that David is an overrated humbug, in spite of his having undeniably overthrown Goliath. The articles are rather more than less interesting for this;

and the paper contains other matter that musicians will find readable.

More than a month ago Mr Macready Chute, of the Prince's Theatre, Bristol, wrote to me: "We have 15 children under 10 years of age out of 32 on the stage. They are principally the same children as were engaged last year, when they had a separate room with a fire in it, a matron, etc., exactly as the magistrates required this year, the only restriction being the hour at which they had to leave the theatre. In fact, I have no hesitation in saying that children in the Prince's Theatre, Bristol, are always treated with the same consideration as they now receive under Act of Parliament." The moral of which is that the Act causes absolutely no hardship whatever to humane managers like Mr Macready Chute, whilst it braces all the sordid or indifferent ones up to his level. I hope, however, that next year Mr Chute will go a step further and try to do without those fifteen children. Meanwhile, I congratulate our good old Mrs Grudden on her new dignity of Parliamentary Matron.

11 March 1890

THE large audience of the Crystal Palace on Saturday may be claimed for Mr Hamish McCunn or for Wagner, according to bias. My own opinion is that the attraction was Mr Edward Lloyd. Bonny Kilmeny is a juvenile work of Mr McCunn's; and although a fairy story set to music could have no better quality than juvenility, yet Mr Manns's platform is hardly the right platform for it. We are accustomed there to pregnant, concentrated, purposeful works, and Mr McCunn's diffuse strains, full of simple feeling and fancy as they are, did once or twice suggest to me that the Sydenham orchestra might be better employed than in accompanying Hogg's verses and tootling the sentimental interludes for the wood wind which occur between every line. The baritone music, exceptionally well sung by Mr Norman Salmond, alone held its ground in spite of the associations of

341

the place. When I first heard this gentleman at a Popular Concert a week or so ago, I was so much struck by the artistic sense with which he used his voice that I thought I would wait and hear him again before committing myself to a favorable verdict that must necessarily seem improbable in a nation which is apt to model itself, when it sings bass, upon Mr Santley and Signor Foli. However, my impression is confirmed: Mr Salmond is undoubtedly a considerable acquisition for our concert *entrepreneurs*. Schubert's symphony in B minor showed off the orchestra to perfection; but the sudden transition to the Homeric bustle and breadth of the Pegnitz scene from Die Meistersinger knocked it to pieces for some dozens of bars at the beginning. When the band had pulled themselves together, Mr Albert Fairbairn (vice Mr Andrew Black, *hors de combat* with influenza) began his impossible task of singing the part of Sachs at sight, with dismal results. Except for Mr Lloyd's prize song, and for the interesting way in which some of the orchestral points came out under concert conditions, the performance can hardly be regarded as a successful one. Mr McCunn's Land of the Mountain and the Flood, a charming Scotch overture that carries you over the hills and far away, was much applauded. I object, by the bye, to the "working out" section, which Mr McCunn would never have written if his tutors had not put it into his head. I know a lady who keeps a typewriting establishment. Under my advice she is completing arrangements for supplying middle sections and recapitulations for overtures and symphonies at twopence a bar, on being supplied with the first section and coda.

I was considerably disappointed to find such a crowd at the orchestral concert given in Prince's Hall by the students of the Royal College of Music. Doubtless the students were glad to see the gallery full; but the effect on me was to force me to buy a stall, and to sit among the nobility and gentry instead of in a modest shilling seat. Some of the orchestral students were already familiar to me. For instance, that promising lad, Master W. B. Wotton, is progressing satisfactorily with his bassoon; and the way in which G. Case, C. Geard, and J. Matt handled the trombones would have done credit to any College. W. L. Barrett plays the flute, and H. G. Lebon the oboe quite in a professional manner. (The foregoing is an elaborate and side-splitting joke, the gentlemen named being skilled professors and no students at all.) All the violins were in the hands of students: fourteen lasses and ten lads; and they played capitally: the influence of King Cole at South Kensington appears to have developed fiddling at the college in an extraordinary degree. Miss Polyxena Fletcher, a young lady with a rich oriental tone in her complexion, gained great and deserved applause by playing Brahms' second pianoforte concerto courageously and even aggressively; for she occasionally, in the abounding strength of her young blood, thumped the keyboard as if it were Brahms' head. And she was quite right: why should she forbear at that age, with an orchestra thundering emulously in her ears? The madrigals and part songs had been well prepared and went with praiseworthy precision; but there was one unsubduable treble voice which pierced through the others like a steam siren, and spoiled the homogeneity of the upper part in the harmony. Mr Pringle's scene from an Italian opera (MS.), with the startling title of Messalina—what on earth do these young spirits know about our friend Messalina?—was sung by Miss Maggie Davies, a very clever young lady whom I heard as Bianca in the students' performance of Goetz's Taming of the Shrew last year, and by Mr E. Branscombe. Miss Davies's Italian vowels have been looked after; but Mr Branscombe remains an Englishman, and considers that a British "two" is equal to an Italian "tu" any day. I must affirm that the performance was highly creditable to the Royal College, and to the conductor, Mr Villiers Stanford.

I USED to think myself rather an advanced musician; but Time is overtaking me at last. In five years I shall be an old fogey. A few weeks ago, when Sir Charles Hallé played Beethoven's E flat concerto in Edinburgh, the critics of that town voted it poor stuff, and called it arid, diffuse, and all manner of disparaging epithets. Whereupon Sir Charles up and told them that no person with any musical knowledge could have talked such nonsense. And The Musical World accused them of "an ape-like passion for wanton and destructive mischief"; lamented that it could visit them with nothing worse than "execration"; and called them "venomous fools" and "witlings who, unable to lift their feeble intellects to the level of works to which the world pays grateful homage, endeavour to bring such works down to the lower plane on which they grovel." People call me severe; but I wonder what they would say if I went on in that style.

I submit two points in defence of the Edinburgh critics. 1. If they thought the concerts overrated, arid, and diffuse, they were right to say so. 2. Perhaps the performance *was* arid. Hamlet is a very fine play; but with Charles Mathews in the leading part, it would seem a trifle long and dry. Are you quite sure, Mr Musical World, that if you were unfamiliar with the Emperor concerto, and heard it for the first time from Hallé in his seventieth year, you would rise fully to the occasion? Besides, listen to what they are beginning to say in London. Last Tuesday a leading evening paper, criticising the Royal College concert at Prince's Hall, said calmly: "Brahms' E flat concerto is full of inspiration; and the day will come when the most famous pianoforte concerto in this key will be that, not of Beethoven, but of Brahms." That is the sort of statement that sets one looking for grey hairs and thin places on one's crown.

The significance of such criticism lies in its being probably the first sign of a reaction in favor of abstract or "absolute" music against the great Wagnerian cult of tone poetry

344

and music drama. An eclipse of reputation always becomes
visible at Greenwich soon after its possessor's canonization.
To take minor cases, Macaulay is only just emerging from
the shadow, and George Eliot is in the very black of it. To
take major ones, the Restoration conception of Shakespear
as vapid and old-fashioned corresponds exactly to the Victorian conception of Mozart, a conception against which
the Mozart idolatry of such writers as Oublicheff availed
nothing. Neither, I suppose, will the many books of
Wolzogen avail Wagner when his turn comes. When it does
come we shall have two consolations. First, these eclipses
are made by critical fashion rather than by popular feeling.
Second, when the Wagnerian criticism becomes the mode,
it will soon be so vulgarized that we shall be glad to shelve
it until its professors are all dead.

I did not go to the Goddard concert on Tuesday, as it
was one of those occasions on which a critic's room is worth
a guinea more than his company. Besides, the Norwegian
colony in London had bidden me to a *soirée* at which they
said they were going to entertain Madame Backer-Gröndahl.
Needless to say, when I arrived, I found Madame Gröndahl
entertaining them. Presently the floor was taken by a violinist who was no stranger to me: to wit, Alexander Bull,
son of the famous Ole of that ilk.

Now, nothing will persuade me that Bull knows how to
play the fiddle any more than I do. He always reminds me of
the too celebrated amateur who being asked could he play
the violin, replied that he had no doubt he could if he tried.
Bull grabs the instrument cautiously by the shoulder, and
considers how he can best tackle it. Finally deciding that he
had better proceed like a man cutting a wedding cake exactly in two, he very carefully draws the bow across it in
that manner, keeping a wary eye on the instrument in case
it should, in some unlooked for way, resent such treatment.
In his inspired moments he stands it on his shoulder and
plays in mid air. Each performance has the same odd appearance of being his first attempt; and though he makes

less faults than most professional violinists, yet there is something strange about them, because they are not the usual faults. He solves the ordinary player's difficulties by natural magic, and then falls into difficulties of his own which an ordinary player would settle offhand. But his tone is so fine and nervous, and so full of subtle and unexpected inflexions; and his playing is so unflaggingly imaginative that I receive a much more vivid musical and poetic impression from him than I do from Joachim, for instance, or from Ysaÿe, who, they say, can play unbroken chords on four strings with an ordinary bow and bridge, and who is declared by experts the most dexterous of living fiddlers. I can answer for it that he is the most bumptious; but I do not rank bumptiousness high as an artistic quality: perhaps because I am myself singularly free from it. Now Bull is not in the least bumptious: he is chronically apologetic for not being able to play as well as his father. It must be a terrible thing to have such a father if you want to be an artist; for of course he will not teach you, and nobody else will venture to interfere. But the result in Bull's case goes to show that if you miss a good deal under such circumstances, you also escape something. I never heard his father; but his own playing seems to me unique of its kind.

Madame Backer-Gröndahl will at last appear in her right place at the Popular Concerts tomorrow and on Monday. If the Philharmonic Society will only give us an opportunity of hearing her play Schumann's concerto, we shall have nothing left to complain of.

The other evening I made one of those appalling sacrifices of my own comfort which are the price of a comprehensive knowledge of contemporary music. It takes all sorts to make a world; and each sort must have its music. There is the stupid sort, for instance: the people who cannot follow the thread of any connected entertainment; whose attention cannot stand a ten minutes' strain; who are so credulous that they will sit open-mouthed and, in a well-meaning, joyless, wondering way, applaud anything that goes on in a room which they are not allowed to enter for less than a shilling. No competent musical critic could possibly enjoy an entertainment suited to these worthy people; but since they are eminently gullible, it is his duty occasionally to suffer for an evening in order to see that no inordinate advantage is taken of their artistic imbecility. It was with a vague notion of doing some good in this direction that I lately visited "the unique and incomparable Bohee Operatic Minstrels" at the International Hall over the Café Monico. I took the title as a guarantee that the audience would be tolerably simple folk.

They were. But I do not think that the Brothers Bohee presumed unduly on their simplicity. If the singers—especially the comic singers—suppose that the audience can distinguish a single word of their songs without carefully reading the printed copy in the program, most of them deceive themselves enormously; and I must say I am not convinced that if, in choosing subjects, an occasional relief from the deathbeds of darling angel mothers were ventured upon, it would not be rather welcome than otherwise. I will even go the length of suggesting that rhymed balderdash must be quite as troublesome to a dull intelligence as rhymed reason. Still, the verses were inoffensive, the tunes innocuous as bread pills, the tambourines full of spirit, and the choruses deeply affecting when repeated, as they always were, pianissimo. The musical conventions of the minstrel style are curious; but I shall reserve a full description of them for my treatise on modern music, which I hope to get through the Press shortly before 1950.

The Bohee Brothers themselves are banjoists, and would have me believe that the Czar of Russia affects that weapon. Had I known this last Sunday, I should have made a much more vigorous speech in Hyde Park at the demonstration on behalf of the Siberian exiles. If it be true that the Prince of Wales banjoizes, then I protest against his succession to the throne. The further suggestion that Mr Gladstone "favors the instrument" is enough to bring that statesman down to the International Hall with his axe. The banjo may be as fashionable as the chimney-pot hat; but the Brothers Bohee could no more reconcile me to the one than Messrs Lincoln and Bennett to the other. The more featly they twanged the more evident they made it that no skill of handling could extenuate the enormities of the Ethiopian lute.

17 *March* 1890

PROVIDENCE did itself credit at the Pop on Saturday. Everybody played well: Madame Neruda and Madame Backer-Gröndahl played very well. Not that those who only knew Madame Gröndahl from her playing here this season yet know all that she is capable of unless they have caught the full significance of one or two movements in the Grieg concerto at the Crystal Palace, or in the last movement of the violin sonata on Saturday. The fact is, Madame Gröndahl has been rather reserved with us this time. Last year she played so as to let us into all her secrets. This time, having no doubt found out how unworthy a horde of Philistines we are, she has kept us at a certain distance, giving us a great deal, but not all. Personally, I feel snubbed. If that state of mind were more generally intelligible in this town, we should gain that confidence from great artists which alone can win them to make us their favorite confidants. Madame Backer-Gröndahl's technique can be bought; and well worth its price it is; but if you want her to play to you as to a friend whom she glories in pleasing, then you have got to convince her that you are artistically capable of that intimate relationship. On Saturday she played Schumann's Novelette in F, which was, of course, mere child's play, though it would, I admit, take an uncommonly forward infant to manage the modulations of the trio as delicately as Madame Gröndahl did. Chopin's prelude in D flat began the serious business of the concert. She played it with a wonderful concentration, holding the thread of it with a grip that never relaxed or lost its sensitiveness, though the web of accompaniment

that wraps it up like an atmosphere was all the time floating
as if her fingers had nothing else to do but to weave it, and
her attention was perfectly free. This indelible impressing
on me of a theme; this exhaustion of its uttermost content
without abandonment, without passion, without joyousness,
with unfailing self-containment and unflagging sense of
beauty, put me completely out of countenance when it had
been continued throughout Mendelssohn's study in B flat
minor, which we could not help encoring, though she had
been so terribly severe with us. I was particularly curious to
hear how she would get on with Madame Neruda in the
Grieg sonata; for I had a vivid recollection of how she ruled
Johannes Wolff with a rod of iron when he played it at
Prince's Hall with her last year; and I knew that Madame
Neruda has a will of her own. But there was no gainsaying
Madame Gröndahl's way; and at the end the two artists
got into such perfect accord that the performance must
stand as so far incomparably the finest yet heard of that
sonata in London. I neither expect nor desire to hear a
better one. Madame Gröndahl unbent a little, too, in the
finale; and I was consoled as by a human caress after an
angelic discourse. I really have more sympathy now with a
gentleman who said to me ruefully after the Crystal Palace
concert: "She doesnt even play any wrong notes."

Mrs Henschel sang very prettily; and there was something else; but it escapes my memory for the moment.

21 *March* 1890

THE Star printers are getting so musical that I can no
longer depend on having my plain and studiously untechni-
cal language set up faithfully. The other day I wrote about
"a couple of moments" during a performance; and it came
out "a couple of movements." What I wanted to say about
the Popular Concert was, that it introduced to us a pianoforte quintet by Giovanni Sgambati, a Roman composer
who is pretty well known here. My objection to him is that

though he is at Rome he does not do as the Romans do, but writes academic music in sonata form, as the Germans and the English, in spite of my remonstrances, persist in doing.

The fact is, that musicians fail to see the real difficulties of the sonata form through allowing their teachers to engross their attention with a horrible conceit of its technical difficulties, which any fool can master. There is no more to prevent you or I from turning out a string of bars in the form of a sonata than to prevent us from turning out a string of lines in the form of a sonnet or a tragedy in five acts and in blank verse. It is not the form that baulks us of a Shakespearean immortality, but the inordinate quantity of first-class stuffing that is required to make these forms, long, severe, and tedious as they are in themselves, interesting, or even endurable, to any but the performers or the author. You really must have something very important to say to a man, if you expect him to allow you to buttonhole him and claim his undivided attention for even twenty minutes at a stretch, much more (as in the case of a tragedy) for a whole evening.

Sgambati had matter enough in hand to amuse an audience for eight or nine minutes. But in trying to make a whole quintet with it, he had so to wire-draw it and to pad it with desperate commonplaces, culminating in that last resource of musical bankruptcy, a *fugato*, that he failed to amuse us at all. Madame Backer-Gröndahl managed to scatter a handful of pearls here and there over the dull fabric; but the general feeling (I always speak of my own private sensations as the general feeling) was that of Christopher Sly at The Taming of the Shrew: "Would 'twere done!" The Schubert quintet (C major) went beautifully, Joachim being in excellent form.

And here a question occurs to me. Joachim is famous for the austerity of his repertoire. He will play nothing meretricious: he stands inflexibly by the classics; and will none of your Sarasate dance tunes and national airs. A pupil of his once flatly refused to believe me when I mentioned that I

350

had heard him play in public an air by Félicien David. But I cannot, for the life of me, see that Joachim has any valid standard of criticism. It seems to me that if he is prepared to tolerate second-hand Mozart, faked by Spohr, and mechanical padding by Sgambati, he is hardly in a position to turn up his nose at the free and original compositions of Sarasate and Wieniawski. Joachim cannot be sufficiently applauded for teaching his pupils to refuse to play unworthy music. He might with equal righteousness urge them not to keep the company of unworthy persons. But as, in the latter instance, the adoption of a tall hat and an income of not less than £1000 a year as the criterion of worth, would at once reduce the wise counsellor to the level of a most malignant snob, I suggest that the acceptance of conformity to any special form as the criterion of worth in a musical composition is the snobbery of art. Imagine the state of soul of a neophyte who should interpret Joachim's precept and example as meaning that any fiddler who considered folk music beneath his notice, would be entitled to consider himself as superior in artistic rank to Ole Bull or Sarasate!

I have nothing more to say about the concert except to chronicle the three recalls, culminating in an encore, which formally stamped Madame Backer-Gröndahl as an indispensable addition to Mr Chappell's list of artists without whom no Monday Popular spring season is complete. I should like to remonstrate with Miss Liza Lehmann for singing some unsuitable triviality about Robin: come and kiss me, in response to an invitation to repeat a song of Stopford Brooke's, set by Mr Somervell; but I had perhaps better let my indignation cool first.

The other day I met Mr William Archer, fresh from a study of the theatre at Copenhagen. I am specially interested in the publication of his observations, because my sanity was seriously called in question a year ago, when I suggested that Mr Harris should offer Coquelin an engagement to play Leporello in Don Giovanni. However, I am but mad nor'-nor'-west: when the wind is in the south I do not know a

hawk from a hernshaw, for I am no ornithologist; but I
know what I am talking about. In Denmark the most famous
actors belong to the operatic as well as the dramatic staff of
their theatre; and the same man will play Shylock in Shake-
pear's Merchant of Venice and Mephistopheles in Gounod's
Faust.

25 *March* 1890

ON reaching St James's Hall on Saturday afternoon, I found
that the room was full. This seemed a very extraordinary
success for Mr Arthur de Greef, whom I had come specially
to hear. But I presently noticed that the program included
Bach's concerto in D minor for two violins. "There!" I said,
as I turned away from the ticket office and made for Prince's
Hall: "that is the true attraction." Now a foreigner might
suppose from this that we are so far advanced in music in
this city that Bach is our first favorite. Would it were so!
The truth is that Bach had nothing to do with the crowd.
When Boswell disparaged Vauxhall, and said it was not
worth half a guinea, Johnson pointed out that the real consideration for the money was relief from the stigma of not
having been to Vauxhall. In London no person can pretend
to musical culture unless he or she has heard Joachim and
Norman Neruda. As they do not usually play at the same
concert, this costs, as a rule, two shillings. But when they
play together in Bach's concerto, then you can kill two birds
with one stone, getting your diploma as one who has heard
both Joachim and Neruda, at half-price. When Lady Hallé
played the same work with Mr Willy Hess, and when Joachim
played it with Mr Gompertz, I got a seat easily enough.
   At Prince's Hall I found Miss Frederika Taylor and Miss
Teresa Aungier giving a concert. Señor Guetary, of whose
singing particular mention has been made here and there of
late, gave us *Come gentil!* He reminded me of Gayarre. This
unfortunately means that his singing is not to my taste.
The actor who moved Hamlet so deeply had "a broken voice,

and his whole function suiting with forms to his conceit."
I confess I bar the broken voice in a lyric artist, even when
he sings dramatic music. Not, of course, that Gayarre's
voice was actually broken, any more than Señor Guetary's
is. But it was harsh, acute, piercing, disquieting: its finish
and polish were like those of a circular saw. This did not
prevent so great a critic as Wagner from placing Gayarre in
the front rank of Lohengrins; and Señor Guetary may, for
all that his voice does not happen to please me, achieve a
reputation as great as De Reszke's; but it will not be a
reputation for beauty of tone or for realizing the summer
night charm of the irresistible Don Pasquale serenade. Were
I Saul, and De Reszke David, his singing would do me good.
But if Gayarre or Guetary were David I should get mad
and shy javelins.

On trying the Popular Concerts again on Saturday, I
found Mr de Greef still there, but the crowd gone. Yet I will
swear that Joachim was better worth hearing in the Beethoven quartet (Rasoumowski in E minor) than in the Bach
concerto. It was as fine a piece of playing as any mortal has
a right to expect. It is all very well for me to protest against
Joachim's abortive struggles with Bach fugues, and to point
out that his intonation is no longer to be depended on in
prolonged quick movements; but every quartet I have heard
him lead this season has renewed and increased my admiration for him. Mr de Greef is a true Belgian, spirited, brilliant, neat, confident, clever, and intensely happy in the
consciousness of being all that. His execution is extremely
ambidexterous; and he has a prodigious musical gift, besides having a fair share of sense and taste. Señor Albeniz
will find in him a formidable rival; but I do not think that
Stavenhagen or Madame Gröndahl need fear the strength
of his youth. I base upon his reading of the Chopin scherzo
the opinion that he is not a very deep player. However, this
must not be taken as final: if he gives a recital, I shall be
open to further light on the subject.

It is one of the inevitable evils of my profession that I

am asked to go to all manner of places; but hitherto I have drawn the line at going to church. Among the pious I am a scoffer: among the musical I am religious. What has a man who knows Die Zauberflöte, the Schiller Ode to Joy as set in the Ninth Symphony, and Parsifal to do with your collects and rubrics and Jackson in F and all the rest of it? I do not believe that many of the people who compound for their essential irreligiousness by putting in a couple of penitential hours in church once or twice every Sunday have any better motive than escaping damnation, in which case they are plainly damned up to the neck already, though they do not know it. However, since I know it, I am bound to look on the poor devils in a friendly and forbearing spirit, as becomes a happier and more fortunate soul. Anyhow I went to church on Tuesday last, to St Nicholas Cole-Abbey.

I had some difficulty in finding St Nicholas. He has an old Tower in Thames Street, among the warehouses; but a glance at it convinced me that if there was an organ inside, there would be no room for me. Besides, there was no sign of its having been opened since the great fire of London; so I made for a red brick mansion which I took to be the Saint's private house, and was there directed by a young lady to go back to Queen Victoria Street and look about me, which I had no sooner done than I perceived St Nicholas staring me in the face on the other side of that spacious thoroughfare. Inside I found some sixty people listening to Mr John Runciman, who was compelling a loud-mouthed intractable organ to discourse to the following effect: 1. *Andante con moto* from Beethoven's C minor symphony. 2. The Parsifal prelude. 3. Bach's organ fugue in A minor. 4. The Death March from the Götterdämmerung. 5. Mr Marshall Hall's Witenagemot music. 6. The prelude to the third act of Lohengrin.

This is exactly the right sort of program for an organ recital in a church. An organist who plays Guilmant and Lemmens, finishing up with a transcription of the Hallelujah chorus, and perhaps throwing in the fugue which he

354

wrote for his Doctor's degree, would be much better employed outside with a mechanical piano, to which the girls could at least dance. But he who sticks to Wagner and Bach, and can play them, as Mr Runciman did, in an imaginative way, will eventually get the choicest spirits in the parish into the way of coming to the church and learning something there. In some churches it might even end in the organist educating the parson; though that is not necessary at Cole-Abbey, where, I blush to say it, the parson (Canon Shuttleworth, a muscular Christian Socialist) sometimes finds it hard enough to educate the organists.

It is a curious sort of church, architecturally, this of St Nicholas. I cannot help suspecting that it was designed in the days of St Nicholas Without and St Walker Within, alluded to by Anthony Weller. The altar reminds me feebly of that church of St Carlo Borromeo at Antwerp, from which, after one glance, I fled with yells of agony and disgust. The platitudinous ceiling suggests Cannon Street Hotel. The rack in which the Rev. George Allen hoists the program number of each piece has a touch—quite welcome and congruous in view of the labors of the Church and Stage Guild —of the music hall. The stained glass is not so bad as I naturally expected it to be—always excepting the rose window, with its plausible, empty, conventional representation of the figure that ought to be more real and deeply felt than any other in the place. But the mother and child over the south door, by Mr Heaton, is all sunshine; and the two large windows behind the altar, though they are hopelessly off the lines of the great glass painters, are dignified, rich in local color and in design, and contain a couple of expressively drawn figures.

The organ recitals, let me add, take place every Tuesday at one o'clock.

LONDON MUSIC IN 1888–89

5 April 1890

THE Philharmonic Society is, I fear, hardly to be held responsible for its actions. It is very old; and it never even in its best days had much sense. Some years ago it brought itself to the verge of extinction by its conservatism. Since then it has been desperately spurting to get abreast of the times—trying new composers, new conductors, new virtuosos, new everything. Now if the Philharmonic had any musical intelligence it would stick to its old line by bringing forward only what is new in that line. It should concern itself mainly with abstract music and the very highest class of dramatic music: that class of dramatic music which may be called secularly religious music. But whatever else it may see fit to do—and Providence only knows what it will be up to next—it had better avoid such senseless vagaries as its last effort at a concert program.

First, by way of shewing that it has learnt nothing and forgotten nothing, it put down the Naïades overture, a genteel musical mongrel which would be a musical description of the Rhine if it were not meant to be a formal concert overture, and which would be a formal concert overture if it were not meant to be a musical description of the Rhine, the net result being, of course, that it is neither the one nor the other. At this time of day, wasting the Philharmonic orchestral forces on it is about as sensible as engaging Rubinstein to play pieces by Stephen Heller would be. Mr Joseph Bennett helps out the society by bravely eulogizing the work in his analytical program as "enjoying universal recognition as among the most beautiful of its kind" (observe that the mischief is just that it is of no kind at all), and by peppering in such adjectives as "divine" and the like; but who is taken in thereby? We all know that Mr Bennett loves Mendelssohn with a love that overflows upon Mendelssohn's most slavish imitator; and how firmly persuaded he is that Wagner wrote music only to revenge himself by its ugliness on the Parisians for not producing Rienzi

356

at the Grand Opera in 1840; but the value of these opinions is a purely historical one, like that of the fossils in the Jermyn Street museum. When I want to impress a young man with the vastness of my musical experience, I hand him the criticisms of Mr Bennett on Wagner and Mendelssohn, and say, "Young man: I can remember the days when everybody talked like that." To which the neophyte always reverently responds, "Indeed, sir?" meaning "Poor old buffer!"

Therefore I would counsel the Philharmonic to drop Sterndale Bennett until they begin to find their audiences falling off for lack of his attraction, when they can easily recover the lost ground by devoting an entire concert to his works, with a few antiques by Smart or Bishop, a novelty by Sir Arthur Sullivan, and a song from Costa's Eli, thrown in for the sake of variety. Such a concert would be crowded with old associations; but otherwise there would be plenty of room at it.

The selection of Haydn's symphony in B flat (The Queen of France) was dictated by all that is good in the conservatism of the Philharmonic. Haydn would have been among the greatest had he been driven to that terrible eminence; but we are fortunate in having had at least one man of genius who was happy enough in the Valley of Humiliation to feel no compulsion to struggle on through the Valley of the Shadow of Death to attain only a moment's glimpse of the Celestial City from the summit of the Delectable Mountains. However, that is not the question just now. We are justified in expecting a very fine performance of a Haydn symphony from an orchestra like that of the Philharmonic Society. That it should be perfectly smooth and neat is nothing: technically a Haydn score is child's play to men accustomed to tackle Berlioz and Wagner. Yet there was nothing more than that in the performance last week. The charming tender Romance in E flat went as mechanically as upon a musical box; and, what was worse, there was a touch of that traditional haste to get the slow movement

357

over before there was time to go asleep which is quite the most ignoble of all the Philharmonic traditions. I do not allude to the omission of the repeats; though why they should be omitted in the Romance, where they are not unwelcome, and observed piously in the allegro, where they are tedious and obsolete, passes my understanding.

When Haydn and Sterndale Bennett were solemnly disposed of, a wild rush to the opposite extreme followed. What has the Philharmonic Society to do with Peter Benoit, of all composers? His Lucifer conclusively shewed that he was an excitable and imaginative musician, without the slightest originality as a composer or depth as a poet. The essential poverty of his scores was only emphasised by their bigness, their ferocity, their grandiosity, their mechanical extravagance. Anyone with two pennorth of critical faculty and experience could have seen that the sort of overture and *entr'actes* he would be likely to compose for a drama on the subject of Charlotte Corday would attain the maximum of unsuitability for a Philharmonic concert. And so, of course, it proved. The music was very strenuous: the Marseillaise was duly intoned and the *Ça ira* madly whistled on "red fool fury of the Seine" lines; the wood wind went into the greenroom and played a waltz, of which I only heard the flute part (which did not happen to be the theme); but we thought of Egmont—indeed, it would have been sufficient almost to think of Struensee—and felt that the Philharmonic was making an idiot of itself.

Yet it was not Mr Benoit who suffered in person for the stupidity of the program. There was another composer in the bill, a Mr Huberti, who followed with a couple of unconscionably spun-out songs in the sentimental manner of Gounod, one of which he accompanied very prettily on the organ. But they took so long, and the hour was so late, and the listeners were so afraid that they would not be able to wait for Ysaÿe's second piece, that they fell on the unfortunate stranger with hisses: actually with hisses! so mortally alarmed were they lest Mr Blauwaert, the singer, should take the slightest applause for an encore. So poor Mr Blauwaert retired, an astonished man; and Ysaÿe came on at last. Ysaÿe was on his mettle: he had probably heard that London is under the impression that Joachim can play Bach; and he accordingly gave us the prelude and gavotte in E, just to shew us what real Bach playing meant. He had already astonished the audience to the extent of three furorious recalls by his playing of Vieuxtemps' fourth concerto; and in both works his performance must have opened the eyes of those who have accepted the concerto playing of Joachim and Lady Hallé today as examples of what a great executant can do in his prime. Even Sarasate is five or six years past attacking a concerto—a true violinist's concerto —with the superb, prodigious, transcendent impetus of Ysaÿe. Of course he overdid it. Instead of being content with a speed which would have been impossible to any other violinist, he dashed into a speed impossible to himself; but what he succeeded in doing without sacrificing the accuracy of his intonation or the quality of his tone, was astonishing. And he knew it, and revelled in it. As I said the other day, Ysaÿe is bumptious. But then he has a good deal to bounce about, and must have paid a heavy price in labor for his dexterity.

I am full of admiration for the vigor and enterprise of Miss Caroline Holland, who has just introduced Tinel's oratorio Franciscus to us with the aid of her own choir, her own piano, a harp, and a triangle. Under these restricted conditions, the thing could hardly have been better done; and I only wish that those who have larger opportunities would make half as good use of them. But I cannot agree with her that Franciscus is a "magnificent work." Musically it is as barren as Benoit's Lucifer, though its poem is much superior to the vaporing nonsense of that huge ado about nothing. I do not at all doubt that it created a great sensation in Brussels. The city which municipalized Wiertz's show as a temple of Miltonic genius, and regards Léon Gallait as a great painter, is capable of admiring anything that has

359

nothing in it; but for my part, I must beg to be excused. I give much more credit to Miss Holland for the performance than to Tinel for the composition.

The following letter, signed with an Italian name, has reached me. "Let me correct your paralytic version of a favorite old wheeze *re* the fiddler in The Star of a day or two ago. You say he replied, 'I daresay I could play the fiddle if I tried,' or words to that effect. That is leprous nonsense. The only true version is thus. Being asked if he could play the fiddle he answered, 'I dont know: I have never tried.' There is some humor, some point in this. But in your version—?"

I do not deny that there is more humor and more point in the above way of describing the incident. But my business in this column is not to be funny, but to be accurate. My version, whatever its artistic shortcomings may be, is the true one; for *I was present on the occasion,* and can positively answer for it that the gentleman replied in the exact terms I attributed to him. I hope this will teach my correspondent to be a little more careful henceforth in dogmatizing on subjects of which his knowledge is but secondhand. As to the pamphlet which he enclosed, proving vegetarianism to be an enfeebling and ultimately fatal practice, I confute it by the simple statement that I—Corno di Bassetto—have been a vegetarian these ten years. Pamphlet or no pamphlet, a mind of the calibre of mine cannot derive its nutriment from cows.

11 *April* 1890

I AM strongly of opinion that the Channel Tunnel should be proceeded with at once. There are worse things than foreign invasions, worse things even than foreign conquest, worse things than the extinction of England as a nation, if you come to that. I came over yesterday morning from Calais; and—but enough! The subject is not dignified; and it is hackneyed. All I will say is, that never again whilst I live— and yet I have made the same vow before, and broken it.

Still, do not suppose that that silver streak of which you are
so proud does not cost you something in the way of Continental musical news in the course of the year. But for it,
The Star would be as great a musical power in Europe as
it is in England.

Paris is, as usual, imposing on American greenhorns and
British Philistines as a city artistic before everything, with
specialties in cookery and well-dressed women. I am not an
artistic novice, English or American; and I am not to be
taken in. Paris is what it has always been: a pedant-ridden
failure in everything that it pretends to lead. Mozart found
it so more than a hundred years ago: Wagner found it so half
a century ago: Corno di Bassetto regrets to say that he finds
it so today. In music, it prides itself on its Opera, which is
about twenty years behind Covent Garden; and Covent
Garden, as everybody knows, is thirty years behind time:
even New York leaving it nowhere. I went to the Paris
Opera on Monday to fulfil my mission of hearing Saint-
Saëns' new opera Ascanio. I need not waste many words on
the music of it. There is not an original phrase in it from
beginning to end. The tragic scenes are secondhand Verdi;
the love scenes are secondhand Gounod; the "historic"
scenes are secondhand Meyerbeer. A duller potboiler I would
not desire to hear anywhere. The orchestra is hardly better
than the Covent Garden orchestra was in the seventies,
before we got tired of the Gye-Mapleson managements that
learned nothing and forgot nothing, and passed Vianesi, the
conductor, on to Paris, where his immense industry, his
cleverness, his ostentation, and his thorough superficiality
enabled him to take root at once. Vianesi looks younger
than ever, and is still on the alert for opportunities of turning conspicuously to the wood wind and brass, and offering
them superfluous leads to shew how completely he has the
score at his finger-ends; whilst the men have cultivated his
slap-dash, noisy style—or want of style—to the highest
imperfection.

As to the singers, there is Lassalle, who brings down the

361

house in a roaring duet with the tenor in the second act, and moves it to sentimental admiration in a mock pathetic passage in the fourth, beginning, "Enfants: je ne vous en veux pas." Lassalle can hardly believe in the part of Benvenuto Cellini; but he believes immensely in Lassalle, and so manages to make things go with an effective air of conviction. Madame Adiny is undeniably what we call a fine figure of a woman; but her tremolo and her superb screaming power leave in the shade even the lady who played Desdemona here in Verdi's Otello at the Lyceum last year. Plançon, as Francis I, and Madame Eames, as Colombe, sang pleasantly enough; and I have no right to find fault with Madame Bosman as a capable if not highly distinguished representative of the old-fashioned type of "dramatic" singer, merely because I object to the entire species. The acting was the old impossible Richardson's Show strutting and swaggering, pitiful to see; and the libretto, like the music, was a string of commonplaces, culminating in Madame Adiny keeping Madame Bosman in a golden shrine in a public room for three days, at the expiry of which Madame Bosman was found dead "for Benvenuto's sake," which was the more affecting inasmuch as there was not the smallest reason why she should have got into the shrine in the first place or forborne to call on somebody to let her out in the second.

On the whole, I am afraid I must dismiss Ascanio as an elaborate and expensive tomfoolery, and applaud the wisdom of those frequenters who came only for the ballet, which, though artificial as it well could be—classical, in short—was good of its kind. Yet Ascanio bored me less than Barbier's Joan of Arc at the Porte St Martin, with Gounod's music, and Sarah Bernhardt in the title part. Barbier, as everybody knows, is the man to go to if you want a great subject debased for operatic purposes. He can turn a masterpiece by Shakespear or Goethe into a trashy melodrama in the twinkling of an eye. He fell on Joan of Arc years ago and fixed her up (no other expression conveys the process) for the Gaieté. Now she is dragged to light again with considerable excisions—all heartily welcome—for Madame Bernhardt. In the music, Gounod imitates himself almost as mechanically as Saint-Saëns, and more exclusively. The best number is the vision of St Margaret and St Catherine. Even now, when his fount runs yet drier than in the last decade, Gounod can always write heavenly music. But Sarah is really too bad. We all know her way of pretending to act when there is no part for her—how sweetly she intones her lines and poses like a saint. This is what she does in Joan. There is no acting because there is no play; but she sends the lines out in a plaintive stream of melody throughout which only a fine ear can catch the false ring. You would almost swear that they meant something and that she was in earnest. Not until the final scene at the stake does the affair become thin enough for even the American and British tripper to see through it. Sarah did not wink once: perhaps because she did not catch my eye, perhaps because she was in no humor for making fun of herself. It must be wearisome to keep up that make-believe night after night, knowing all the time that her serious work is going on without her at the Français.

Of course, I went to the Français for the sake of the traditions of the house of Molière, and found them to consist of equal parts of gag and horseplay, in no way superior—distinctly the contrary, in fact—to those established only the other day in Mr Benson's company for Hamlet and The Taming of the Shrew. But if the traditions are feeble, the acting is not; and not many things are more enjoyable than an Easter Monday afternoon performance of Le Bourgeois Gentilhomme by the Comédie Française. Monsieur Jourdain can only be enjoyed in Paris, because he is himself bourgeois Paris incarnate. When the play is over you can continue your study of his flunkeyism in his petrified Lord-Mayor's-coach of an opera house; his helpless incapacity for art, and consequent subjection to any pedant who will talk to him about something that he can understand (something quite beside the purpose of art, necessarily) in the Louvre; and his petty rationalism and delight in unreasonable scraps of logic anywhere you please. If I ever take to playwriting (one never knows how low one may fall) I shall do a London Bourgeois Gentilhomme—quite as curious a creature in his way.

However, my main business here is not with the Comédie Française, but with a certain "Soirée Musicale et Littéraire du Vendredi Saint" at the Winter Circus. The sensation here was the appearance of the divine Sarah in a divine character—that of the Virgin Mary, no less. She did more than this, however: she doubled her part with that of Mary Magdalen. Philippe Garnier confined himself to the leading character of Jesus; and Brémont compendiously undertook Pilate, Annas, Caiaphas, Peter, and Judas Iscariot. The work was described as "a mystery in five parts" by Edmond Haraucourt, and was entitled The Passion. A large dose of Berlioz, Beethoven, and Wagner was administered first to get us into the proper frame of mind; and then the mystery began. Sarah, in a dress of the purest, softest white, and with her complexion made up with really exquisite delicacy into a faint blush that could hardly have been more virginal, was well received. The Passion began amid a hush of expectation, and soon proved to be fully equal in depth of thought and novelty of illustration to our finest specimens of modern oratorio libretti. Sarah sang—sung as usual, holding the book in her right hand and waving her left in the air with a rhythmic persuasiveness that did wonders in soothing the distressing cough that soon became epidemic. On the whole the audience bore up bravely until Garnier rose to deliver a sort of Sermon on the Mount some forty minutes long. In quarter of an hour or so the coughing took a new tone: it became evident that the more impatient spirits were beginning to cough on purpose, though their lungs were as sound as Garnier's own. Then came a voice crying, "Music, music," followed by applause, laughter, and some faint protest. Garnier went on, as if deaf. Presently another voice, in heartfelt appeal, cried, "Enough, enough." The reception of this was unmistakeably sympathetic; and Sarah's shoulders gathered themselves expressively; but Garnier held on like grim death; and again the audience held their hand for a moment on the chance of his presently stopping; for it seemed impossible that he could go on much longer. But he did; and the storm broke at last all the more furiously because it had been so long pent up. In the midst of it a gentleman rushed down the grades of the amphitheatre; crossed the arena; and shook hands demonstratively with Sarah, then Garnier, then with Brémont. This was Haraucourt himself; and he capped his protest by shaking his fist at the audience, who reiterated their fundamental disagreement with him on the merits of his poem by yells of disapproval. Hereupon, exasperated beyond endurance, he took the extreme step of informing them that if they persisted in their behavior he would there and then leave the room. The threat prevailed. An awestruck silence fell upon the multitude: and the poet was moving loftily towards his seat when a lady, presumably his wife, threw herself on his neck and rained kisses on him. This affecting spectacle moved the gentlemen in the neighborhood to offer him their hands, which he took in an impressive attitude. Then he sat down; and the imperturbable Garnier started again. But soon the conviction spread that even at the risk of Haraucourt fulfilling his terrible threat, the speech must be stopped. Garnier, whose demeanor throughout was a model of perfect taste, at last exchanged glances with his colleagues, and then with the politest deprecation began: "Ladies and gentlemen: if you dont wish it"—whereupon the people in the arena expressed their opinion that the conduct of the five franc snobs was disgraceful, and the snobs in question vehemently gave Garnier to understand that there was no "if" at all in the question—that they didnt wish it and wouldnt have it. Sarah, in lively pantomime, conveyed her thanks to the arena; but I could not help suspecting that she was privately of the gallery's opinion. At last the three artists held a consultation, at the end of which Garnier sat down, and Sarah started at a scene only a few pages from the end.

The audience accepted the compromise; Haraucourt made no further protest except by applauding occasionally; and the remainder of The Passion was dispatched without further interruption.

The anti-Wagner party was present in full force. It consists of six old gentlemen, more or less like the Duke of Cambridge in personal appearance, who make faces and stop their ears whenever an unprepared major ninth occurs in the harmony. As the audience was some thousands strong, and enthusiastically opposed to the veterans, they did not make much headway. Wagner always maintained that the great Tannhäuser fiasco was a success with the gallery; and there is no serious reason to doubt that he was right. Lamoureux's orchestra played with refinement and precision; but the first movement of the C minor symphony was taken in the old empty, hurried, vapidly elegant way; and in the overture to Tannhäuser the brass, reinforced by two extra cornets and a fourth trombone (a monstrous license), played like a coarse cavalry band, and blared out the Pilgrims' March in a most detestable manner, making the famous violin figure quite inaudible. One moral of which is that London, which declined to accept Lamoureux as a great conductor, and took Richter to its bosom, is as far ahead of Paris in musical judgment as in most other things.

I have only had one peep at the Carl Rosa company. That was last night at Mignon. For the present, I shall say no more than that the performance was a very creditable one—much more enjoyable than that at the Paris Opera, for instance.

I have returned to Mr F. R. Benson a couple of stalls which he has been kind enough to send me for his Hamlet at the Globe Theatre; and I shall make my reason public. The tickets were inscribed "Evening dress indispensable for stalls, dress circle, and private boxes." Now, I object to being forced into the uniform of any class—most of all that of the class of gentlemen to which I do not belong, and should be ashamed to belong. I need not here repeat the refutation of

366

the stale pretence that the evening dress regulation ensures
decency and cleanliness. A man can be just as offensively
unclean in evening dress as in any other costume. It is, as I
have said, a class uniform and nothing else. Now I submit to
it at the opera (in London) because I cannot effectively
challenge Mr Harris's right to place his theatre on the footing of a West-End drawing room as long as the West-End
people pay up the subvention which in France comes from
the nation. But I submit reluctantly, and take a distinct
pleasure in the fact that my evening suit is by far the seedi-
est article of clothing I possess. When Mr Benson tries on
the same tyranny without the same excuse, I object. I prefer
to pay two shillings and go into the pit, where I can wear
what I like. That is what I did some weeks ago, when I went
to see Mr Benson as Hamlet on my own initiative, and re-
marked that he keeps up the pleasant old tradition by
which the Danish court enters to the strains of the march
from Judas Maccabaeus. The performance is an interesting
and enjoyable one; and Mr Benson is better as Hamlet than
in any other of the parts he has played here this season. But
he is not going to force his inky cloak and customary suits
of solemn black on me, for all that. And his attempt to do so
makes me half suspect him of being a relative of the archbishop after all.

14 *April* 1890

SATURDAY was an eventful day in my musical life. After two
hours of Wagner at the Crystal Palace, I heard Lurline for
the first time. Evidently indeed for the first time; since, if I
pretended that, having ever before heard Wallace's masterpiece, anything short of being in love with one of the performers could have induced me to go a second time, I should
not be believed by any expert. No: once is enough, if not
once too much. And yet there are several moments in the
opera in which the string of hackneyed and trivial shop
ballad stuff rises into melody that surges with genuine emo-

tion. During the first half of the overture you say to your-self, "Now, if he can only keep this up, Lurline will come out at the head of modern English operas." But he does not keep it up; and presently you are wallowing in banalities that are fully worthy of the desperate trash—the naked and unashamed nonsense—of Fitzball's libretto. If Wallace had taken his art seriously, he would no more, in his mature age, have set a line of such fustian to music than Wagner would have turned aside from the score of Parsifal, to set Scribe's Robert the Devil. And the poor silly public forgave Wallace for the sake of Sweet Spirit, hear my prayer, just as they make much of that other absurdity The Bohemian Girl, for the sake of When other lips, and I dreamt that I dwelt.

I cannot say that the performance was much less ridiculous than the piece itself. Obviously a good deal might be done with the Rhine scenery, and the changes from the depths of the river to its surface. The problem of making Lurline look like a water spirit without exposing her to an undue risk of catching cold is also one for a costumier of genius. But Mr Harris knows the value of Lurline too well to spend an extra five shillings on it. As for the costumes, Madame Georgina Burns boldly followed the example of Mrs Leo Hunter at the fancy ball, and put on a silk gown with spangles—a thing not to be contemplated without amazement and laughter. Mr Crotty, as the Rhine King, fell back on the habiliment of a pantomime demon, and left to the monster the distinction of being the sole representative of rational dress.

Madame Burns secured a great success as Lurline. I hinted the other day that Madame Adiny, of the Paris Opera, had considerable power of making herself audible; but I had not then heard Madame Burns in her latest phase. In the concerted piece in the last scene of the second act, she had much to contend against. The brass blared; Mr Lely roared; Mr Crotty shouted; Mr Eugene bellowed; and the chorus lent a willing hand; but Madame Burns was able for them all. She sent her voice ripping, tearing, piercing through the hurly burly until the gallery, astounded and almost hysterical, madly demanded a repetition of the unparalleled sensation. It was magnificent; but it was not singing. However, it brought down the house; and if that is all Madame Burns cares for, I have only to congratulate her on her entire success. Her other efforts were comparatively lustreless. The first lines of Sweet Spirit were not ill sung; but Take this cup of sparkling wine was given in a fashion which in London is generally confined to the music hall; and the shakes which she introduced were made up of wrong notes—not even the right notes sung flat, but actually of notes far remote from those which she intended to sing. Mr Crotty sang his ballad in the second act very well; and the hearty encore he got was the heartiest of the evening. I have only to beg him to reconsider the advisability of treating London to such an unheard-of provincialism as beginning a high note with a double attack. Mr Lely got on fairly as Rudolph the Ridiculous; but Mr Eugene, whether his cramped attitude disabled him, or whether his Neptune-like beard got into his mouth, could do nothing with the florid passages in the drinking song. Not that it mattered: the song is not worth singing well, because it is not worth singing at all. The work will be repeated on Tuesday, on which occasion I shall make a point of being elsewhere.

18 *April* 1890

I HOPE the Carl Rosa Company will get severe criticism and plenty of it during their stay in London. "The Italian Opera" is a class affair at best; and its influence in the country generally is small. But these Carl Rosa people play everywhere. They are at it practically all the year round; and the rising generation in the provinces—from which, be it remembered, the future critics and connoisseurs of London will be largely recruited—will have its ideas formed by witnessing the sort of thing now proceeding at Drury Lane. Consequently I regard every member of the company as saddled with a heavy national responsibility. I wonder how many of them have any adequate sense of this!

The company has yet to recover from the effects of what was in many respects a bad start. Carl Rosa was a sensible, pertinacious, shrewd man of business, with a turn for music, but without that quick keen sympathy with the artistic instinct in its human vehicles—that confidence, power, and tact in developing it and stimulating it to courageous action, which make the really able impresario. For if anybody supposes that operatic companies, or dramatic companies, or, for the matter of that, political parties can be made by simply enrolling a number of more or less clever individuals, and then expecting them to do spontaneously what they have undertaken to do, such a one knows little of the incapacity of his species for concerted action. In the old times I never saw in the Carl Rosa Company much more than a fortuitous assemblage of middle-class amateurs competing with one another for applause under a certain factory discipline. Of artistic discipline there was very little. The singers were allowed to play to the gallery by introducing such alterations and interpolations as their vanity and ignorance suggested. They were allowed to take sham Italian names, and to sing broken English that would not have imposed on a moderately intelligent cockney poodle. How vulgar and offensive the follies of the Italian stage become when they are aped by young people of the Irish and American middle classes need not be described. Carl Rosa could have checked it if he had cared to: there is never any difficulty in checking practices that do not pay. As they were not checked, I think it is fair to conclude that he had no adequate sense of the mischief they did in his company; and I would earnestly impress on the surviving members thereof that instead of having a great past to live up to, they have an inglorious and third-rate record to retrieve by renouncing all the lusts of operatic vanity and making it their sole aim every evening, not that this song shall be encored, or that popular favorite called before the curtain, but that they shall collectively achieve a representation of the work in hand as nearly perfect as their individual shortcomings will allow.

The operatic stage is improving, like other things. But it is still possible for a prima donna to bounce on the stage and throw her voice at the heads of the audience with an insolent insistence on her position as a public favorite, and hardly the ghost of a reference to the character she is supposed to impersonate. An ambitious young artist may easily be misled by illustrious examples of stage misconduct. To tell an average young opera singer that she is a Patti or a Nilsson is to pay her the highest compliment she desires. Yet Madame Patti's offences against artistic propriety are mighty ones and millions. She seldom even pretends to play any other part than that of Adelina, the spoiled child with the adorable voice; and I believe she would be rather hurt than otherwise if you for a moment lost sight of Patti in your preoccupation with Zerlina, or Aïda, or Caterina. Nilsson, a far greater dramatic artist, so far stood on her dignity that she never came before the curtain to bow until there had been applause enough to bring out her rival at least six times (Patti will get up and bow to you in the very agony of stage death if you only drop your stick accidentally); and yet it is not sixteen years since I saw Madame Nilsson, in the wedding scene in Il Trovatore, turn to the tenor at the end of *Ah, si ben mio*, and slap him on the back with a loud "Bravo" that was audible—and meant to be audible—all over the house. Try to imagine Miss Ellen Terry doing that to Mr Irving after the "palace lifting to eternal summer" speech in The Lady of Lyons; and you will begin to realize how far the opera house is behind the theatre in England, and how any young lady, by the exercise of the simplest good sense and taste, may attain a higher normal level of dramatic sincerity than the two most famous of her predecessors.

And this reminds me of a writer in The Musical World, who last week advocated the abolition of applause. I wish there were any chance of his suggestion being carried out. The writer supposes that it has been abolished at Bayreuth; but he is wrong: it has only been reduced to the comparative innocence of a burst at the end of the representation, acknowledged by raising the curtain for a moment on the last tableau; and I am by no means sure that when they come to perform Mozart's masterpieces there, it will be possible to avert an encore of *La ci darem* or *Voi che sapete*. I am against applause on the balance of its advantages (to which I am keenly sensible) and disadvantages. The latter are enormous, especially at dramatic representations, where the interruption of the illusion is an obvious and conclusive objection. Further, it enables a noisy minority to tyrannize over a silent and disgusted majority; it gives a false importance to claptrap which does nothing to attract audiences to the theatre, however much it may excite them when they are once inside; and its quantity and frequency are necessarily in inverse ratio to the preoccupation of the audience with the drama. The worst offenders are the people who clap because they are constitutionally ready to be goodnatured when it costs them nothing, and those who clap because the others do. For my own part, I always regard the money I pay at the doors as sufficient evidence of my appreciation of the performers; and in the normal course of things I hardly ever applaud. When I do, it is usually to join in some personal demonstration apart from the merit of any particular performance.

For instance, at the Crystal Palace last Saturday Mr Manns marked his appreciation of the occasion (the afternoon was devoted entirely to Wagner) by discarding his velvet jacket and appearing in a frock coat, as if he had been marrying or burying somebody. At the end, the audience, instead of rushing off to the tea-room to snatch a refresher before the half-past five train, felt a common impulse to give Mr Manns a spontaneous assurance of their unaltered affection for him. So they waited long enough to disconnect their projected ovation from the effect produced by the performance of the Kaisermarsch which had just ended the concert, and then gave a great salvo of clapping, which soon brought the frock coat back from the depths. Thus was a pestiferous custom for once turned to account conveniently, appropriately, sensibly, and feelingly; and I joined in the applause with much satisfaction to myself and no harm to anyone else.

I have been for some time waiting for an opportunity of saying a word about Mrs Langtry's revival of As You Like It at the St James's Theatre. I submit that the play is spoiled by the ruthless cutting to bits of the last half of it. This has been forced on the management by want of skill and want of thought on the part of the actors. The problem is to get through a play of so many lines between eight o'clock and eleven. Any fool can solve this in the fashion of Alexander (I allude to the man who stopped a hole to keep the wind away, and not to the lessee of the Avenue Theatre) by cutting out a chunk here and a scrap there until the lines are few enough to fit. But, somehow, the shorter you make your play in this fashion, the more tedious it becomes. The proper way is to divide your play into movements like those of a symphony. You will find that there are several sections which can be safely taken at a brisk *allegro*, and a few that may be taken *prestissimo*: those, for instance, which serve only to explain the mere mechanism of the plot. Each *allegro* will improve the representation if it is judiciously chosen and managed. Mr Benson has introduced one or two in Hamlet with the happiest effect. Of course the thing must be honestly done: the familiar star system trick of making the minor characters slur their work in order to leave plenty of time for the mock pregnant pauses, head waggings, and elaborate business of the leading actor, is vile, and shows a pitiful ambition in the fool that uses it. The star must not take a minute more than his lines are worth, or put off the third murderer with a minute less. Under these conditions, I believe it would be quite feasible to play As You Like It right through in a little over three hours without sacrificing a point.

However, it would be necessary to get another Jacques than Mr Bourchier, or else to rudely shake his conviction that the secret of effective elocution is to pause at every third word, and look significantly out of the corners of his eyes at anybody who happens to be in that direction before letting out the fourth. Mr Bourchier can easily make himself a competent Jacques; but he may take it from me that he is at present as bad a one as London has seen for some years. Mrs Langtry makes a very womanly Rosalind, and succeeds better than any other actress within my recollection in making her love for Orlando the keynote of the part. I may remark that in spite of the beauty of the verse and the deep feeling for sylvan and pastoral scenery which pervades the play, the human part of it is excessively conventional, and might almost have been planned by Tom Taylor. Like Henry V., it belongs to that moment of sympathy with the common morality and thought of his time which came between the romanticism of Shakespear's early plays and the independent thought of his later one; and this is why it is so easily played by any company with a fair share of sense and skill. There is no confounded insight required in the business.

One member of the cast, dressed as a young god (Hymen, in fact) seemed to me to be no other than Carl Armbruster fresh from a rejuvenating dose of the elixir of life. The play-bill explained that Hymen is Carl's daughter. I have been so accustomed to regard him as one in whom the energy and vehement enthusiasms of early manhood will achieve a perfect balance and mellowness on his attaining middle age, that I cannot quite believe that this young lady of eighteen is his daughter. When she was at school with the Moravians at Neuwied, and subsequently went to Miss Genevieve Ward to study for the stage, it was hard to give her father credit for a daughter of more than ten at the outside; but it appears that Time was, as usual, hurrying faster than I thought. I shall be a grand old man myself presently.

374

LONDON MUSIC IN 1888–89

19 *April* 1890

I AM not disposed to quarrel with the Carl Rosa Opera Company over L'Étoile du Nord on no better ground than that the principal parts are entirely beyond the means of their principal singers. *Le mieux est l'ennemi du bien*; and it is perhaps better to play Meyerbeer's operas with half the bravura left out and the other half more or less botched than not to play them at all. Besides, the inadequacy is not really greater in L'Étoile du Nord than in many other works which are regarded as the natural prey of English opera companies. It only appears so because Meyerbeer's music leaves no latitude for that unaffected slovenliness which makes life comparatively easy for the Carl Rosaists, in spite of their hard work in the provinces. A Meyerbeer opera requires extreme mechanical precision of execution and un-flagging energy and attention. Everybody must be smart, polished, alert; there must be no hitch, no delay, no fluking or trusting to *laisser-aller*. It follows that the company must be clever and in good condition, fresh as paint every time. Now I do not say that the Carl Rosa Company is not clever, nor do I deny that it is always ready to do rough and ready work with a will. But if it is jolly it is also a little jaded, and has come to think itself lucky if it gets through its seven operas a week without an actual breakdown; so that though it never gets quite down to the level of a subscription night during the regular Italian season, yet it certainly does fall considerably short of the Meyerbeer standard of finish.

It must not be supposed that completeness has been aimed at in adapting The Star of the North to the require-ments of the Carl Rosa Company. The camp scene is given in full, except for an ugly cut in the quintet in the tent scene (which should, by the bye, have been taken more swiftly and delicately), and the necessary excision for Madame Burns' sake of the brilliant coda to the trio in which Peter drinks Catherine's health. But the first act was vigorously scissored. Danilowitz's polonaise, the trio in which Catherine

375

describes her visit to Prascovia's father, and even the great
duet in which Catherine fires Peter's ambition, were all
sacrificed, whilst the third act was simply gutted, nothing
being left but a verse of Peter's song, an air for Prascovia,
and Catherine's scena cut all to ribbons. The act would bear
with advantage the restoration of Danilowitz's charming air
in E flat, and the concerted piece for Peter, Danilowitz and
Gritsenko, which is given in dialogue.

I am not going to shoot at the performers, though I am
by no means prepared to admit that they all did their best.
Mr Celli might have sung "By thy side, oh beauty cruel" a
little more carefully, even if he had substituted mere vocalizing for the impossibly ridiculous words of Chorley. Mr
Aynsley Cook can scarcely be quite incapable of giving at
least some suggestion of Gritsenko's eccentric devotion to
discipline, which eventually leads the monomaniacal Cos-
sack to approve of the Czar's proposal to shoot him. That
very rough diamond, Mr Child, may rest assured that a
spell of patient practice would open his ears to some of the
refinements of Meyerbeer; but unfortunately I cannot believe that practice is encouraged in the company: it would
give the artist who tried it a mean advantage over the others.
At least it seems to me that the average Carl Rosa execution is that of singers who have not worked at their scales
for years. The minor parts were well done; the chorus, which
is ordinarily too much addicted to shouting, acquitted itself
capitally; and the military bands covered themselves with
well-earned glory. The orchestra was not so good: it was
sluggish and blurred in many passages where neatness and
delicacy were needed: for instance, the excellently imagined
accompaniment to Catherine's scene on her entry in the
third act. Mr Goossens seemed to me to be imperfectly in
sympathy with the electrical Meyerbeerian atmosphere. On
the whole, however, I think the audience felt that they had
had their money's worth. The immense adroitness and
genuine fire of the camp scene were sufficiently brought out
to interest and please the house in an exceptional degree.

P.S. Is it an established English custom to speak of the Ukraine as the You-Crane? I do not know whether it is good Russian to call it the Oookra-eena; but it is much prettier.

25 April 1890

I CONFESS to a weakness, not altogether musical, for Madame Sophie Menter. There is an enormous exhilaration and sense of enlarged life and freedom communicated to me by her superlative and victorious power and adroitness. I worship her magnetic muscle: I admire her puissant hands: I expand in the reflection of her magnificent strength, her suppleness, her swiftness, her inexhaustible, indefatigable energy. I grant that this may be the rebellion of the old Adam in me—a diabolic turbulence of the unchastened will-to-live, inherited from my beefsteak eating ancestors: I even insist on the superiority of the plane upon which I am raised by the spiritual intensity and purely musical instinct of a player like Madame Backer-Gröndahl, whose right arm seems frailer than Madame Menter's little finger. All the same, I have no intention of restraining my enjoyment of her immense execution, which places her beside the violinist Ysaÿe at the head of the musical athletes of the world.

No doubt the admirers of Schumann were disappointed with the performance of his concerto by Madame Menter at the Crystal Palace on Saturday. But what could they expect? To the superb Sophie, solid, robust, healthy, with her mere self-consciousness an example and sufficient delight to her, playing Schumann was like bringing a sensitive invalid into the fields on a sunshiny day and making him play football for the good of his liver. You could hear Schumann plaintively remonstrating in the orchestra, and the piano coming down on him irresistibly, echoing his words with goodnatured mockery, and whirling him off in an endless race that took him clean out of himself and left him panting. Never were the quick movements finished with less regard for poor Schumann's lungs.

The intermezzo delighted me beyond measure. Ordinarily, no man can put into words those hushed confidences that pass in it between piano and orchestra, as between a poet and a mistress. But I can give you what passed on Saturday, word for word. Here it is:

> SOPHIE: Now, then, Bob, are you ready for another turn?

> SCHUMANN: Yes. Just half a moment, if you dont mind. I havnt quite got my wind yet.

> SOPHIE: Come! you feel all the better for it, dont you?

> SCHUMANN: No doubt, no doubt. The weather is certainly very fine.

> SOPHIE: I should think so. Better than sticking indoors at that old piano of yours and sentimentalizing, anyhow.

> SCHUMANN: Yes: I know I should take more exercise.

> SOPHIE: Well, you have got wind enough by this time. Come along, old man: hurry up.

> SCHUMANN: If you wouldnt mind going a bit slower——

> SOPHIE: Oh, bother going slow. You just stick to me and I'll pull you through. You'll be all right in a brace of shakes. Now: one, two, three, and——

> (*attacca subito l'allegro*).

And it really did Schumann good.

Pray do not suppose that Madame Menter is a hard, bloodless, unsympathetic: in a word, an unkind player. Not a bit of it. When, after an indescribable performance of a piece by Scarlatti and a Hungarian rhapsody by Liszt, she was recalled once, twice, thrice, four times, and eventually seized bodily by the intrepid Mr Manns and led in custody back to the piano, she played Liszt's transcription of Beethoven's Wonne der Wehmuth, and by that selection, as well as by the strong tenderness with which she played, completed the conquest of the already heavily-smitten Bassetto.

The orchestra was in fine form; and I cannot recall a performance of the Pastoral Symphony which has afforded me more pleasure. But the vocalist, Mr Charles Manners, who, if I recollect aright, first burst on London as the meditative sentinel in Iolanthe, threw away a chance of distinguishing himself by finishing The Two Grenadiers with an interpolation which he honestly meant to be decorative, and to give the song a rounding-off which Schumann had not been equal to. I hope that Mr Manners is under no illusion as to the effect he produced. The minority who applauded him may have distracted his attention from the eloquently grim expression of the majority who did not. If so, let him take my word for it that his cadenzas had better be reserved for his next tour to Juan Fernandez. As it is the custom to sing *Qui sdegno* sharp, and to spoil the end by going down to the low E, I do not greatly blame him for that. But as he seems to have a genuine love of his profession, and considerable qualifications for success in it, I can do no less than warn him against those failings in taste and good sense which, more than any deficiency in voice or musical aptitude, keep so many of our singers in the second or third rank as artists.

Miss Dell Thompson made me laugh so exceedingly at the soirée given by the Norwegian Club some time ago that there was no difficulty in inducing me to go to her recital at Prince's Hall this day week. I will not attempt to describe her personally, because I do not know which is the real Miss Thompson: the small girl of three feet high, with staring eyes, infantile mouth, elbowless little sticks of arms, and absurdly laughably childlike squeak of a voice, or the young woman who is like any other well-favored and graceful young woman, except in respect of being clever and able to do something. Anyhow, she is gifted in a remarkable degree with the qualities needed for distinguished success in naturalist comedy. As a reciter, what she wants at present is a little criticism from the London point of view; and that is what I now propose respectfully to offer her.

First, then, as to her selection of pieces for recitation. She laid a good deal of stress on The Chariot Race from Ben

Hur, which I took to be a novel in the manner of Mr Rider Haggard. It is without literary grace, being as business-like a piece of three-volume prose as ever was penned; and the chariot race is imagined in a perfectly commonplace way. There is nothing in it that specially suits Miss Thompson's style; and she adds nothing to it; indeed, she finds the incidental specifications of the arena so hopelessly insusceptible of artistic treatment, that her air of intelligent explanation verges harder upon the ridiculous than I quite like to say. And when, in a hopeless effort to churn the literary skim milk into some presentable sort of oleo-margarine, she lavishes all the vigor of her young lungs on it, the strain on the patience of the audience becomes severe. There were people who hissed on Friday, as well as people who applauded. Both were fools for their pains: they should have let Ben Hur fall with his own unaided flatness. Miss Dell Thompson is clever enough to see, on reflection, that it would serve him right. I certainly think she has formed either an over-estimate of Ben, or an under-estimate of the taste of London.

Another point. Miss Thompson has an irresistible American accent: merely to hear her say "Tom" sets me wondering whether, if she whispered the more euphonious "Corno di Bassetto," it would be possible to refuse her anything. But when she passes from impersonation to description—from the first person to the third—from dramatic utterance to abstract recitation, then I confess that the need for classical diction asserts itself imperatively, and I involuntarily make notes of such words as bawlcony, fahllowed, invahlved, invahlunterry, necesserrily (with a stress on the third syllable worthy of Mr Henry George himself), sympithy, equil, tern for turn, dew for do, and a ringing nasal ah-oo which is sometimes charming, but which does not seem at its best in words like bound, round, etc. Then Miss Thompson has deliberately cultivated an R which is neither the no R at all of Middlesex nor the clean trilled R which is the only pleasant alternative to it. She just rolls her tongue up and treats us to a thick guttural R which makes such a word as "neared" (for example) an ugly obstruction in the middle of the silver stream of her speech.

London is full not only of cockneys who have too many and horrible defects of their own to leave them any excuse for fastidiousness, but of provincials and Americans who have got the better of the ugly features of their native dialects, and who are therefore rather intolerant of professional speakers who shew any indisposition to take the same trouble. I am myself disposed to insist on the right of the individual to the widest latitude; but obviously a line must be drawn somewhere; and it should be drawn higher for one who professes speaking as an art than for a private person or a propagandist lecturer. My own diction when I speak in public is perhaps slightly less artistic than that of Coquelin; and Mrs Victoria Claflin Woodhull falls considerably short of Miss Ada Rehan as an American exponent of the art of diction. Nevertheless, the critic who should object to our lectures on that ground would be justly contemned as an unmitigated prig. Not so in the case of Miss Dell Thompson. It is her business to be word-perfect; and nobody who heard her recite "What my lover said" can doubt her capacity for the most delicate degree of excellence, if she chooses to set about attaining it. Nobody can even doubt that her artistic insight will compel her to insist on attaining it the moment she becomes conscious of the smallest refinement not yet mastered by her.

As I do not wish to confine myself exclusively to destructive criticism, I may as well point out to Miss Thompson that she has a substitute for Ben Hur of the highest order ready to her hand in William Morris's Atalanta's Race, which she will find in The Earthly Paradise. Further, it may interest her to know that The Owl Critic is played out here, and that our very souls loath Poor Little Jo and the quagmire of sloshy false sentiment to which he belongs. Besides, only artists who are born third-rate ever really succeed with third-rate stuff. I suspect that Miss Dell Thompson's future will be chiefly devoted to the stage; but in the meantime I hope she will not mistrust herself and us so far as to play low down in her selections. If I were a reciter I should get up a single program and stump the country with it. Here it is:

PART I

The Ancient Mariner—S. T. Coleridge.

PART II

John Gilpin—Cowper.

2 May 1890

ALTHOUGH Mr Manns was inconsiderate enough to select the very wettest day he could find for his benefit, the audience was of the largest; and as they all had umbrellas to thump with, the applause was exceptionally effective. Not so the program. The Freischütz overture, played without the Wagnerian interpretation of the *decrescendo* mark over the chord preceding the entry of the "feminine theme" in the coda, was as fresh as ever; though, with all respect to Mr Manns, Wagner was assuredly right. The Tannhäuser overture was equally welcome. But then the Freischütz was played at three and the Tannhäuser at five; and between the two were two mortal hours of music which did nothing to restore that alacrity of spirit which the rain had washed out of me.

There was Dr Sapellnikoff's playing of Tschaikowsky's pianoforte concerto in G (No. 2) for the first time in England. The apology made by Sir George Grove in the program for the absence of an analysis was the less needed because the work contains nothing new. It is impulsive, copious, difficult, and pretentious; but it has no distinction, no originality, no feeling for the solo instrument, nothing to rouse the attention or to occupy the memory. It left me without any notion of Sapellnikoff's rank as a player: he is, of course, swift and powerful with his fingers; but six bars of a Mozart sonata would have told me more about his

382

artistic gift than twenty whole concertos of the Tschai-kowsky sort.

And here let me remark that whenever you hear of a great composer from Russia, or from Hungary, or from any other country which is far behind us in social development, the safest plan is not to believe in him. You cannot be too intensely insular on the art question in England. If England wants music to reach her own highest standard, she must make it for herself. The adolescent enthusiasms, the revolutionary ardors, the belated romanticism of Slav and Czech can produce nothing for England except toys for her young people. Wagner himself is, on some points, too sentimental for us: we must have an English Wagner: perhaps he is starving somewhere whilst I write. If we would only give a chance to every potential Wagner among our millions—that is, secure him adequate schooling and adequate grub—we should have an actual one in two generations at latest.

Perhaps you doubt the national capacity for music of Wagnerian depth and strength. No Englishman, you think, has a Meistersinger in him. Pinchbeck Handel and second-hand Mendelssohn, with words by Mr Joseph Bennett: that, according to your experience, is English music. But every nation has its plague of "kapellmeister's music"; and if the critics are fools enough to mistake such academic trifling for genuine art, so much the worse for them and not much the better for the kapellmeisters and Mr Joseph Bennett. Not all the good-natured puffing of Mr Bennett's colleagues will get as much wear out of Mr Cowen's Thorgrim or Mr Parry's Judith as I shall get out of my second best pair of boots before they descend into the blind cave of eternal night. As to where an English Meistersinger is to come from, all I know is that long before Wagner was born England produced Henry Purcell's Yorkshire Feast, a work cognate with the Meistersinger in its most characteristic feature. We cannot count on another Purcell; but in my opinion England's turn in art is coming, especially since there is a growing disposition among us to carry our social aims further than providing every middle-class dog with his own manger as soon as he is able to pay for it.

Some time ago I suggested that Mr Manns should give us some medieval trombone and organ music at the Saturday concerts. Consequently I should be praising myself if I were to applaud the selection of Heinrich Schütz's Lamentatio Davidis for performance on Saturday. Besides, the chief credit on this score must surely be due to Mr George Case, who probably induced the Wind Instrument Society to bring it forward at a concert last month. I guess this because I first heard the work in 1885 at South Kensington, where he played it with Mr Geard and Messrs J. and Antoine Matt, the voice part (taken by Mr Henschel on Saturday) being sung by Mr Stanley Smith. On that occasion they also played Luther's Eine feste Burg, which I can recommend to Mr Manns if he feels disposed for more trombone music. We all know the trombone in its melodramatic moods; but its noblest qualities never come out so impressively as when it is treated in what I may call a spirit of pure counterpoint.

I have to apologize to Mr Harold and Miss Ethel Bauer for missing their concert on Monday. I allowed myself to be seduced by the management of the Prince of Wales's Theatre into attending the 100th night of Marjorie, intending to leave after an act or two and go on to the concert. But my Herculean frame suddenly yielded to the strain which the present stress of pictures, politics, and music put on a critic who is engaged in all three departments simultaneously. I settled down lazily in my stall and never budged until the curtain fell. Not that the performance, though it amused me, can be said to have enthralled me. I can tell you very little about it—not even how often Mr Coffin kissed Miss Broughton. He seemed to me to be kissing everybody with a reckless disregard of propriety. I must say that Mr Coffin, being a handsome young man, and considerably under-parted to boot, had an easy time of it. Had he been trying his prentice hand at Iago or Don Juan I should have set my brains seriously to the task of criticism; but Marjorie is child's play for him. As a singer he has been better, and he will some day again be better, than he is today. He insists too much on the manly roughness of his voice, and is, it seems to me, actually impatient of the delicate color and the rich, light, smooth tone with which he started, and which was the cause of his success; for anybody can produce the rough, loud article if he sets himself at it. Mr Coffin has only to cast back after his old charm to get two stops to his organ. Then skill and taste in their employ-ment, with the dramatic intelligence of which, even in this Marjorie nonsense, he shews plenty, will keep him in the front rank when he becomes a middle-aged operatic villain, and takes to serious business.

Mr Slaughter has not allowed the better to become the enemy of the good in composing Marjorie. The score is sufficient for its purpose; but I think he really might have devised some worthier climax for Mr Coffin's song in the third act than a hackneyed waltz refrain. Marjorie com-pares favorably with Dorothy as to the book: unfavorably as to the music. The book of Dorothy was not only silly, but stupid. The book of Marjorie is also silly, but it is amusing. On the other hand, the music of Dorothy was pretty, and had a certain elegance and technical finish which belonged to the Mendelssohn-Sterndale Bennett traditions in which Mr Cellier, like Sir Arthur Sullivan, was trained. Mr Slaughter has been less fastidious; and his share in the suc-cess of Marjorie is proportionately less than that of Mr Cellier in the success of Dorothy, which, by the way, is still ravaging the provinces.

I must bring these disjointed remarks to a close. The fact is, I have been at the Royal Academy all day, "Press-viewing" it; and my mind is unhinged by the contemplation of so much emptiness and so much bungling. My wits were in a sufficiently unsettled condition before I went there: for last week I described how Madame Sophie Menter played Liszt's transcription of Beethoven's *Wonne der Wehmuth*, whereas what she did play was—as I heard with my own ears and knew perfectly well—his transcription of Mendelssohn's *Auf Flugeln des Gesanges*. I have before this gone to a performance of Don Giovanni, and begun my notice thereof with half a column about Fidelio before, in trying to remember how the statue came into the prison scene, the truth flashed on me. I therefore give warning that I will not be answerable for the accuracy of any statement that may appear in this column—or out of it, for that matter.

P.S. I forgot to say that the omission of any reference to Dvorak's new symphony is due to that idiotic body the Executive Committee of the London Liberal and Radical Union, which selected for a council meeting the night fixed long beforehand for the Philharmonic concert. These Goths think that a concert is a thing of no importance. If it were a horserace now——!

9 *May* 1890

I occasionally get letters from artists whom I have criticized, explaining away their misdeeds, or thanking me for my valuable suggestions, or arguing the point with me, or threatening me with personal violence, either to relieve their feelings or to follow up a small opening. Some of them mean nothing more than to nobble me with a little flattery; and these are the wise ones; for I need not say that I delight in flattery. Even when there is no mistaking it for sincere admiration, I am pleased to find that anybody attaches sufficient importance to my opinion to spend a postage stamp on an attempt to humbug me. Therefore let no diplomatic young singer be deterred from paying me compliments by the certainty of my seeing through them. Flatter by all means; and remember that you cannot lay it on too thick. The net pleases the bird no less than the bait. But be particularly careful not to discuss artistic points with me; for nothing is easier than to drop some remark that will make me your enemy for life.

For instance, I have before me a letter from a singer who wrote to me to ask whether a certain song should not be sung with a high note interpolated at the end for the sake of effect. As the song was by Mozart, my reply may be imagined. The following is the astonishing rejoinder of my correspondent: "I see plainly that you are quite right; and when I sing at another *classical* concert I shall act on your view. But you will, of course, agree with me that a singer must try to be popular; and therefore at ballad concerts, etc., if he finds a high note brings him success and secures him the applause of the public, it is only common sense for him to do it. I confess it is inartistic; but what is one to do? To earn my living I must please my audience."

Imagine my feelings on being calmly told that "of course I will agree" with the assumption that it is "only common sense" to act against your conscience whenever there is money to be made by doing so. However, this is not really the position taken by my correspondent. He does not feel that the high note is inartistic at all: he only knows that certain cranks like myself, who are supposed to be authorities on the subject, say that it is inartistic; and he agrees as a pure matter of convention. Consequently, the high note is not against his conscience: it is only against mine, which is not morally binding on him, though he supposes himself let in for admitting that I know better than he. Therefore I now say to my correspondent, Go on singing the high note. If you like it better than Mozart's ending, or if the repugnance you feel to the alteration is so slight as to be profitably compensated by the applause which the note brings you from people who have not even that slight repugnance then fire away. Your artistic sense will be satisfied: mine will be outraged. You guarantee the applause from the audience: I guarantee the slating from at least one critic. The fact is, that if the singers felt about these interpolations as a cultivated musician does, they could not sing them without an intolerable sense of discomfort and humiliation. And until a singer has that sense it is idle for him to suppose

387

that the word "inartistic" has any genuine significance for him.

As to the distinction between classical and popular concerts, it conveniently describes the difference between a Crystal Palace Saturday concert and one of Messrs Boosey's ballad concerts. But it does not mean that the right way to sing a song by Mozart at one concert is the wrong way at another. At a ballad concert you may substitute the music of Milton Wellings for the music of Mozart; but you most certainly may not substitute the wrong way of singing Mozart for the right way.

Here is an affectionate comment of The Musical World on the unmusical World:

"We have more than once pointed out, with friendly amusement, the harmless mistakes which have been made in speaking of English art by our excellent contemporary 'Le Menestrel.' But there is a limit to our toleration. When it asserts, as in its last issue, that Mr Louis Engel is a member of our staff, we are bound to protest. We do not pretend to know what evil days may be in store for The Musical World; but our readers may be assured that these days are not yet."

Now, in the name of all that is easy-going, why this unprovoked onslaught? Ordinarily, I have only one fault to find with Mr Jaques (that is the M.W.'s name). It is that he is scandalously good-natured: so much so, that he wrapped up the nakedness of the bitter truth about Thorgrim in an article 500,000 words long, in order to spare the feelings of Mr Cowen and Mr Bennett. I believe that the indignation unnaturally pent up by this effort demanded an outlet; and so feeling that he must have somebody's blood, he flew at the unfortunate L. E., and wreaked on him the rage that ought to have laid Thorgrim low. This sort of Berserkerism must not be encouraged; for how do I know who may be the next victim? myself, perhaps!

Some time ago a weekly paper, criticizing a performance of Gounod's Ave Maria by Madame Patti, took occasion to observe that the harmonium *obbligato* was vilely played. It was L. E. who played it; and he played it with admirable discretion; but the critic evidently despised The World's musical column, and felt that he must assassinate its author. Now the reason L. E. is thus pursued is that he is beyond all comparison the best musical critic of his school in London, as far as my knowledge goes. His school (mid-century Parisian) is not mine: I was brought up in it, and soon had enough of it, finding its arch enemy Wagner more to my taste; but that does not prevent me from seeing that he knows his business, and that he has the force to write individually, originally, making his mark with every opinion he delivers. Of how many critics in London is it possible to say as much? When one thinks of the average critic, with his feeble infusion of musical dictionary and analytical program, the man who has no opinion, and dare not express it if he had, who is afraid of his friends, of his enemies, of his editor, of his own ignorance, of committing an injustice (as if there were any question of abstract justice involved in the expression of a critic's tastes and distastes), it is impossible not to admire L. E., who, at an age at which all ordinary journalists are hopelessly muzzled by the mere mass of their personal acquaintance, can still excite these wild animosities in the breasts of his colleagues.

Another critic, Mr Clement Scott, has been describing how he was boycotted in the early days of his warfare against the managers. But my advice to managers and concert givers is Boycott all good critics. I am myself vigorously boycotted; and I take it as a sincere compliment. Concert givers are perfectly well aware that my criticism will be exactly the same whether I pay for my seat or not; and they naturally think they may as well have my money as well as my notice. In my opinion the whole system of complimentary tickets for the Press should be discontinued. The managers have only to combine against the free list, and the thing is done. The papers must have criticisms; the critics must see the plays; and the proportion between praise and blame must remain practically the same, however freely and sincerely expressed. Unfortunately, the initiative in the matter ought to come from the critics and not from the managers. Just as waiters will have their wages made precarious by the tipping system until they have the sense to refuse tips; so managers will send tickets as long as the critics will accept them. We should form a Critics' Trade Union, and pledge ourselves never to enter a place of public entertainment without paying (and charging the price to our paper). If we are anything like so highly skilled as we ought to be, there could be no danger of blacklegs taking our places on papers of any pretension to high-class literary matter. Who will join? There would be no gain or loss to speak of, except to ourselves in independence. The managers would make the papers pay for the stalls; but then the papers would make the managers pay for advertisements to replace the purely complimentary puffs which are a feature of the present system.

Miss Elsie Hall is an infant phenomenon of the latest fashion, that is, a twelve-year-old pianist. She played last Monday at Steinway Hall with all the vigor and enjoyment of her age, and as dexterously as you please, being a hardy wiry girl, with great readiness and swiftness of execution, and unbounded alacrity of spirit. At the same time, there is not the slightest artistic excuse for exploiting her cleverness at concerts; I hope we may not hear of her again in public until she is of an age at which she may fairly be asked to earn her living for herself. And this reminds me of a matter I omitted to mention in connection with Marjorie last week [May 2]. It is that the stage is "dressed" with children in the first set, quite unnecessarily. I again urge on the notice of our legislators the cynical unscrupulousness with which the loophole made in the Act for the purpose of enabling Richard III to have his little Duke of York on the stage has been abused to the extent of making the Act, so far as the stage is concerned, almost a dead letter.

I deserted Miss Meredyth Elliott's concert on Wednes-

day to hear Dr John Todhunter's pastoral entitled A Sicilian
Idyll at the little theatre of the club in Bedford Park. It is
not every poet who could reconcile me to an hour's transparent Arcadian make-believe in the classic Sicily of Theo-
critus; but Dr Todhunter did it. There is nothing in music
more beautiful in its way than blank verse in its early
simplicity of line by line, each beautiful and complete in
itself. Marlowe's line was not "mighty": blank verse did not
become mighty until the lines had grown together into the
great symphonic movements of Shakespear's final manner;
but it was tuneful, exquisitely emphasized, and sometimes
gorgeous in its sound color. Sometimes on the other hand, it
was vulgar and swaggering. Now Dr Todhunter writes a
line that is guiltless of swagger. It is melodious, tender,
delicately colored, and with that convincing cadence that
only comes from perfect fitness of emphasis. It was quite
enchanting to sit listening to it, and to escape from the
realistic drama of modern life for a whole hour. The performance was very creditable. Music, dancing, costumes,
scenery were all excellent. Mr Paget (Alcander) seemed to
me to have no experience of using his voice except for
private conversation: there was not enough tone and weight
in his lines; but I have no other fault to find with him.
Florence Farr's striking and appropriate good looks no
doubt helped her to a success that would have cost a plainer
woman more to achieve; but her intelligence and her instinct for the right fall of the line was never at fault. Miss
Linfield's ear is perhaps not quite so sure as that of her
lover Daphnis, enacted by "Mr John Smith." I may mention that Dr Todhunter has evidently never experienced the
vicissitudes known as "having the brokers in." He has
therefore never heard the terrible word "inventory" pronounced. If he ever does (*absit omen!*) he will discover that
the accent is on the first syllable instead of, as he supposes,
on the second.

I CANNOT quite account for the crowded state of the concert-room at the Philharmonic last week. And they were so enthusiastic, too. Young Mr Borwick is hardly an established favorite as yet (it was his first appearance in England); and Signor Mancinelli, though he has conducted for a few seasons at Covent Garden, is not absolutely the idol of London. I could not help thinking that both these gentlemen must have been treated very liberally by the Society in the matter of complimentary tickets. Nothing could be more natural under the circumstances; but the effect, as far as the public is concerned, is much the same as if the *claque* system had been introduced for the evening. For instance, I do not believe that the desire to hear the third movement of Signor Mancinelli's Venetian suite was as general among those who had paid for their tickets as among those who had not. The orchestration is after the pattern of that glittering sample which Signor Mancinelli showed us in his finale to Bizet's Pêcheurs de Perles at Covent Garden. The success of its execution by "the famous Philharmonic orchestra" was a melancholy proof of the sort of work which that kid-gloved body is now fit for. It is an unapproachably noiseless, delicate, well-bred band, too superfine for the vulgarities of Beethoven or the democratically unreticent Wagner, but incomparable for a Venetian suite or a quadrille at a Court ball.

Mr Leonard Borwick would have made a greater success if he had not been a little over-newspapered beforehand. I have no fault to find with his playing: it is well studied, accurate, and earnestly and enthusiastically set about, as it should be; but he is still a pupil and not a master. Whether Mr Borwick will be spoken of hereafter only once a year (after his benefit concert) as "that excellent pianist and well-known professor," or whether he will be current throughout Europe as "Borwick" *sans phrase*, is a question which the Philharmonic concert has left unsettled. It is sufficiently

392

high praise for the present to say that it was not settled adversely.

Mr Cowen's conducting reminded me rudely of the flight of time. We have been so long accustomed to regard Mr Cowen as a young man that the sudden discovery of such signs of age as slowness, timidity, exhaustion of musical eagerness, come upon us with a shock: at least, they do on me. I forget Mr Cowen's exact age; but if I were to judge of the funereal way in which he led the Frischka of Liszt's Fourth Hungarian Rhapsody—one of the maddest of them —I should put him not far from eighty. The allegro of *Dove sono* was also far too tame. Miss Macintyre, whose popularity increases each time she sings, got through it very creditably; but if I were to say that she sang it quite satisfactorily I should imply that she is a singer of the very highest rank, which she can hardly yet claim to be.

It seems to me that there are more champion pianists in the world at present than any previous age has seen. Possibly the introduction and general use of the street piano has raised the standard of swiftness and certainty in execution. However that may be, mere technique, which used to suffice to stamp as a "great player" any dullard who had perseverance enough to become a finger acrobat, is now a drug in the market; and the seat of the higher faculties of the pianist is no longer supposed to be the left wrist. Consequently I went to hear the famous Paderewski without the slightest doubt that his execution would be quite as astonishing as everybody else's; and I was not disappointed. He plays as clearly as Von Bulow—or as nearly so as is desirable, and he is much more accurate. He has not enough consideration for the frailty of his instrument; his *fortissimo*, instead of being serious and formidable like that of Stavenhagen, is rather violent and elate. He goes to the point at which a piano huddles itself up and lets itself be beaten instead of unfolding the richness and color of its tone. His charm lies in his pleasant spirit and his dash of humor: he carries his genius and his mission almost jauntily, which is more than can be said for Stavenhagen, whose seriousness, however, is equally admirable in its way. He began with Mendelssohn, and knocked him about rather unceremoniously; then he took the Harmonious Blacksmith and spoiled it by making it a stalking-horse for his sleight-of-hand—playing it too fast, in fact; then he went on to Schumann's Fantasia, which seems so hard to fathom because there is next to nothing in it; and then the way was cleared for Chopin. His playing of that great composer's studies—three of them—was by far the best thing he did. The other Chopin pieces were not specially well played; and his execution of the Liszt rhapsody at the end was by no means equal to Sophie Menter's. Still his Parisian vogue is not to be wondered at: he makes a recital as little oppressive as it is the nature of such a thing to be.

I desire to thank Mr William Stead publicly for getting out The Review of Reviews in time for the Bach Choir concert on Saturday afternoon, and so lightening for me the intolerable tedium of sitting unoccupied whilst the Bachists conscientiously maundered through Brahms' Requiem. Mind, I do not deny that the Requiem is a solid piece of music manufacture. You feel at once that it could only have come from the establishment of a first-class undertaker. But I object to requiems altogether. The Dead March in Saul is just as long as a soul in perfect health ought to meditate on the grave before turning lifewards again to a gay quickstep, as the soldiers do. A requiem overdoes it, even when there is an actual bereavement to be sympathized with; but in a concert-room when there is nobody dead, it is the very wantonness of make-believe. On such occasions the earnest musician reads The Review of Reviews; and the Culture Humbug sits with his longest face, pretending to drink in that "solemn joy at the commencement of a higher life" which Mr Bennett, in the analytical programme, assures him is the correct emotion for the occasion. By the bye, I must quote Mr Bennett's opening remark, as it put me into high spirits for the whole afternoon. "This Requiem," he writes, "was composed in 1867 as a tribute by the composer to the memory of his mother, a sentiment which lends especial interest to the soprano solo." For boldness of syntactical ellipsis, and farfetched subtlety of psychologic association, Mr Bennett must be admitted the master of us all.

Somebody is sure to write to me now demanding, "Do you mean Mozart's Requiem?" I reply, that in the few numbers—or parts of numbers—in that work which are pure Mozart, the corpse is left out. There is no shadow of death anywhere on Mozart's music. Even his own funeral was a failure. It was dispersed by a shower of rain; and to this day nobody knows where he was buried or whether he was buried at all or not. My own belief is that he was not. Depend on it, they had no sooner put up their umbrellas and bolted for the nearest shelter than he got up, shook off his bones into the common grave of the people, and soared off into universality. It is characteristic of the British middle class that whenever they write a book about Mozart, the crowning tragedy is always the dreadful thought that instead of having a respectable vault all to himself to moulder in for the edification of the British tourist, he should have been interred cheaply among the bodies of the lower classes. Was it not the Rev. H. R. Haweis who waxed quite pathetic over this lamentable miscarriage of propriety, and then called his book Music and Morals!?

However, I am not yet done with the Bach concert. It turned out that the Requiem was only a clever device of Mr Stanford's to make his setting of Tennyson's Revenge seem lively by force of contrast. But it would have needed half a dozen actual funerals to do that. I do not say that Mr Stanford could not set Tennyson's ballad as well as he set Browning's Cavalier songs, if only he did not feel that, as a professional man with a certain social position to keep up, it would be bad form to make a public display of the savage emotions called up by the poem. But as it is, Mr Stanford is far too much the gentleman to compose anything but drawing-room or class-room music. There are moments here and there in The Revenge during which one feels that a conductor of the lower orders, capable of swearing at the choir, might have got a brief rise out of them; and I will even admit that the alternating chords for the trombones which depict the sullen rocking of the huge Spanish ship do for an instant bring the scene before you; but the rest, as the mad gentleman said to Mrs Nickleby, is gas and gaiters. It is a pity; for Mr Stanford is one of the few professors who ever had any talent to lose.

16 *May* 1890

"We are losing, we are sorry to say, Corno di Bassetto. The larger salary of a weekly organ of the classes has proved too much for the virtue even of a Fabian, and he has abandoned us. We wish him well, and twice even the big salary that is coming to him from the bloated coffers of the organ of the aristocracy. Let us give his adieu to The Star readers, with whom he has been on terms of such pleasant intercourse, in his own words."—T.P.

After the malediction, the valediction. I have now to make a ruinous, a desolating, an incredible announcement. This is the last column from the hand of Corno di Bassetto which will appear in The Star. Friday will no longer be looked forward to in a hundred thousand households as the day of the Feast of Light. The fault is not mine. I proposed long ago that not only this column, but the entire paper, political leaders and all, should be conducted on Bassettian lines, and practically dictated by me. This perfectly reasonable proposition, which would have spared the editor much thought and responsibility, he refused with such an entire blindness to its obvious advantages that I could do no less than inform him that he knew nothing about politics. It will hardly be believed that he retorted by aspersing my capacity as a musical critic. One memorable Friday, when the machines failed to keep pace with the demand for the paper, he declared that the newly-issued report of the Parnell Commission, and not my column, was the attraction. He even said that nobody ever read my articles; and I then felt that

I owed it to myself to affirm that nobody ever read anything else in the paper.

At last our relations became so strained that we came to the very grave point of having to exchange assurances that we esteemed one another beyond all created mortals, and that no vicissitude should ever alter those feelings of devotion. Upon this brotherly basis I had no hesitation in magnanimously admitting that a daily paper requires, in the season at least, a daily and not a weekly chronicle and criticism of musical events. Such a chronicle I am unable to undertake. A man who, like myself, has to rise regularly at eleven o'clock every morning cannot sit up night after night writing opera notices piping hot from the performance. My habits, my health, and my other activities forbid it. Therefore I felt that my wisest course would be to transfer myself to a weekly paper, which I have accordingly done. I ask some indulgence for my successor, handicapped as he will be for a time by the inevitable comparison with one whom he can hardly hope to equal, much less to surpass. I say this on my own responsibility, as he has not invited me to make any such appeal on his behalf, perhaps because it is not yet settled who he is to be. Whoever he is, I hope he will never suffer the musical department of The Star to lose that pre-eminence which has distinguished it throughout the administration of "Corno di Bassetto."

SPOOF OPERA

By a Ghost from the 'Eighties

THE institution called variously a busman's or a stage-door-keeper's holiday has never been called a musical critic's holiday. The musician who has been a professional critic knows, better even than Wagner, that music is kept alive on the cottage piano of the amateur, and not in the concert rooms and opera houses of the great capitals. He will not go to public performances when he is no longer paid for his soul-destroying sufferings. I wonder how many of our critics at last become quite clearly conscious that what they have to listen to in these places is not music. Sometimes the horrible thought comes that perhaps some of them have never heard music in their lives, but only public performances, and therefore honestly believe that these sounds, produced for so many guineas a week, and synchronized by an official called a conductor, really make music, and that there is no other sort of music. But such a state of damnation is hardly possible; for it happens from time to time within the experience of every opera or concert goer that the pentecostal miracle recurs, and for a few bars, or a whole number, or even for a whole evening, the guineas' worth of notes organize themselves into living music. Such occasions are very rare; but they are frequent enough to give every critic some moments of the real thing to compare with the simulacrum. Yet the critics seldom venture to face the conclusion that the difference is not between a bad performance and a good one, but between the waste and heartbreak of a vain search, and the supreme satisfaction of a glorious discovery.

Still, the miracle being always possible, there is hope, as long as the performers are really trying. Sometimes, if only for a moment, there is success. But they are not always trying. Worst of all, they are sometimes guying. Our orchestras become so stale with their endless repetitions of work which contains no durably interesting orchestral detail nor presents any technical difficulty, that nothing but a high standard of artistic self-respect and honesty in their public obligations will make them do their work seriously if the conductor either sympathizes with their attitude or lacks the authority which is not to be trifled with. When these saving conditions are lacking, you get spoof opera. The accompaniments are a derisive rum-tum. The fortissimo chords are music-hall crashes, pure charivari, in which the players play any note that comes uppermost, and then laugh to one another. The joke is kept from the audience, partly by its own ignorance, and partly by the fact that as the *farceurs* are in a minority, most of the players are playing the notes

398

set down in their parts because that is the easiest thing to do, and because they are not all in the humor for horseplay, not to mention that some of them are artists to whose taste and conscience such tomfoolery is detestable.

Verdi was the victim of a riot of this sort which lately came under my ghostly notice. I haunted a famous London theatre one evening in time to hear the last two acts of what was the most popular opera of the nineteenth century until Gounod's Faust supplanted it: an opera so popular that people who never dreamt of going to the opera as a general habit, and never in all their lives went to any other opera, went again and again to hear Il Trovatore whenever they had a chance.

Il Trovatore is, in fact, unique, even among the works of its own composer and its own country. It has tragic power, poignant melancholy, impetuous vigor, and a sweet and intense pathos that never loses its dignity. It is swift in action, and perfectly homogeneous in atmosphere and feeling. It is absolutely void of intellectual interest: the appeal is to the instincts and to the senses all through. If it allowed you to think for a moment it would crumble into absurdity like the garden of Klingsor. The very orchestra is silenced as to every sound that has the irritant quality that awakens thought: for example, you never hear the oboe: all the scoring for the wind that is not mere noise is for the lower registers of the clarionets and flutes, and for the least reedy notes of the bassoon.

Let us admit that no man is bound to take Il Trovatore seriously. We are entirely within our rights in passing it by and turning to Bach and Handel, Mozart and Beethoven, Wagner and Strauss, for our music. But we must take it or leave it: we must not trifle with it. He who thinks that Il Trovatore can be performed without taking it with the most tragic solemnity is, for all the purposes of romantic art, a fool. The production of a revival of Il Trovatore should be supervised by Bergson; for he alone could be trusted to value this perfect work of instinct, and defend its integrity from the restless encroachments of intelligence.

The costumes and scenery need to be studied and guarded with the most discriminating care. For example, there is only one costume possible for the Count di Luna. He must wear a stiff violet velvet tunic, white satin tights, velvet shoes, and a white turban hat, with a white puggaree falling on a white cloak. No other known costume can remove its wearer so completely from common humanity. No man could sit down in such a tunic and such tights; for the vulgar realism of sitting down is ten times more impossible for the Count di Luna than for the Venus of Milo. The gipsy must be decorated with sequins and Zodiacal signs: as well put a caravan on the stage at once as relate her by the smallest realistic detail to any gipsy that ever sold uncouth horses at St Margaret's Fair or kept a shooting-gallery. The harp of Manrico must be, not "the harp that once," but the harp that never. It should be such an instrument as Adams decorated ceilings with, or modern piano-makers use as supports for the pedals of their instruments. Give Manrico an Erard harp—a thing that he could possibly play—and he is no longer Manrico, but simply Man; and the un-plumbed depths of the opera dry up into an ascertained and disilluding shallow. And the scenes in which these un-bounded and heart-satisfying figures move must be the scenery of Gustave Doré at his most romantic. The moun-tains must make us homesick, even if we are Cockneys who have never seen a mountain bigger or remoter than Primrose Hill. The garden must be an enchanted garden: the convent must be a sepulchre for the living: the towers of Castellor must proclaim the dungeons within.

I should say that a production of Il Trovatore is perhaps the most severe test a modern impresario has to face; and I suggest that if he cannot face it, he had better run away from it; for if he pretends to make light of it, no one will laugh with him.

Well knowing all this, I haunted, as aforesaid, half a performance of this wonderful opera a few nights ago. It cost me six-and-sixpence.

Let the six-and-sixpence go: I do not ask for my money back, except, perhaps the sixpence that went as tax to the Government, which might have stopped the performance by virtue of Dora, and didnt. But except for the unorganized individual feats of the singers, it was not worth the money. The Count of Luna not only wore an ugly historical costume (German, I think), in which he could have sat down, but actually did sit down, and thereby killed the illusion without which he was nothing. The scenery was the half playful scenery of the Russian opera and ballet. The soldiers, instead of being more fiercely soldierly than any real soldiers ever were on sea or land, were wholly occupied in demonstrating their unfitness to be combed out; and though, unlike the old Italian choristers, they had voices, they seemed to have picked up their music by ear in the course of a demoralizing existence as tramps. Worst of all, the humorists of the orchestra were guying what they regarded as the poor old opera quite shamelessly. There was some honorable and fine playing in the wood wind: Leonora could not have desired a more dignified and sympathetic second than the flute in her opening of the last act; but there were others, of whom I cannot say that they treated Verdi, or the audience, or their own professional honor, handsomely.

In their defence, I will say just this: that the cue was given to them by mutilations of the score for which the management must be held responsible. In the wedding scene, Verdi demands that Leonora shall wear a bridal veil and make it clear that her intentions are honorable. But here Leonora scandalously wore her walking dress. Manrico shamelessly sang his love song; and then, instead of giving Leonora a chance in the touching little antiphony which introduces the organ and gives the needed ritual character to the scene, besides saving the lady's character, he went straight on to the final war song with the bolero accompaniment, and thus made the whole scene a licentious concert. The end of it was quite senselessly botched in a way that must have given somebody a good deal of unnecessary trouble. The first interlude between the bolero blood-and-thunder song and its repetition was cut out, and replaced by the second; yet the song was repeated, so that when it ended there was nothing to be done but set the chorus and band to demonstrate at random, in the key of C or thereabouts, whilst the tenor brought down the curtain and the house by delivering that note "all out," as motorists say, above the din. If there was any more design in the business than this, all I can say is that it was not discernible: the finish seemed to me to be pure spoof. In any case, I see no reason why any gentleman employed about the theatre should have been called on to improve Verdi, who knew how to arrange that sort of climax very well. As the thrown-open window, and the blaze of red fire which tells the audience that Manrico's high C is extracted from him by the spectacle of his mother at the stake, were omitted (too much trouble in the hot weather, doubtless), nobody had the least notion of what he was shouting about.

Again, in the prison scene, when one was expecting the little stretto for the three singers which leads to Leonora's death, and which is happily not a stunt for any of them, but a very moving dramatic passage which completes the musical form of the scene, the lady suddenly flopped down dead; the tenor was beheaded; and the curtain rushed down: this barbarous cut announcing plainly that the object was to get the silly business over as soon as possible when there were no more solos for the principals.

Yet that is not the worst thing of the kind I have heard lately. I went to hear Figaro's Wedding, by Mozart, at another theatre a few weeks ago; and they not only made a cut of several pages in the finale of the last act, including one of the most beautiful passages in the whole work, but positively stopped the music to speak the words set to the omitted music, and then calmly resumed the finale, leaving me gasping. They had much better have taken a collection. There would have been some sense in that. And they began the proceedings with the National Anthem, which almost makes the matter one of high treason.

And now may I ask the critics why they, the watch-dogs of music, suffer these misdemeanors to pass unmentioned and unreproved? They may know so little of Italian opera, and have so low an opinion of it, that the cuts in Il Trovatore may escape them; and they may really believe that all that spoof and charivari is genuine Verdi. But if they know anything about the forms of music at all, they must know that the interruption of a Mozart finale for a spell of dialogue is as impossible as a step-dance by a dean in the middle of an anthem. Several numbers of the opera were also omitted; but the omission of complete separate numbers is not mutilation: circumstances may make it reasonable; for instance, the artists may not be able to sing them, or it may be desirable to shorten the performance. But if such cuts as I have just described are allowed to pass without remonstrance, we shall soon have all the connective tissue of opera either left out or supplied by spoof, the residue consisting of star turns. Needs there a ghost from the criticism of the eighteen-eighties to tell the public that they are not getting full measure? Why, even the dramatic critics only the other day missed Polonius's blessing from Hamlet when Mr Harry Irving cut it. When his father omitted about a third of King Lear, the critics of that day did not miss a line of it, and only wondered mildly what on earth the play was about. If dramatic criticism can progress, why should musical criticism, which used to be the senior branch, be left behind?

What makes me touchy about Il Trovatore is that the materials for a better performance than I have ever heard were present. In the nineteenth century, Verdi, Gounod, Arthur Sullivan, and the rest wrote so abominably for the human voice that the tenors all had goat-bleat (and were proud of it); the baritones had a shattering vibrato, and could not, to save their lives, produce a note of any definite pitch; and the sopranos had the tone of a locomotive whistle without its steadiness: all this being the result of singing parts written for the extreme upper fifth of voices of exceptional range, because high notes are pretty. But to-day our singers, trained on Wagner, who shares with Handel the glory of being great among the greatest writers for the voice, can play Verdi, provided they do not have to do it too often. There was no spoof about the singing of Leonora and Manrico: they threw about high Cs like confetti, and really sang their music. I have never heard the music of the prison scene sung as it was by the tenor. He was, by the way, remarkably like Mr Gilbert Chesterton, who would certainly have a very pleasant voice if he took to opera (I hope he will); and the illusion was strongly reinforced by the spectacle of Mr Belloc seated in a box in evening dress, looking like a cardinal in mufti. A better Leonora was impossible: there is nothing more in the part than she got out of it. Though the opera was supposed to be in English, they all exhorted her to lay a Nora whenever they addressed her; and I am afraid they thought they were pronouncing her name in the Italian manner. I implore them to call her Leeonora, like Sir James Barrie's heroine, in future; for that is at least English. Layanora is nothing but simple mispronunciation. I do not think either the conductor or the chorus knew much about the opera except the tunes they had picked up from the ghosts of the old barrel-organs (where they heard them, goodness only knows); but the Count knew his part; and the result in the trio at the end of the third act, where there is a very jolly counterpoint to be pieced out in mosaic by the Count, Ferrando, and the chorus, was amusing, as the Count got in his bits of the mosaic, whilst the bewildered chorus merely muttered distractedly, and the conductor raced madly to the end to get it all over and enable the gipsy to cover his disgrace by answering repeated curtain calls, which she deserved, not only for her courageous singing against a very unsympathetic accompaniment, but for the self-restraint with which she refrained from committing murder.

England's musical obligations to the artistic director of

this enterprise are so enormous that it seems ungrateful to ask him to add to them by taking Il Trovatore in hand himself next time I drop in. But I really can say no less than I have said above. Even at that, I am surprised at my own moderation.

By the way, incredible as it may seem, there really was a Manrico in the fifteenth century who fought a Di Luna, who was not a Count, but a Constable (not a police-constable). Di Luna was not his brother, and did not cut his head off; but as Manrico was the founder of Spanish drama, perhaps it would have been better if he had.

The Nation, 7th July 1917

A WORD MORE ABOUT VERDI

I HAVE read most of the articles on Verdi elicited by his death, and I have blushed for my species. By this I mean the music-critic species; for though I have of late years disused this learned branch I am still entitled to say to my former colleagues, *"Anch'io son critico."* And when I find men whom I know otherwise honorable glibly pretending to an intimate acquaintance with Oberto, Conte di San Bonifacio, with Un Giorno di Regno, with La Battaglia di Legnano; actually comparing them with Falstaff and Aïda, and weighing, with a nicely judicial air, the differences made by the influence of Wagner, well knowing all the time that they know no more of Oberto than they do of the tunes Miriam timbrelled on the shores of the divided Red Sea, I say again that I blush for our profession, and ask them, as an old friend who wishes them well, where they expect to go after such shamelessly mendacious implications when they die.

For myself, I value a virtuous appearance above vain erudition; and I confess that the only operas of Verdi's I know honestly right through, as I know Dickens's novels, are Ernani, Rigoletto, Il Trovatore, Un Ballo, La Traviata, Aïda, Otello, and Falstaff. And quite enough too, provided one also knows enough of the works of Verdi's forerunners and contemporaries to see exactly when he came in and where he stood. It is inevitable that as younger and younger critics come into the field, more and more mistakes should be made about men who lived as long as Verdi and Wagner, not because the critics do not know their music, but because they do not know the operas that Wagner and Verdi heard when they were boys, and are consequently apt to credit them with the invention of many things which were familiar to their grandfathers.

For example, in all the articles I have read it is assumed that the difference between Ernani and Aïda is due to the influence of Wagner. Now I declare without reserve that there is no evidence in any bar of Aïda or the two later operas that Verdi ever heard a note of Wagner's music. There is evidence that he had heard Boito's music, Mendelssohn's music, and Beethoven's music; but the utmost that can be said to connect him with Wagner is that if Wagner had not got all Europe into the habit of using the whole series of dominant and tonic discords as freely as Rossini used the dominant seventh, it is possible that Falstaff might have been differently harmonized. But as much might be said of any modern pantomime score. Verdi uses the harmonic freedom of his time so thoroughly in his own way, and so consistently in terms of his old style, that if he had been as ignorant of Wagner as Berlioz was of Brahms, there is no reason to suppose that the score of Falstaff would have been an unprepared thirteenth the worse.

I am, of course, aware that when Aïda first reached us, it produced a strong impression of Wagnerism. But at that time nothing of Wagner's later than Lohengrin was known to us. We thought the Evening Star song in Tannhäuser a precious Wagnerian gem. In short, we knew nothing of Wagner's own exclusive style, only his operatic style, which was much more mixed than we imagined. Everybody then thought that a recurring theme in an opera was a Wagnerian Leitmotif, especially if it stole in to a *tremolando* of the strings and was harmonized with major ninths instead of

406

sub-dominants; so when this occurred in Aïda's scena, *Ritorna vincitor*, we all said, "Aha! Wagner!" And, as very often happens, when we came to know better, we quite forgot to revise our premature conclusion. Accordingly, we find critics taking it for granted to-day that Aïda is Wagnerized Verdi, although, if they had not heard Aïda until after Siegfried and Die Meistersinger, they would never dream of connecting the two composers or their styles.

The real secret of the change from the roughness of Il Trovatore to the elaboration of the three last operas, is the inevitable natural drying up of Verdi's spontaneity and fertility. So long as an opera composer can pour forth melodies like *La donna è mobile* and *Il balen*, he does not stop to excogitate harmonic elegancies and orchestral sonorities which are neither helpful to him dramatically nor demanded by the taste of his audience. But when in process of time the well begins to dry up; when instead of getting splashed with the bubbling over of *Ah si, ben mio*, he has to let down a bucket to drag up *Céleste Aïda*, then it is time to be clever, to be nice, to be distinguished, to be impressive, to study instrumental confectionery, to bring thought and knowledge and seriousness to the rescue of failing vitality. In Aïda this is not very happily done: it is not until Otello that we get dignified accomplishment and fine critical taste; but here, too, we have unmistakably a new hand in the business, the hand of Boito. It is quite certain that Boito could not have written Otello; but certain touches in Iago's Credo were perhaps either suggested by Boito, or composed in his manner in fatherly compliment to him; and the whole work, even in its most authentic passages, shews that Verdi was responding to the claims of a more fastidious artistic conscience and even a finer sensitiveness to musical sound than his own was when he tried to turn Macbeth into another Trovatore, and made Lady Macbeth enliven the banquet scene with a florid drinking song. The advance from romantic intensity to dramatic seriousness is revolutionary. Nothing is more genial in Verdi's character than this docility, this respect for the demands of a younger man, this recognition that the implied rebuke to his taste and his coarseness showed a greater tenderness for his own genius than he had shown to it himself.

But there is something else than Boito in Otello. In the third act there is a movement in six-eight time, Essa t'avvince, which is utterly unlike anything in the Trovatore period, and surprisingly like a rondo in the style of Beethoven. That is to say, it is pre-Wagnerian; which at such a date is almost equivalent to anti-Wagnerian. In Falstaff, again, in the buck-basket scene there is a light-fingered and humorous *moto perpetuo* which might have come straight out of a Mendelssohn concerto. Unfortunately it is ineffectively scored; for Verdi, brought up in the Italian practice of using the orchestra as pure accompaniment, was an unskilled beginner in German symphonic orchestration. These are the only passages in the later works which are not obviously the old Verdi developed into a careful and thoughtful composer under the influence of Boito and the effect of advancing age on his artistic resources. I think they would both be impossible to a composer who had not formed an affectionate acquaintance with German music. But the music of Beethoven and Mendelssohn is the music of a Germany still under that Franco-Italian influence which made the music of Mozart so amazingly unlike the music of Bach. Of the later music that was consciously and resolutely German and German only; that would not even write *allegro* at the head of its quick, or *adagio* at the head of its slow movements, because these words are not German; of the music of Schumann, Brahms, and Wagner, there is not anywhere in Verdi the faintest trace. In German music the Italian loved what Italy gave. What Germany offered of her own music he entirely ignored.

Having now, I hope, purged myself of the heresy that Verdi was Wagnerized, a heresy which would never have arisen if our foolish London Opera had been as punctual with Lohengrin as with Aïda, instead of being nearly a

quarter of a century late with it, I may take Verdi on his
own ground. Verdi's genius, like Victor Hugo's, was hyper-
bolical and grandiose: he expressed all the common passions
with an impetuosity and intensity which produced an effect
of sublimity. If you ask, What is it all about? the answer
must be that it is mostly about the police intelligence melo-
dramatized. In the same way, if you check your excitement
at the conclusion of the wedding scene in Il Trovatore to
ask what, after all, *Di quella pira* is, the answer must be
that it is only a common bolero tune, just as *Strida la vampa*
is only a common waltz tune. Indeed, if you know these
tunes only through the barrel organs, you will need no telling. But in the theatre, if the singers have the requisite
power and spirit, one does not ask these questions: the
bolero form passes as unnoticed as the saraband form in
Handel's *Lascia ch'io pianga*, whereas in the more academic
form of the aria with caballetto, which Rossini, Bellini, and
Donizetti accepted, the form reduces the matter to absurdity. Verdi, stronger and more singly dramatic, broke away
from the Rossinian convention; developed the simpler cavatina form with an integral codetta instead of a separated
cabaletto; combined it fearlessly with popular dance and
ballad forms; and finally produced the once enormously
popular, because concise, powerful, and comparatively natural and dramatic type of operatic solo which prevails in
Il Trovatore and Un Ballo. A comparison of this Italian
emancipation of dramatic music from decorative form with
the Wagnerian emancipation shews in a moment the utter
unthinkableness of any sort of connection between the two
composers. No doubt the stimulus given to Verdi's self-
respect and courage by his share in the political activity of
his time, is to some extent paralleled by the effect of the
1848 revolution on Wagner; but this only accentuates the
difference between the successful composer of a period of
triumphant nationalism and the exiled communist-artist-
philosopher of The Niblung's Ring. As Wagner contracted
his views to a practicable nationalism at moments later on,

I can conceive a critic epigrammatically dismissing the
Kaiser March as a bit of Verdified Wagner. But the critic
who can find Wagner in Otello must surely be related to the
gentleman who accused Bach of putting forth the accompaniment to Gounod's Ave Maria as a prelude of his own
composition.

By this Mascagni-facilitating emancipation of Italian
opera, Verdi concentrated its qualities and got rid of its
alloys. Il Trovatore is Italian opera in earnest and nothing
else: Rossini's operas are musical entertainments which are
only occasionally and secondarily dramatic. Moses in Egypt
and Semiramis, for example, are ridiculous as dramas,
though both of them contain one impressively splendid number to shew how nobly Rossini could have done if the silly
conditions of the Italian opera houses had given their composers any chance of being sensible. "I could have achieved
something had I been a German," said Rossini humbly to
Wagner; "*car j'avais du talent.*" Bellini, Donizetti, and the
Italianized Jew Meyerbeer pushed the dramatic element in
opera still further, making it possible for Verdi to end by
being almost wholly dramatic. But until Verdi was induced
by Boito to take Shakespear seriously they all exploited the
same romantic stock-in-trade. They composed with perfect
romantic sincerity, undesirous and intolerant of reality, un-
troubled by the philosophic faculty which, in the mind of
Wagner, revolted against the demoralizing falseness of their
dramatic material. They revelled in the luxury of stage woe,
with its rhetorical loves and deaths and poisons and jeal-
ousies and murders, all of the most luscious, the most enjoyable, the most unreal kind. They did not, like Rossini,
break suddenly off in the midst of their grandiosities to
write *excusez du peu* at the top of the score, and finish with a
galop. On the contrary, it was just where the stage business
demanded something elegantly trivial that they became embarrassed and vulgar. This was especially the case with
Verdi, who was nothing if not strenuous, whereas Bellini
could be trivially simple and Donizetti thoughtlessly gay on

occasion. Verdi, when he is simple or gay, is powerfully so. It has been said, on the strength of the alleged failure of a forgotten comic opera called Un Giorno di Regno, that Verdi was incapable of humor; and I can understand that an acquaintance limited to Ernani, Il Trovatore, La Traviata, and Aïda (and acquaintances of just this extent are very common) might support that opinion. But the parts of the Duke and Sparafucile in Rigoletto could not have been composed by a humorless man. In Un Ballo again we have in Riccardo the Duke's gaiety and gallantry without his callousness; and at the great moment of the melodrama Verdi achieves a master-stroke by his dramatic humor. The hero has made an assignation with the heroine in one of those romantically lonely spots which are always to be found in operas. A band of conspirators resolves to seize the opportunity to murder him. His friend Renato, getting wind of their design, arrives before them, and persuades him to fly, taking upon himself the charge of the lady, who is veiled, and whose identity and place of residence he swears as a good knight to refrain from discovering. When the conspirators capture him and find that they have the wrong man they propose to amuse themselves by taking a look at the lady. Renato defends her; but she, to save him from being killed, unveils herself and turns out to be Renato's own wife. This is no doubt a very thrilling stage climax: it is easy for a dramatist to work up to it. But it is not quite so easy to get away from it; for when the veil is off the bolt is shot; and the difficulty is what is to be said next. The librettist solves the problem by falling back on the chaffing of Renato by the conspirators. Verdi seizes on this with genuine humorous power in his most boldly popular style, giving just the right vein of blackguardly irony and mischievous mirth to the passage, and getting the necessary respite before the final storm, in which the woman's shame, the man's agony of jealousy and wounded friendship, and the malicious chuckling of the conspirators provide material for one of those concerted pieces in which Italian opera is at its

411

best.

And here may I mildly protest that the quartet in Rigoletto, with its four people expressing different emotions simultaneously, was not, as the obituary notices almost all imply, an innovation of Verdi's. Such concerted pieces were *de rigueur* in Italian opera before he was born. The earliest example that holds the stage is the quartet in Don Giovanni, *Non ti fidar*; and between Don Giovanni and Rigoletto it would be difficult to find an Italian opera without a specimen. Several of them were quite as famous as the Rigoletto quartet became. They were burlesqued by Arthur Sullivan in Trial by Jury; but Verdi never, to the end of his life, saw anything ridiculous in them; nor do I. There are some charming examples in Un Ballo, of which but little seems to be remembered nowadays.

In Otello and Falstaff there is some deliberate and not unsuccessful fun. When Cassio gets too drunk to find his place in Iago's drinking song it is impossible not to burst out laughing, though the mistake is as pretty as it is comic. The fugue at the end of Falstaff so tickled Professor Villiers Stanford that he compromised himself to the extent of implying that it is a good fugue. It is neither a good fugue nor a good joke, except as a family joke among professional musicians; but since Mozart finished Don Giovanni with a whizzing fughetta, and Beethoven expressed his most wayward fits by scraps of fugato, and Berlioz made his solitary joke fugually, the Falstaff fugue may be allowed to pass.

However, to show that Verdi was occasionally jocular does not prove that he had the gift of dramatic humor. For such a gift the main popular evidence must be taken from the serious part of Falstaff; for there is nothing so serious as great humor. Unfortunately, very few people know The Merry Wives of Windsor as it was when Falstaff was capably played according to the old tradition, and the playgoer went to hear the actor pile up a mighty climax, culminating in "Think of that, Master Brook." In those palmy days it was the vision of the man-mountain baked in the buck-

412

basket and suddenly plunged hissing hot into the cool stream
of the Thames at Datchet that focused the excitement of
the pit; and if the two conversations between Ford and
Falstaff were played for all they were worth, Shakespear
was justified of his creation, and the rest was taken cheerfully as mere filling up. Now, it cannot be supposed that
either Boito or Verdi had ever seen such a performance; and
the criticisms of modern quite futile productions of The
Merry Wives have shown that a mere literary acquaintance
with the text will not yield up the secret to the ordinary un-
Shakespearean man; yet it is just here, on Ford and Falstaff,
that Verdi has concentrated his attack and trained his
heaviest artillery. His Ford carries Shakespear's a step
higher: it exhausts what Shakespear's resources could only
suggest. And this seems to me to dispose of the matter in
Verdi's favor.

The composition of Otello was a much less Shakespearean
feat; for the truth is that instead of Otello being an Italian
opera written in the style of Shakespear, Othello is a play
written by Shakespear in the style of Italian opera. It is
quite peculiar among his works in this aspect. Its characters
are monsters: Desdemona is a prima donna, with handkerchief, confidante, and vocal solo all complete; and Iago,
though certainly more anthropomorphic than the Count di
Luna, is only so when he slips out of his stage villain's part.
Othello's transports are conveyed by a magnificent but
senseless music which rages from the Propontick to the
Hellespont in an orgy of thundering sound and bounding
rhythm; and the plot is a pure farce plot: that is to say, it is
supported on an artificially manufactured and desperately
precarious trick with a handkerchief which a chance word
might upset at any moment. With such a libretto, Verdi
was quite at home: his success with it proves, not that he
could occupy Shakespear's plane, but that Shakespear could
on occasion occupy his, which is a very different matter.
Nevertheless, such as Othello is, Verdi does not belittle it as
Donizetti would have done, nor conventionalize it as Rossini

actually did. He often rises fully to it; he transcends it in his setting of the very stagey oath of Othello and Iago; and he enhances it by a charming return to the simplicity of real popular life in the episodes of the peasants singing over the fire after the storm in the first act, and their serenade to Desdemona in the second. When one compares these choruses with the choruses of gypsies and soldiers in Il Trovatore one realizes how much Verdi gained by the loss of his power to pour forth *Il balens* and *Ah, che la mortes*.

The decay and discredit which the Verdi operas of the Trovatore type undoubtedly brought on Italian opera in spite of their prodigious initial popularity was caused not at all by the advent of Wagner (for the decay was just as obvious before Lohengrin became familiar to us as it is now that Tristan has driven Manrico from the Covent Garden stage), but by Verdi's recklessness as to the effect of his works on their performers. Until Boito became his artistic conscience he wrote inhumanly for the voice and ferociously for the orchestra. The art of writing well for the voice is neither recondite nor difficult. It has nothing to do with the use or disuse of extreme high notes or low notes. Handel and Wagner, who are beyond all comparison the most skilled and considerate writers of dramatic vocal music, do not hesitate to employ extreme notes when they can get singers who possess them. But they never smash voices. On the contrary, the Handelian and Wagnerian singer thrives on his vocal exercises and lasts so long that one sometimes wishes that he would sing Il Trovatore once and die.

The whole secret of healthy vocal writing lies in keeping the normal plane of the music, and therefore the bulk of the singer's work, in the middle of the voice. Unfortunately, the middle of the voice is not the prettiest part of it; and in immature or badly and insufficiently trained voices it is often the weakest part. There is, therefore, a constant temptation to composers to use the upper fifth of the voice almost exclusively; and this is exactly what Verdi did without remorse. He practically treated that upper fifth as the

414

whole voice, and pitched his melodies in the middle of it instead of in the middle of the entire compass, the result being a frightful strain on the singer. And this strain was not relieved, as Handel relieved his singers, by frequent rests of a bar or two and by long ritornellos: the voice has to keep going from one end of the song to the other. The upshot of that, except in the case of abnormally pitched voices, was displacement, fatigue, intolerable strain, shattering tremolo, and finally, not, as could have been wished, total annihilation, but the development of an unnatural trick of making an atrociously disagreeable noise and inflicting it on the public as Italian singing, with the result that the Italian opera singer is now execrated and banished from the boards of which he was once the undisputed master. He still imposes himself in obscure places; for, curiously enough, nothing dumbs him except well-written music. Handel he never attempts; but Wagner utterly destroys him; and this is why he spread the rumour through Europe that Wagner's music ruined voices.

To the unseductive bass voice, Verdi always behaved well; for since he could not make it sensuously attractive, it forced him to make the bass parts dramatically interesting. It is in Ferrando and Sparafucile, not in Charles V. and the Count di Luna, that one sees the future composer of Falstaff. As to the orchestra, until Boito came, it was for the most part nothing but the big guitar, with the whole wind playing the tune in unison or in thirds and sixths with the singer.* I am quite sure that as far as the brass was concerned this was a more sensible system, and less harshly crushing to the singer, than the dot and dash system of using trumpets and drums, to which the German school and its pupils in England clung pedantically long after the employment of valves had made it as unnecessary as it was

* Elgar, the greatest of all orchestral technicians, maintained that the big guitar business has a genuine skilled technique, and that, for instance, such scores as Rossini's Stabat Mater, in the apparently crude and crushing accompaniment to *Cujus animam*, in performance sound exactly right, and help the singer instead of annihilating him.

ugly and absurd. But beyond this, I do not feel called upon
to find excuses for Verdi's pre-Boitian handling of the orchestra. He used it unscrupulously to emphasize his immoderate demands for overcharged and superhuman passion,
tempting the executants to unnatural and dangerous as-
sumptions and exertions. It may have been exciting to see
Edmund Kean revealing Shakespear "by flashes of lightning," and Robson rivalling him in burlesque; but when the
flashes turned out to be tumblers of brandy, and the two
thunder-wielders perished miserably of their excesses, the
last excuse for the insufferable follies and vulgarities of the
would-be Keans and Robsons vanished. I speak of Kean
and Robson so as not to hurt the survivors of the interreg-
num between Mario and De Reszke, when bawling troopers,
roaring Italian porters, and strangulating Italian newspaper
criers made our summer nights horrible with Verdi's for-
tissimos. Those who remember them will understand.

But in his defects, as in his efficiencies, his directness,
and his practical common sense, Verdi is a thorough un-
adulterated Italian. Nothing in his work needs tracing to
any German source. His latter-day development of declamatory recitative can be traced back through the recitatives in
Rossini's Moses right back to the beginning of Italian opera.
You cannot trace a note of Wotan in Amonasro or Iago,
though you can trace something of Moses in the rhythms of
Wotan. The anxious northern genius is magnificently assimi-
lative: the self-sufficient Italian genius is magnificently im-
pervious. I doubt whether even Puccini really studies
Schumann, in spite of his harmonic Schumannisms. Certainly, where you come to a strong Italian like Verdi you
may be quite sure that if you cannot explain him without
dragging in the great Germans, you cannot explain him at
all.

At all events, Verdi will stand among the greatest of the
Italian composers. It may be that, as with Handel, his
operas will pass out of fashion and be forgotten whilst the
Manzoni Requiem remains his imperishable monument.

Even so, that alone, like Messiah, will make his place safe
among the immortals.

The Anglo-Saxon Review
March 1901

SIEGFRIED'S TOD

I DO not wish to hurt your feelings, O respectable reader;
but do you really think a man of genius would feel much
more at home in your company than you would in the
galleys? Your objection to a galley-slave, after all, is only
that he is a coarser fellow than yourself, insensible to the
extremes of your points of honor in decency and morality;
tolerant of sights, sounds, and deeds that are horrible to
you; and callously reckless, even to bodily violence, of the
delicacies and amenities which are to you the indispensable
conditions of bearable human intercourse. Among such creatures, shrinking and constant apprehension would be your
lot; and yet it would not be safe to shew your fear any more
than if you were in a den of hyenas and jackals. I submit to
you, then, as politely as such a thing may be submitted, that
since Plato, Dante, Shakespear, Goethe, and men of that
kind are esteemed great only because they exceed us average
persons exactly as we exceed the galley-slave, it follows that
they must walk through our world much as through a
strange country full of dangerous beasts. It must, therefore,
take something like a lion-tamer's nerve to be a man of
genius; and when the man of genius is timid—and fear is the
beginning of wisdom—he must suffer much more than the
ordinary coward, who can, at any rate, choose a safer pursuit than lion-taming, whereas your hapless man of genius
is born into the den and must stay there until he is carried
out in his coffin.

Obviously, I have never seen Goethe or Shakespear or
Plato: they were before my time. But I have seen Richard
Wagner, who was so vehemently specialized by Nature as a
man of genius that he was totally incapable of anything

417

ordinary. He fought with the wild beasts all his life; and when you saw him coming through a crowded cage, even when they all felt about him as the lions felt about Daniel, he had an air of having his life in his hand, as it were, and of wandering in search of his right place and his own people, if any such there might be. When he had nothing else to do he would wander away to the walls and corners, apparently in search of some door or stairway or other exit from the world, not finding which he would return disconcerted, and either sit down in desperation for a moment before starting off on a fresh exploration, or else—being a most humane man—pet one of the animals with a little conversation.

In 1883 Wagner wandered to Venice, and there at last stumbled upon that long-sought exit, since when he has not been seen by mortal man. You may well believe, then, how ghostly a sensation I had when, at Queen's Hall in London ten years later, I saw, making its guarded way through the crowd on the platform, a phantom Wagner, again, in Bunyan's phrase, "walking through the wilderness of this world." Of course I knew perfectly well that it was really Siegfried Wagner, son of Richard, and grandson of Liszt; for had I not come there expressly to see him? But, for all that, what appeared to me was the father in his habit as he lived, the old face with immortal youth in it, the set expression of endurance, the apprehensive step, and the unmistakable feeling of supernaturalness among the wild beasts.

This illusion did not wear off so soon as I expected: it came back again and again whilst Siegfried was conducting. It only broke up completely when, in response to the applause, he turned round smiling; made a series of boyish bows which had all the pleasant qualities of friendly nods; and became quite a young fellow in his earliest manhood. When he got to work again, the old look came back: there was something of the quaint gravity of an old-fashioned child: one remembered, in trying to account for it, that his father was over fifty when he was born, and his mother, though much younger than that, still a mature woman. His handling of the music, too, was very Wagnerian, more so even than that of Wagner himself; for Wagner had roots in the past which have been pulled up since before Siegfried's time. No man born in 1813, as Richard Wagner was, could have conducted Les Preludes or the Siegfried Idyll with such a complete detachment from the mechanical swing of the old dance and march measures from which their forms are descended.

We are certainly all old fogies compared to this young man, who shews not only a perfect comprehension of the poetic side of his father's and grandfather's music—a much less troubled and turbid comprehension at certain points than the composers themselves had—but an instinctive gentleness and strong patience of handling of the finest masculine quality, complemented by a sensitiveness of feeling of the finest feminine quality. He gave us the Mephisto Waltzes without a whiff of brimstone, the Flying Dutchman overture without a touch of violence. He treated the overture's atmosphere of curse and storm, its shrieking tempest and scurrying damnation, with scrupulous artistic care and seriousness, albeit with a certain youthful share in the excitement which was perhaps not far remote from amusement; but it was with the theme of love and salvation that he opened the music to its very depths. And this is the clue to him as a conductor, and to those complaints of sentimentality which have been made against him by critics who were in an unregenerate mood and missed the violence and the brimstone—missed the bitterness of death in his beatific version of Isolde's Liebestod—found heaven, in short, rather dull after London. For my part, I was touched, charmed, more than satisfied. I can appreciate Richter's grandeur of tone and breadth of style. I like the thunder of Mottl's drums, the splendid energy of his accents, and the fastidious polish and refinement of his manner. But there is a place left —and a very high one—for this old-young conductor, with his rare combination of insight and innocence, and his purity and delicacy of sentiment, not to mention complete technical knowledge of his business and a first-rate standard of orchestral execution. It is of course as impossible for him as it was for Mottl to make the immense impression here as a conductor that Richter made, not because Richter is a greater conductor than either Mottl or Siegfried, but because they have had to follow Richter, whereas Richter had only to follow Cusins, Costa, Carl Rosa, and Vianesi, by comparison with whom the pupil of Wagner could not help appearing a demi-god. Except Mr August Manns at the Crystal Palace, nobody in London at Richter's advent could possibly have known what modern orchestra handling meant. Siegfried Wagner is, at a moderate computation, about six hundred times as great a conductor as Cusins, Costa, Carl Rosa, and Vianesi rolled into one, with Dr Mackenzie, Dr Villiers Stanford, Mr Cowen, Sir Arthur Sullivan, Mr Randegger, and Signor Bevignani thrown in as makeweights; but he would certainly make no greater claim as against Richter than Michael Angelo made against Brunelleschi: "Different, but not better."

There is little more to be said. The penetrating musical criticism of our day, which nothing escapes, has pointed out already that Siegfried conducts with his left hand, and that he uses a score. I can add nothing except to say that the concert, though it left Siegfried's ability as a symphony conductor unsettled, there being nothing in sonata form in the program, placed his talent as an interpreter of tone poetry beyond all doubt. He comprehended everything; and it was gratifying to find that though he did not take command of the army like Richter, nor head the charge like Mottl, but simply gave the band plenty of time to turn in, and trusted without misgiving or embarrassment to the rightness of his own reading, he got their very best work out of the players. They surpassed the Bayreuth orchestra not only in volume of tone—a sort of superiority which is a foregone conclusion in London, our instruments being better— but ran Bayreuth hard in point of smoothness of combination, delicacy, and precision in the execution of what may be

called the stage effects of the Wagner scores. It seems to me
—though in this I may be wrong, since I am only guessing
by the general effect, and not by any particular instance
that I can put my finger on—that more trouble has been
taken at these concerts to secure accuracy in the band parts
than has ever been taken before.

The Pall Mall Budget
15 *November* 1894

POSTSCRIPT, 1937. I grieve to have to add that the
magic of Siegfried's first concert was not maintained at the
second. The orchestra had thrown itself wholeheartedly into
making a success of his first appearance; but he must have
got on the wrong side of his players after this; for at the
second concert they were not helpful; and the evening fell
rather flat. Siegfried, it appeared, was the sort of conductor
his father most abhorred: a gentleman conductor, meaning
a conductor who is a gentleman first and a conductor afterwards, an order of things which ends in his not being a conductor at all. In short, a snob conductor. Our universities
produced a succession of them which made the advent in
London of Richter with Wagner in 1877 a revelation and a
revolution. It was many, many years before Siegfried came
to London again to conduct a concert at the Albert Hall.
He was then an elderly person, still extremely gentlemanly.
His conducting was too depressing to be describable as mad-
dening; but it made us all feel as if we were at a garden party
in a cathedral town being welcomed by a highly connected
curate who failed to find any tea for us. There was in the
program a harmless little piece by himself: the elegant
diversion of a superior person who dabbled in light composition. The farewell and fire music from Die Walküre was
handled as it had never within our experience been handled
before, and will, I trust, never be handled again. The trombones echoing Wotan's final *Wer meines Speeres Spitze
fürchtet* sounded like an evening hymn, slow and sweet, all
but *sotto voce*. The critics, I think (I was no longer one of

them) got up and left after this; for the man seemed hopeless; and the politeness of the applause was deadlier than
silence.

Then an incredible thing happened. The last item in the
program was the overture to Die Meistersinger. The last,
and, as it at once promised, the worst. Its slowness, its
genteelness, made me doubt whether I was not dreaming. I
felt that the overture would certainly peter out and stop
from sheer inertia if he did not speed up the final section.
Instead, to my amazement, he achieved the apparently impossible feat of slowing it down. And the effect was magical.
The music broadened out with an effect that is beyond
description. It was immense, magnificent. At the end the
audience, which ten minutes before would have murdered
him but for the police, was frantically recalling him to the
platform again and again and again and yet again. The next
we heard of him was that he was dead. It was his swan song.

INDEX

423

INDEX

425

428

INDEX

INDEX

431

INDEX

INDEX

INDEX